T0261263

Machine Learning:
a Concise Introduction

WILEY SERIES IN PROBABILITY AND STATISTICS

Established by *Walter A. Shewhart and Samuel S. Wilks*

Editors: *David J. Balding, Noel A. C. Cressie, Garrett M. Fitzmaurice, Geof H. Givens, Harvey Goldstein, Geert Molenberghs, David W. Scott, Adrian F. M. Smith, Ruey S. Tsay*

Editors Emeriti: *J. Stuart Hunter, Iain M. Johnstone, Joseph B. Kadane, Jozef L. Teugels*

The *Wiley Series in Probability and Statistics* is well established and authoritative. It covers many topics of current research interest in both pure and applied statistics and probability theory. Written by leading statisticians and institutions, the titles span both state-of-the-art developments in the field and classical methods.

Reflecting the wide range of current research in statistics, the series encompasses applied, methodological and theoretical statistics, ranging from applications and new techniques made possible by advances in computerized practice to rigorous treatment of theoretical approaches. This series provides essential and invaluable reading for all statisticians, whether in academia, industry, government, or research.

A complete list of titles in this series can be found at http://www.wiley.com/go/wsps

Machine Learning: a Concise Introduction

Steven W. Knox

WILEY

This edition first published 2018
This work is a U.S. Government work and is in the public domain in the U.S.A.
Published 2018 by John Wiley & Sons, Inc

The right of Steven W. Knox to be identified as the author of this work has been asserted in accordance with law.

Registered Office(s)
John Wiley & Sons, Inc., 111 River Street, Hoboken, NJ 07030, USA

Editorial Office
111 River Street, Hoboken, NJ 07030, USA

For details of our global editorial offices, customer services, and more information about Wiley products visit us at www.wiley.com.

Wiley also publishes its books in a variety of electronic formats and by print-on-demand. Some content that appears in standard print versions of this book may not be available in other formats.

Library of Congress Cataloging-in-Publication Data

Names: Knox, Steven W., author.
Title: Machine learning : a concise introduction / by Steven W. Knox.
Description: Hoboken, New Jersey : John Wiley & Sons, 2018. | Series: Wiley series in probability and statistics |
Identifiers: LCCN 2017058505 (print) | LCCN 2018004509 (ebook) | ISBN 9781119439073 (pdf) | ISBN 9781119438984 (epub) | ISBN 9781119439196 (cloth)
Subjects: LCSH: Machine learning.
Classification: LCC Q325.5 (ebook) | LCC Q325.5 .K568 2018 (print) | DDC 006.3/1–dc23
LC record available at https://lccn.loc.gov/2017058505

Cover image: © Verticalarray/Shutterstock
Cover design by Wiley

Set in 10/12pt TimesStd by Aptara Inc., New Delhi, India

10 9 8 7 6 5 4 3 2 1

Contents

Preface

> The goal of statistical data analysis is to extract the maximum information from the data, and to present a product that is as accurate and as useful as possible.
>
> —David Scott, *Multivariate Density Estimation: Theory, Practice and Visualization*, 1992

My purpose in writing this book is to introduce the mathematically sophisticated reader to a large number of topics and techniques in the field variously known as machine learning, statistical learning, or predictive modeling. I believe that a deeper understanding of the subject as a whole will be obtained from reflection on an intuitive understanding of many techniques rather than a very detailed understanding of only one or two, and the book is structured accordingly. I have omitted many details while focusing on what I think shows "what is really going on." For details, the reader will be directed to the relevant literature, or to the exercises, which form an integral part of the text.

No work this small on a subject this large can be self-contained. Some undergraduate-level calculus, linear algebra, and probability is assumed without reference, as are a few basic ideas from statistics. All of the techniques discussed here can, I hope, be implemented using this book and a mid-level programming language (such as C),[1] and explicit implementation of many techniques using R is presented in the last chapter.

The reader may detect a coverage bias in favor of classification over regression. This is deliberate. The existing literature on the theory and practice of linear regression and many of its variants is so strong that it does not need any contribution from me. Classification, I believe, is not yet so well documented. In keeping with what has been important in my experience, loss functions are completely general and predictive modeling is stressed more than explanatory modeling.

The intended audience for these notes has an extremely diverse background in probability, ranging from one introductory undergraduate course to extensive

---

[1] There is one exception: the convex programming needed to implement a support vector machine is omitted.

graduate work and published research.[2] In seeking a probability notation which will create the least confusion for all concerned, I arrived at the non-standard use of $P(x)$ for both the probability of an event x and a probability mass or density function, with respect to some measure which is never stated, evaluated at a point x. My hope, which I believe has been borne out in practice, is that anyone with sufficient knowledge to find this notation confusing will have sufficient knowledge to work through that confusion.

---

[2] This book is designed for two kinds of people: those who know what $P(Y \mid X)$ means but do not know the Radon–Nikodym theorem, and those who know what $P(Y \mid X)$ means only because they know the Radon–Nikodym theorem. I have tried to communicate with the first group, at the cost of possibly irritating the second.

Organization—How to Use This Book

The core material of this book is laid out in Chapters 1 through 7. These chapters are intended to be read in order, as each chapter builds on the previous ones. Chapters 1 and 2 introduce problems which machine learning methods can solve, and also introduce the fundamental ideas and terminology used to describe these problems and their solutions. Chapter 3 gives a brief introduction to regression.[1]

Chapter 4 presents many methods for classification, grouped according to how they approach the problem. Chapter 5 discusses bias–variance trade-off, a topic essential to understanding the design principles behind ensemble methods. Chapter 6 presents various ensemble methods, focusing on how each method can be understood as trading off bias for variance, or vice versa. Chapter 7 concludes the core material with methods for risk estimation and model selection. By the end of Chapter 7, the reader will have encountered many useful methods for approaching classification and regression problems, and (I hope) will appreciate how each method works and why each method approaches classification or regression the way it does.

After Chapter 7, the reader can select from among the remaining seven chapters in any order, best suiting the reader's goals or needs. For example, some readers might wish to follow

a path toward machine learning practice or consultancy:

- Chapter 9, Clustering, and then Chapter 11, High-Dimensional Data
- Chapter 10, Optimization
- Chapter 12, Communication with Clients
- Chapter 14, R Source Code (optional—recommended if the reader plans to use R)

---

[1] The reader who has a thorough background in regression may choose to skip Chapter 3, or skim it for notation.

Other readers might wish to follow

a path toward machine learning research:

- Chapter 8, Consistency
- Chapter 11, High-Dimensional Data (optionally preceded by Chapter 9, Clustering)
- Chapter 10, Optimization (optional)
- Chapter 13, Current Challenges in Machine Learning

Other readers might wish to develop insight empirically, through hands-on experience working with the methods covered in the core material of Chapters 1 through 7, before progressing on to later chapters. Such readers can proceed directly to Chapter 14, R Source Code, which illustrates how to apply and interpret many of the classification methods from Chapters 4 and 6. Finally, some readers might wish to learn specifically about deep neural networks. Feed-forward deep neural networks[2] are a combination of several ideas, and these ideas are presented separately because each is individually useful: feed-forward neural networks in Section 4.7, stochastic gradient descent optimization in Sections 10.1 and 10.6, autoencoders in Section 11.3, and parameter regularization in Section 11.4.

Three of the later chapters—8 (Consistency), 10 (Optimization), and 12 (Communication with Clients)—may seem unusual in an introductory book on machine learning. Chapter 8 is about consistency, which addresses whether or not a given supervised learning method converges to an optimal solution as the number of data, n, increases without bound, either for a given problem or for *any* problem. This statistical topic is present because some readers of Chapters 4, 5, and 6 may, upon being presented with approximately 20 methods to solve classification problems, conclude that the richness and diversity of methods is a sign that no one actually knows yet how to deal with classification. Such readers might feel that there ought to be one method which solves all classification or regression problems optimally, at least as $n \to \infty$. Such readers may be comforted, or saved reinventing the wheel, by learning of the large body of theory which addresses this issue.

Chapter 10 presents useful techniques in optimization, a topic which is required in order to apply most methods in machine learning.[3] Indeed, a common theme running through Chapters 3, 4, 6, 7, 9, and 11 (most of the practical content of the book) is the transformation of a classification, clustering, regression, density estimation, or dimension-reduction problem into an optimization problem: find the best estimate θ of a vector of model parameters θ, find the best trained model in a class of trained models, find the best features to use or the best low-dimensional representation

---

[2] Recurrent neural networks are not covered in this book.

[3] Despite its importance, optimization is a topic which is often either taken for granted or ignored.

of features, etc. Thus, in order to solve real-world problems, the machine learning practitioner needs to be able to solve various kinds of optimization problems. Even when relying on existing software for optimization, a machine learning practitioner can be more effective if he or she understands a variety of optimization methods, and their strengths and weaknesses.

Chapter 12 is about communication with clients. In the author's experience, machine learning practitioners do not generally work for themselves, in the sense that they are not the ultimate beneficiary of a machine learning solution they create for some real-world application. Instead, a machine learning practitioner's work is typically performed for a client, or customer, or mission stakeholder, or scientific colleague. *It is the client's subjective judgment which matters* in determining what is a good solution to a problem, and what kind of trade-offs are acceptable in error, computation, and model interpretability. A machine learning practitioner—no matter how smart, how well trained, or how gifted in computational resources—is doomed to failure if he or she cannot elicit from a client what is really needed, or cannot communicate to a client what the machine learning practitioner needs and can provide.

Acknowledgments

This book was written to train mathematicians, computer scientists, data scientists, and others at the National Security Agency (NSA), where it has been used, in various editions, since 2005. This book is respectfully dedicated to the silent professionals—past, current, and future—who use this material in the intelligence services of the United States and its allies. The views and opinions expressed are those of the author and do not reflect those of NSA/CSS.

This book has been improved through many discussions with teachers, students, and colleagues. Most of these people cannot be listed here by name, so I will simply say I am grateful to you all.

Steven W. Knox

About the Companion Website

This book is accompanied by a companion website:

www.wiley.com/go/Knox/MachineLearning

The website includes:

- Solutions to some of the exercises in the book.

1

Introduction—Examples from Real Life

> To call in a statistician after the experiment is done may be no more than asking him to perform a postmortem examination: he may be able to say what the experiment died of.
>
> —R. A. Fisher, *Presidential Address*, 1938

The following examples will be used to illustrate the ideas of the next chapter.

Problem 1 ("Shuttle"). *The space shuttle is set to launch. For every previous launch, the air temperature is known and the number of O-rings on the solid rocket boosters which were damaged is known (there are six O-rings, and O-ring damage is a potentially catastrophic event). Based on the current air temperature, estimate the probability that at least one O-ring on a solid rocket booster will be damaged if the shuttle launches now.*

This is a regression problem. Poor analysis, and poor communication of some good analysis (Tufte, 2001), resulted in the loss of the shuttle *Challenger* and its crew on January 28, 1986.

Problem 2 ("Ballot"). *Immediately after the 2000 US presidential election, some voters in Palm Beach County, Florida, claimed that a confusing ballot form caused them to vote for Pat Buchanan, the Reform Party candidate, when they thought they*

Machine Learning: a Concise Introduction, First Edition. Steven W. Knox.
© This publication is a US Government work and is in the public domain.
Published 2018 by John Wiley & Sons, Inc.
Companion Website: http://www.wiley.com/go/Knox/MachineLearning

were voting for Al Gore, the Democratic Party candidate. Based on county-by-county demographic information (number of registered members of each political party, number of people with annual income in a certain range, number of people with a certain level of education, etc.) and county-by-county vote counts from the 1996 presidential election, estimate how many people in Palm Beach County voted for Buchanan but thought they were voting for Gore.

This regression problem was studied a great deal in 2000 and 2001, as the outcome of the vote in Palm Beach County could have decided the election.

Problem 3 ("Heart").   *A patient who is suffering from acute chest pain has entered a hospital, where several numerical variables (for example, systolic blood pressure, age) and several binary variables (for example, whether tachycardia present or not) are measured. Identify the patient as "high risk" (probably will die within 30 days) or "low risk" (probably will live 30 days).*

This is a classification problem.

Problem 4 ("Postal Code").   *An optical scanner has scanned a hand-written ZIP code on a piece of mail. It has approximately separated the digits, and each digit is represented as an 8 × 8 array of pixels, each of which has one of 256 gray-scale values, 0 (white), ..., 255 (black). Identify each pixel array as one of the digits 0 through 9.*

This is a classification problem which affects all of us (though not so much now as formerly).

Problem 5 ("Spam").   *Identify email as "spam" or "not spam," based only on the subject line. Or based on the full header. Or based on the content of the email.*

This is probably the best known and most studied classification problem of all, solutions to which are applied many billions of times per day.[1]

Problem 6 ("Vault").   *Some neolithic tribes built dome-shaped stone burial vaults. Given the location and several internal measurements of some burial vaults, estimate how many distinct vault-building cultures there have been, say which vaults were built by which culture and, for each culture, give the dimensions of a vault which represents that culture's ideal vault shape (or name the actual vault which best realizes each culture's ideal).*

This is a clustering problem.

---

[1] In 2013, approximately 182.9 billion emails were sent *per day*, on average, worldwide (Radicati and Levenstein, 2013).

2

The Problem of Learning

Far better an approximate answer to the *right* question, which is often vague, than an *exact* answer to the wrong question, which can always be made precise.

—John Tukey, *The Future of Data Analysis*, 1962

This book treats *The Problem of Learning*, which can be stated generally and succinctly as follows.

The Problem of Learning. *There are a known set $\mathcal{X}$ and an unknown function f on $\mathcal{X}$. Given data, construct a good approximation $\hat{f}$ of f. This is called learning f.*

The problem of learning has been studied in many guises and in different fields, such as statistics, computer science, mathematics, and the natural and social sciences. An advantage of this situation is that the set of methods now available for addressing the problem has benefited from a tremendous diversity of perspective and knowledge. A disadvantage is a certain lack of coherence in the language used to describe the problem: there are, perhaps, more names for things than there are things which need names, and this can make the study of the problem of learning appear more complicated and confusing than it really is.

This chapter introduces the main ideas which occur in almost any applied problem in learning, and introduces language commonly used to describe these ideas. The ideas and language introduced here will be used in every other chapter of this book.

Machine Learning: a Concise Introduction, First Edition. Steven W. Knox.
© This publication is a US Government work and is in the public domain.
Published 2018 by John Wiley & Sons, Inc.
Companion Website: http://www.wiley.com/go/Knox/MachineLearning

2.1 Domain

The set $\mathcal{X}$ is called *feature space* and an element $X \in \mathcal{X}$ is called a *feature vector* (or an *input*). The coordinates of X are called *features*. Individual features may take values in a continuum, a discrete, ordered set, or a discrete, unordered set.

In Problem 1 ("Shuttle"), $\mathcal{X}$ is an interval of possible air temperatures: $(-60, 140)$ Fahrenheit, say, or $[0, \infty)$ Kelvin. In Problem 4 ("ZIP Code"), $\mathcal{X}$ is the set of all 8×8 matrices with entries in $\{0, 1, \ldots, 255\}$. In Problem 2 ("Ballot"), $\mathcal{X}$ is $\{0, 1, 2, \ldots\}^m$ for the given number of features m, each feature being a count of people or votes, though in practice $\mathcal{X}$ might well be taken to be the m-dimensional real numbers, $\mathbb{R}^m$.

2.2 Range

The range $f(\mathcal{X})$ is usually either a finite, unordered set, in which case learning is called *classification*,[1] or it is a continuum, in which case learning is called *regression*.[2] An element $Y \in f(\mathcal{X})$ is called a *class* in classification and a *response* in regression.

In Problem 1 ("Shuttle"), $f(\mathcal{X}) = [0, 1]$, the set of probabilities that an O-ring is damaged.[3] In Problem 4 ("Postal Code"), $f(\mathcal{X}) = \{$"0", "1", "2", "3", "4", "5", "6", "7", "8", "9"$\}$, the quotes indicating that these are unordered labels rather than numbers. In Problem 2 ("Ballot"), $f(\mathcal{X})$ is the set of non-negative integers less than or equal to the number of registered voters in Palm Beach County, but in practice $f(\mathcal{X})$ would usually be taken to be $\mathbb{R}$, the set of real numbers.

2.3 Data

In principle, data are random draws (X, Y) from a probability distribution P on $\mathcal{X} \times f(\mathcal{X})$. Depending on the problem at hand, the data which are observed may either consist of domain-range pairs (X, Y) or just domain values X: learning is called *supervised* in the former case and *unsupervised* in the latter.

---

[1] Classification is sometimes referred to as *pattern recognition*, a term not to be confused with *pattern search* (a general class of optimization algorithms) or *pattern theory* (Grenander, 1993, 1996).

[2] If the range $f(\mathcal{X})$ is a finite, ordered set, learning is called *ordinal regression*. The reader is directed to Agresti (1984) for information on ordinal regression.

[3] Problem 1 ("Shuttle") could be either classification or regression, depending on the exact wording of the question asked. It is a regression problem if the question asks for the probability that at least one O-ring will be damaged ($f(\mathcal{X}) = [0, 1]$) or asks for the expected number of O-rings which will be damaged ($f(\mathcal{X}) = [0, 6], [0, 12]$, or $[0, 18]$ depending on the specific booster design and on which O-rings are being counted). It is a classification problem if the question asks whether or not any O-rings will be damaged ($f(\mathcal{X}) = \{$yes, no$\}$). In applied problems, it is important to be clear about what kind of question is being asked. Answering a different question than the one asked may sometimes be beneficial, but it should never be done unknowingly or unacknowledged.

In *supervised learning*, the data are

$$(x_1, y_1), \ldots, (x_n, y_n) \in \mathcal{X} \times f(\mathcal{X}),$$

where each (x_i, y_i) is drawn from a joint probability distribution $P(X, Y)$ on $\mathcal{X} \times f(\mathcal{X})$. Such data are called *marked data*.[4] It is sometimes useful to consider the data as produced by a two-step process, in one of two ways: by drawing y from marginal distribution $P(Y)$ on $f(\mathcal{X})$ and then drawing a corresponding feature vector x from conditional distribution $P(X \mid Y = y)$ on $\mathcal{X}$; or by drawing feature vector x from marginal distribution $P(X)$ on $\mathcal{X}$ and then drawing a corresponding y from conditional distribution $P(Y \mid X = x)$ on $f(\mathcal{X})$. These two points of view correspond to the two factorizations,[5]

$$P(X, Y) = P(Y) P(X \mid Y) = P(X) P(Y \mid X).$$

Both are useful in classification. The latter is more useful in regression, where the function f to be learned is often, though not necessarily, the expected value of the conditional distribution of $Y \mid X$, that is,

$$f(x) = \mathrm{E}[Y \mid X = x].$$

In *unsupervised learning*, the data are[6]

$$x_1, \ldots, x_n \in \mathcal{X}.$$

Such data are called *unmarked data*. The range $f(\mathcal{X})$ is either assumed to be finite, in which case unsupervised learning is called *clustering*, or it is $[0, \infty)$ and the function f to be learned is the mass or density function of the marginal distribution of the features,

$$f(x) = P(X = x),$$

in which case unsupervised learning is called *density estimation*. In clustering problems, the size of the range, $|f(\mathcal{X})|$, may or may not be known: usually it is not.

Problem 1 ("Shuttle") is supervised learning, since the data are of the form

(temperature, number of damaged O-rings).

Problem 6 ("Vaults") is unsupervised learning, and $|f(\mathcal{X})|$ is unknown (though archaeologists might have other evidence outside the data — such as artifacts recovered from the vaults or related sites — which indicates that, for example, $4 \leq |f(\mathcal{X})| \leq 10$).

---

[4] It may happen that two data points (x_i, y_i) and (x_j, y_j) agree in their features ($x_i = x_j$) but not their response or class ($y_i \neq y_j$). This does not mean that f is multivalued, but that the data are noisy. The goal of learning is to find a deterministic function $\hat{f}$ on $\mathcal{X}$ which approximates f.

[5] We shall see in Chapter 4 that this relatively trivial piece of mathematics has a profound influence on the design of practical machine learning algorithms.

[6] It may be useful to think of $x_1, \ldots, x_n \in \mathcal{X}$ as being drawn originally as $(x_1, y_1), \ldots, (x_n, y_n) \in \mathcal{X} \times f(\mathcal{X})$, but then $y_1, \ldots, y_n$ were lost or somehow unobserved. That is, to think of $y_1, \ldots, y_n$ as *latent variables*.

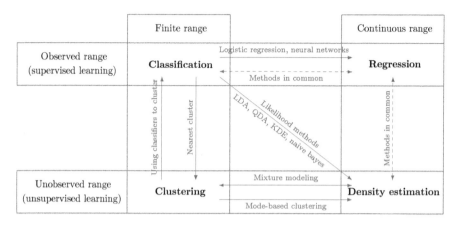

Figure 2.1   Four categories of learning problems, in bold type, split according to whether the range of f is finite (and unordered) or continuous, and whether or not elements of the range are observed directly. Some solutions to these problems are devised by transforming one problem into another: examples of this are shown in red and described in Chapters 3, 4, 6, and 9.

Figure 2.1 summarizes some of the terminology introduced so far and illustrates some connections between the four learning problems mentioned.

Sometimes both marked and unmarked data are available. This situation is called *semi-supervised learning.*[7]

2.4   Loss

What does "a good approximation" mean? This is specified by a *loss function*

$$\text{L} : f(\mathcal{X}) \times \widehat{f}(\mathcal{X}) \rightarrow \mathbb{R},$$

where for each $(x, y) \in \mathcal{X} \times f(\mathcal{X})$, $\text{L}(y, \widehat{f}(x))$ is the loss, or penalty, incurred by approximating y with $\widehat{f}(x)$. Common examples are:

squared-error loss	(regression)	$\text{L}(y, \widehat{f}(x)) = (y - \widehat{f}(x))^2$
absolute-error loss	(regression)	$\text{L}(y, \widehat{f}(x)) = \|y - \widehat{f}(x)\|$
zero-one loss	(classification)	$\text{L}(y, \widehat{f}(x)) = \begin{cases} 0 & \text{if } y = \widehat{f}(x) \\ 1 & \text{if } y \neq \widehat{f}(x) \end{cases}$

In classification, an arbitrary loss function can be specified by the cells of a $C \times C$ *loss matrix*, usually with all-zero diagonal elements and positive off-diagonal elements

---

[7] Semi-supervised learning is not covered in this book.

(so correct classification incurs no loss and misclassification incurs positive loss). Zero-one loss is represented by the $C \times C$ matrix with 0's on the diagonal and 1's everywhere off the diagonal.

Some techniques for solving classification problems focus on estimating the conditional probability distribution on class labels, given the feature vector,

$$(P(Y = 1 \mid X), \dots, P(Y = C \mid X))$$

(such techniques translate a classification problem into a regression problem, following the top-most red arrow in Figure 2.1). Let

$$(\widehat{P}(Y = 1 \mid X), \dots, \widehat{P}(Y = C \mid X))$$

denote an estimate of this vector. Predicted class labels, $\widehat{f}(X)$, are obtained from this estimated probability distribution in some way: for example, by predicting the most probable class. Techniques which do this essentially convert a classification problem into a regression problem, solve the regression problem, and apply the solution to classification. A loss function[8] often used in such cases is

$$cross\text{-}entropy\ loss \text{ (classification) } L\left(y, (\widehat{P}(Y = c \mid X = x))_{c=1}^{C}\right)$$
$$= -\log \widehat{P}(Y = y \mid X = x).$$

The choice of loss function is subjective and problem-dependent.[9] An asymmetric loss function is sometimes appropriate: for example, in Problem 3 ("Heart"), declaring a healthy person to be sick may be viewed as a much less costly error than declaring a sick person to be healthy.[10] That said, loss functions are often chosen for convenience and computational tractability.[11] Exercises in Sections 3.6 and 4.6,

---

[8] It may seem strange that here, a loss function is comparing a class to a probability distribution. A formal justification is given in Exercise 2.1.

[9] This means, among other things, that the choice of loss function depends on information which is not in the data. And subjective decisions ought usually to be elicited from our clients, not ourselves!

[10] Choice of loss function may depend not only on the consequences of misclassifying particular cases, but on the aggregate consequences of misclassifying. Here is an example. Suppose there are two tests, A and B, to screen for a rare, fatal, but treatable disease. Test A can be done in a doctor's office or clinic but is not completely accurate, while test B is perfectly accurate but requires a sophisticated medical lab to perform. Whatever the "real" loss of misclassifying a person with test A is, test A must not declare so many healthy people to be sick that the total capacity of medical labs to perform test B as a follow-up is exceeded. Thus practical considerations may force the parameters of test A to be set so that the probability of declaring a sick person to be healthy with test A is higher than really desired.

[11] Many machine learning methods require solving optimization problems through iterative numerical procedures because no closed-form solutions are known. This is addressed at length in Chapter 10. It has been found empirically that some loss functions lead to easier optimization problems than others, and that sometimes changing a loss function to make an optimization problem easier, say by replacing cross-entropy loss with squared-error loss in a neural network, results in a better solution, even in terms of the original loss function. Choice of loss function based on convenience does not necessarily go against Tukeys' advice at the beginning of this chapter.

respectively, derive squared-error loss and cross-entropy loss from the (subjective) principle that the best model in a class of models is one which assigns maximal likelihood to the observed data.

Exercise 2.1 *The Kullback–Leibler information*[12] *(also called cross-entropy) for discriminating between discrete probability distributions p and q on the set* $\{1, \ldots, C\}$ *is*

$$\mathrm{KL}\,(p,\,q) = \sum_{c=1}^{C} p_c \, \log \frac{p_c}{q_c}.$$

It is sometimes interpreted as "the cost of using q in place of p when the true distribution is p," where the "cost" refers to loss of efficiency in encoding data drawn from distribution p (see Cover and Thomas (2006) for a full explanation). When a datum is class y, the true class probability vector is $t = (0, \ldots, 0, 1, 0, \ldots, 0)$, *where the single 1 occurs in position y.*[13] *Show that cross-entropy loss is the same as Kullback–Leibler information:*

$$\mathrm{L}\left(y, (\widehat{\mathrm{P}}(Y = c \mid X = x))_{c=1}^{C}\right) = \mathrm{KL}\left(t, (\widehat{\mathrm{P}}(Y = c \mid X = x))_{c=1}^{C}\right).$$

2.5   Risk

A standard criterion for a "good" approximation $\widehat{f}$ of f is one which minimizes the expected loss,[14] known as the *generalization error* or *risk*. Usually the expectation is with respect to the joint probability distribution P on points $(X, Y) \in \mathcal{X} \times f(\mathcal{X})$.

The *risk of approximation* $\widehat{f}$ *at point* $x \in \mathcal{X}$ is the expected loss incurred by using $\widehat{f}(x)$ in place of Y for new data (X, Y) such that $X = x$,

$$\mathrm{R}(\widehat{f} \mid X = x) = \mathrm{E}_{Y \mid X=x}[\mathrm{L}(Y, \widehat{f}(x))] = \int_{f(\mathcal{X})} \mathrm{L}(y, \widehat{f}(x))\,\mathrm{P}(Y = y \mid X = x)\,dy.$$

The response variable Y is treated as random, with the conditional distribution $\mathrm{P}(Y \mid X = x)$, while the input $X = x$ and trained classifier $\widehat{f}$ are treated as fixed.[15]

---

[12] Kullback–Leibler information will be seen again in Section 10.7, in the context of the expectation-maximization algorithm.

[13] This is called a *one-hot encoding* of the class y.

[14] Two other criteria for a "good" approximation, different from "minimize the expected loss," are the *minimax* criterion—"minimize the maximum possible loss, $\max_{(x,y) \in \mathcal{X} \times f(\mathcal{X})} \mathrm{L}(y, \widehat{f}(x))$"—and the *structural risk minimization* criterion—"minimize a provable and computable upper bound for the true risk based on training risk."

[15] If the notation $\widehat{f} \mid X = x$ seems odd, keep in mind that $\widehat{f}$ is a deterministic function of a random variable X, and thus is also a random variable.

Choosing an approximation $\widehat{f}$ to minimize the risk of $\widehat{f}$ at a specific point (or finite set of points) in $\mathcal{X}$ is called *transductive learning*. It is of use when the entire set of points at which predictions are to be made is known at the time that $\widehat{f}$ is constructed.[16] The risk of $\widehat{f}$ at a point $x \in \mathcal{X}$ is also useful theoretically—see Exercise 2.3 and Section 4.1.

The *risk of approximation* $\widehat{f}$ is the expected loss incurred by using $\widehat{f}(X)$ in place of Y for new data (X, Y),

$$R(\widehat{f}) = E_{(X,Y)}[\, L(Y,\widehat{f}(X))\,].$$

Data point (X, Y) is treated as random while the trained classifier $\widehat{f}$ is treated as fixed. The risk of approximation $\widehat{f}$ is also the expected value (with respect to the distribution on X) of the risk at X,

$$R(\widehat{f}) = E_X[R(\widehat{f} \mid X)] = \int_{\mathcal{X}} \int_{f(\mathcal{X})} L(y,\widehat{f}(x))\, P(Y = y \mid X = x)\, dy\, P(X = x)\, dx.$$

Choosing an approximation $\widehat{f}$ to minimize the risk of $\widehat{f}$ is done when the points at which $\widehat{f}$ is to make a prediction are not known at the time that $\widehat{f}$ is constructed, but will be drawn from the distribution $P(X)$ on $\mathcal{X}$ at some future time. This is the typical situation in applied machine learning.

An *approximation method* is a function which maps training datasets to approximations of f. It maps a set $S \in (\mathcal{X} \times f(\mathcal{X}))^n$ of n observed data to a function $\widehat{f}_S$, where $\widehat{f}_S$ is in the set of all functions which map $\mathcal{X} \to f(\mathcal{X})$. Actually, approximations $\widehat{f}_S$ lie in a method-specific proper subset of the set of all functions $\mathcal{X} \to f(\mathcal{X})$, about which more will be said later. The probability distribution on $\mathcal{X} \times f(\mathcal{X})$ extends to training datasets S and thence to approximations $\widehat{f}_S$, so approximations $\widehat{f}_S$ are random variables.

The *risk of an approximation method (trained on datasets of size n)* is the expected loss incurred by drawing a random training set[17] S of size n, constructing an approximation $\widehat{f}_S$ from it, and using $\widehat{f}_S(X)$ in place of Y for new data (X, Y),

$$R_n = E_{(S,X,Y)}[\, L(Y,\widehat{f}_S(X))\,].$$

---

[16] For example, the problem of determining who wrote which articles in *The Federalist* (Mosteller and Wallace, 1963) is transductive learning.

[17] It may seem strange to treat the training data as random, when in any particular problem it is fixed and known. It is, however, the "orthodox" (*frequentist*) point of view in Statistics that the data are random. This might be justified by declaring our goal to be finding approximation methods which are good, on average, for constructing approximations $\widehat{f}_S$ on future, as-yet-unobserved training datasets S. That is, the frequentist point of view is that of the algorithm designer, who wants an algorithm to perform well on a large number of as-yet-unknown problems. In contrast, the *Bayesian* viewpoint might be called that of the applied practitioner, who is more interested in what can be inferred from the particular dataset at hand than in the performance of an algorithm on other problems.

The risk of an approximation method is also the expected value of the risk of a classifier trained by the method on a random dataset of n points,

$$R_n = E_S[R(\hat{f}_S)]$$
$$= \int_{s \in (\mathcal{X} \times f(\mathcal{X}))^n} \int_{x \in \mathcal{X}} \int_{y \in f(\mathcal{X})} L(y, \hat{f}_s(x)) \, P(Y = y \mid X = x) \, dy \, P(X = x) \, dx \, P(S = s) \, ds.$$

The risk of a particular approximation $\hat{f}_S$, $R(\hat{f}_S)$, can be viewed as the risk of the approximation method conditional on the training dataset S. Choosing an approximation method $S \mapsto \hat{f}$ to minimize the risk of the approximation method is done by algorithm designers, whose goal is to produce approximation methods which are useful in a wide variety of as-yet-unseen applied problems. A caveat for the applied machine learning practitioner to keep in mind is that a low-risk approximation method may, in any given application, produce a high-risk approximation $\hat{f}$.

Exercise 2.2 *Consider the following situation, which will be revisited in Exercises 4.3, 4.7, and Section 12.1. There are $C = 2$ classes, and the marginal probabilities of the two classes are*

$$P(Y = 1) = p \qquad and \qquad P(Y = 2) = 1 - p$$

for some given value of p, $0 < p < 1$. There is a one-dimensional feature X: for data of class 1 it is distributed $N(\mu_1, 1)$ and for data of class 2 it is distributed $N(\mu_2, 1)$, where means $\mu_1 < \mu_2$ are given, so

$$P(X = x \mid Y = 1) = \frac{1}{\sqrt{2\pi}} e^{-\frac{1}{2}(x - \mu_1)^2} \qquad and \quad P(X = x \mid Y = 2) = \frac{1}{\sqrt{2\pi}} e^{-\frac{1}{2}(x - \mu_2)^2}.$$

Approximations to the true class label function f are assumed to have a particular form: predict class 1 if the feature falls below a threshold, τ, and otherwise predict class 2, that is,

$$\hat{f}_\tau(x) = \begin{cases} 1 & if \; x \le \tau \\ 2 & if \; x > \tau \end{cases}.$$

Express the following in terms of the given quantities p, μ_1, and μ_2 and, where appropriate, the threshold τ and given losses $L(1, 2) > 0$ and $L(2, 1) > 0$:

(A) the conditional probabilities of the classes, $P(Y = 1 \mid X)$ and $P(Y = 2 \mid X)$;

(B) the risk of approximation $\hat{f}_\tau$ at a point x, $R(\hat{f}_\tau \mid X = x)$;

(C) the risk of approximation $\hat{f}_\tau$, $R(\hat{f}_\tau)$;

(D) the unique value τ_{min} of the threshold τ which produces the minimum-risk approximation.

(E) Show that if $L(1, 2) = L(2, 1)$ and $p = \frac{1}{2}$, then τ_{min} is the midpoint between μ_1 and μ_2.

Except in special cases, risk cannot be computed exactly because $P(Y \mid X)$ and $P(X)$ are unknown. In supervised learning, the risk of approximation $\hat{f}$ can be approximated (poorly) from training data

$$(x_1, y_1), \ldots, (x_n, y_n)$$

by the *training risk*, or *apparent risk*,

$$\hat{R}_{train}(\hat{f}) = \frac{1}{n} \sum_{i=1}^{n} L(y_i, \hat{f}(x_i)).$$

Better approximations of risk will be discussed in Chapter 7.

Exercise 2.3 *Show that if the risk of approximation $\hat{f}_1(x)$ is no more than the risk of approximation $\hat{f}_2(x)$ at each point $x \in \mathcal{X}$, then the overall risk of $\hat{f}_1$ is no more than the overall risk of approximation $\hat{f}_2$. Thus point-wise improvement in the risk of $\hat{f}$, if it can be done without making the risk worse somewhere else, always results in overall improvement of the risk of $\hat{f}$.*

Exercise 2.4 *Explain why training risk is a bad approximation of risk.* **Hint:** *Design a classification algorithm, using 0–1 loss and assuming for convenience that the probability of seeing two identical feature vectors X is zero, such that the training risk is 0 for any set of training data but the risk is $\frac{C-1}{C}$, where C is the number of classes.*

Exercise 2.5 **Open-Ended Challenge.** *Propose a better approximation of risk than training risk (without looking at Chapter 7).*

Exercise 2.6 *A figure of merit sometimes used for classification is the so-called* class-averaged accuracy,

$$\frac{1}{C} \sum_{c=1}^{C} P(\hat{f}(X) = c \mid Y = c),$$

or equivalently the class-averaged inaccuracy,

$$\frac{1}{C} \sum_{c=1}^{C} P(\hat{f}(X) \neq c \mid Y = c).$$

Show that the class-averaged inaccuracy of $\hat{f}$ is the risk $R(\hat{f})$ corresponding to the loss function

$$L(y, \hat{f}(x)) = \begin{cases} 0 & \text{if } y = \hat{f}(x) \\ \dfrac{1}{C\,P(Y = y)} & \text{if } y \neq \hat{f}(x) \end{cases}.$$

Does it make sense for a loss function to depend on the number of classes? Does it make sense for a loss function to depend on the marginal distribution of the class labels?

2.6   The Reality of the Unknown Function

A reasonable question to ask at this point is whether the unknown function f, or the joint probability distribution $P(X, Y)$, actually exists. One quick and easy answer is that this is a mathematical model which is rich enough to be broadly applicable and simple enough to analyze, and as such, it is defensible on purely utilitarian grounds.

A somewhat more nuanced answer is that we use the language of probability to express our imperfect state of knowledge about the world. The data which we observe were generated by a process which we do not fully understand: we introduce $P(X, Y)$ as a name for this process, and use the theory of probability both to derive names for various aspects of the unknown process (such as the conditional distribution $P(X \mid Y)$ and the marginal distribution $P(Y)$) and also to enable us to quantify our uncertainty about the process. If we accept using probability in this way, and accept as our goal the development of a function $\widehat{f}$ which has low risk when used for prediction (recall that the idea of risk follows from $P(X, Y)$ but does *not* require that we accept the existence of an unknown function f), then the existence of an unknown function f to be learned is straightforward. Given the joint distribution $P(X, Y)$ and a point $X = x$ at which to predict a response or class Y, compute the risk of predicting every possible value of Y at $X = x$, and predict a value of Y which corresponds to the minimal risk, breaking any ties, if there are multiple distinct values of Y which are minimal-risk predictions at x, in some deterministic but arbitrary way.[18] Define f to be the function which makes these minimal-risk predictions. This will be revisited in the context of classification with the development of the Bayes classifier in Section 4.1.

2.7   Training and Selection of Models, and Purposes of Learning

Given a practically computable optimality criterion (training risk, for example) for approximations of f, a major goal is to find an optimal approximation $\widehat{f}$ in the set of all functions $\mathcal{X} \to f(\mathcal{X})$. Generally, this set is too large to search effectively. The purpose of each regression or classification method is to specify a subset $\mathcal{F}$ of the set functions mapping $\mathcal{X} \to f(\mathcal{X})$ which is simultaneously small enough that an

---

[18] Ties could be broken randomly, but making f random without gaining anything in terms of risk needlessly complicates the problem of learning.

approximately optimal approximation $\widehat{f} \in \mathcal{F}$ can be found and big enough that $\widehat{f}$ is close to f, the true function, in many applications.

Specification of $\mathcal{F}$ is called *model assumption* and, given $\mathcal{F}$, computation of $\widehat{f_S} \in \mathcal{F}$ from a dataset S is called *training a model*. Sometimes $\mathcal{F}$ can be described by a finite number of scalar parameters, in which case the method which gave rise to it is called a *parametric method*. Otherwise, the method is called a *non-parametric method*.[19]

There are at least two reasons for solving the Problem of Learning. The first reason is that in the future, we will be presented with unmarked feature vectors, $X_{n+1}, \ldots,$ and will be asked to make predictions $\widehat{f}(X_{n+1}), \ldots$ of the unobserved responses or class labels. Solving the Problem of Learning in this case is *predictive learning* or *predictive modeling*.

The second reason for solving the Problem of Learning is to find relationships between observed features vectors $x_1, \ldots, x_n$ and their corresponding observed response or class labels $y_1, \ldots, y_n$, in order to enhance human understanding of the process by which the data were generated. This enhanced understanding often serves an applied purpose, or it may be a goal in and of itself. The data of Problem 2 ("Ballot"), for example, might reveal relationships between demographic features and voting behavior which could be used by political parties in various ways. Solving the Problem of Learning in this case is *explanatory learning* or *explanatory modeling*.

In any given application, the two reasons for solving the Problem of Learning are not necessarily exclusive. One may wish both to predict and to explain.[20] The relative emphasis on prediction or explanation may influence the choice of approximation method. An approximation method might not be used for explanatory modeling, even if it has low risk, if the structure of the approximation $\widehat{f}$ it produces does not reveal easily interpreted relationships between $x_1, \ldots, x_n$ and $y_1, \ldots, y_n$. Such an approximation method also might not be used for predictive modeling, as some clients are reluctant to trust an approximation $\widehat{f}$ which has not been validated through interpretation by experts in the field of the application. This book focuses primarily on predictive modeling, because it has been called for more often than explanatory modeling in the author's experience.

2.8   Notation

Throughout this book, unobserved feature vectors and responses (or classes), thought of as random variables on $\mathcal{X}$ and $f(\mathcal{X})$, are denoted by upper-case letters X and Y respectively. Specific values of feature vectors and responses (or classes), thought of

---

[19] *Non-parametric* does not mean that a method uses no parameters. It refers to a method where the number of parameters is determined in part by the data (in particular, where the number of parameters can grow with the number of data).

[20] For interesting further discussion, see Breiman (2001b).

as fixed points in $\mathcal{X}$ and $f(\mathcal{X})$, are denoted by lower-case letters x and y respectively (sometimes y is replaced by c or d in the case of classes). Context should prevent confusion in the rare exceptions. A list of notation is provided in Appendix A.

The letter P denotes both the probability of an event *and* a probability density or mass function. In the latter case, the density or mass function may be multiplied by a positive, non-unit constant. Application and convenience determine whether P integrates or sums to one or to some other positive number. By way of example, consider $P(Y = y \mid X = x)$ and $P(X = x)$ in the expression of the risk of an approximation $\widehat{f}$:

$$R(\widehat{f}) = \int_{\mathcal{X}} \int_{f(\mathcal{X})} L(y, \widehat{f}(x)) \, P(Y = y \mid X = x) \, dy \, P(X = x) \, dx.$$

If we are asked to choose, from a set of approximations, an optimal one, then these density or mass functions can be multiplied by any positive constant without changing the result: in particular, normalizing constants of certain statistical models can be ignored for analytical or computational convenience. But if we are asked what is the risk of a particular approximation, these functions must integrate or sum to one.

3

Regression

A statistical model involves the identification of those elements of our problem which are subject to uncontrolled variation and a specification of that variation in terms of probability distributions.
—David J. Bartholomew, *Unobserved Variables: Models and Misunderstandings*, 2013

Essentially, all models are wrong, but some are useful.
—George E. P. Box and Norman R. Draper, *Empirical Model Building and Response Surfaces*, 1987

This is the one chapter in this book which is dedicated to regression, and it presents regression mostly from the classical, statistical, least-squares point of view. We open the discussion of practical learning methods with least-squares regression for (at least) four reasons. First, it is *useful:* the underlying model assumptions are, in many applications, close enough to correct that this method has been widely used in the literature of many scientific domains.[1] Second, it is *relatively easy to treat analytically*, and a study of the analysis and the closed-form solutions it yields can provide insight into "what is going on" with this approach to regression. The author hopes this will lead to more informed application. The exercises of this chapter are an integral part of the analytic development (solutions, as always, can be found in Appendix B). Third, it enables *the transformation of classification problems into regression problems*, which is an approach taken by logistic regression and neural networks in Chapter 4. Finally,

---

[1] This is not to say that every use has been appropriate.

Machine Learning: a Concise Introduction, First Edition. Steven W. Knox.
© This publication is a US Government work and is in the public domain.
Published 2018 by John Wiley & Sons, Inc.
Companion Website: http://www.wiley.com/go/Knox/MachineLearning

the thorough understanding we have of least-squares regression sets the bar high for what is to follow in later chapters where, generally speaking, our theoretical understanding is not as complete.[2] Perhaps the contrast will motivate some readers to improve the current state of the art.

For simplicity, in Sections 3.1 through 3.7, the domain of the function f which is to be learned is assumed to be the m-dimensional real numbers, $\mathbb{R}^m$. Categorical features are addressed in Section 3.8 and adding flexibility to a linear model by expanding and transforming the features or response is addressed in Section 3.9. The range of f will always be $\mathbb{R}$, except as briefly mentioned in Section 3.10.

Linear regression is an old technique[3] and the subject of a large and excellent literature. The reader is directed to Rawlings et al. (2001) for a thorough introduction to the theory and practice of fitting linear regression models to data, and to Searle (1971) for more in-depth development of the theory.

3.1 General Framework

The model assumption of linear regression is that the function to be learned, $f : \mathbb{R}^m \to \mathbb{R}$, is linear.[4] This means that, given a vector $x_i \in \mathbb{R}^m$, $f(x_i)$ is the vector inner product

$$f(x_i) = f_\theta(x_i) = [\, 1 \quad x_{i1} \quad x_{i2} \quad \cdots \quad x_{im} \,] \begin{bmatrix} \theta_0 \\ \theta_1 \\ \vdots \\ \theta_m \end{bmatrix} = \theta_0 + x_{i1}\theta_1 + \cdots + x_{im}\theta_m$$

for some fixed real $(m+1)$-vector of parameters $\theta = (\theta_0, \theta_1, \ldots, \theta_m)^{\mathrm{T}}$. Observed data $(x_1, y_1), \ldots, (x_n, y_n)$ are taken to be

$$y_i = f_\theta(x_i) + e_i$$

for each i, where $e_1, \ldots, e_n$ are realizations of independent, identically distributed random variables with mean zero and unknown variance, σ^2. We do *not* assume that $e_1, \ldots, e_n$ are Gaussian-distributed, although we will make this assumption later, starting in Section 3.6. In matrix notation with n observations, the data satisfy

$$\begin{bmatrix} y_1 \\ y_2 \\ \vdots \\ y_n \end{bmatrix} = \begin{bmatrix} f_\theta(x_1) + e_1 \\ f_\theta(x_2) + e_2 \\ \vdots \\ f_\theta(x_n) + e_n \end{bmatrix} = \begin{bmatrix} 1 & x_{11} & x_{12} & \cdots & x_{1m} \\ 1 & x_{21} & x_{22} & \cdots & x_{2m} \\ \vdots & \vdots & \vdots & & \vdots \\ 1 & x_{n1} & x_{n2} & \cdots & x_{nm} \end{bmatrix} \begin{bmatrix} \theta_0 \\ \theta_1 \\ \vdots \\ \theta_m \end{bmatrix} + \begin{bmatrix} e_1 \\ e_2 \\ \vdots \\ e_n \end{bmatrix}.$$

---

[2] Practice usually runs ahead of theory, and this can be observed in many aspects of machine learning. See, in particular, Chapters 5 and 6.

[3] Least-squares linear regression goes back to Legendre or Gauss.

[4] Some readers, particularly those with a background in geometry or algebra, may insist that f as defined here be called an *affine function* rather than a *linear function* unless $\theta_0 = 0$. It is common in statistics to ignore this distinction, and to call f linear whether $\theta_0 = 0$ or not: we follow the statistical usage in this book.

Written more compactly,

$$\mathbf{y} = \mathbf{x}\theta + \mathbf{e},$$

where the $n \times (m + 1)$ matrix $\mathbf{x}$ (the *design matrix*), the n-long column vectors $\mathbf{y}$ and $\mathbf{e}$, and the $(m + 1)$-long parameter vector θ in the last equation are defined to be the corresponding vectors and matrices in the one above it.

3.2 Loss

Although choice of loss function is subjective, squared-error loss

$$L(y, \hat{y}) = (y - \hat{y})^2$$

is by far the most commonly used, with absolute-error loss

$$L(y, \hat{y}) = |y - \hat{y}|$$

a distant second. This is partly a matter of computational and analytic convenience, though Exercise 3.7 shows that squared-error loss also arises naturally from an additional model assumption and a widely used parameter estimation criterion. An advantage of absolute-error loss is that the fitted model is more robust to outliers in the data and so regression with absolute-error loss is sometimes called *robust regression*. This chapter addresses squared-error loss exclusively.

Exercise 3.1 *Suppose that there are no observable features, and that the response Y is real-valued, so the linear model of Section 3.1 is $Y = \theta_0$ plus mean-zero noise. The predicted value for future Y's is θ_0. Compute the risk of predicting any given value of θ_0, and find the risk-minimizing value or values of θ_0, under*

(A) squared-error loss, and

(B) absolute-error loss.

Hint: *The answers will be in terms of the distribution of Y. For part (B), the fact that $|Y - \theta_0| = \int_{-\infty}^{\theta_0} [Y \leq t] dt + \int_{\theta_0}^{\infty} [Y > t] dt$ may be useful, and it may be assumed that the cumulative distribution function of Y is continuous on $\mathbb{R}$ or, even more, that Y has a density function on $\mathbb{R}$.*

3.3 Estimating the Model Parameters

Given an $(m + 1)$-long (column) parameter vector θ, the linear model predicts that at point

$$x_i = (x_{i1}, \ldots, x_{im})$$

in feature space, the response will be

$$(1, x_i)\theta.$$

The difference between an actual response y_i from observed datum (x_i, y_i) and the predicted response $(1, x_i)\theta$ is

$$e_i = y_i - (1, x_i)\,\theta.$$

Viewed this way, e_i is what is left over from the observed response, after the effect of the model has been removed. For this reason, $e_1, \ldots, e_n$ are called *residuals*.

Using training risk as an estimate of risk, searching for a minimum-risk approximation to f_θ is equivalent to searching for a parameter vector θ which minimizes the training risk,

$$\begin{aligned} n \times \widehat{R}_{\text{train}}(f_\theta) &= \textstyle\sum_{i=1}^{n} \left(y_i - (1, x_{i1}, \ldots, x_{im})(\theta_0, \theta_1, \ldots, \theta_m)^{\mathrm{T}} \right)^2 \\ &= (\mathbf{y} - \mathbf{x}\theta)^{\mathrm{T}} (\mathbf{y} - \mathbf{x}\theta) = \mathbf{e}^{\mathrm{T}}\mathbf{e} = \textstyle\sum_{i=1}^{n} e_i^2 = \text{RSS}. \end{aligned}$$

Note that the training risk is equal to the sum of the squares of the residuals: it is called the *residual sum of squares* and denoted RSS. Since minimizing training risk is equivalent to minimizing the residual sum of squares, fitting a linear model under squared-error loss is called *least-squares linear regression*.[5] Minimizing the quadratic form $(\mathbf{y} - \mathbf{x}\theta)^{\mathrm{T}} (\mathbf{y} - \mathbf{x}\theta)$ over $\theta \in \mathbb{R}^{m+1}$ is an exercise in multivariate calculus.

Exercise 3.2 *Show that the unique minimizer of* $\widehat{R}_{\text{train}}(f_\theta) = \frac{1}{n} (\mathbf{y} - \mathbf{x}\theta)^{\mathrm{T}} (\mathbf{y} - \mathbf{x}\theta)$ *is*

$$\hat{\theta} = (\mathbf{x}^{\mathrm{T}}\mathbf{x})^{-1}\mathbf{x}^{\mathrm{T}}\,\mathbf{y},$$

when $\mathbf{x}$ *is of full rank.*[6]

---

[5] The term *regression*, coined by Francis Galton in the 19th century, has its origin in "regression toward mediocrity" which he observed in the height of adult children of exceptionally tall or exceptionally short parents. Specifically, Galton's fitted model was

$$\text{adult child's height} = \tfrac{1}{3} \text{ population mean height} + \tfrac{1}{3} \text{ father's height} + \tfrac{1}{3} \text{ mother's height.}$$

In fitting this model, Galton multiplied all female heights by 1.08 "so that no objection grounded on the sexual difference of stature need be raised when I speak of averages" (Galton, 1886). Thus Galton's models are actually

$$\text{adult son's height} = \tfrac{1}{3} \text{ population mean height} + \tfrac{1}{3} \text{ father's height} + \tfrac{1.08}{3} \text{ mother's height.}$$

and

$$\text{adult daughter's height} = \tfrac{1}{3.24} \text{ population mean height} + \tfrac{1}{3.24} \text{ father's height} + \tfrac{1}{3} \text{ mother's height.}$$

The fact that the mother's coefficient is larger than the father's has drawn comment (Pagano and Anoke, 2013).

[6] When $\mathbf{x}$ is not of full rank, the inverse of $\mathbf{x}^{\mathrm{T}}\mathbf{x}$ in the expression for the least-squares estimate for $\hat{\theta}$ must be replaced by a generalized inverse. In this case, there is a (translated) non-trivial linear subspace of parameter vectors θ, all of which minimize $(\mathbf{y} - \mathbf{x}\theta)^{\mathrm{T}} (\mathbf{y} - \mathbf{x}\theta)$. By convention, the shortest such vector is presented as the least-squares solution, together with a basis for the subspace. Full details are given in Searle (1971).

With respect to squared-error loss, using training risk to estimate risk, the optimal linear approximation is $\hat{f}_\theta(x) = f_{\hat{\theta}}(x)$.

3.4   Properties of Fitted Values

Let $\hat{\theta}$ denote the least-squares estimate for θ found in Exercise 3.1, $\hat{\theta} = (\mathbf{x}^T\mathbf{x})^{-1}\mathbf{x}^T\mathbf{y}$. These are the *fitted model parameters*. Let $\mathbf{i}$ denote the $n \times n$ identity matrix and let $\mathbf{h}$ denote the $n \times n$ matrix $\mathbf{x}\left(\mathbf{x}^T\mathbf{x}\right)^{-1}\mathbf{x}^T$. The *fitted response* and the *fitted residuals* are respectively

$$\hat{\mathbf{y}} = \mathbf{x}\hat{\theta} = \mathbf{h}\,\mathbf{y} \qquad \text{and} \qquad \hat{\mathbf{e}} = \mathbf{y} - \hat{\mathbf{y}} = (\mathbf{i} - \mathbf{h})\,\mathbf{y}.$$

Given a new feature vector x_{n+1} which does not appear in the training data, the *predicted response* at x_{n+1} is

$$\hat{y}_{n+1} = \hat{f}_\theta(x_{n+1}) = f_{\hat{\theta}}(x_{n+1}) = (1, x_{n+1})\hat{\theta}.$$

Exercise 3.3 *The symmetric $n \times n$ matrix $\mathbf{h} = \mathbf{x}(\mathbf{x}^T\mathbf{x})^{-1}\mathbf{x}^T$ is called the* hat matrix *because multiplication by $\mathbf{h}$ "puts the hat on $\mathbf{y}$" in the sense that $\hat{\mathbf{y}} = \mathbf{h}\mathbf{y}$. Prove three properties of the hat matrix:*

(A) $\mathbf{h}\mathbf{h} = \mathbf{h}$, *that is, $\mathbf{h}$ is idempotent;*

(B) $\mathbf{h}\mathbf{x} = \mathbf{x}$, *that is, $\mathbf{h}$ acts as the identity map on the column space of the design matrix $\mathbf{x}$;*

(C) $\mathbf{h}\mathbf{z} = 0$ *for any n-long vector $\mathbf{z}$ orthogonal to the column space of $\mathbf{x}$.* **Hint:** *This will be useful in Exercises 3.4 and 3.5.*

Together, parts (A), (B), and (C) of Exercise 3.3 say that left multiplication by $\mathbf{h}$ is a linear projection of $\mathbb{R}^n$ into the column space of $\mathbf{x}$. The column space of $\mathbf{x}$ is precisely the set of n-long vectors of the form

$$\begin{bmatrix} 1 & x_{11} & x_{12} & \cdots & x_{1m} \\ 1 & x_{21} & x_{22} & \cdots & x_{2m} \\ \vdots & \vdots & \vdots & & \vdots \\ 1 & x_{n1} & x_{n2} & \cdots & x_{nm} \end{bmatrix} \begin{bmatrix} \theta_0 \\ \theta_1 \\ \vdots \\ \theta_m \end{bmatrix},$$

that is, the column space of $\mathbf{x}$ is the space of n-long vectors which can be realized as the response of some linear model applied to the inputs $x_1, x_2, \ldots, x_n$ with no error.

The fundamental random thing in the linear model is the vector of residuals, $\mathbf{e}$, with

$$E[\mathbf{e}] = 0 \qquad \text{and} \qquad \text{Var}[\mathbf{e}] = \sigma^2 \mathbf{i}.$$

From this, it follows that $\mathbf{y}$ is also random,[7] with

$$E[\mathbf{y}] = \mathbf{x}\theta \qquad \text{and} \qquad \text{Var}[\mathbf{y}] = \sigma^2 \mathbf{i},$$

and therefore all of the fitted and predicted values, being linear functions of $\mathbf{y}$, are also random.

Exercise 3.4 *Show that the expected values and variances of the fitted and predicted values are as follows, where x_{n+1} is a feature vector not in the training data and $\widehat{y}_{n+1}$ is the estimated response at x_{n+1}:*

$$
\begin{aligned}
E[\widehat{\theta}] &= \theta & \text{Var}[\widehat{\theta}] &= \sigma^2 (\mathbf{x}^\mathsf{T}\mathbf{x})^{-1} \\
E[\widehat{\mathbf{y}}] &= E[\mathbf{y}] & \text{Var}[\widehat{\mathbf{y}}] &= \sigma^2 \mathbf{h} \\
E[\widehat{y}_{n+1}] &= (1, x_{n+1})\theta & \text{Var}[\widehat{y}_{n+1}] &= \sigma^2 (1, x_{n+1}) (\mathbf{x}^\mathsf{T}\mathbf{x})^{-1} (1, x_{n+1})^\mathsf{T} \\
E[\widehat{\mathbf{e}}] &= 0 & \text{Var}[\widehat{\mathbf{e}}] &= \sigma^2 (\mathbf{i} - \mathbf{h}).
\end{aligned}
$$

Note that σ^2 and θ are unknown, while $\mathbf{y}, \mathbf{x}, \mathbf{h}, \mathbf{i}$, and x_{n+1} are known. **Hint:** *Recall that the variance of a real random variable Z satisfies* $\text{Var}[Z] = E[Z^2] - E[Z]^2$.

The exercise shows that the fitted and predicted values are unbiased estimates of the quantities they are estimating: the *bias* of an estimator $\widehat{z}$ of a fixed quantity z is $E[\widehat{z}] - z$, and an estimator is *unbiased* if its bias is zero. In particular, $\widehat{\theta}$ is an unbiased estimate of the model parameters, θ. Historically, unbiasedness has been considered a desirable property, and effort concentrated on finding optimal unbiased estimates, where *optimal* usually meant *minimal variance* under certain restrictions. Since the 1960's, however, it has been appreciated that biased parameter estimates can lead to better predictive linear models, and that there is a *bias–variance trade-off* to be managed. Chapter 5 is devoted entirely to the bias–variance trade-off, beginning with the case of least-squares regression.

Two other sums of squares will be useful later: the *total sum of squares* is

$$\text{TSS} = \sum_{i=1}^{n}(y_i - \bar{y})^2,$$

where $\bar{y} = \frac{1}{n}\sum_{i=1}^{n} y_i$ is the mean response in the data. The TSS measures the overall variability of the observed response about its mean: it is $(n-1)$ or n times the sample

---

[7] It may strike the reader as strange that $\mathbf{y}$, a vector of responses which has been observed, is random. The reader may also be surprised to learn that the unknown parameter vector θ is *not* random. This is the traditional statistical viewpoint: it is not the only one, or necessarily the best one.

variance of the response.[8] It is a property only of the data, not of the linear model.[9] The *model sum of squares* is

$$\text{MSS} = \sum_{i=1}^{n} (\hat{y}_i - \bar{y})^2.$$

The MSS measures the overall variability of the fitted values about the mean observed response. When MSS is large relative to TSS, the fitted values vary about the mean, and they can only do so through the presence of some estimated linear effect (that is, because some of the components of $\hat{\theta}$ are not zero). Conversely, when MSS is small relative to TSS, this suggests that the fitted linear model does not explain much of the variability in the data. In terms of fitted values, the residual sum of squares is

$$\text{RSS} = \sum_{i=1}^{n} (y_i - \hat{y}_i)^2,$$

and it measures the variability of the observed response around the fitted response: a way to interpret this is as the variability in the data *not* explained by the linear model.

Exercise 3.5 *Show that*

$$TSS = MSS + RSS.$$

Hint: *TSS, MSS, and RSS are the squared lengths of certain vectors. Show that one of these vectors is the sum of the other two, and that the two summands are orthogonal to each other.*

A statistic for assessing the quality of a fitted model, denoted R^2, is defined in terms of RSS, MSS, and TSS:

$$R^2 = 1 - \frac{\text{RSS}}{\text{TSS}} = \frac{\text{MSS}}{\text{TSS}}.$$

It is interpreted as the proportion of the variation in the observed response which is explained by the model. See Section 7.9 for further discussion, including a modification of R^2, called *adjusted* R^2, which balances the proportion of variation explained against the number of non-zero parameters in the model.

---

[8] Depending on whether one divides by $(n-1)$ or n in computing the sample variance.

[9] Another way to view TSS is as the residual sum of squares of a linear model consisting only of parameter θ_0, the least-squares estimate of which is $\hat{\theta}_0 = \bar{y}$.

Exercise 3.6 *Show that $R^2 = r^2$, where r is the sample correlation of the vector of observed responses $(y_1, \ldots, y_n)$ with the vector of fitted responses $(\hat{y}_1, \ldots, \hat{y}_n)$,*

$$r = \frac{\frac{1}{n-1} \sum_{i=1}^{n} (y_i - \bar{y})(\hat{y}_i - \bar{y})}{\sqrt{\frac{1}{n-1} \sum_{i=1}^{n} (y_i - \bar{y})^2} \sqrt{\frac{1}{n-1} \sum_{i=1}^{n} (\hat{y}_i - \bar{y})^2}}.$$

Hint: *In the numerator of r, write $y_i - \bar{y}$ as $y_i - \hat{y}_i + \hat{y}_i - \bar{y}$. In the process of solving Exercise 3.5, one shows that the vector $\hat{\mathbf{y}} - \bar{y}\mathbf{1}$ is orthogonal to the vector $\hat{\mathbf{e}}$, where $\mathbf{1}$ is the n-long vector $(1, 1, \ldots, 1)$.*

3.5   Estimating the Variance

There is another parameter in the model to be addressed: σ^2, the variance of the residuals. It is not important for determining the least-squares estimate of the model parameters θ—we have seen that $\hat{\theta} = (\mathbf{x}^T\mathbf{x})^{-1}\mathbf{x}^T\mathbf{y}$—but estimating σ^2 is essential for making statistical inferences about the response in terms of fitted or predicted values.

The last line of Exercise 3.4 ($\mathrm{E}[\hat{\mathbf{e}}] = 0$ and $\mathrm{Var}[\hat{\mathbf{e}}] = \sigma^2(\mathbf{i} - \mathbf{h})$) and an intermediate deduction needed in solving Exercise 3.5 (the fact that $\mathrm{RSS} = \hat{\mathbf{e}}^T\hat{\mathbf{e}}$) can be applied to show that

$$\mathrm{E}[\mathrm{RSS}] = \sum_{i=1}^{n} \mathrm{E}\left[\hat{e}_i^2\right] = \sum_{i=1}^{n} \mathrm{E}\left[\hat{e}_i^2\right] - \mathrm{E}\left[\hat{e}_i\right]^2 = \sum_{i=1}^{n} \mathrm{Var}[\hat{e}_i]$$

$$= \sum_{i=1}^{n} \sigma^2 (1 - \mathbf{h}_{ii}) = \sigma^2 (n - \mathrm{tr}(\mathbf{h})).$$

Recalling a result from linear algebra, and assuming $\mathbf{x}$ is full rank,[10]

$$\mathrm{tr}(\mathbf{h}) = \mathrm{tr}(\mathbf{x}(\mathbf{x}^T\mathbf{x})^{-1}\mathbf{x}^T) = \mathrm{tr}((\mathbf{x}^T\mathbf{x})^{-1}\mathbf{x}^T\mathbf{x})$$
$$= \mathrm{tr}((m + 1) \times (m + 1)\text{identity matrix}) = m + 1,$$

so

$$\mathrm{E}[\mathrm{RSS}] = \sigma^2 (n - m - 1).$$

Thus an unbiased estimate for the residual variance σ^2 is

$$\hat{\sigma}^2 = \frac{\mathrm{RSS}}{n - m - 1}.$$

---

[10] The trace of a square $n \times n$ matrix $\mathbf{h}$ is the sum of the diagonal elements, $\mathrm{tr}(\mathbf{h}) = \sum_{i=1}^{n} \mathbf{h}_{ii}$. Generally, the trace $\mathrm{tr}(\mathbf{h})$ is the rank of $\mathbf{h}$. For any two matrices A and B, $\mathrm{tr}(AB) = \mathrm{tr}(BA)$.

3.6   A Normality Assumption

We now add the assumption that the residuals are Gaussian-distributed, that is, that $e_1, \ldots, e_n$ are independent, identically distributed $N(0, \sigma^2)$. It then follows that $\mathbf{y}$, $\hat{\theta}$, $\hat{\mathbf{y}}$, $\hat{y}_{n+1}$, and $\hat{\mathbf{e}}$ are also Gaussian-distributed with the means and variances given in Exercise 3.4.

Furthermore, for $i = 1, \ldots, m$, let

$$t_i = \frac{\frac{\hat{\theta}_i - \theta_i}{\sqrt{(\mathbf{x}^{\mathsf{T}}\mathbf{x})_{ii}^{-1}}}}{\sqrt{\frac{\text{RSS}}{n - m - 1}}} \tag{3.1}$$

and let

$$F = \frac{\frac{\text{MSS}}{m}}{\frac{\text{RSS}}{n - m - 1}} = \frac{n - m - 1}{m} \left(\frac{\text{TSS}}{\text{RSS}} - 1 \right). \tag{3.2}$$

From the theory of quadratic forms of Gaussian random variables,[11] it can be shown that statistics t_i have Student's t distribution,

$$t_i \sim t_{n-m-1},$$

and, if $\theta_1 = \theta_2 = \cdots = \theta_m = 0$, statistic F has Snedecor's F distribution,

$$F \sim F_{m, n-m-1}.$$

These two facts play a central role in testing hypotheses about the parameter vector of a linear model.

For any given value v, both the hypothesis that $\theta_i = v$ and the hypothesis that $\theta_i \leq v$ can be tested by computing the statistic t_i of (3.1) with $\theta_i = v$. The null hypothesis that $\theta_i \leq v$ is rejected (in favor of the alternative hypothesis that $\theta_i > v$) if the probability that a t_{n-m-1}-distributed random variable exceeds the observed value of t_i is below a user-specified threshold, τ. The null hypothesis that $\theta_i = v$ is rejected (in favor of the alternative hypothesis that $\theta_i \neq v$) if the probability that the absolute value of a t_{n-m-1}-distributed random variable exceeds the observed absolute value of t_i is below a user-specified threshold, τ. The hypothesis that the ith feature plays no real role in the fitted linear model, and therefore should be excluded from the model, is equivalent to the hypothesis $\theta_i = 0$.

The hypothesis that $\theta_1 = \theta_2 = \cdots = \theta_m = 0$ is tested by computing the statistic F of (3.2). This hypothesis is rejected (in favor of the alternative hypothesis that $\theta_i \neq 0$ for some $1 \leq i \leq m$) if the probability that an $F_{m,n-m-1}$-distributed random variable exceeds the observed value of F is below a user-specified threshold, τ.

---

[11] See, for example, Mardia et al. (1979).

Under the assumption of independent $N(0, \sigma^2)$-distributed residuals, the likelihood of the data for a given parameter vector θ is

$$P(y_1, \ldots, y_n \mid x_1, \ldots, x_n, \theta, \sigma^2) = \prod_{i=1}^{n} \left((2\pi\sigma^2)^{-\frac{1}{2}} \exp\left(-\frac{(y_i - (1, x_i)\theta)^2}{2\sigma^2} \right) \right), \quad (3.3)$$

or, equivalently, the log-likelihood is

$$\log P(y_1, \ldots, y_n \mid x_1, \ldots, x_n, \theta, \sigma^2) = -\frac{n}{2} \log(2\pi\sigma^2) - \frac{1}{2\sigma^2} \sum_{i=1}^{n} (y_i - (1, x_i)\theta)^2.$$

Exercise 3.7 *Show that the parameter estimates $\hat{\theta} = (\mathbf{x}^T\mathbf{x})^{-1}\mathbf{x}^T\mathbf{y}$ and $\hat{\sigma}^2 = \dfrac{RSS}{n}$ maximize the likelihood of the data in (3.3). Compare these estimates to the least-squares estimate of θ and the unbiased estimate of σ^2.*

Exercise 3.7 shows that under the normality assumption, the least-squares parameter estimate $\hat{\theta}$ is the *maximum-likelihood estimate* for θ. Thus squared-error loss in the learning problem can arise implicitly in regression from a decision to use a maximum-likelihood estimate for a model with independent, Gaussian-distributed residuals. Maximum-likelihood estimates have many useful properties and are commonly used as estimates. Note that the maximum-likelihood estimate for σ^2 is not the unbiased estimate derived in Section 3.5.

The assumption that errors are Gaussian-distributed should be checked. This can be done graphically with a quantile–quantile plot or by applying tests in D'Agostino and Stephens (1986), Mardia et al. (1979), or Thode (2002).

3.7   Computation

In practice, $\hat{\theta} = (\mathbf{x}^T\mathbf{x})^{-1}\mathbf{x}^T\mathbf{y}$ is not found by computing a matrix inverse.[12] Instead, the QR-decomposition of $\mathbf{x}$, $\mathbf{x} = \mathbf{QR}$, is computed and $\hat{\theta}$ is obtained as follows.[13]

Exercise 3.8 *Assuming that $\mathbf{x}$ is full rank, show that $\hat{\theta}$, the least-squares parameter estimate, is the solution of the $(m + 1) \times (m + 1)$ triangular system of equations*

first $m + 1$ coordinates of $\mathbf{R}\theta = $ first $m + 1$ coordinates of $\mathbf{Q}^T\mathbf{y}$

where $\mathbf{x} = \mathbf{QR}$ is the QR-decomposition of $\mathbf{x}$.

---

[12] A famous academic statistician once threatened his entire Statistical Computing class with death if any of them were caught estimating θ by inverting $\mathbf{x}^T\mathbf{x}$ (the author was a student in this class).

[13] In the QR-decomposition of $\mathbf{x}$, $\mathbf{Q}$ is a $n \times n$ *orthogonal matrix* (meaning $\mathbf{Q}^T = \mathbf{Q}^{-1}$) and $\mathbf{R}$ is a $n \times (m + 1)$ upper triangular matrix. The obvious way to compute the QR-decomposition, by Gram–Schmidt orthonormalization, is numerically unstable. The QR-decomposition should be computed by one of the methods described in Gentle (1998) or Golub and Van Loan (1996).

In light of Exercise 3.8, it is sufficient to compute the n-long vector $\mathbf{Q}^T\mathbf{y}$ directly rather than computing the $n \times n$ orthogonal matrix $\mathbf{Q}$ and then multiplying it by $\mathbf{y}$. This is what is done in practice (Gentle, 1998; Golub and Van Loan, 1996).

3.8   Categorical Features

A categorical feature taking values in an unordered set of size K can be encoded in a set of K or $K - 1$ binary (and hence real-valued) features by the use of indicator functions. For simplicity, say the model input consists of a single categorical feature, so the ith input is $x_i = (x_{i1})$, and identify the set in which x_i takes values with the (unordered) set $\{1, \ldots, K\}$. One way to encode the categorical feature is to define vectors $z_1, \ldots, z_n$ by

$$z_i = x_i\text{th standard basis vector of } \mathbb{R}^K = \underbrace{(0, \ldots, 0, 1, 0, \ldots, 0)}_{\substack{1 \text{ in coordinate } x_i, \\ 0\text{'s elsewhere,}}}$$

and to use the real K-dimensional feature vectors z_i as input to a linear model. The binary indicator variables $z_{i1}, \ldots, z_{iK}$ are called *dummy variables* for the categorical variable x_i and the vector of dummy variables $(z_{i1}, \ldots, z_{iK})$ is called a *one-hot encoding* of the categorical variable x_i.

For example, if feature x_1 is categorical and takes values in the set {orange, blue, purple}, and if we arbitrarily identify orange with 1, blue with 2, and purple with 3, then the design matrix

$$\mathbf{x} = \begin{bmatrix} 1 & \text{blue} \\ 1 & \text{orange} \\ 1 & \text{orange} \\ 1 & \text{purple} \\ 1 & \text{blue} \\ \vdots & \vdots \\ 1 & \text{purple} \end{bmatrix} \quad \text{is encoded as} \quad \mathbf{x} = \begin{bmatrix} 1 & 0 & 1 & 0 \\ 1 & 1 & 0 & 0 \\ 1 & 1 & 0 & 0 \\ 1 & 0 & 0 & 1 \\ 1 & 0 & 1 & 0 \\ \vdots & \vdots & \vdots & \vdots \\ 1 & 0 & 0 & 1 \end{bmatrix}.$$

In this encoding, the single categorical column of $\mathbf{x}$ has been expanded into three binary columns: the first binary column is the indicator for orange, the second binary column is the indicator for blue, and the third binary column is the indicator for purple.

This leads to a complication, since the design matrix

$$\mathbf{x} = \begin{bmatrix} 1 & z_{11} & z_{12} & \cdots & z_{1K} \\ 1 & z_{21} & z_{22} & \cdots & z_{2K} \\ \vdots & \vdots & \vdots & & \vdots \\ 1 & z_{n1} & z_{n2} & \cdots & z_{nK} \end{bmatrix}$$

is no longer full rank. The original categorical feature x_{i1} takes exactly one value among the K categories, so $z_{i1} + \cdots + z_{iK} = 1$ for all i, and therefore for all $i = 1, \ldots, n$,

$$(1, z_{i1}, \ldots, z_{iK}) \begin{bmatrix} -1 \\ 1 \\ \vdots \\ 1 \end{bmatrix} = -1 + z_{i1} + \cdots + z_{iK} = 0.$$

Thus the binary encoding of a categorical variable has resulted in a design matrix which has a column space of dimension K (instead of $K + 1$).

One way to address this complication is to omit the explicit intercept (represented by the column of 1's in the design matrix and model parameter θ_0). This only works when there is exactly one categorical variable.[14] Another way to address this complication is to expand a categorical feature with K categories into $K - 1$ binary features such that the corresponding $K - 1$ columns of the design matrix span a $(K - 1)$-dimensional subspace of $\mathbb{R}^n$ orthogonal to the n-long vector of all 1's. This could be done, for example, by truncating the last coordinate off the z_i's defined above. The choice of approach affects the interpretation of the model parameters. If the intercept is omitted, then model parameter θ_j is the expected response, given that x_i takes the value j. If the intercept is retained but the last coordinate of the z_i's is truncated, then value K becomes a default value of x_i, and model parameter θ_j is the effect, or *contrast*, due to x_i taking the value j instead of K.

In the example above, if

$$\mathbf{x} = \begin{bmatrix} 0 & 1 & 0 \\ 1 & 0 & 0 \\ 1 & 0 & 0 \\ 0 & 0 & 1 \\ 0 & 1 & 0 \\ \vdots & \vdots & \vdots \\ 0 & 0 & 1 \end{bmatrix}$$

then the model parameters would be denoted as $(\theta_1, \theta_2, \theta_3)$—because θ_0 is usually reserved to denote an intercept term, and there is none in this model—and θ_i would be interpreted as the mean response for data with a feature x belonging to category i (in

---

[14] This observation seems to have originated with Suits (1957).

the example, $\theta_1 \leftrightarrow$ mean effect for being orange, $\theta_2 \leftrightarrow$ mean effect for being blue, and $\theta_3 \leftrightarrow$ mean effect for being purple). If instead

$$\mathbf{x} = \begin{bmatrix} 1 & 0 & 1 \\ 1 & 1 & 0 \\ 1 & 1 & 0 \\ 1 & 0 & 0 \\ 1 & 0 & 1 \\ \vdots & \vdots & \vdots \\ 1 & 0 & 0 \end{bmatrix}$$

then the model parameters would be denoted as $(\theta_0, \theta_1, \theta_2)$, and θ_0 would be interpreted as the mean response for all data, which by default are in category 3 (purple). For $i = 1, 2$, θ_i would be interpreted as the contrast in mean response due to the feature belonging to category i instead of category 3 (in the example, $\theta_1 \leftrightarrow$ difference in mean effect for being orange instead of purple and $\theta_2 \leftrightarrow$ difference in mean effect for being blue instead of purple).

3.9 Feature Transformations, Expansions, and Interactions

Linear regression can be made to capture non-linear relationships between the features and the response by transformations of variables and expansion of bases. For example, the model assumption could be that f is a quadratic function without cross terms, which in practice is written as a linear function in an expanded basis,

$$f_\theta(x_i) = \theta_0 + \sum_{j=1}^{m} x_{ij}\theta_j + \sum_{j=1}^{m} x_{ij}^2 \theta_{2j}$$

or the model assumption could be that f is a quadratic function with cross terms (called *interactions*),

$$f_\theta(x_i) = \theta_0 + \sum_{j=1}^{m} x_{ij}\theta_j + \sum_{j=1}^{m} x_{ij}^2 \theta_{2j} + \sum_{j=1}^{m} \sum_{k=j+1}^{m} x_{ij} x_{ik} \theta_{(j,k)}.$$

A continuous feature can be made categorical if there is reason to believe that what is important is not so much the value of the feature as whether the feature exceeds one or more thresholds. Such discretization can be done following the outline in Section 3.8.

Exercise 3.9 *Suppose feature vector $x = (x_1, \ldots, x_m)$ measures the amount of each of m possible ingredients in a serving of food, and that a linear model $f_\theta(x)$ is used to approximate how much a person likes the item described by the ingredients x (large positive values of $f_\theta(x)$ are interpreted as "likes strongly" and large negative values* *are interpreted as "dislikes strongly"). In an item of food, let x_a represent the amount of asparagus, let x_b represent the amount of bacon, and let x_c represent the amount of chocolate. Assume the linear model $f_\theta(x)$ includes quadratic terms and interactions, as above.*

(A) *Give values of θ_a and θ_c indicating that the person dislikes food containing asparagus but likes food containing chocolate.*

(B) *Give values of θ_c and θ_{2c} indicating that the person likes food containing chocolate up to a certain amount, but dislikes food containing too much chocolate.*

(C) *Give values of θ_a, θ_c, and $\theta_{(a,c)}$ indicating that the person likes food containing asparagus and likes food containing chocolate, but dislikes food containing both asparagus and chocolate.*

(D) *Give values of θ_a, θ_c, and $\theta_{(a,c)}$ indicating that the person likes food containing asparagus and likes food containing chocolate, and especially likes these two ingredients in combination.*

(E) *What is the meaning of θ_0 in this model?*

(F) *Suggest a discrete replacement of feature x_b and a value of θ_b to indicate that a person strongly dislikes food containing any amount of bacon, without regard to how much bacon is in the food.*

3.10   Variations in Linear Regression

The brief treatment of linear regression given in this chapter concludes with an even briefer description of a few of the many variants which have been developed. Many more can be found in books such as Rawlings et al. (2001).

Ridge regression is a technique which explicitly seeks to optimize a *bias–variance trade-off*, about which much more will be said in Chapter 5. Given a value of a parameter $\lambda \geq 0$, the ridge regression estimate of the linear model parameters θ is the value $\widehat{\theta}_\lambda$ which minimizes

$$\text{RSS} + \lambda \sum_{i=1}^{m} \theta_i^2.$$

The *ridge parameter* λ is chosen to minimize some estimate of the risk of the fitted model. Note that when $\lambda = 0$, ridge regression is least-squares regression and when $\lambda > 0$, parameters $\theta_1, \ldots, \theta_m$ will tend to be smaller than they would be for least-squares regression. Note also that the intercept coefficient θ_0 is not penalized. Ridge regression tends to produce lower-risk models than least-squares regression, particularly when the features are highly correlated. This will be revisited in Section 11.4.

Exercise 3.10 *Given the ridge parameter* λ*, show that the ridge regression parameter estimates for the model*

$$
\begin{bmatrix} y_1 \\ y_2 \\ \vdots \\ y_n \end{bmatrix} =
\begin{bmatrix}
1 & x_{11} & x_{12} & \cdots & x_{1m} \\
1 & x_{21} & x_{22} & \cdots & x_{2m} \\
\vdots & \vdots & \vdots & & \vdots \\
1 & x_{n1} & x_{n2} & \cdots & x_{nm}
\end{bmatrix}
\begin{bmatrix} \theta_0 \\ \theta_1 \\ \vdots \\ \theta_m \end{bmatrix}
$$

are the same as the least-squares parameter estimates for the model

$$
\begin{bmatrix} y_1 \\ y_2 \\ \vdots \\ y_n \\ 0 \\ 0 \\ \vdots \\ 0 \end{bmatrix} =
\begin{bmatrix}
1 & x_{11} & x_{12} & \cdots & x_{1m} \\
1 & x_{21} & x_{22} & \cdots & x_{2m} \\
\vdots & \vdots & \vdots & & \vdots \\
1 & x_{n1} & x_{n2} & \cdots & x_{nm} \\
0 & \sqrt{\lambda} & 0 & \cdots & 0 \\
0 & 0 & \sqrt{\lambda} & \cdots & 0 \\
\vdots & \vdots & \vdots & & \vdots \\
0 & 0 & 0 & \cdots & \sqrt{\lambda}
\end{bmatrix}
\begin{bmatrix} \theta_0 \\ \theta_1 \\ \vdots \\ \theta_m \end{bmatrix}.
$$

Thus computing parameter estimates for ridge regression has approximately the same computational cost as computing parameter estimates for ordinary least-squares regression (provided $m \ll n$*).*

A technique related to ridge regression is the *lasso*,[15] which minimizes

$$
\text{RSS} + \lambda \sum_{i=1}^{m} |\theta_i|.
$$

Computing the lasso-fitted parameters is more expensive than the ridge or least-squares-fitted parameters. Lasso performs a useful sort of automatic feature selection: see Section 11.4 and Hastie et al. (2001).

Cases where additive noise terms are uncorrelated but have different variances can be treated by a method called *weighted least squares*. Suppose that instead of

$$
\text{Var}\,[\mathbf{e}] =
\begin{bmatrix}
\sigma^2 & & & \\
& \sigma^2 & & \\
& & \ddots & \\
& & & \sigma^2
\end{bmatrix}
$$

---

[15] Lasso stands for "least absolute selection and shrinkage operator" in Tibshirani (1996b). A slightly earlier approach was called the *nonnegative garrote* (Breiman, 1995).

we have, for some $k_1^2, \ldots, k_n^2$,

$$\mathrm{Var}\,[\mathbf{e}] = \begin{bmatrix} k_1^2\sigma^2 & & & \\ & k_2^2\sigma^2 & & \\ & & \ddots & \\ & & & k_n^2\sigma^2 \end{bmatrix}.$$

Define matrix

$$W = \begin{bmatrix} k_1^{-2} & & & \\ & k_2^{-2} & & \\ & & \ddots & \\ & & & k_n^{-2} \end{bmatrix}.$$

The linear model

$$\mathbf{y} = \mathbf{x}\theta + \mathbf{e}$$

can be transformed to

$$W^{\frac{1}{2}}\,\mathbf{y} = W^{\frac{1}{2}}\,\mathbf{x}\,\theta + W^{\frac{1}{2}}\,\mathbf{e},$$

where $\mathrm{Var}\,[W^{\frac{1}{2}}\mathbf{e}] = \sigma^2 I$. The least-squares estimate of the parameters of the transformed model is

$$\widehat{\theta} = \left(\mathbf{x}^\mathsf{T} W\mathbf{x}\right)^{-1}\mathbf{x}^\mathsf{T}\,W\,\mathbf{y}.$$

Exercise 3.11 *Show that $\widehat{\theta}$ above minimizes the weighted sum of squares*

$$\sum_{i=1}^{n} k_i^{-2}(y_i - (1, x_{i1}, \ldots, x_{im})(\theta_0, \theta_1, \ldots, \theta_m)^\mathsf{T})^2.$$

Weighted least squares can be used to assign greater or lesser importance to certain observations. Cases where additive noise terms are correlated can be treated similarly, taking $W^{\frac{1}{2}}$ to be an inverse Cholesky factor[16] of the covariance matrix: that is, $W^{\frac{1}{2}}$ is a non-diagonal $n \times n$ matrix such that

$$\left((\mathrm{Cov}[Y_i, Y_j])_{i,j=1}^n\right)^{-1} = W^{\frac{1}{2}\mathsf{T}}\,W^{\frac{1}{2}}.$$

---

[16] The Cholesky decomposition of a positive-definite real matrix M is a lower-triangular matrix W such that $M = WW^\mathsf{T}$. Every positive-definite real matrix has a unique Cholesky decomposition.

Linear regression can be expanded naturally to the case where f is vector-valued, $f : \mathbb{R}^m \to \mathbb{R}^k$. The vector-valued model assumption is

$$
\begin{bmatrix}
y_{11} & y_{12} & \cdots & y_{1k} \\
y_{21} & y_{22} & \cdots & y_{2k} \\
\vdots & \vdots & & \vdots \\
y_{n1} & y_{n2} & \cdots & y_{nk}
\end{bmatrix}
=
\begin{bmatrix}
1 & x_{11} & x_{12} & \cdots & x_{1m} \\
1 & x_{21} & x_{22} & \cdots & x_{2m} \\
\vdots & \vdots & \vdots & & \vdots \\
1 & x_{n1} & x_{n2} & \cdots & x_{nm}
\end{bmatrix}
\begin{bmatrix}
\theta_{01} & \theta_{02} & \cdots & \theta_{0k} \\
\theta_{11} & \theta_{12} & \cdots & \theta_{1k} \\
\vdots & \vdots & & \vdots \\
\theta_{m1} & \theta_{m2} & \cdots & \theta_{mk}
\end{bmatrix}
$$

$$
+
\begin{bmatrix}
e_{11} & e_{12} & \cdots & e_{1k} \\
e_{21} & e_{22} & \cdots & e_{2k} \\
\vdots & \vdots & & \vdots \\
e_{n1} & e_{n2} & \cdots & e_{nk}
\end{bmatrix}.
$$

The least-squares solution is found exactly as in the scalar-valued case.

Logistic regression is a technique for estimating probabilities, that is, continuous response vectors $(p_1, \ldots, p_k)$ such that $p_i \geq 0$ for all i and $p_1 + \cdots + p_k = 1$. It does this by mapping the range of f from the simplex of k-long probability vectors

$$
\{(p_1, \ldots, p_k) \in \mathbb{R}^k : p_1 \geq 0, \ldots, p_k \geq 0, p_1 + \cdots + p_k = 1\}
$$

into $\mathbb{R}^{k-1}$ by the map

$$
(p_1, \ldots, p_k) \mapsto \left(\log \frac{p_2}{p_1}, \ldots, \log \frac{p_k}{p_1} \right)
$$

and fitting a linear model by maximum-likelihood estimation, using a different statistical framework than additive Gaussian-distributed noise—see Section 4.6. Logistic regression is an example of a *generalized linear model*, in which the observed response is not itself a linear function of the features, but the result of applying some other function, called the *link function*, to the output of a linear function of the features.

Sometimes feature vectors in the data are themselves a random sample from a population, and inference about the whole population is desired. In this case, the features are known as *random effects*, as opposed to non-random features which are called *fixed effects*. In a *random effects model* there should be multiple observations of the response for each feature vector. A simple *analysis of variance* (ANOVA) example is

$$
y_{ij} = \theta_0 + \theta_i + e_{ij},
$$

where y_{ij} is the jth observation of a response from the ith feature vector, θ_0 is an intercept, θ_i is the effect for the ith feature vector (θ_i is a random variable with with mean 0 and variance σ_θ^2) and e_{ij} is the usual error in the response (e_{ij} is a random variable with mean 0 and variance σ_e^2). Inference about θ_0 and σ_θ^2 is inference about the population from which the features were drawn. A model with both random and fixed effects is a *mixed effects model*.

3.11 Nonparametric Regression

There are many regression techniques which do not rely on a linear model, or even on any statistical model at all. Many of the techniques for classification, presented in Chapter 4, have analogous regression techniques. Looking ahead to Chapter 4, we conclude this section with two examples, *k-nearest-neighbor regression* and *regression trees*. The reader may wish to read Chapter 4, at least up through Section 4.8, and then return to this section.

A *k-nearest-neighbor regressor* is exactly like a *k*-nearest-neighbor classifier in Section 4.5, except that instead of predicting the minimum-risk class for a new point based on the class of *k* neighbors, the minimum-risk response is predicted based on the response of *k* neighbors. For squared-error loss, the mean response of the *k*-nearest-neighbors is predicted.

A *regression tree* is trained and used exactly as a classification tree in Section 4.8, except that instead of predicting the minimum-risk class for a new point entering a leaf node t of the tree based on the class of the data in t, the minimum-risk response is predicted based on the response of the data in t. For squared-error loss, the mean response of the data in t is predicted,

$$\mu(t) = \frac{1}{|\text{training data entering node } t|} \sum_{\substack{\text{training data } (x_i, y_i) \\ x_i \in t}} y_i,$$

For squared-error loss, the impurity of a node is the sum over the data which enter it of the squared deviations of the response around its mean,

$$I(t) = \sum_{\substack{\text{training data } (x_i, y_i) \\ x_i \in t}} (y_i - \mu(t))^2,$$

that is, $I(t)$ is the sample variance of the responses of the data in leaf node t.

Regression trees and *k*-nearest-neighbor regression are *non-parametric regression methods*, because the number of parameters (the splitting criteria of non-leaf nodes and the estimated response returned by leaf nodes in the case of trees, the number of training data in the case of *k*-nearest-neighbors) are not fixed prior to training.

4

Survey of Classification Techniques

Understand the modeling premises implicit in the tools you use. And, if you don't, understand that, too.

—Mark Jacobson, personal communication, 2006

It's a totally black-box, brainless approach. You don't have to think—it just works.

—Jeremy Howard, referring to random forests
in *Down with Experts*, 2012

The statistician cannot evade the responsibility for understanding the process he applies or recommends.

—R. A. Fisher, *The Design of Experiments*, 1937

This chapter introduces the reader to a wide variety of approaches to the problem of *classification*, that is, to the problem of supervised learning when the range of the unknown function f is a discrete, unordered set of labels. It begins in Section 4.1 by developing an optimal (minimum risk) classifier, the *Bayes classifier*, under the assumption that the joint probability distribution $P(X, Y)$ from which data are drawn in known. This assumption is totally unrealistic, of course, but analyzing the Bayes classifier allows one to perceive and appreciate the role played by our subjectivity, encoded in the loss function $L(Y, \hat{f}(X))$, and the roles played by various aspects of the joint probability distribution $P(X, Y)$.

Machine Learning: a Concise Introduction, First Edition. Steven W. Knox.
© This publication is a US Government work and is in the public domain.
Published 2018 by John Wiley & Sons, Inc.
Companion Website: http://www.wiley.com/go/Knox/MachineLearning

The practical part of the chapter begins in Section 4.2, which contains a brief survey of many ways to approximate components of the Bayes classifier which are unknown in real applications, focusing in particular on the design principles behind practical classification methods. Viewing most methods as approximations of the Bayes classifier provides a common theme uniting the 14 or so practical classification algorithms described in Sections 4.4 through 4.9, which at first glance may appear to be quite different from each other. Some of these methods (quadratic discriminant analysis, linear discriminant analysis, Gaussian mixture models, logistic regression) are based on relatively simple statistical models; some (k-nearest neighbors, histograms, kernel density estimation, support vector machines) are based on geometric insight; and some are based on understanding of how humans solve problems, either at the behavioral level (k-nearest neighbors, classification trees) or at the neurological level (neural networks).

Understanding the design principles behind applied machine learning algorithms can lead to tangible benefits. If one method works considerably better than another on an applied problem, and the practitioner understands how both methods work, then he or she has learned something about the data which should inform the next steps taken (more on this in Section 4.10). If domain knowledge about an applied problem suggests that useful structure relating feature vectors X to class labels Y exists and has a given form, and the practitioner understands which methods are (and are not) capable of efficiently approximating the structure believed to be present in the data, then he or she can select a method or a small set of methods to apply.[1] Finally, classification methods occasionally need to be modified in order to solve applied problems, and understanding the design principles behind the methods leads to better-informed modifications, which lead to a greater chance of applied success.

4.1   The Bayes Classifier

Suppose that one of the following two things is known about how data are generated: either class labels are drawn (independently) from a *known* conditional distribution on the set of class labels $\{1, \ldots, C\}$ given the features,

$$P(Y = c \mid X) \qquad \text{for } c = 1, \ldots, C,$$

---

[1] For example, if the probability of class membership $P(Y \mid X)$ is believed to change suddenly with respect to small changes in a continuous feature, then one would be more inclined to use a classification tree than logistic regression—or if logistic regression were used, one would certainly explore feature transformations of the type described in Section 3.9 to help capture the non-linear behavior.

or class labels are drawn from a *known* marginal distribution on class labels[2] and features are drawn from a *known* conditional distribution of features given the class,

$$P(Y = c) \quad \text{and} \quad P(X \mid Y = c) \quad \text{for } c = 1, \dots, C.$$

The former can be recovered from the latter by Bayes' theorem:[3]

$$P(Y = c \mid X) = \frac{P(X \mid Y = c)P(Y = c)}{P(X)} = \frac{P(X \mid Y = c)P(Y = c)}{\sum_{d=1}^{C} P(X, Y = d)}$$

$$= \frac{P(X \mid Y = c)P(Y = c)}{\sum_{d=1}^{C} P(X \mid Y = d)P(Y = d)}.$$

Taking a Bayesian viewpoint, one can interpret $P(Y = c)$ as the prior probability that the class label of a new datum is c and $P(Y = c \mid X)$ as the posterior probability after observing the feature vector X. Knowledge of either of these things ($P(Y = c \mid X)$ or both $P(Y = c)$ and $P(X \mid Y = c)$, for all c) implies knowledge of the risk (expected loss) of predicting any class c, given a feature vector X:

$$R(c \mid X) = E_{Y \mid X}[L(Y, c)] = \sum_{d=1}^{C} L(d, c) P(Y = d \mid X)$$

$$= \sum_{d=1}^{C} L(d, c) \frac{P(X \mid Y = d) P(Y = d)}{\sum_{e=1}^{C} P(X \mid Y = e) P(Y = e)}$$

$$\propto \sum_{d=1}^{C} L(d, c) P(X \mid Y = d) P(Y = d),$$

the constant of proportionality being the reciprocal of $P(X) = \sum_{d=1}^{C} P(X \mid Y = e) P(Y = e)$.

The *Bayes classifier* classifies a new datum X as the class with minimum risk, conditional on X. That is, at $X = x$ the Bayes classifier predicts

$$\widehat{f}_{\text{Bayes}}(x) = \text{argmin}_{c \in \{1,\dots,C\}} R(c \mid X = x) = \text{argmin}_{c \in \{1,\dots,C\}} E_{Y \mid X = x}[L(Y, c)]. \quad (4.1)$$

Any ties in the argument of the minimum are broken arbitrarily because they have no effect on risk. As indicated by Exercise 2.3, this results in minimum overall risk,

$$R_{\text{Bayes}} = R(\widehat{f}_{\text{Bayes}}) = E_X[\min_{c \in \{1,\dots,C\}} E_{Y \mid X}[L(Y, c)]].$$

---

[2] Explicit knowledge of the marginal distribution of class labels $P(Y = c)$ can be practically quite important: for example, when one class is known to be much rarer than another class, but an equal number of training data of each class are provided.

[3] Bayes' theorem states that $P(Y = c \mid X) = \frac{P(X \mid Y=c)P(Y=c)}{P(X)}$.

The overall risk of the Bayes classifier, denoted R_{Bayes} above, is called the *Bayes risk* or, for 0–1 loss, the *Bayes error rate*. The Bayes classifier is widely regarded as an optimal classifier, because minimization of risk is widely regarded as an optimal strategy for making decisions.[4]

Exercise 4.1 *Knowledge of the conditional distribution $P(Y \mid X)$ enables construction of the Bayes classifier. Show that, in general, knowledge of the Bayes classifier does not enable reconstruction of the conditional distribution $P(Y \mid X)$. In this sense, $P(Y \mid X)$ contains stronger information than $\hat{f}_{\text{Bayes}}$.* **Hint:** *Show that there are distributions $\widetilde{P}(Y \mid X)$ other than $P(Y \mid X)$ which, when substituted for $P(Y \mid X)$ in (4.1), do not change the classification decisions made.*

Exercise 4.2 *Show that under 0–1 loss, the Bayes classifier classifies a new point X as the class with maximum posterior probability,*

$$\text{argmax}_{c \in \{1,\dots,C\}} P(Y = c \mid X).$$

Show that under 0–1 loss, if the prior distribution on classes is uniform then the Bayes classifier classifies X as the class under which X has the greatest likelihood,

$$\text{argmax}_{c \in \{1,\dots,C\}} P(X \mid Y = c).$$

Exercise 4.3 *Explicitly construct the Bayes classifier for Exercise 2.2 as a function of the observed one-dimensional feature X. Does the Bayes classifier have the form "predict class 1 if the feature falls below a threshold, and otherwise predict class 2"?*

Exercise 4.4 *Show that for risk-minimization, the following are equivalent:*

(A) an arbitrary prior distribution $(p_1, p_2, \dots, p_C)$ and a loss function which depends only on the true class, that is,

$$L(d, c) = \begin{cases} \alpha_d & \text{if } d \neq c \\ 0 & \text{if } d = c \end{cases}$$

for non-negative constants $\alpha_1, \dots, \alpha_C$;

(B) the 0–1 loss function and the prior distribution

$$P(Y = c) = \frac{\alpha_c p_c}{\sum_{d=1}^{C} \alpha_d p_d} \quad \text{for} \quad c = 1, \dots, C.$$

---

[4] As noted in Section 2.5, there are other criteria for what makes a classifier "good."

4.2   Introduction to Classifiers

The Bayes classifier classifies a new datum X to be the class c which minimizes the risk,

$$R(c \mid X) = \sum_{d=1}^{C} L(d, c) \, P(Y = d \mid X) \propto \sum_{d=1}^{C} L(d, c) \, P(X \mid Y = d) \, P(Y = d).$$

In real life $P(Y = d \mid X)$, $P(X \mid Y = d)$, and $P(Y = d)$ are unknown. Thus some kind of approximation is needed in order to follow the strategy of the Bayes classifier. The approximation may be of either the conditional distribution on class labels given the features,

$$P(Y = d \mid X),$$

or both the marginal distribution of class labels[5] and the conditional distribution on features given the class label,

$$P(Y = d) \qquad \text{and} \qquad P(X \mid Y = d).$$

Description of what is approximated, and how it is approximated, provides an introduction to the practical algorithms described in Sections 4.4 through 4.9.

A *likelihood method* approximates the likelihood function $P(X \mid Y = d)$ separately for each class d either by positing a specific parametric form for this distribution and using training data to approximate the parameters of this form or by fitting a nonparametric statistical model to the training data of each class separately. Likelihood methods are among methods which require that the marginal distribution of class labels $P(Y = d)$ be specified, or that it be learned from the training data.

A *prototype method* approximates $P(Y = d \mid X)$ by assuming that this probability changes slowly with respect to some kind of distance[6] on $\mathcal{X}$, the set of feature vectors. Given a feature vector X, the distribution $P(Y = d \mid X)$ is approximated by the distribution of the class labels among a set of *prototypical data points* near X (what "near" means may depend on the data). Depending on the specific method employed, prototypical data points may be observed data or may be synthetic points which correspond to no single, observed data point.

---

[5] If it is believed that new data will be generated in approximately the same way as the training data, the proportion of the training data belonging to the cth class, $\frac{n_c}{n}$, is a reasonable value to use for $P(Y = c)$. In some cases, though, very rare classes d are deliberately over-represented in training data, to better enable estimation of $P(X \mid Y = d)$: *in such cases, it is important to estimate the marginal probability* $P(Y = d)$ *by other means than its proportion in the training data!*

[6] A *distance function* δ maps $\mathcal{X} \times \mathcal{X} \to [0, \infty)$ such that $\delta(x_1, x_1) = 0$ and $\delta(x_1, x_2) = \delta(x_2, x_1)$ for all $x_1, x_2 \in \mathcal{X}$. We do not assume that δ satisfies any other properties, such as a triangle inequality, or even that $\delta(x_1, x_2) = 0$ implies $x_1 = x_2$ (that is, we distinguish between the case $x_1 = x_2$ and the case that a particular distance function δ cannot detect any difference between x_1 and x_2).

A *logistic regression* classifier approximates $P(Y = d \mid X)$ by assuming that for classes $d = 2, \ldots, C$, the log-odds in favor of class d over class 1,

$$\log \frac{P(Y = d \mid X)}{P(Y = 1 \mid X)},$$

is a linear function of the features. Thus approximating $P(Y = d \mid X)$ is akin to estimating the parameters of $C - 1$ linear functions

$$\left(\log \frac{P(Y = 2 \mid X)}{P(Y = 1 \mid X)}, \ldots, \log \frac{P(Y = C \mid X)}{P(Y = 1 \mid X)} \right),$$

through regression, as described in Chapter 3.

A *neural network* approximates $P(Y = d \mid X)$ in a way very much like a logistic regression classifier, except that it models the log-odds not as a linear function of the features, but as a linear function of the outputs of other functions called *neurons*. Approximating $P(Y = d \mid X)$ with a neural network means simultaneously estimating the parameters of the linear function and the parameters of the neurons.

A *classification tree* approximates $P(X \mid Y = d)$ by partitioning feature space $\mathcal{X}$ into regions and approximating, for each region t,

$$P(X \in t \mid Y = d).$$

Classification trees are similar both to prototype methods (if feature vector X is in region t, the training data in t are "near" X and used to predict a class label for X) and to likelihood methods (within each region t, $P(X \mid Y = d)$ is approximated by a constant, $P(X \in t \mid Y = d)$). The partitioning of feature space into regions also depends on the training data.

The author does not see how a *support vector machine* fits into this paradigm. Support vector machines use a type of loss function which depends not only on the true and predicted class labels, but also on the point x at which the prediction is made (a support vector machine can incur positive loss for predicting the correct class at $x \in \mathcal{X}$). Support vector machines will be motivated geometrically in Section 4.9.

4.3   A Running Example

A toy example is used throughout this chapter and Chapters 5 and 6 to illustrate the behavior of classification methods: in particular, to show classification decisions made at points in feature space and method-specific details such as estimated likelihood functions for each class. In this example, there are three classes, *orange*, *blue*, and *purple*, and feature vectors are in $\mathcal{X} = \mathbb{R}^2$.

The three classes are equally likely:

$$P(Y) = \begin{cases} \frac{1}{3} & \text{if } Y = \text{orange} \\ \frac{1}{3} & \text{if } Y = \text{blue} \\ \frac{1}{3} & \text{if } Y = \text{purple} \end{cases}.$$

Means defining class densities   **Example training data**

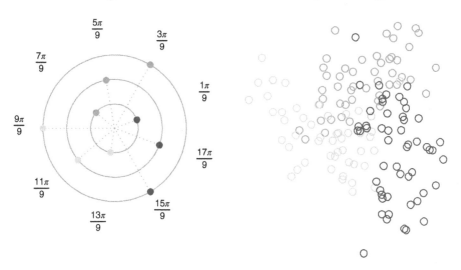

Figure 4.1   The left-hand cell shows a set of nine points which define the class densities of each of three classes, orange, blue, and purple. The points lie on circles of radius 1, 2, and 3 centered at the origin and angularly consecutive points are separated by an angle of $\frac{2\pi}{9}$. The distribution of the data in each class is a mixture of three equally weighted Gaussian distributions with means shown and unit covariance matrix. The right-hand cell shows a set of 150 points drawn randomly from this distribution: there are 48 orange, 49 blue, and 53 purple points. The points shown are used for training classifiers in the examples below.

Within each class, features are distributed as an equal-weight mixture of three two-dimensional Gaussian distributions with unit covariance matrix and different means. The means of the nine Gaussians are shown in the left-hand cell of Figure 4.1, colored according to class. In polar coordinates, the orange means are $\{(3, \frac{3\pi}{9}), (2, \frac{5\pi}{9}), (1, \frac{7\pi}{9})\}$, the blue means are $\{(3, \frac{9\pi}{9}), (2, \frac{11\pi}{9}), (1, \frac{13\pi}{9})\}$, and the purple means are $\{(3, \frac{15\pi}{9}), (2, \frac{17\pi}{9}), (1, \frac{1\pi}{9})\}$. Thus, for example, the distribution of $X \mid (Y = \text{orange})$ has density function

$$
\begin{aligned}
P(X = (x_1, x_2) \mid Y = \text{orange}) = {} & \frac{1}{3} \frac{1}{2\pi} e^{-\frac{1}{2}\left\|(x_1, x_2) - 3\left(\cos\frac{3\pi}{9}, \sin\frac{3\pi}{9}\right)\right\|^2} \\
& + \frac{1}{3} \frac{1}{2\pi} e^{-\frac{1}{2}\left\|(x_1, x_2) - 2\left(\cos\frac{5\pi}{9}, \sin\frac{5\pi}{9}\right)\right\|^2} \\
& + \frac{1}{3} \frac{1}{2\pi} e^{-\frac{1}{2}\left\|(x_1, x_2) - 1\left(\cos\frac{7\pi}{9}, \sin\frac{7\pi}{9}\right)\right\|^2}.
\end{aligned}
$$

Data are generated from this model independently, one at a time, as follows. First a class is chosen from $P(Y)$, that is, uniformly at random from the set {orange, blue, purple}. Then one of the three Gaussian distributions for the chosen class is selected uniformly at random. Then a point in $\mathbb{R}^2$ is drawn randomly from the selected Gaussian distribution.

A randomly drawn set of 150 points from the joint distribution $P(X, Y)$ is shown in the right-hand cell of Figure 4.1: there are 48 points from the orange class, 49 from the blue class and 53 from the purple class. Throughout this and later chapters, classifiers will be trained on this dataset using 0–1 loss. A test set of 50,000 points drawn from the same distribution is used to estimate the risk of trained classifiers.[7] The data illustrated in Figure 4.1 are given in Appendix D, along with fitted parameters of many of the methods described in this chapter.

The likelihood functions for the three classes, and the classification decisions made by the Bayes classifier, are shown in Figure 4.2. The Bayes risk, accurate to six decimal places,[8] is 0.191705.

4.4   Likelihood Methods

Suppose that the data from the cth class is randomly drawn from a distribution with likelihood[9] $P(X \mid Y = c)$ on the sample space, $\mathcal{X}$. A likelihood-based classifier uses training data to compute an estimate $\widehat{P}(X \mid Y = c)$ of the likelihood $P(X \mid Y = c)$. Given the marginal or prior distribution of the classes $P(Y = c)$ (estimated from the training data or obtained another way, as appropriate) the posterior distribution on the classes is estimated by

$$\widehat{P}(Y = c \mid X) = \frac{\widehat{P}(X \mid Y = c)P(Y = c)}{\sum_{d=1}^{C} \widehat{P}(X \mid Y = d)P(Y = d)},$$

and a new data point X is classified to minimize estimated posterior risk.

The first three methods described in this section, quadratic discriminant analysis, linear discriminant analysis, and Gaussian mixture models, are *parametric methods,* because they specify a parametric form for the class densities. These have the advantage of being cheap to implement and the disadvantage that they can produce relatively high-risk approximations $\widehat{f}$ when the model assumptions on which they are

---

[7] The risk estimates reported in this chapter and Chapters 5 and 6, obtained by applying trained classifiers to a 50,000-point test dataset and counting the proportion of errors made, all turned out to have standard deviation about 0.0018 or 0.0019.

[8] The Bayes risk was computed to six decimals of accuracy using numerical integration in *Mathematica,* not estimated using the 50,000-point test set.

[9] The likelihoods $P(X \mid Y = c)$ need not be densities, but the constant of proportionality $\int_{\mathcal{X}} P(x \mid Y = c) \, dx$ must be the same for all classes, that is, $\int_{\mathcal{X}} P(x \mid Y = c) \, dx = \int_{\mathcal{X}} P(x \mid Y = d) \, dx$ for all classes c and d.

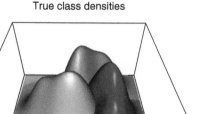

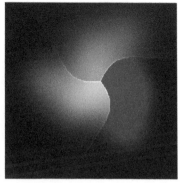

Figure 4.2   The left-hand cell shows the density function for the orange data in orange, the density function for the blue data in blue, and the density function for the purple data in purple. In this example, the prior distribution of the classes is uniform and 0–1 loss is used, so at any point, the Bayes classifier predicts whatever class has the highest density (Exercise 4.2). The regions of points classified by the Bayes classifier as orange, blue, and purple are shown in the right-hand cell, with the class boundaries highlighted in white. Shading in the right-hand cell is proportional to the marginal density of the data, $P(X)$: mistakes in bright areas contribute more to the risk of a classifier than mistakes in dark areas. These plots are for comparison with the plots illustrating the behavior of methods described in this chapter and Chapters 5 and 6. The Bayes risk for this problem is 0.191705.

based are far from the truth. The next two methods, kernel density estimation and histograms, are *non-parametric methods* and can be expensive to implement. The last method, the naive Bayes classifier, can be parametric, non-parametric, or a mixture of the two (in which case it is a *semi-parametric method*).

4.4.1   Quadratic Discriminant Analysis

Suppose that for each class c, the likelihood function $P(x \mid Y = c)$ is a Gaussian density (all features must be real in order to use this method, so $\mathcal{X} = \mathbb{R}^m$),[10]

$$P(x \mid Y = c) = \phi(x \mid \mu_c, \Sigma_c) = |2\pi\Sigma_c|^{-\frac{1}{2}} e^{-\frac{1}{2}(x-\mu_c)^T \Sigma_c^{-1}(x-\mu_c)}.$$

---

[10] When applying likelihood methods which assume a Gaussian distribution, it is worth checking whether the data really are approximately normally distributed. This can be done graphically with a quantile–quantile plot or by applying tests in D'Agostino and Stephens (1986), Mardia et al. (1979), or Thode (2002).

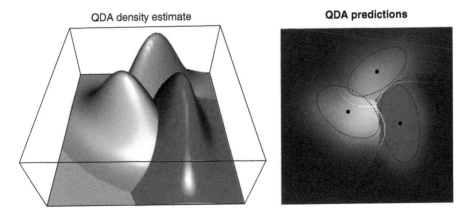

Figure 4.3   Estimated class densities (left) and classification decisions (right) made by quadratic discriminant analysis (QDA) trained on the data of Figure 4.1. The estimated class boundaries are piecewise quadratic. Estimated class means are shown by black dots, and level curves of the estimated densities with 50% of the probability mass inside are shown by dashed lines (see Appendix C for how the level curves were obtained). White curves show the Bayes class boundaries. QDA has estimated risk 0.204.

The cth density is determined by a mean μ_c and a covariance matrix Σ_c, and training the density amounts to estimating these parameters, for example, by maximum likelihood,[11]

$$(\hat{\mu}_1, \dots, \hat{\mu}_C, \hat{\Sigma}_1, \dots, \hat{\Sigma}_C) = \operatorname{argmax}_{(\mu_1, \dots, \mu_C, \Sigma_1, \dots, \Sigma_C)} \prod_{i=1}^{n} P(x_i \mid Y = y_i)$$

$$= \operatorname{argmax}_{(\mu_1, \dots, \mu_C, \Sigma_1, \dots, \Sigma_C)} \prod_{c=1}^{C} \prod_{\substack{i=1 \\ y_i = c}}^{n} P(x_i \mid Y = c).$$

The name of this classifier comes from the fact that the estimated class boundaries (surfaces which partition feature space into regions of homogeneous predicted class) it produces are piecewise quadratic surfaces. Figure 4.3 illustrates the estimated densities $\hat{P}(x \mid Y = c)$ and class predictions made by quadratic discriminant analysis trained on the data of Figure 4.1.

---

[11] Maximum likelihood estimation of parameters, which is typically used in QDA and several other methods described in this section, is seeking a model which explains the training data well. It is not explicitly seeking a model which is good at prediction.

Exercise 4.5 *Let $(x_1, y_1), \dots, (x_n, y_n)$ be n independent draws from the joint distribution (X, Y), where for each class $c = 1, \dots, C$, the feature vector*

$$X \mid Y = c \sim N(\mu_c, \Sigma_c).$$

Show that the parameters $\mu_1, \dots, \mu_C, \Sigma_1, \dots, \Sigma_C$ which maximize the likelihood of the feature vectors $x_1, \dots, x_n$ conditional on the class labels $y_1, \dots, y_n$ are given by

$$\hat{\mu}_c = \frac{1}{n_c} \sum_{\substack{i=1 \\ y_i = c}}^{n} x_i$$

and

$$\hat{\Sigma}_c = \frac{1}{n_c} \sum_{\substack{i=1 \\ y_i = c}}^{n} (x_i - \hat{\mu}_c)(x_i - \hat{\mu}_c)^{\mathrm{T}} = \left(\frac{1}{n_c} \sum_{\substack{i=1 \\ y_i = c}}^{n} x_i x_i^{\mathrm{T}} \right) - \hat{\mu}_c \hat{\mu}_c^{\mathrm{T}}.$$

where n_c is the number of training data of class c. **Hints:** *(1) maximizing the log-likelihood is the same as maximizing the likelihood; (2) use matrix derivative identities (for any vectors v and w, and any invertible, symmetric matrix A, $\frac{\partial}{\partial v} v^{\mathrm{T}} w = w$, $\frac{\partial}{\partial v} v^{\mathrm{T}} A v = 2Av$, $\frac{\partial}{\partial A} \log |A| = A^{-1}$, and $\frac{\partial}{\partial A} v^{\mathrm{T}} A^{-1} v = -A^{-1} v v^{\mathrm{T}} A^{-1}$).*

The total number of parameters for each class is m (for the m-long vector $\hat{\mu}_c$) plus $m + \frac{m(m-1)}{2}$ (for the $m \times m$ symmetric matrix $\hat{\Sigma}_c$), which is quite a lot when m is large. If a class c is relatively rare, this can lead to an estimated covariance matrix $\hat{\Sigma}_c$ which is singular. Sometimes this problem is avoided by replacing $\hat{\Sigma}_c$ by a convex combination of $\hat{\Sigma}_c$ and a covariance matrix $\hat{\Sigma}$ estimated under the assumption that all classes have the same covariance (see below for a definition of $\hat{\Sigma}$)

$$\alpha \hat{\Sigma}_c + (1 - \alpha) \hat{\Sigma},$$

for some parameter $0 \le \alpha \le 1$. This technique is called *regularized discriminant analysis*. Sometimes the number of parameters is reduced to $2m$ per class by assuming that the covariance matrix for each class is diagonal.

4.4.2 Linear Discriminant Analysis

Linear discriminant analysis is the same as quadratic discriminant analysis, except that the covariance matrices of the class densities are assumed to be equal (it is regularized discriminant analysis above with $\alpha = 0$). The estimated class boundaries are piecewise linear, and the common covariance matrix Σ can be estimated from all of the data. Figure 4.4 illustrates the estimated densities $\hat{P}(x \mid Y = c)$ and class predictions made by linear discriminant analysis trained on the data of Figure 4.1.

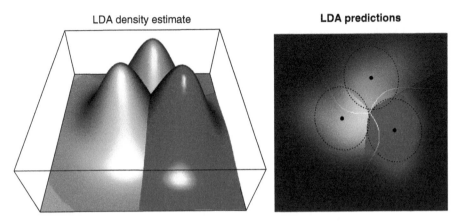

LDA density estimate   **LDA predictions**

Figure 4.4   Estimated class densities (left) and classification decisions (right) made by linear discriminant analysis (LDA) trained on the data of Figure 4.1. The estimated class boundaries are piecewise linear. Estimated class means are shown by black dots, and level curves of the estimated densities with 50% of the probability mass inside are shown by dashed lines (see Appendix C for how the level curves were obtained). Note that the level curves all have the same shape, differing only in location, unlike QDA (Figure 4.3). White curves show the Bayes class boundaries. LDA has estimated risk 0.229.

Exercise 4.6 *Let $(x_1, y_1), \dots, (x_n, y_n)$ be n independent draws from the joint distribution (X, Y), where for each class $c = 1, \dots, C$, the feature vector*

$$X \mid Y = c \sim N(\mu_c, \Sigma).$$

Show that the parameters $\mu_1, \dots, \mu_C, \Sigma$ which maximize the likelihood of the feature vectors $x_1, \dots, x_n$ conditional on the class labels $y_1, \dots, y_n$ are given by

$$\widehat{\mu}_c = \frac{1}{n_c} \sum_{\substack{i=1 \\ y_i = c}}^{n} x_i$$

and

$$\widehat{\Sigma} = \frac{1}{n} \sum_{i=1}^{n} \left(x_i - \widehat{\mu}_{y_i}\right)\left(x_i - \widehat{\mu}_{y_i}\right)^{\mathrm{T}} = \sum_{c=1}^{C} \frac{n_c}{n} \widehat{\Sigma}_c,$$

where n_c is the number of training data of class c. **Hint:** *See the hint for Exercise 4.5.*

Exercise 4.7 *In the case of $C = 2$ classes, the minimum-posterior-risk LDA class boundary is a hyperplane. Establish this and find the equation of the hyperplane,* *given arbitrary priors* $P(Y = 1)$ *and* $P(Y = 2) = 1 - P(Y = 1)$, *an arbitrary loss function* L *with* $L(1,1) = L(2,2) = 0$, *and estimated class densities*

$$\widehat{P}(x \mid Y = c) = \phi(x \mid \widehat{\mu}_c, \widehat{\Sigma}) = |2\pi\widehat{\Sigma}|^{-\frac{1}{2}} \exp\left(-\frac{1}{2}(x - \widehat{\mu}_c)^{\mathsf{T}}\widehat{\Sigma}^{-1}(x - \widehat{\mu}_c)\right).$$

Write the solution in the form "predict x is class 1 if $x \cdot v \le \alpha$*." What happens when* $P(Y = 1) = \frac{1}{2}$ *and* $L(1,2) = L(2,1)$? *Compare your solution to that of Exercise 2.2.*

4.4.3   Gaussian Mixture Models

Suppose that for each class c, the likelihood function $P(x \mid Y = c)$ is a mixture of Gaussian densities,

$$P(x \mid Y = c) = \sum_{j=1}^{J_c} w_{jc}\, \phi(x \mid \mu_{jc}, \Sigma_{jc}),$$

where $\phi(x \mid \mu, \Sigma)$ denotes a Gaussian density function with mean μ and covariance matrix Σ, w_{jc} are non-negative weights with $w_{1c} + \cdots + w_{J_c c} = 1$ for each c, and $J_c > 0$ is the number of mixture components for the cth class. Gaussian mixtures are fit by the expectation-maximization (EM) algorithm described in Section 10.7.[12] The number of mixture components J_c must be determined for each class using a model selection criterion, such as those discussed in Chapter 7 (for example, a cross-validation estimate of risk, or Akaike's information criterion). Setting $J_c = 1$ for all c is equivalent to QDA.

Using a Gaussian mixture model for a likelihood-based classifier can result in an enormous number of parameters to estimate if m is large. Imposing structure on the covariance matrices (such as all being equal to each other, or diagonal, or a scaled identity matrix) can reduce the number of parameters.

Figure 4.5 shows two Gaussian mixture models fit to the data of Figure 4.1. The first model used two Gaussian components for each class ($J_1 = J_2 = J_3 = 2$), and the second model used three Gaussian components for each class ($J_1 = J_2 = J_3 = 3$). It is obvious to the eye that the fitted three-component Gaussian mixture model performs poorly (its risk, estimated from test data, is 0.228): *yet a three-component Gaussian mixture is the correct model, in the sense that the data were truly generated from a Gaussian mixture with three components per class.* As measured by likelihood (shown in Table 4.1), the fitted three-component model fits the training data better than the true model: on average, each data point is assigned approximately 50% higher likelihood under the fitted model than under the true model.

---

[12] In addition to presenting the expectation-maximization algorithm in general, Section 10.7 gives complete details on fitting Gaussian mixture models via EM. In the example shown in Figure 4.5, the Gaussian mixture for each class was fit by applying the expectation-maximization algorithm starting from 1000 random starting states and retaining the single fit with maximal likelihood.

Gaussian-mixture density estimate   **Gaussian-mixture predictions**

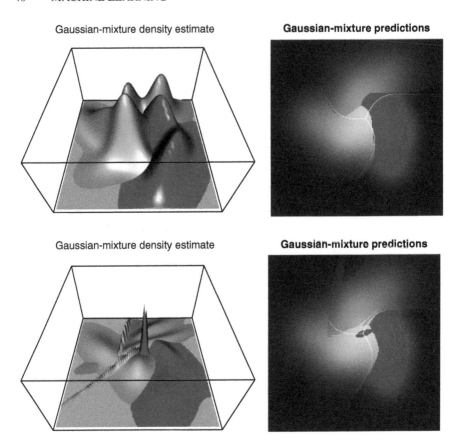

Gaussian-mixture density estimate   **Gaussian-mixture predictions**

Figure 4.5   Estimated class densities (left) and classification decisions (right) made using Gaussian mixture models trained on the data of Figure 4.1. The upper two cells correspond to Gaussian mixtures with two components for each class, and the bottom two cells correspond to Gaussian mixtures with three components for each class (graphing artifacts may cause a sawtooth appearance in densities which are truly smooth). *Note that a three-component Gaussian mixture is the correct model, in the sense that the data were truly generated from a Gaussian mixture with three components per class.* White curves show the Bayes class boundaries. The Gaussian mixture models have estimated risks 0.205 (two components per class) and 0.228 (three components per class).

Some find it counter-intuitive that the "structurally correct" model could produce a trained classifier with quite high risk. The high risk of this fitted model is due to having too many parameters or too little data. In the language of Chapter 5, where this issue will be addressed at length, the Gaussian mixture model with three components for each class has low bias but high variance. Yet there is also merit in the intuition

Table 4.1   The log-likelihood of the data of Figure 4.1, separated by class, under a three-component Gaussian mixture model fitted by approximate maximum likelihood (center column) and under the three-component Gaussian mixture model from which the data were drawn (right column). In each class, the fitted model assigns substantially higher likelihood to the data than the true model.

	Log-likelihood of class c data, fitted three-component model	Log-likelihood of class c data, true three-component model
Class $c = 1$	-136.41	-153.10
Class $c = 2$	-145.45	-168.40
Class $c = 3$	-158.60	-179.53

that knowledge of the parametric form of the correct model should be helpful: see Chapter 8, in particular Theorem 8.5, and also the comment on rates of convergence in Section 4.4.5.

Using mixtures of Student's t distributions in place of mixtures of Gaussians may provide robustness against outliers. The density of Student's t distribution with v degrees of freedom is

$$P(x \mid \mu, \Sigma, v) = \frac{\Gamma\left(\frac{v+m}{2}\right)}{(\pi v)^{\frac{m}{2}} \Gamma\left(\frac{v}{2}\right)} |\Sigma|^{-\frac{1}{2}} \left(1 + v^{-1}(x - \mu)^{\mathsf{T}} \Sigma^{-1}(x - \mu)\right)^{-\frac{v+m}{2}}.$$

For small values of v, Student's t distribution has much heavier tails than the Gaussian distribution, while as $v \to \infty$, it approaches the Gaussian distribution. When $v = 1$, Student's t distribution is called the Cauchy distribution.

4.4.4   Kernel Density Estimation

A *kernel density estimate* estimates the density function which produces a sample of data by placing a probability mass at, and nearby, each observed datum. A kernel density estimate for the data of class c, for $c = 1, \ldots, C$, has the form

$$\widehat{P}(x \mid Y = c) = \frac{1}{n_c} \sum_{\substack{i = 1 \\ y_i = c}}^{n} \frac{1}{h_c^m} K\left(\frac{x - x_i}{h_c}\right),$$

where n_c is the number of training data of class c, $K : \mathcal{X} \to [0, \infty)$ is a *kernel function*, and h_c is a parameter known as *bandwidth*.[13] A kernel function in this context is any function which is relatively large near zero and relatively small away from zero: two

---

[13] Epanechnikov referred to the h_c's by the more descriptive term *spreading coefficients* (Epanechnikov, 1967).

Gaussian kernel

Epanechnikov kernel

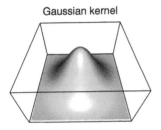

$$K(x) = \phi(x \,|\, 0, \mathbf{i}) = (2\pi)^{-\frac{m}{2}} e^{-\frac{1}{2} x^T x} \qquad K(x) = \begin{cases} \frac{\Gamma(\frac{m}{2}+2)}{\pi^{\frac{m}{2}} (m+4)^{\frac{m}{2}}} \left(1 - \frac{x^T x}{m+4}\right) & \text{if } x^T x < m+4 \\ 0 & \text{else} \end{cases}$$

Figure 4.6   Gaussian (left) and Epanechnikov (right) kernel functions. Both kernels are probability density functions of distributions on $\mathbb{R}^m$ with mean 0 and unit covariance matrix.

commonly used kernel functions, the Gaussian and Epanechnikov kernels, are shown in Figure 4.6.

The kernel density estimate $\widehat{P}(x \,|\, Y = c)$ is large when the point x is near data of class c and gets smaller as x gets farther from data of class c. The bandwidth parameter h_c controls how rapidly $\widehat{P}(x \,|\, Y = c)$ decreases as x gets farther from data of class c. Thus h_c controls the smoothness[14] of the density estimate: if h_c is small, then there is not much smoothing, while if h_c is large, there is a lot of smoothing.

The effect of the bandwidth parameters h_c is illustrated in Figure 4.7, where for simplicity the constraint $h_1 = h_2 = h_3$ was imposed. A value of the bandwidth parameter which is small (relative to the scale of the data) makes the density estimates "spiky" and highly concentrated about the observed data. A middling value of the bandwidth parameter produces density estimates which appear visually similar to the true densities illustrated in Figure 4.1. A large value of the bandwidth parameter results in a density estimate which is almost constant in a large neighborhood around the data.

Multivariate kernel functions are sometimes built up as products of univariate kernel functions. In that case

$$\widehat{P}(x \,|\, Y = c) = \frac{1}{n_c} \sum_{\substack{i=1 \\ y_i = c}}^{n} \left(\prod_{j=1}^{m} \frac{1}{h_{c,j}} K_j \left(\frac{x_j - x_{ij}}{h_{c,j}} \right) \right),$$

where $K_1, \ldots, K_m$ are univariate kernel functions, x_j and x_{ij} denote the jth coordinate of x and x_i respectively, and bandwidth parameters $h_{c,j}$ are allowed to depend on a class c as well as a coordinate j in feature space. This can be useful when features are

---

[14] In this book, the word *smooth* is used in its colloquial sense, not according to any technical definition.

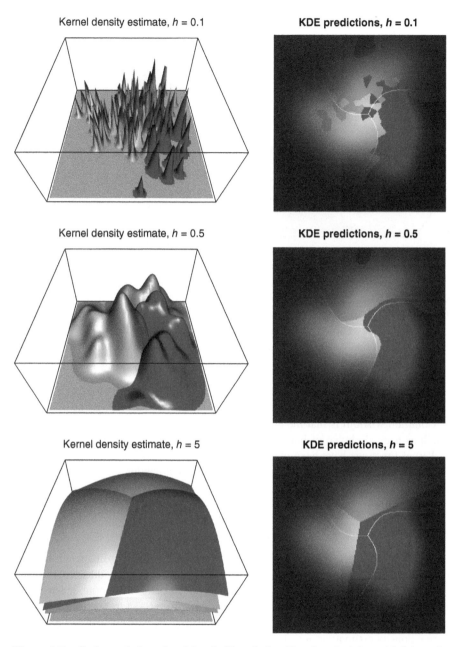

Figure 4.7 Estimated class densities (left) and classification decisions (right) made using a Gaussian kernel density estimate with, from top to bottom, bandwidths $h = 0.1$, 0.5, and 5, trained on the data of Figure 4.1. White curves show the Bayes class boundaries. These kernel density estimates have estimated risks 0.246, 0.203, and 0.261, respectively. Bandwidth $h = 0.5$ was selected as approximately optimal using leave-one-out cross-validation, described in Section 7.3, to estimate risk from the training data.

Product kernel density estimate

Product KDE predictions

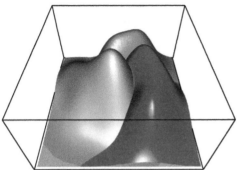

Figure 4.8   Estimated class densities (left) and classification decisions (right) made using a product Gaussian kernel density estimate, trained on the data of Figure 4.1 with bandwidths obtained from the normal reference rule, $h_{1,1} = 0.76$, $h_{1,2} = 0.62$, $h_{2,1} = 0.79$, $h_{2,2} = 0.67$, $h_{3,1} = 0.49$, and $h_{3,2} = 0.98$. White curves show the Bayes class boundaries. This kernel density estimate has estimated risk 0.199, although leave-one-out cross-validation prefers the bandwidth $h = 0.5$ classifier shown in the center cells of Figure 4.7.

measured on very different scales. The m-dimensional Gaussian kernel is a product of m one-dimensional Gaussian kernels.

Common wisdom is that the choice of kernel function does not matter nearly as much as a good choice of bandwidth parameter, although theoretical comparisons of kernel functions have been made[15] (Epanechnikov, 1967; Scott, 1992). Rules of thumb have been developed for approximately optimal bandwidth selection, such as the *normal reference rule* (Scott, 1992), which for product kernels is

$$h_{c,j} = \left(\frac{4}{n_c(m + 2)} \right)^{\frac{1}{m+4}} \hat{\sigma}_{c,j},$$

where $\hat{\sigma}_{c,j}$ is the sample standard deviation of the jth feature coordinate among data of class c. Note, however, that such rules generally select bandwidths which minimize the risk of the kernel density estimate as an estimate of the true density with respect to squared-error loss, and that optimality with respect to that criterion does not imply optimality of a classifier based on the kernel density estimate. When using kernel density estimation in a classifier, bandwidths should be tuned to optimize the estimated risk of the classifier (though Figure 4.8 shows that the normal reference rule can do well).

---

[15] For some computational purposes, it is convenient to use a kernel function which is strictly positive on all of $\mathcal{X}$. The Gaussian kernel has this property, but the Epanechnikov kernel does not.

Although the number of bandwidth parameters $h_1, \ldots, h_C$ is fixed in advance, note that each observed datum (x_i, y_i) adds a term $K(\frac{x-x_i}{h_c})$ to one of the density estimates, and thus in effect the data are also parameters of the kernel density estimate, so the number of parameters increases without bound as $n \to \infty$. In this sense, kernel density estimation is a non-parametric method. Since evaluation of $\widehat{P}(x \mid Y = c)$ for each class c involves one evaluation of the kernel function for each data point, KDE can be expensive to implement when the number of data, n, is large.

4.4.5 Histograms

A histogram is a step-function approximation of a density function. As in kernel density estimates, histograms have a bandwidth parameter which must be chosen carefully. For each class c, a bandwidth-dependent tiling of feature space $\mathcal{X}$ into rectangular cells is given. When $\mathcal{X} = \mathbb{R}^m$, these cells are

$$R_c(i_1, \ldots, i_m)$$
$$= \{(x_1, \ldots, x_m) \in \mathbb{R}^m : i_1 h_{c,1} \le x_1 < (i_1 + 1)h_{c,1}, \ldots, i_m h_{c,m} \le x_m < (i_m + 1)h_{c,m}\},$$

indexed by $(i_1, \ldots, i_m) \in \mathbb{Z}^m$, where $h_{c,j}$ is a bandwidth parameter for the jth feature and the cth class. Given any feature vector x and any class c, let

$$R_c(x)$$

denote the rectangle $R_c(i_1, \ldots, i_m)$ which contains x: the index vector $(i_1, \ldots, i_m)$ is found by setting

$$i_j = \left\lfloor \frac{x_j}{h_{c,j}} \right\rfloor$$

for $j = 1, \ldots, m$, where $\lfloor r \rfloor$ represents the integer floor of a real number r. For any feature vector x and any class c, let $n_c^{R_c(x)}$ denote the number of training data of class c which fall in the rectangle $R_c(x)$. The histogram density function estimate is

$$\widehat{P}(x \mid Y = c) = \frac{n_c^{R_c(x)}}{n_c}.$$

This situation is illustrated in Figure 4.9.

Note that unlike kernel density estimates, histogram density estimates depend on a choice of origin in $\mathcal{X}$ in addition to bandwidth. The rectangular cells defined above can be translated by addition of any constant vector in $[0, h_{c,1}) \times \cdots \times [0, h_{c,m})$ to give additional flexibility to the classifier. As with product kernel density estimates, rectangular cells with different edge lengths $h_{c,1}, \ldots, h_{c,m}$ accommodate features measured on different scales.

The effect of the bandwidth parameters $h_{c,i}$ is illustrated in Figure 4.10, where for convenience the constraint $h_{1,1} = h_{1,2} = h_{2,1} = h_{2,2} = h_{3,1} = h_{3,2}$ was imposed and

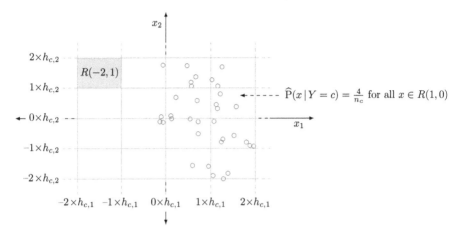

Figure 4.9   A partition of $\mathcal{X} = \mathbb{R}^2$ into a grid of $h_{c,1} \times h_{c,2}$ rectangles $R_c(i,j)$, shown with some of the purple data of Figure 4.1.

the lower-left corner of cell $R(0, 0)$ is located at the origin for each class. A value of the bandwidth parameter which is small (relative to the scale of the data) makes the density estimates "spiky" and highly concentrated about the observed data. It also causes many histogram cells to contain no data at all. In cells where $R_1(x) = \cdots = R_C(x) = 0$, the histogram classifier treats $P(X = x \mid Y = c)$ as the same small, positive number for all classes c, and uses the estimate $P(Y = c \mid X = x) \propto P(Y = c)$ for $c = 1, \ldots, C$. A middling value of the bandwidth parameter produces density estimates which appear visually similar to the true densities illustrated in Figure 4.1. A large value of the bandwidth parameter results in a density estimate which is constant in large rectangular regions.

Histograms are computationally more efficient than kernel density estimates, since histogram cells are typically far fewer than the number of training data (this is shown explicitly by the development of a histogram classifier using hash tables in Section 14.9). On the other hand, histograms use the training data less efficiently than kernel density estimates in the sense that, with bandwidths chosen appropriately (and in dimension $m = 1$), the mean squared error of a histogram density estimate is $O(n^{-\frac{2}{3}})$ while the mean squared error of a kernel density estimate is $O(n^{-\frac{4}{5}})$. For comparison, the mean squared error of a parametric density estimate is $O(n^{-1})$ when the parametric model is correct. See Scott (1992) for details.

Histograms are particularly useful when knowledge about the data suggests that there is a natural way for it to be binned into rectangular cells. Categorical features, for example, have this property.

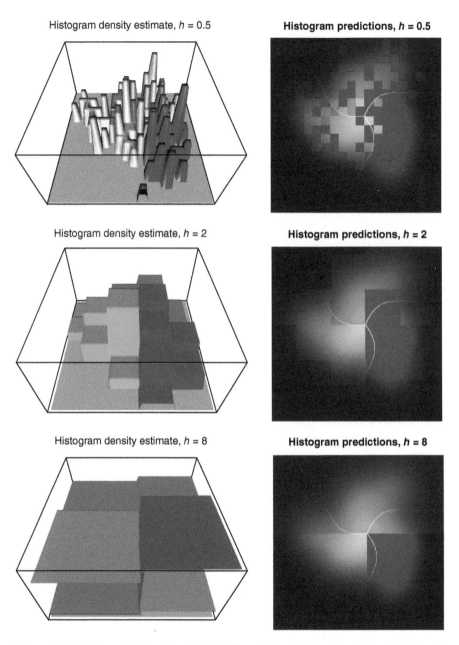

Figure 4.10 Estimated class densities (left) and classification decisions (right) made using a histogram density estimate with, from top to bottom, bandwidths $h = 0.5$, 2, and 8, trained on the data of Figure 4.1. These histogram density estimates have estimated risks 0.444, 0.260, and 0.281, respectively. Bandwidth $h = 2$ was selected as approximately optimal using leave-one-out cross-validation, described in Section 7.3, to estimate risk from the training data. Points in empty histogram cells are predicted to be the most frequent class (purple), which is the minimum-risk prediction based on the estimated marginal distribution $P(Y = c) = n_c/n$.

Exercise 4.8 *Suppose that in a histogram classifier, the prior distribution on classes* $(P(Y = 1), \ldots, P(Y = C))$ *is estimated from the training data,*

$$P(Y = c) = \frac{n_c}{n}$$

for $c = 1, \ldots, C$. *Show that at a feature vector* x, *the classifier predicts*

$$\text{argmin}_{c=1,\ldots,C} \sum_{d=1}^{C} L(d, c) n_d^{R_d(x)}.$$

Show that if, additionally, the classifier uses 0–1 loss, then the classifier predicts

$$\text{argmax}_{c=1,\ldots,C}\, n_c^{R_c(x)}.$$

4.4.6   The Naive Bayes Classifier

The *naive Bayes classifier* is a likelihood method which is based on the assumption that the features (coordinates of X) are all independent, at least approximately. This means that the likelihood function $P(x \mid Y = c)$ for each class can be expressed as a product of m marginal likelihoods: at the point $x = (x_1, \ldots, x_m)$,

$$P(x \mid Y = c) = \prod_{j=1}^{m} P(x_j \mid Y = c).$$

The naive Bayes classifier is trained by estimating the one-dimensional coordinate density $P(x_i \mid Y = c)$ for each class c and feature i in some way (any of the ways above, for example) and plugging the estimates into the product. Figure 4.11 illustrates kernel density estimates of marginal densities $\hat{P}(x_1 \mid Y = c)$ and $\hat{P}(x_2 \mid Y = c)$, the resulting estimated joint densities $\hat{P}(x \mid Y = c)$, and class predictions made by the naive Bayes classifier trained on the data of Figure 4.1. This technique should not be neglected merely because of its pejorative name.[16]

Exercise 4.9 *Show that a naive Bayes classifier where all features are assumed to be Gaussian-distributed is equivalent to a quadratic discriminant classifier where all covariance matrices are assumed to be diagonal.*

4.5   Prototype Methods

The general idea behind prototype methods is to classify new data points by considering the classes of nearby training data points, where "nearby" is defined in terms of some kind of distance which makes sense for the application at hand. Training

---

[16] The naive Bayes classifier is also known as the *independence Bayes classifier*, the *simple Bayes classifier*, and the *idiot's Bayes classifier* Hand and Yu (2007).

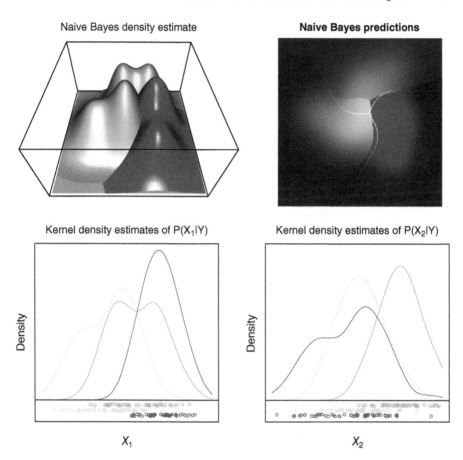

Figure 4.11   Estimated class densities (upper left) and classification decisions (upper right) made using a naive Bayes density estimate trained on the data of Figure 4.1. The density estimate is formed from the product of two one-dimensional kernel density estimates which used Gaussian kernels and bandwidth 0.7, shown in the lower two cells (with one-dimensional projections of the data for reference). The naive Bayes classifier has estimated risk 0.212. Bandwidth 0.7 was selected as approximately optimal using leave-one-out cross-validation, described in Section 7.3, to estimate risk from the training data.

data are represented by *prototypes*, which are feature vectors in $\mathcal{X}$. Prototypes may be observed data points or may be idealized data points.

4.5.1 k-Nearest-Neighbor

Given training data $(x_1, y_1), \ldots, (x_n, y_n)$ and a new point x, the k-nearest-neighbor (KNN) algorithm classifies x to the most frequent class of the k nearest training data (ties, when possible, are usually decided randomly).[17] Small values of k result in wiggly class boundaries, while large values result in smooth ones. Taking $k > 1$ can provide robustness in the presence of mislabeled training data. *Every* data point is a prototype in the k-nearest-neighbor classifier.

The effect of the number-of-neighbors parameter k is illustrated in the left-hand cells of Figure 4.12. A small value of k makes the behavior of the classifier sensitive to particular data points. Note how the 1-nearest-neighbor classifier predicts that a region in the top center of the upper-left cell is purple, due to the single out-lying purple data point visible in at the top center of the right-hand cell of Figure 4.1. Moderate values of k strike a balance between sensitivity to local variations in the class densities and smoothing away noise in the data. Large values of k result in classifiers which are relatively insensitive to local variations in the class densities.

Straightforward implementation of a k-nearest-neighbor classifier requires computation of the distance between each new point $X \in \mathcal{X}$ to be classified and every training data point: $O(n)$ work per point to be classified. If the number of points to be classified is sufficiently large, a more efficient implementation of k-nearest-neighbor can be achieved using a data structure called a *multidimensional binary search tree* or, more commonly, a *k-d tree* (Bentley, 1975). A k-d tree requires $O(n \log n)$ work to construct, but using a k-d tree requires only $O(\log n)$ work, on average, per point to be classified.

This is a very old classification method: 1-nearest-neighbor goes back to a 1951 technical report of the United States Air Force School of Aviation Medicine (Fix and Hodges, 1951). General k-nearest-neighbor is due to Cover and Hart (1967).

4.5.2   Condensed k-Nearest-Neighbor

Condensed k-nearest-neighbor is an attempt to get the performance of k-nearest-neighbor at lower cost (Hart, 1968). Given training data $(x_1, y_1), \ldots, (x_n, y_n)$, a condensed set S is formed in the following way: initially, $S = \{(x_1, y_1)\}$. For $i = 2$, $3, \ldots, n$, if x_i is misclassified by the k-nearest-neighbor classifier trained on S, then (x_i, y_i) is added to S and otherwise is discarded. Once S has been constructed using all of the training data, the condensed k-nearest-neighbor classifier is the k-nearest-neighbor classifier trained on the subset $S \subseteq \{(x_1, y_1), \ldots, (x_n, y_n)\}$. The condensed set S is a set of prototypes which are actual data points. Of course, instead of training the k-nearest neighbor classifier on S, one can use other classifiers—such as condensed k-nearest-neighbor.

4.5.3   Nearest-Cluster

Nearest-cluster is another attempt to reduce the cost of k-nearest-neighbor. The idea is simple: run a clustering algorithm on the training data from each class separately

---

[17] The knn() function in R's class package splits ties randomly for classification.

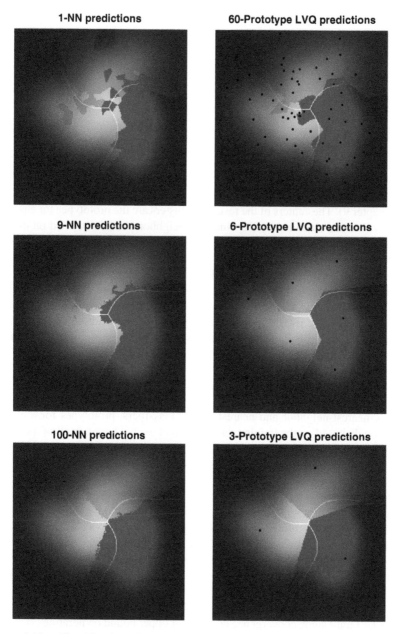

Figure 4.12 Classification decisions made using k-nearest-neighbors (left) and learning vector quantization (right), trained on the data of Figure 4.1. Numbers of nearest neighbors $k = 1$, 9, and 100 produce estimated risks 0.248, 0.202, and 0.247, respectively. Numbers of LVQ prototypes 60, 6, and 3 (20, 2, and 1 per class, shown in black) produce estimated risks 0.213, 0.195, and 0.245, respectively. The values $k = 9$ and 6 LVQ prototypes were selected as approximately optimal using leave-one-out cross-validation, described in Section 7.3, to estimate risk from the training data.

> (1) Draw a point (x, y) from the training data uniformly at random.
> (2) Find the nearest prototype p to x and the distance $d(p, x)$ between them.
> (3) If p is a class-y prototype,
> (4)   move p towards x by distance $\epsilon\, d(p, x)$
> (5) else
> (6)   move p away from x by distance $\epsilon\, d(p, x)$.
> (7) Update ϵ.

Figure 4.13   The learning vector quantization algorithm.

(see Chapter 9). The centers of the resulting clusters are the prototypes for each class, and new data are classified by the k-nearest-neighbor classifier trained on the set of prototypes (the class of a prototype is the class of the data from which it is constructed).

The class prototypes constructed by the nearest-cluster classifier need not be actual training data points, as they were in k-nearest-neighbor and condensed k-nearest-neighbor. For example, if $\mathcal{X} = \mathbb{R}^m$ and the k-means[18] clustering algorithm (described in Section 9.2) were used, the prototypes typically would not be observed feature vectors. On the other hand, if the k-medoids clustering algorithm (described in Section 9.6) were used, then the prototypes would be observed feature vectors.

4.5.4   Learning Vector Quantization

In the k-nearest-neighbor and nearest-cluster classifiers, prototypes for a class are selected only based on the training data for that class, not based on all of the training data.[19] Learning vector quantization (LVQ), first described in Kohonen (1986), uses all of the training data to choose the class prototypes. For each class, some number of initial prototypes are chosen: this could be done by randomly sampling the training data for each class or by using a clustering algorithm as in the nearest-cluster classifier. Training the prototype set (which is the same as training the LVQ classifier) is done by moving the prototypes toward data points of their own class and away from data points of any other class. The trained LVQ classifier predicts the class at a point x to be the class of the nearest prototype to x. Application of LVQ requires that feature space $\mathcal{X}$ be such that a point $x \in \mathcal{X}$ can move a given distance in a given direction (for example, $\mathcal{X} = \mathbb{R}^m$).

The training algorithm starts with a step size $\epsilon < 1$ and iterates the steps shown in Figure 4.13 until some convergence criterion or upper bound on iterations is reached.

---

[18] The value of k in the k-nearest-neighbor classifier and the value of k in k-means or k-medoids clustering may be different. The double use of the letter k is an unfortunate collision in standard terminology.

[19] While the k-nearest-neighbor and nearest-cluster classifiers choose prototypes to be representatives of their class, the condensed k-nearest-neighbor and LVQ classifiers choose prototypes specifically for their utility in performing the classification task at hand.

Some versions of LVQ decrease ϵ in step (7) of every iteration, for example, by using the update rule

$$\epsilon_i = \epsilon_0 \left(1 - \frac{i}{I}\right),$$

where index i counts the iterations of the algorithm from 0 up to $I - 1$, and I is a user-specified number of iterations to perform. Another, more sophisticated version of LVQ[20] uses different values of ϵ for each class c, updating ϵ_c in step (7) by the rule

$$\epsilon_c = \begin{cases} \frac{\epsilon_c}{1+\epsilon_c} & \text{if } x \text{ and } p \text{ are of the same class} \\ \min\left(\epsilon, \frac{\epsilon_c}{1-\epsilon_c}\right) & \text{if } x \text{ and } p \text{ are of different classes,} \end{cases}$$

where c is the class of prototype p and $\epsilon < 1$ is the initial value of $\epsilon_1, \ldots, \epsilon_C$. Thus the training algorithm shrinks ϵ_c when it finds evidence that LVQ is performing well on class c, and increases ϵ_c (up to a maximum of ϵ) when it finds evidence that LVQ is performing poorly on class c.

The effect of the number of prototypes k is illustrated in the right-hand cells of Figure 4.12. In these examples, the prototypes were initialized by selecting proportion $P(Y = c)$ of the k points from feature vectors of class c uniformly at random without replacement, for each $c = 1, \ldots, C$. The "more sophisticated" update rule was used with each ϵ_c initialized to $\epsilon = 0.3$, and 6000 iterations were performed. Larger values of k make the behavior of the LVQ classifier sensitive to particular data points, while smaller values of k make the behavior less sensitive to particular data points. In the extreme case of one prototype per class ($k = C$), the boundary between each pair of classes is linear.

4.6 Logistic Regression

Logistic regression solves the classification problem by turning it into a regression problem, explicitly estimating the vector of class probabilities

$$(P(Y = 1 \mid X), \ldots, P(Y = C \mid X)).$$

Specifically, the model assumption made by logistic regression is that the $(C - 1)$-long vector of log-odds with respect to some specified class, which without loss of generality may as well be class 1,

$$\left(\log \frac{P(Y = 2 \mid X)}{P(Y = 1 \mid X)}, \ldots, \log \frac{P(Y = C \mid X)}{P(Y = 1 \mid X)}\right),$$

---

[20] This version is implemented in the R library class as function olvq1().

is a linear function of the feature vector X. That is, it is assumed that

$$
\begin{bmatrix}
\log \frac{P(Y=1\,|\,X)}{P(Y=1\,|\,X)} \\[4pt]
\log \frac{P(Y=2\,|\,X)}{P(Y=1\,|\,X)} \\[4pt]
\log \frac{P(Y=3\,|\,X)}{P(Y=1\,|\,X)} \\[2pt]
\vdots \\[2pt]
\log \frac{P(Y=C\,|\,X)}{P(Y=1\,|\,X)}
\end{bmatrix}
=
\begin{bmatrix}
0 & 0 & \cdots & 0 \\
\theta_{2,0} & \theta_{2,1} & \cdots & \theta_{2,m} \\
\theta_{3,0} & \theta_{3,1} & \cdots & \theta_{3,m} \\
\vdots & \vdots & & \vdots \\
\theta_{C,0} & \theta_{C,1} & \cdots & \theta_{C,m}
\end{bmatrix}
\begin{bmatrix}
1 \\ X_1 \\ \vdots \\ X_m
\end{bmatrix}
\tag{4.2}
$$

for some $C \times (m+1)$ matrix of real parameters ($m+1$ of which are constrained to be zero)

$$
\theta =
\begin{bmatrix}
0 & 0 & \cdots & 0 \\
\theta_{2,0} & \theta_{2,1} & \cdots & \theta_{2,m} \\
\theta_{3,0} & \theta_{3,1} & \cdots & \theta_{3,m} \\
\vdots & \vdots & & \vdots \\
\theta_{C,0} & \theta_{C,1} & \cdots & \theta_{C,m}
\end{bmatrix}
=
\begin{bmatrix}
\theta_1 \\ \theta_2 \\ \theta_3 \\ \vdots \\ \theta_m
\end{bmatrix},
$$

where θ_c denotes row c of θ.

Given a value of matrix θ, class-membership probabilities can be recovered from (4.2). For $c = 1, \dots, C$, define linear functions

$$
T_c = T(X, \theta_c) = [\theta_{c,0}, \theta_{c,1}, \dots, \theta_{c,m}]
\begin{bmatrix}
1 \\ X_1 \\ \vdots \\ X_m
\end{bmatrix}
= \theta_{c,0} + \sum_{j=1}^{m} \theta_{c,j} X_j,
$$

and note that $T_1 = T(X, \theta_1) = 0$. Linear function $T(X, \theta_c)$ is the logistic regression estimate of the log-odds in favor of class c over class 1, $\log \frac{P(Y=c\,|\,X)}{P(Y=1\,|\,X)}$, for $c = 1, \dots, C$.

Exercise 4.10 *Show that under the logistic regression model assumption (4.2), the probability that a feature vector X belongs to class c is*[21]

$$
P(Y = c \,|\, X) = \frac{\exp(T(X, \theta_c))}{\sum_{d=1}^{C} \exp(T(X, \theta_d))}.
\tag{4.3}
$$

---

[21] In the case of $C = 2$ classes, this results in one-dimensional real-valued functions,

$$
P(Y = 1 \,|\, X) = \frac{1}{1 + \exp(T(X, \theta_2))} \quad \text{and} \quad P(Y = 2 \,|\, X) = \frac{\exp(T(X, \theta_2))}{1 + \exp(T(X, \theta_2))} = \frac{1}{1 + \exp(-T(X, \theta_2))}.
$$

Thus $P(Y = 1 \,|\, X)$ and $P(Y = 2 \,|\, X)$ are the *logistic function* $q(z) = \frac{1}{1+\exp(-z)}$, applied to the linear functions $\mp T(X, \theta_2)$. The logistic function first arose as the solution of a boundary value problem for the differential equation $q'(z) = q(z)(1 - q(z))$, and was named *logistique* by Verhulst (1838, 1844).

Training a logistic regression classifier means finding an estimate $\widehat{\theta}$ of matrix θ. The training data are assumed to be independent, which means that the class label Y_i is a single draw from the multinomial distribution with probability parameter $P(Y_i | X_i = x_i)$,

$$Y_i | (X_i = x_i) \sim \text{Multinomial}\,(1, (P(Y_i = 1 | X = x_i), \dots, P(Y = C | X = x_i))).$$

Thus the log-likelihood[22] of the data $(x_1, y_1), \dots, (x_n, y_n)$ is

$$\sum_{i=1}^{n} \log P(y_i | X = x_i) = \sum_{i=1}^{n} T(x_i, \theta_{y_i}) - \sum_{i=1}^{n} \log \left(\sum_{d=1}^{C} \exp(T(x_i, \theta_d)) \right).$$

An estimate $\widehat{\theta}$ of θ is found by (approximately) maximizing this log-likelihood using a numerical optimization algorithm.[23] Details, including computation of the gradient of the log-likelihood (equivalently, by Exercise 4.11, the gradient of the training estimate of risk under cross-entropy loss) may be found in Chapter 10. The trained classifier is then

$$\widehat{f}(x) = \text{argmin}_{c \in \{1, \dots, C\}} \sum_{d=1}^{C} L(d, c)\, \widehat{P}(Y = d | X = x),$$

where, for $c = 1, \dots, C$,

$$\widehat{P}(Y = c | X) = \frac{\exp(T(X, \widehat{\theta}_c))}{\sum_{d=1}^{C} \exp(T(X, \widehat{\theta}_d))}.$$

Exercise 4.11 *Show that estimating θ by maximizing the multinomial likelihood above is equivalent to estimating θ by minimizing training risk with respect to cross-entropy loss (defined in Chapter 2).*

As in linear discriminant analysis, the estimated class boundaries produced by logistic regression are piecewise linear. Classification decisions made by logistic regression trained on the data of Figure 4.1 are shown in Figure 4.14.

---

[22] The probability mass function of the Multinomial $(s, (p_1, \dots, p_k))$ distribution is

$$P((z_1, \dots, z_k)) = \frac{s!}{z_1! \cdots z_k!} p_1^{z_1} \cdots p_k^{z_k}$$

where $z_1 + \cdots + z_k = s$. In the case $s = 1$, this simplifies to $P((z_1, \dots, z_k)) = p_i$ where i is the unique index such that $z_i = 1$.

[23] Two standard algorithms for this are the quasi-Newton methods called *iteratively reweighted least squares*, which is used in the R function glm(), and the *Broyden-Fletcher-Goldfarb-Shanno (BFGS) algorithm*, which is used in the R functions multinom() and nnet(). BFGS is described in Chapter 10.

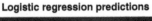

Logistic regression predictions

Logistic regression log-odds vs 'orange'   Logistic regression estimates of P(Y|X)

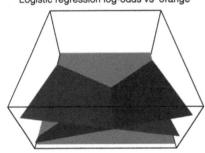   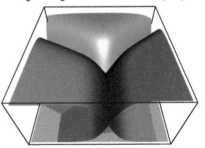

Figure 4.14   Classification decisions made using logistic regression trained on the data of Figure 4.1 are shown in the upper cell. The class boundaries are piecewise linear. The lower-left cell shows the three linear functions T_c: the blue plane is $T_2 = T(x, \widehat{\theta}_2)$, the log-odds in favor of the blue class over the orange class; the purple plane is $T_3 = T(x, \widehat{\theta}_3)$, the log-odds in favor of the purple class over the orange class; and the orange plane is $T_1 = 0$. The lower-right cell shows the three estimated probabilities $\widehat{P}(Y = c \mid x)$ for $c = 1, 2, 3$, plotted as functions of the features x. Logistic regression has estimated risk 0.220.

4.7   Neural Networks

4.7.1   Activation Functions

A neural network classifier requires an *activation function*, which is often a "soft" (piecewise differentiable) version of an indicator function. Most commonly used is the *sigmoid*[24] function,

$$\sigma(v) = \frac{1}{1 + e^{-v}},$$

---

[24] The word *sigmoid* applies to any function shaped like the letter S, not just the logistic function shown here.

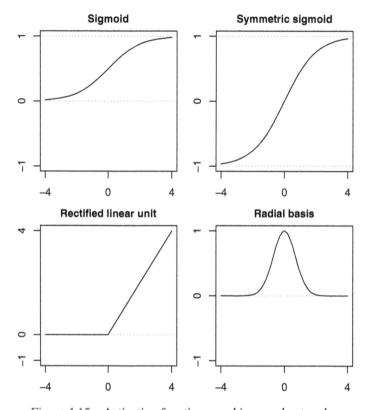

Figure 4.15   Activation functions used in neural networks.

which is a soft version of the indicator function[25] $[v \geq 0]$. This activation function is graphed in the upper-left cell of Figure 4.15.

Other activation functions used sometimes in neural networks are the *symmetric sigmoid*,

$$\sigma(v) = 2\,\frac{1}{1 + e^{-v}} - 1 = \frac{1 - e^{-v}}{1 + e^{-v}} = \tanh\left(\frac{v}{2}\right),$$

which is a sigmoid shifted and scaled to take values in $(-1, 1)$, the *rectified linear unit* (ReLU),

$$\sigma(v) = \begin{cases} 0 & v \leq 0 \\ v & v > 0 \end{cases},$$

and the *radial basis function*,

$$\sigma(v) = \exp(-v^2),$$

---

[25] This is Iverson bracket notation: [statement] is 1 or 0 accordingly as the statement is true or false.

which is a soft version of the indicator function $[v = 0]$. These activation functions are graphed Figure 4.15. For specificity, we will use the sigmoid function $\sigma(v) = \frac{1}{1+e^{-v}}$ in the rest of this section.

4.7.2   Neurons

The fundamental unit of a neural network is a *neuron*, which is the composition of an activation function σ and a linear map $\mathbb{R}^k \to \mathbb{R}$ specified by a $(k + 1)$-long parameter vector $\theta = (\theta_0, \theta_1, \dots, \theta_k)$. It will be convenient sometimes to think of the parameter vector as the concatenation of a scalar parameter[26] θ_0 and a k-long vector $\theta_\star = (\theta_1, \dots, \theta_k)$. A neuron, then, is the composition[27]

$$
\sigma\left([\theta_0, \theta_1, \dots, \theta_k]\begin{bmatrix} 1 \\ v_1 \\ \vdots \\ v_k \end{bmatrix}\right) = \sigma(\theta_0 + \theta_\star v) = \sigma\left(\theta_0 + \sum_{i=1}^{k} \theta_i v_i\right),
$$

where vector $v = (v_1, \dots, v_k)$ is the input to the neuron. The geometric meaning of a neuron becomes more apparent when the length of vector $\theta_\star$ is separated from its direction, $\theta_\star = \frac{\theta_\star}{\|\theta_\star\|}\|\theta_\star\|$. The unit vector $\frac{\theta_\star}{\|\theta_\star\|}$, length $\|\theta_\star\|$ and the scalar parameter θ_0 define a hyperplane $H(\theta_\star, \theta_0)$ in $\mathbb{R}^k$,

$$
H(\theta_\star, \theta_0) = \{v : \theta_0 + \theta_\star v = 0\} = \left\{v : \frac{\theta_0}{\|\theta_\star\|} + \frac{\theta_\star}{\|\theta_\star\|} v = 0\right\}
$$

$$
= \left\{v : \frac{\theta_\star}{\|\theta_\star\|} v = -\frac{\theta_0}{\|\theta_\star\|}\right\}.
$$

The neuron specified above is a soft version of the indicator function

$$
\left[\frac{\theta_\star}{\|\theta_\star\|} v \geq -\frac{\theta_0}{\|\theta_\star\|}\right],
$$

which is 1 when input v is in the direction of $\theta_\star$ from hyperplane $H(\theta_\star, \theta_0)$ and is 0 when input v is in the direction of $-\theta_\star$ from hyperplane $H(\theta_\star, \theta_0)$. The geometry of this situation is illustrated in Figure 4.16.

The length of the k-long vector $\|\theta_\star\|$, is called the *activation rate* and affects how sensitive the neuron is to its input. If $\|\theta_\star\|$ is large, then the value of the neuron changes quickly from nearly 0 (or 1) to nearly 1 (or 0) as v crosses from one side of $H(\theta_\star, \theta_0)$ to the other—so the neuron closely approximates an indicator function. If $\|\theta_\star\|$ is small, the value of the neuron changes slowly as v moves from one side of

---

[26] In the context of neural networks, the scalar parameter θ_0 is called the *bias* of the neuron.

[27] Throughout this section, parameter vectors θ and $\theta_\star$ are row vectors, and inputs to neurons are column vectors.

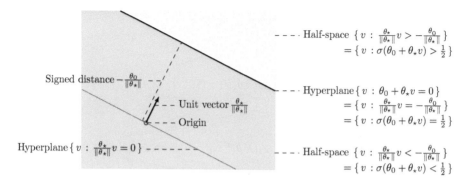

Figure 4.16   For any scalar θ_0 and k-long real vector $\theta_\star$, the set of points $H(\theta_\star, \theta_0) = \{v \in \mathbb{R}^k : \theta_0 + \theta_\star v = 0\}$ is a hyperplane in $\mathbb{R}^k$. The hyperplane lies at distance $\frac{|\theta_0|}{\|\theta_\star\|}$ from the origin, either in the direction of $\theta_\star$ (if $-\frac{\theta_0}{\|\theta_\star\|} > 0$, that is, if $\theta_0 < 0$) or in the direction of $-\theta_\star$ (if $-\frac{\theta_0}{\|\theta_\star\|} < 0$, that is, if $\theta_0 > 0$). The hyperplane $H(\theta_\star, \theta_0)$ cuts $\mathbb{R}^k$ into two half-spaces. The neuron $\sigma(\theta_0 + \theta_\star v)$ increases from $\frac{1}{2}$ as v moves away from $H(\theta_\star, \theta_0)$ in the direction of $\theta_\star$, eventually approaching the value 1. The neuron $\sigma(\theta_0 + \theta_\star v)$ decreases from $\frac{1}{2}$ as v moves away from $H(\theta_\star, \theta_0)$ in the direction of $-\theta_\star$, eventually approaching the value 0. This notation will be used again in Section 4.9.

$H(\theta_\star, \theta_0)$ to the other—so for a substantial set of v's, the neuron is approximately a linear function of v with gradient $\theta_\star$.

4.7.3   Neural Networks

A *neural network* composes multiple neurons into a single function.[28] Some of the neurons in a neural network use the feature vector as input, some use the output of other neurons as input, and some may use a combination of the two.[29] The parameters of a neural network are the parameters of the neurons (including the way in which the neurons are connected together) and the parameters of an *output layer* of linear functions defined as in logistic regression,

$$T(v, \theta) = \theta_0 + \theta_\star v,$$

but unlike logistic regression, none of the linear output functions are constrained to be zero. Neurons are typically arranged in layers according to what kind of input they

---

[28] It is difficult to define exactly what a neural network is, because there is great diversity among algorithms which go by that name. What is being defined here is a common or "classical" type, sometimes called a *feed-forward neural network*, or a *perceptron*.

[29] In a *recurrent neural network*, some neurons use their own output as input.

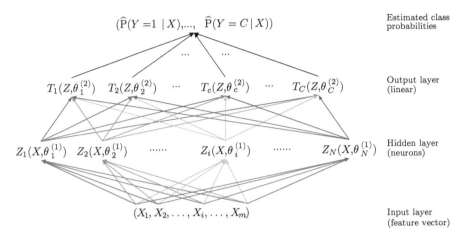

Figure 4.17   A single-hidden-layer neural network with N hidden nodes. The ith hidden node is $Z_i = Z_i(X, \theta_i^{(1)}) = \sigma(\theta_{i,0}^{(1)} + \theta_{i,\star}^{(1)} X)$, a neuron. The cth output node is $T_c = T_c(Z, \theta_c^{(2)}) = \theta_{c,0}^{(2)} + \theta_{c,\star} Z$, a linear function. Given estimates of parameters $\theta^{(1)}$ and $\theta^{(2)}$, the estimated probability of the cth class, given feature vector X, is $\hat{P}(Y = c \mid X) = \exp(T_c) / \sum_{d=1}^{C} \exp(T_d)$.

receive. The *input layer* of neurons receives feature vectors as input, while any layer other than the input or output layers is called a *hidden layer* of neurons.

Figure 4.17 shows a neural network with an output layer of C linear functions, $T_1, \ldots, T_C$, and a single hidden layer of N neurons, $Z_1, \ldots, Z_N$. Each neuron in the hidden layer receives as input the entire feature vector, $X = (X_1, \ldots, X_m)$. Each linear function in the output layer receives as input the entire vector of values of the hidden neurons, $Z = (Z_1, \ldots, Z_N)$. The parameters of this neural network can be written as two matrices,

$$\theta^{(1)} = \begin{bmatrix} \theta_{1,0}^{(1)} & \theta_{1,1}^{(1)} & \cdots & \theta_{1,m}^{(1)} \\ \theta_{2,0}^{(1)} & \theta_{2,1}^{(1)} & \cdots & \theta_{2,m}^{(1)} \\ \vdots & \vdots & & \vdots \\ \theta_{N,0}^{(1)} & \theta_{N,1}^{(1)} & \cdots & \theta_{N,m}^{(1)} \end{bmatrix}$$

which governs how the hidden-layer neurons respond to a feature vector, and

$$\theta^{(2)} = \begin{bmatrix} \theta_{1,0}^{(2)} & \theta_{1,1}^{(2)} & \cdots & \theta_{1,N}^{(2)} \\ \theta_{2,0}^{(2)} & \theta_{2,1}^{(2)} & \cdots & \theta_{2,N}^{(2)} \\ \vdots & \vdots & & \vdots \\ \theta_{C,0}^{(2)} & \theta_{C,1}^{(2)} & \cdots & \theta_{C,N}^{(2)} \end{bmatrix}$$

which governs how the output-layer linear functions respond to the vector of hidden-layer neuron outputs. The total number of parameters is $N(m + 1) + C(N + 1)$.

The output of the ith neuron in the hidden layer is

$$
Z_i = \sigma\left(\left[\theta_{i,0}^{(1)}, \theta_{i,1}^{(1)}, \ldots, \theta_{i,m}^{(1)}\right]\begin{bmatrix} 1 \\ X_1 \\ \vdots \\ X_m \end{bmatrix}\right) = \sigma\left(\theta_{i,0}^{(1)} + \theta_{i,\star}^{(1)} X\right) = \sigma\left(\theta_{i,0}^{(1)} + \sum_{j=1}^{m} \theta_{i,j}^{(1)} X_j\right).
$$

Applying σ to a vector coordinatewise, the entire hidden layer may be written as

$$
\begin{bmatrix} Z_1 \\ \vdots \\ Z_N \end{bmatrix} = \sigma\left(\begin{bmatrix} \theta_{1,0}^{(1)} & \theta_{1,1}^{(1)} & \cdots & \theta_{1,m}^{(1)} \\ \theta_{2,0}^{(1)} & \theta_{2,1}^{(1)} & \cdots & \theta_{2,m}^{(1)} \\ \vdots & \vdots & & \vdots \\ \theta_{N,0}^{(1)} & \theta_{N,1}^{(1)} & \cdots & \theta_{N,m}^{(1)} \end{bmatrix}\begin{bmatrix} 1 \\ X_1 \\ \vdots \\ X_m \end{bmatrix}\right),
$$

or, in more compact notation, writing $\theta_0^{(1)}$ for the first column of $\theta^{(1)}$ and $\theta_\star^{(1)}$ for the rest of $\theta^{(1)}$, as

$$
Z = \sigma\left(\theta_0^{(1)} + \theta_\star^{(1)} X\right).
$$

The cth linear output function is

$$
T_c = T\left(Z, \theta_c^{(2)}\right) = \left[\theta_{c,0}^{(2)}, \theta_{c,1}^{(2)}, \ldots, \theta_{c,N}^{(2)}\right]\begin{bmatrix} 1 \\ Z_1 \\ \vdots \\ Z_N \end{bmatrix} = \theta_{c,0}^{(2)} + \theta_{c,\star}^{(2)} Z = \theta_{c,0}^{(2)} + \sum_{i=1}^{N} \theta_{c,i}^{(2)} Z_i.
$$

The entire output layer may be written as

$$
\begin{bmatrix} T_1 \\ \vdots \\ T_c \end{bmatrix} = \begin{bmatrix} \theta_{1,0}^{(2)} & \theta_{1,1}^{(2)} & \cdots & \theta_{1,N}^{(2)} \\ \theta_{2,0}^{(2)} & \theta_{2,1}^{(2)} & \cdots & \theta_{2,N}^{(2)} \\ \vdots & \vdots & & \vdots \\ \theta_{C,0}^{(2)} & \theta_{C,1}^{(2)} & \cdots & \theta_{C,N}^{(2)} \end{bmatrix}\begin{bmatrix} 1 \\ Z_1 \\ \vdots \\ Z_N \end{bmatrix}
$$

$$
= \begin{bmatrix} \theta_{1,0}^{(2)} \\ \theta_{2,0}^{(2)} \\ \vdots \\ \theta_{C,0}^{(2)} \end{bmatrix} + \begin{bmatrix} \theta_{1,1}^{(2)} & \cdots & \theta_{1,N}^{(2)} \\ \theta_{2,1}^{(2)} & \cdots & \theta_{2,N}^{(2)} \\ \vdots & & \vdots \\ \theta_{C,1}^{(2)} & \cdots & \theta_{C,N}^{(2)} \end{bmatrix}\sigma\left(\begin{bmatrix} \theta_{1,0}^{(1)} & \theta_{1,1}^{(1)} & \cdots & \theta_{1,m}^{(1)} \\ \theta_{2,0}^{(1)} & \theta_{2,1}^{(1)} & \cdots & \theta_{2,m}^{(1)} \\ \vdots & \vdots & & \vdots \\ \theta_{N,0}^{(1)} & \theta_{N,1}^{(1)} & \cdots & \theta_{N,m}^{(1)} \end{bmatrix}\begin{bmatrix} 1 \\ X_1 \\ \vdots \\ X_m \end{bmatrix}\right),
$$

or, in more compact notation, as

$$
T = \theta_0^{(2)} + \theta_\star^{(2)} Z = \theta_0^{(2)} + \theta_\star^{(2)}\sigma\left(\theta_0^{(1)} + \theta_\star^{(1)} X\right).
$$

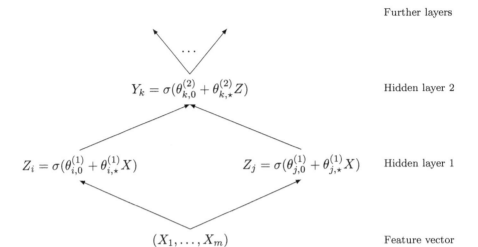

Figure 4.18   Part of a neural network considered in Exercise 4.12.

The vector of outputs $T = (T_1, \ldots, T_C)$ is transformed into a vector of probabilities just as in logistic regression,[30]

$$\widehat{P}(Y = c \mid X) = \frac{\exp(T_c)}{\sum_{d=1}^{C} \exp(T_d)}.$$

In a neural network context, the map

$$(T_1, \ldots, T_C) \mapsto \frac{\exp(T_c)}{\sum_{d=1}^{C} \exp(T_d)}$$

is called the *softmax* function. As in logistic regression, a new data point is classified to minimize estimated risk.

Neural networks can have multiple hidden layers. A two-hidden-layer neural network could be made from the one shown in Figure 4.17 by using the vector Z as input to another layer of neurons (possibly a different number of them than in the first layer), the output of which is then used as input to the linear functions $T_1, \ldots, T_C$.

Training a neural network means estimating values of all of the parameters. Neural networks are trained by minimizing squared-error or cross-entropy loss[31] on training data using a numerical optimization method (for example, the fitted neural networks shown in Figure 4.18 were trained by applying the BFGS algorithm, described in

---

[30] That is, the model assumes $\log P(Y = c \mid X) \propto T_c$, with the same constant of proportionality for all $c = 1, \ldots, C$.

[31] For large neural networks, it has sometimes been found useful to include a penalty term on the parameters, similar to penalization used in ridge regression and lasso described in Section 3.10, and classification trees and support vector machines described in Sections 4.8 and 4.9. Parameter penalization is

Chapter 10, to 1000 randomly generated initial states and retaining the single fit with maximum likelihood). An important computational element of neural networks is *back-propagation*, which refers to an efficient method of computing the gradient of the training risk for use in a gradient descent algorithm. Details, including computation of the gradient of the training estimate of risk under cross-entropy loss, may be found in Chapter 10. A technique which has been found useful in training deep networks (that is, networks with many layers) is described in Section 11.3.11.

Geometrically, the N hyperplanes corresponding to the N hidden neurons in Figure 4.17 partition $\mathbb{R}^m$ into $\binom{N}{0} + \cdots + \binom{N}{\min(m,N)} \leq 2^N$ polyhedra (except in degenerate cases, where there are even fewer polyhedra) (Buck, 1943), and the complete state of the hidden layer, $Z = (Z_1, \ldots, Z_N)$, may be viewed as a soft version of a binary codeword which identifies the polyhedron containing input X. The linear functions of the output layer can, then, be viewed as linear functions of (approximate) binary codewords.

Exercise 4.12 *For the partial neural network shown in Figure 4.18, for given constants α_1 and α_2, provide explicit values of the scalar and vector parameters $\theta_{i,0}^{(1)}, \theta_{i,\star}^{(1)}, \theta_{j,0}^{(1)}, \theta_{j,\star}^{(1)}, \theta_{k,0}^{(2)}, \theta_{k,\star}^{(2)}$ so that the output Y_k of the second-layer neuron is an arbitrarily close approximation to the following Boolean functions:*

(A) $[X_1 > \alpha_1 \text{ and } X_2 > \alpha_2]$

(B) $[X_1 > \alpha_1 \text{ and } X_2 < \alpha_2]$

(C) $[X_1 < \alpha_1 \text{ and } X_2 > \alpha_2]$

(D) $[X_1 < \alpha_1 \text{ and } X_2 < \alpha_2]$.

What modification of the parameters in each of (A) through (D) converts the logical "and" operation to "nand" ("not and")? Any Boolean function can be constructed as a composition of nands, so this exercise shows that a sufficiently deep neural network can approximate, arbitrarily well, any Boolean function of inequality statements about its inputs. Hint: Express the answer in terms of a parameter r, so that as r → ∞, output Y_k converges pointwise to $[X_1 > \alpha_1 \text{ and } X_2 > \alpha_2]$ (or other Boolean function, as appropriate).

Classification decisions made by a single-hidden-layer neural network trained on the data of Figure 4.1 are shown in Figure 4.19. This figure illustrates the effect of the number N of hidden states in a single-hidden-layer neural network: in one extreme, the case $N = 1$ forces all class boundaries to be mutually parallel hyperplanes; as more neurons are added, the classifier becomes more sensitive to particular data points.

Figure 4.20 shows details of the two-neuron network[32] whose classification decisions are shown in the upper-right cell of Figure 4.19. The bottom two cells of

---

discussed more generally in Section 11.4. In the context of neural networks, parameter penalization is called *weight decay*.

[32] The fitted parameters for this network can be found in Appendix D.

1-Neuron network predictions   **2-Neuron network predictions**

3-Neuron network predictions   **4-Neuron network predictions**

5-Neuron network predictions   **256-Neuron network predictions**

Figure 4.19   Classification decisions made using a single-hidden-layer neural network trained on the data of Figure 4.1. Numbers of hidden-layer neurons 1, 2, 3, 4, 5, and 256 produce estimated risks 0.401, 0.201, 0.213, 0.224, 0.235, and 0.246 respectively. A range of two to five hidden-layer neurons was selected as approximately optimal using leave-one-out cross-validation, described in Section 7.3, to estimate risk from the training data. Dashed black lines show hyperplanes on which a fitted hidden neuron outputs the value $\frac{1}{2}$ (omitted in the 256-neuron network).

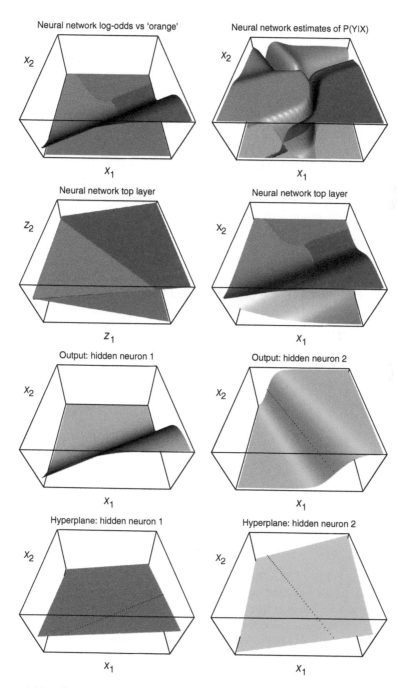

Figure 4.20 Components of the neural network with two hidden neurons whose performance is shown in Figure 4.18. Bottom: linear functions inside the two neurons. Second-from-bottom: output of the neurons. Second-from-top: the output functions, as functions of both Z and X. Top: estimated log-odds and posterior class probabilities.

Figure 4.20 show (from left to right) the linear functions of the two-dimensional feature vector (X_1, X_2),

$$\theta_1^{(1)} \cdot (1, X_1, X_2) = \theta_{1,0}^{(1)} + \theta_{1,1}^{(1)} X_1 + \theta_{1,2}^{(1)} X_2 \qquad \text{and}$$

$$\theta_2^{(1)} \cdot (1, X_1, X_2) = \theta_{2,0}^{(1)} + \theta_{2,1}^{(1)} X_1 + \theta_{2,2}^{(1)} X_2,$$

which define the two hidden neurons. Dashed lines show where these linear functions take the value 0. These dashed lines are "hyperplanes" in $\mathcal{X}$, and the neurons are soft indicators of which side of these hyperplanes a point $(X_1, X_2) \in \mathcal{X}$ falls on.

The second-from-bottom two cells of Figure 4.20 show (from left to right) the values taken by the two hidden neurons,

$$Z_1 = \sigma\big(\theta_1^{(1)} \cdot (1, X_1, X_2)\big) \qquad \text{and} \qquad Z_2 = \sigma\big(\theta_2^{(1)} \cdot (1, X_1, X_2)\big).$$

Hidden neuron Z_1 only gets excited when feature vector X is in the extreme lower-right corner of its domain, while hidden neuron Z_2 gets excited when feature vector X is roughly in the right half of its domain. Dashed lines show where the neurons take the value $\frac{1}{2}$, which is the value corresponding to "being on the hyperplane" determined by the neuron.

In the second-from-top two cells of Figure 4.20, the left-hand cell shows the three linear output functions as functions of the hidden layer output $Z = (Z_1, Z_2)$,

$$T_1 = \theta_1^{(2)} Z = \theta_{1,0}^{(2)} + \theta_{1,1}^{(2)} Z_1 + \theta_{1,2}^{(2)} Z_2 \qquad \text{(orange plane)}$$

$$T_2 = \theta_2^{(2)} Z = \theta_{2,0}^{(2)} + \theta_{2,1}^{(2)} Z_1 + \theta_{2,2}^{(2)} Z_2 \qquad \text{(blue plane)}$$

$$T_3 = \theta_3^{(2)} Z = \theta_{3,0}^{(2)} + \theta_{3,1}^{(2)} Z_1 + \theta_{3,2}^{(2)} Z_2 \qquad \text{(purple plane)}$$

and the right-hand cell shows the three output functions as functions of the feature vector X,

$$T_1 = \theta_{1,0}^{(2)} + \theta_{1,1}^{(2)} \sigma\big(\theta_1^{(1)} \cdot (1, X_1, X_2)\big) + \theta_{1,2}^{(2)} \sigma\big(\theta_2^{(1)} \cdot (1, X_1, X_2)\big) \qquad \text{(orange surface)}$$

$$T_2 = \theta_{2,0}^{(2)} + \theta_{2,1}^{(2)} \sigma\big(\theta_1^{(1)} \cdot (1, X_1, X_2)\big) + \theta_{2,2}^{(2)} \sigma\big(\theta_2^{(1)} \cdot (1, X_1, X_2)\big) \qquad \text{(blue surface)}$$

$$T_3 = \theta_{3,0}^{(2)} + \theta_{3,1}^{(2)} \sigma\big(\theta_1^{(1)} \cdot (1, X_1, X_2)\big) + \theta_{3,2}^{(2)} \sigma\big(\theta_2^{(1)} \cdot (1, X_1, X_2)\big) \qquad \text{(purple surface)}$$

(recall that $\log P(Y = c \mid X) \propto T_c$, with the same constant of proportionality for all $c = 1, \dots, C$). In the left-hand cell, the orange plane is above the blue and purple planes in an almost invisible triangular region consisting of values of Z_1 which are nearly zero, and medium-to-large values of Z_2.

In the top two cells of Figure 4.20, the left-hand cell shows the log-odds in favor of each class relative to the orange class ($c = 1$), as functions of the feature vector X. This is obtained by subtracting the output function for the orange class, T_1, from each output function, forming

$$
\begin{array}{ll}
T_1 - T_1 = 0 & \text{log-odds of orange over itself} \\
T_2 - T_1 & \text{log-odds of blue over orange} \\
T_3 - T_1 & \text{log-odds of purple over orange.}
\end{array}
$$

The right-hand cell of the top row shows the estimated posterior probability $\widehat{P}(Y = c \mid X)$ for $c = 1, 2, 3$, as functions of X, obtained as

$$\widehat{P}(Y = 1 \mid X) = \frac{e^{T_1}}{e^{T_1} + e^{T_2} + e^{T_3}} \qquad \text{(orange surface)}$$

$$\widehat{P}(Y = 2 \mid X) = \frac{e^{T_2}}{e^{T_1} + e^{T_2} + e^{T_3}} \qquad \text{(blue surface)}$$

$$\widehat{P}(Y = 3 \mid X) = \frac{e^{T_3}}{e^{T_1} + e^{T_2} + e^{T_3}} \qquad \text{(purple surface)}.$$

4.7.4   Logistic Regression and Neural Networks

Consider a neural network with no hidden layer, shown in Figure 4.21. The output vector of class probabilities is

$$\left(\frac{\exp\left(T_c\left(X, \theta_c^{(1)}\right)\right)}{\sum_{d=1}^{C} \exp\left(T_d\left(X, \theta_d^{(1)}\right)\right)} \right)_{c=1}^{C}.$$

Without loss of generality, it can be assumed that any one of $\exp(T_1(X, \theta_1^{(1)})), \ldots,$ $\exp(T_C(X, \theta_C^{(1)}))$ has any given positive value by scaling them all (the scaling factor, which depends on X and $\theta^{(1)}$, cancels out in normalization). In particular it can be assumed that $\exp(T_1(X, \theta_1^{(1)}))$ is identically one, which is equivalent to assuming that its parameter vector $\theta_1^{(1)}$ is identically zero. This is exactly logistic regression.

This remark gives another interpretation of neural networks. A neural network with a single hidden layer is logistic regression performed on a basis of "soft" indicator functions of disjoint polyhedra, where the polyhedra are chosen adaptively when the

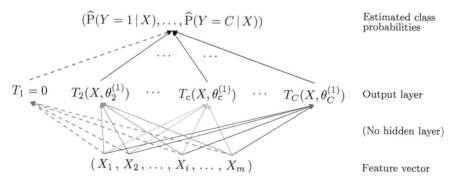

Figure 4.21   Logistic regression drawn as a no-hidden-layer neural network. The dashed arrows indicate that constant output node $T_1 = 0$ may be regarded as a function of the feature vector (with fixed parameter vector $\theta_1^{(1)} = 0$) or may be omitted from the network.

neural network is trained. Neural networks with multiple hidden layers are logistic regression on more complex adaptive bases.

4.8   Classification Trees

A classification tree is a decision tree algorithm which assigns class labels to data. All data enter the root node of the tree, and each internal (non-leaf) node partitions the data in some way, based on the feature vectors. Each leaf (terminal node) assigns a particular class label to all data which enter it. Figure 4.22 shows a small classification tree.

4.8.1   Classification of Data by Leaves (Terminal Nodes)

Let a tree be given, and let t denote a leaf node of the tree. The event "datum (X, Y) enters node t" will be denoted $X \in t$: by construction, at least one training point enters each leaf node of the tree. Let n_c denote the number of training data of class c, n_c^t denote the number of training data of class c which enter node t, and $n^t = \sum_{c=1}^{C} n_c^t$ denote the total number of training data which enter node t.

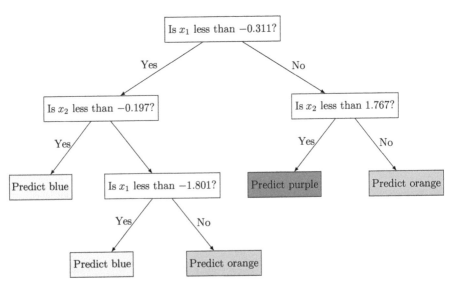

Figure 4.22   A classification tree which maps an input vector $(x_1, x_2) \in \mathbb{R}^2$ to one of three classes. The root node is at the top. This tree was trained on the data of Figure 4.1, and pruned to have five leaf nodes.

The probability that a datum (X, Y) enters node t, given that its class is c, is estimated by the proportion of training data of class c which enter it,[33]

$$\widehat{P}(X \in t \mid Y = c) = \frac{n_c^t}{n_c}.$$

This estimate is then used to make predictions as a likelihood classifier. That is, the estimated posterior probability that a datum (X, Y) is class c, given that it enters node t, is

$$\widehat{P}(Y = c \mid X \in t) = \frac{\widehat{P}(X \in t \mid Y = c) \, P(Y = c)}{\widehat{P}(X \in t)},$$

where

$$\widehat{P}(X \in t) = \sum_{d=1}^{C} \widehat{P}(X \in t, Y = d) = \sum_{d=1}^{C} \widehat{P}(X \in t \mid Y = d) \, P(Y = d).$$

Node t classifies all data which enter it as the class c which minimizes the estimated posterior risk,

$$\widehat{R}(c \mid X \in t) = \sum_{d=1}^{C} L(d, c) \widehat{P}(Y = d \mid X \in t) \propto \sum_{d=1}^{C} L(d, c) \frac{n_d^t}{n_d} P(Y = d).$$

Exercise 4.13 *Show that if the prior distribution is estimated from the training data such that* $P(Y = c) = \frac{n_c}{n}$, *then*

$$\widehat{P}(X \in t) = \frac{n^t}{n}$$

and

$$\widehat{P}(Y = c \mid X \in t) = \frac{n_c^t}{n^t}.$$

Show that with this prior, under 0–1 loss, a leaf node classifies all data which enter it to be the most common class among the training data which enter it.

4.8.2   Impurity of Nodes and Trees

The *impurity of a leaf node t* is a function, $I(t)$, of the estimated posterior distribution on the class of a datum (X, Y) given that $X \in t$,

$$(\widehat{P}(Y = 1 \mid X \in t), \dots, \widehat{P}(Y = C \mid X \in t)),$$

---

[33] When training trees on samples of the training data (as, for example, when training trees used by a random forest classifier as described in Chapter 6), it may happen that $n_c = 0$, in which case $\widehat{P}(X \in t \mid Y = c)$ is defined to be zero.

which measures how diffuse the distribution is on the set of values $\{1, \ldots, C\}$. Commonly used measures of impurity are:

proportion not of the majority class $\qquad I(t) = 1 - \max_{c \in \{1, \ldots, C\}} \widehat{P}(Y = c \mid X \in t)$

entropy $\qquad I(t) = - \sum_{c=1}^{C} \widehat{P}(Y = c \mid X \in t) \log \widehat{P}(Y = c \mid X \in t)$

Gini index of diversity[34] $\qquad I(t) = 1 - \sum_{c=1}^{C} \widehat{P}(Y = c \mid X \in t)^2$

$$= \sum_{c \neq d} \widehat{P}(Y = c \mid X \in t) \widehat{P}(Y = d \mid X \in t).$$

Under each of these definitions, the impurity $I(t)$ is non-negative, is uniquely maximized when the probability distribution $(\widehat{P}(Y = 1 \mid X \in t), \ldots, \widehat{P}(Y = C \mid X \in t))$ is the uniform distribution, and is minimal and equal to zero when this distribution assigns probability one to one class and probability zero to all other classes.

The *impurity of a tree* is the expected impurity of a leaf node with respect to probability distribution $\widehat{P}(X \in t)$ on leaf nodes,

$$\sum_{\text{all leaf nodes } t} I(t) \widehat{P}(X \in t).$$

Exercise 4.14 *Show that when the impurity of a leaf node is measured by the Gini index of diversity, the impurity of the whole tree can be expressed as:*

$$1 - \sum_{\text{all leaf nodes } t} \frac{\sum_{c=1}^{C} (\widehat{P}(X \in t \mid Y = c) P(Y = c))^2}{\widehat{P}(X \in t)}.$$

4.8.3 Growing Trees

A classification tree is trained ("grown") by beginning with a single node, which is the root node and also a leaf, and iteratively splitting leaf nodes in the following way. Let t be a leaf node, let

$$R = \{(x_i, y_i) : x_i \in t\}$$

---

[34] The Gini index of diversity is the probability that two class labels drawn independently at random from $\widehat{P}(Y \mid X \in t)$ are not equal. The Gini index preceded Shannon's (1948) definition of entropy historically, but it can be viewed as a quadratic approximation of entropy since

$$- \sum_{c=1}^{C} \widehat{P}(Y = c \mid X \in t) \log \widehat{P}(Y = c \mid X \in t) \approx \sum_{c=1}^{C} \widehat{P}(Y = c \mid X \in t)(1 - \widehat{P}(Y = c \mid X \in t))$$

$$= 1 - \sum_{c=1}^{C} \widehat{P}(Y = c \mid X \in t)^2.$$

The approximation is not very good when $\widehat{P}(Y = c \mid X \in t)$ is small. See Breiman et al. (1984), Sections 4.2 and 4.3, for arguments in favor of the Gini index as a splitting criterion.

be the set of training data which enter t, and suppose that at least two distinct classes are represented in R, that is, $|\{y_i : x_i \in t\}| \geq 2$. Consider all partitions of R into two non-empty subsets, $R = R_1 \cup R_2$, which arise by splitting the data according to the jth feature, for each $j = 1, \ldots, m$, as follows. If the jth feature is continuous, splitting is performed by applying a threshold τ,

$$R_1 = \{(x_i, y_i) \in R : x_{ij} \leq \tau\} \quad \text{and} \quad R_2 = \{(x_i, y_i) \in R : x_{ij} > \tau\}.$$

There are infinitely many possible values of τ, but only finitely many such partitions to consider, since R is a finite set. If the jth feature is categorical, splitting is performed by partitioning the range of the categorical feature,

$$R_1 = \{(x_i, y_i) \in R : x_{ij} \in S_1\} \quad \text{and} \quad R_2 = \{(x_i, y_i) \in R : x_{ij} \in S_2\},$$

where $S_1 \cup S_2$ is a partition into two nonempty subsets of the finite set of values attainable by the jth feature. Each partition[35] of R corresponds to the addition of two new leaf nodes t_1 and t_2 to the tree extending from t, which is no longer a leaf node: R_1 is the set of training data which enter t_1 and R_2 is the set of training data which enter t_2. The split which minimizes the impurity of the tree is retained, meaning that the new nodes t_1 and t_2 are added to the tree.[36]

The splitting process is repeated, and splitting continues until each leaf node satisfies a stopping criterion, for example, leaf nodes may be split until each satisfies at least one of the following conditions: its training data are all of one class; its training data all have the same feature vector; it contains no more than some specified number of training data.

Figure 4.23 shows the first four steps of training of a classification tree on the data of Figure 4.1. At each step, the partition of the data shown is that which minimizes the impurity of the tree with the empirical prior distribution ($\frac{48}{150}, \frac{49}{150}, \frac{53}{150}$) on the three classes.[37] The classification tree corresponding to the lower-right cell of Figure 4.23 is represented in Figure 4.22 as a decision tree algorithm. The predictions made by this tree are shown in the upper-right cell of Figure 4.24. Any tree with only two leaf nodes, such as that shown in the upper-left-hand cell of Figure 4.23, is called a *stump*.

Exercise 4.15 *Show that when the impurity of a leaf node is measured by the Gini index of diversity, the split which minimizes the impurity of the tree (and thus is*

---

[35] It appears that when splitting according to a categorical feature with k categories, $2^{k-1} - 1$ splits must be considered. In two important special cases, an optimal split can be found with far less work: it is sufficient to consider only k splits in the case of *binary* classification (Breiman et al., 1984, Theorem 4.5, p. 101) and only $k - 1$ splits the case of regression (Breiman et al., 1984, Proposition 8.16, p. 247).
[36] The split node is the *parent node* of t_1 and t_2, and t_1 and t_2 are each a *child node* of their parent.
[37] There are 48 orange, 49 blue, and 53 purple points in the training data.

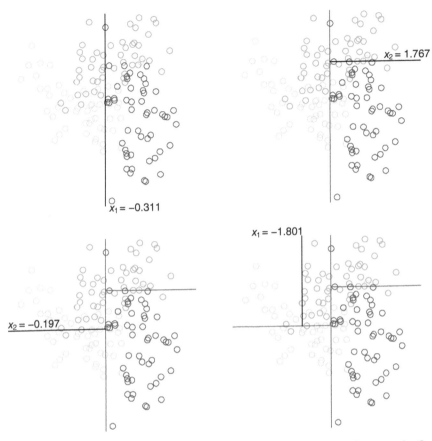

Figure 4.23   These four pictures show, from left to right and top to bottom, the first four steps of training a classification tree on the data of Figure 4.1. The lower-right cell corresponds to the tree shown in Figure 4.22, and to the predictions shown in the upper-right cell of Figure 4.24.

retained) is the split which maximizes

$$-\frac{\sum_{c=1}^{C}(\widehat{P}(X \in t \mid Y = c)\,P(Y = c))^2}{\widehat{P}(X \in t)}$$
$$+\frac{\sum_{c=1}^{C}(\widehat{P}(X \in t_1 \mid Y = c)\,P(Y = c))^2}{\widehat{P}(X \in t_1)} + \frac{\sum_{c=1}^{C}(\widehat{P}(X \in t_2 \mid Y = c)\,P(Y = c))^2}{\widehat{P}(X \in t_2)}.$$

over all leaf nodes t and all splits of t into two new leaf nodes, t_1 and t_2. **Hint:** *Use Exercise 4.14.*

1-Leaf tree predictions   **5-Leaf tree predictions**

15-Leaf tree predictions   **25-Leaf tree predictions**

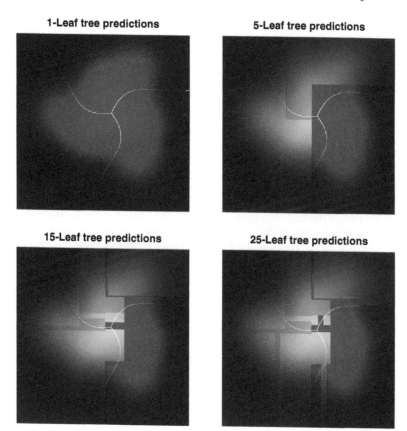

Figure 4.24   Classification decisions made using a classification tree trained on the data of Figure 4.1. The numbers 1, 5, 15, and 25 of leaf nodes correspond to cost-complexity parameter α values of about 2^{-1}, 2^{-4}, 2^{-7}, and 0, respectively, and produce respective estimated risks 0.665, 0.236, 0.243, and 0.259. The 15-leaf tree was selected as approximately optimal using leave-one-out cross-validation, described in Section 7.3, to estimate risk from the training data, though *in this case the 5-node tree has significantly lower risk on test data.*

4.8.4   Pruning Trees

As explained so far, trees are trained until they have zero misclassification error on the training data (unless there are training data with identical feature vectors but different class labels) or some other stopping criterion is met. This suggests that they may be badly over-fit (see Chapter 5 and Chapter 7). There are two ways to avoid over-fit trees. The first is to stop growing the tree according to some criterion, such as if all nodes either pass a (non-zero) threshold on the measure of impurity or contain fewer than some number of training points. The second, recommended by Breiman et al. (1984), is to grow the tree completely and then to prune it back to a subtree of the full-grown tree.

Breiman et al. (1984) recommend pruning a full-grown tree in the following way. For a given value of a tuning parameter $\alpha > 0$, find the subtree of the full tree which minimizes the *cost-complexity criterion*,

$$\alpha \times \text{(number of leaf nodes)}$$

$$+ \sum_{\text{all leaf nodes } t} \left(\min_{c \in \{1,\ldots,C\}} \sum_{d=1}^{C} L(d,c) \widehat{P}(Y = d \mid X \in t) \right) \widehat{P}(X \in t).$$

The first term penalizes the size of the tree, the second penalizes the training estimate of the risk of the tree, and parameter α sets the relative importance of these two terms[38] ($\alpha = 0$ puts no penalty on the size of the tree, in which case no nodes are pruned, and as $\alpha \to \infty$, the tree will be pruned back to the root node). Chapter 10 of Breiman et al. (1984) shows how to compute efficiently the optimal subtree, in terms of cost-complexity criterion, for any given α. An approximately optimal value of α is chosen by cross-validation or some other method of risk estimation—see Chapter 7.

Exercise 4.16 *Show that under 0–1 loss, the cost-complexity criterion is*

$$\alpha \times \text{(number of leaf nodes)} + \sum_{\text{all leaf nodes } t} \left(1 - \max_{c \in \{1,\ldots,C\}} \widehat{P}(Y = c \mid X \in t) \right) \widehat{P}(X \in t).$$

One of the strengths of trees is that they are very easy to interpret, and trees have even been designed for implementation by hand. For example, the pocket-sized book *Berry Finder: A Guide to Native Plants with Fleshy Fruits* by Dorcas S. Miller, illustrated by Cherie Hunter Day, contains a 54-page implementation of a classification tree consisting of approximately 120 leaf nodes and 150 internal nodes (some of which have more than two child nodes). Internal nodes are queries about features of a plant (leaves, stems, fruit, growing location, etc.) and leaf nodes predict a distinct species.[39]

---

[38] The R tree-training function `rpart()` scales the cost-complexity criterion, dividing it by the training estimate of risk for a one-leaf tree (that is, a tree consisting only of a root node), $\widehat{R}_0$. Function `rpart()` allows the user to control parameter α by assigning a value to $\alpha/\widehat{R}_0$, a quantity it names cp.

[39] Here is one example of a descent through the tree in Miller and Day (1986). If a berry grows on a woody plant with broad leaves which is → an erect shrub or small tree with many small stems → and leaves alternate on the stem → and leaves are divided → and the berries are black or dark purple and the plant is spiny → and the berries are not in umbels (many small stalks radiating from a common point), and fruit separates from the plant → and the berries do not have a central receptacle → it is a black raspberry. With due consideration for the asymmetric loss function involved ("miss eating fruit" vs. "be poisoned"), the author ate the berry predicted to be a black raspberry by this classification tree. It tasted like a black raspberry, and the author suffered no ill effects. Note that descent through the tree

4.8.5   Regression Trees

Trees are also used for regression. Impurity measures used for regression trees are

variance $I(t) = \text{Var}[Y \mid X \in t] = \text{E}[(Y - \text{E}[Y \mid X \in t])^2 \mid X \in t]$
mean absolute deviation $I(t) = \text{E}[|Y - \text{median}[Y \mid X \in t]| \mid X \in t]$

At a leaf node t, a regression tree predicts $\text{E}[Y \mid X \in t]$ when squared-error loss is used, and median $[Y \mid X \in t]$ when absolute-error loss is used.

4.9   Support Vector Machines

The last classification method covered in this chapter is the support vector machine. Support vector machines are somewhat different from all of the other methods in this chapter, in that they are not explicit approximations of the Bayes classifier. Support vector machines are motivated by a geometric idea of what makes a classifier "good" and we shall see that this results in a loss function which is different from the loss functions encountered in Chapters 2, 3, and 4 (indeed, which violates the definition of a loss function given in Chapter 2). In particular, we shall encounter a loss function which takes into account *the location of a feature vector* relative to a class boundary, and *which may penalize correctly classified data* if their feature vectors are too close to this boundary.

4.9.1   Support Vector Machine Classifiers

Suppose there are $C = 2$ classes, that the feature space $\mathcal{X}$ is $\mathbb{R}^m$ and that the two classes are *linearly separable* in the feature space, which means that there exists a hyperplane[40]

$$H(\theta_\star, \theta_0) = \{v \in \mathbb{R}^m : \theta_\star v + \theta_0 = 0\} = \left\{ v \in \mathbb{R}^m : \frac{\theta_\star}{\|\theta_\star\|} v + \frac{\theta_0}{\|\theta_\star\|} = 0 \right\}$$

such that all data of one class lie on one side of $H(\theta_\star, \theta_0)$ and all data of the other class lie on the other side. Data with two linearly separable classes are shown in Figure 4.25. Suppose also that our goal is to classify new data using a linear classification boundary: that is, we must choose a hyperplane in $\mathbb{R}^m$ and declare all points on one side to be class 1 and all points on the other side to be class 2. What is the best hyperplane to choose?

---

determines which features are used, and that potentially only a few of many features need be collected for any particular item to be classified.

[40] As in Sections 4.6 and 4.7, we think of the m-long parameter vector $\theta_\star$ as a row vector, and of points in $\mathbb{R}^m$ as column vectors.

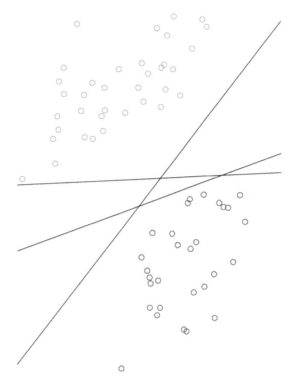

Figure 4.25   Subsets of the orange and purple data of Figure 4.1, selected so that the two classes are linearly separable. Three distinct hyperplanes (lines) which separate the two classes are shown: there are, of course, infinitely many such lines. A geometric definition of what makes a line separating the two classes "good" motivates support vector machine (SVM) classifiers.

One answer to this question is the following. First, restrict the choice to the set of hyperplanes which separate the training data. These and only these hyperplanes will produce a classifier with zero training error.[41] For any of these hyperplanes H, there is a minimum distance d_1 from H to the data in class 1 and a minimum distance d_2 from H to the data in class 2, and so H can be widened into a slab of width $d_1 + d_2$ which separates the two classes. The width $d_1 + d_2$ is called the *margin* of the classifier based on H. The basic assumption of a support vector machine classifier is that *under 0–1 loss and uniform prior distribution on class, the "best" two-class linear classifier is a separating hyperplane with maximum margin such that $d_1 = d_2$.*

---

[41] Zero training error is not necessarily a good thing (see Exercise 2.4 and Chapter 7) but is useful here for motivation.

Let the two class labels be encoded so that the response variables Y_i are in $\{-1, 1\}$. Data $(x_1, y_1), \ldots, (x_n, y_n)$ are separated by a hyperplane if and only if there is a hyperplane $H(\theta_\star, \theta_0)$ such that, for all i,

$$y_i = \begin{cases} 1 & \text{if } \theta_\star x_i + \theta_0 \geq 1 \\ -1 & \text{if } \theta_\star x_i + \theta_0 \leq -1, \end{cases} \tag{4.4}$$

which is written more compactly as

$$y_i(\theta_\star x_i + \theta_0) \geq 1 \quad \text{for all } i. \tag{4.5}$$

The geometry of the situation, illustrated in Figure 4.26, is more apparent if the normal vector of the separating hyperplane is made to be a unit vector,

$$y_i \left(\frac{\theta_\star}{\|\theta_\star\|} x_i + \frac{\theta_0}{\|\theta_\star\|} \right) \geq \frac{1}{\|\theta_\star\|} \quad \text{for all } i. \tag{4.6}$$

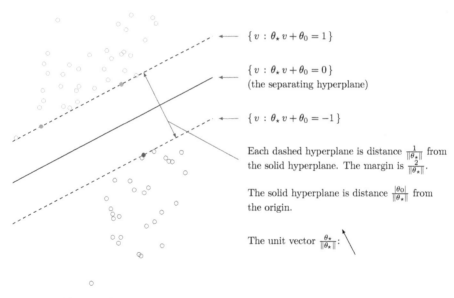

$\{v : \theta_\star v + \theta_0 = 1\}$

$\{v : \theta_\star v + \theta_0 = 0\}$
(the separating hyperplane)

$\{v : \theta_\star v + \theta_0 = -1\}$

Each dashed hyperplane is distance $\frac{1}{\|\theta_\star\|}$ from the solid hyperplane. The margin is $\frac{2}{\|\theta_\star\|}$.

The solid hyperplane is distance $\frac{|\theta_0|}{\|\theta_\star\|}$ from the origin.

The unit vector $\frac{\theta_\star}{\|\theta_\star\|}$:

Figure 4.26   The linearly separable data of Figure 4.25, with the maximum-margin separating hyperplane (solid line) and the two hyperplanes which define the margin (dashed lines). The unit vector $\frac{\theta_\star}{\|\theta_\star\|}$ is shown at the lower right. The orange dots are class "1" and the purple dots are class "-1," and all data points (x_i, y_i) satisfy the inequality $y_i(\theta_\star x_i + \theta_0) \geq 1$. The three filled dots—two orange and one purple—are the support vectors, that is, the data points satisfying $y_i(\theta_\star x_i + \theta_0) = 1$.

Written this way, it is easy to see that the distance from feature vector x_i to the separating hyperplane $H(\theta_\star, \theta_0)$ is

$$\left| \frac{\theta_\star}{\|\theta_\star\|} x_i + \frac{\theta_0}{\|\theta_\star\|} \right|,$$

and this is bounded below by $\frac{1}{\|\theta_\star\|}$.

Maximizing the margin, then, means solving the optimization problem[42]

$$\begin{aligned} &\text{minimize over } \theta_\star \text{ and } \theta_0: &&\tfrac{1}{2}\|\theta_\star\|^2 \\ &\text{subject to, for all } i: && y_i(\theta_\star x_i + \theta_0) \geq 1. \end{aligned} \qquad (4.7)$$

This is done (approximately) by quadratic programming techniques, resulting in trained parameter values $\widehat{\theta}_\star$ and $\widehat{\theta}_0$. A trained support vector machine consists of the trained parameters together with the classification rule "given a feature vector X, predict the class to be the sign of $\widehat{\theta}_\star X + \widehat{\theta}_0$." The margin of the trained support vector machine is $2/\|\widehat{\theta}_\star\|$. Any training data point (x_i, y_i) which satisfies (4.5) with equality, that is, satisfies $y_i(\theta_\star x_i + \theta_0) = 1$, is a *support vector*.

While the details of quadratic programming are beyond the scope of this book, there are some points which are essential to mention here. The optimization problem (4.7) is solved by solving a dual problem in which the objective function depends on the data only through the set of inner products $(x_i^T x_j)_{i,j=1}^n$. Solving this dual problem results in estimation of an n-long parameter vector $\psi = (\psi_1, \ldots, \psi_n)$, with the property that $\widehat{\psi}_i \neq 0$ only if the training data point (x_i, y_i) is a support vector. In terms of the dual parameter ψ, the predicted class of a new feature vector X is

$$\text{sign}\left(\widehat{\theta}_0 + \sum_{i=1}^n \widehat{\psi}_i y_i x_i^T X \right) = \text{sign}\left(\widehat{\theta}_0 + \sum_{\substack{i\,:\,(x_i,y_i) \text{ is a} \\ \text{support vector}}} \widehat{\psi}_i y_i x_i^T X \right) = \text{sign}(\widehat{\theta}_0 + \widehat{\theta}_\star^T X),$$

where $\widehat{\theta}_\star = \sum_{\substack{i\,:\,(x_i,y_i) \text{ is a} \\ \text{support vector}}} \widehat{\psi}_i y_i x_i^T$.

If the classes are not linearly separable, as shown in Figure 4.27, then the inequality condition (4.5) cannot be satisfied. A weakened form of (4.5) can be satisfied, though, by introducing *slack variables*[43]

$$\xi_i = \max(0, 1 - y_i(\theta_\star x_i + \theta_0))$$

and changing (4.5) to

$$y_i(\theta_\star x_i + \theta_0) \geq 1 - \xi_i \qquad \text{and} \qquad \xi_i \geq 0 \qquad \text{for all } i. \qquad (4.8)$$

---

[42] In (4.7), the term to minimize is $\|\theta_\star\|^2$ rather than $\|\theta_\star\|$ because the former is a quadratic function. The constant $\frac{1}{2}$ is present to make notation clean when taking derivatives: we will not need it for that, but include it to be consistent with later notation.

[43] The variables $\theta_\star$ and θ_0 are then called *decision variables*.

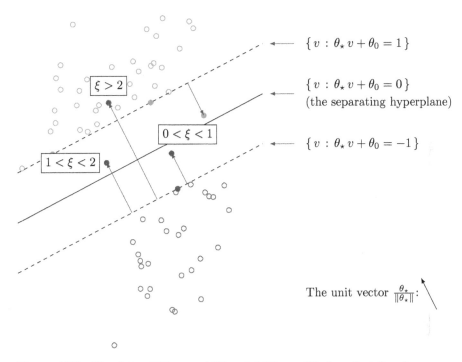

Figure 4.27   The data of Figures 4.25 and 4.26, modified so that the classes are not linearly separable. The data with positive slack variables are indicated by gray arrows. The purple dots above the solid line are data with slack variables $\xi_i > 1$ and are misclassified by the linear classifier. The purple dot below the solid line but above the dashed line, and the orange dot above the solid line but below the dashed line, are data with slack variables $0 < \xi_i < 1$: they contribute to the penalty without being misclassified.

Slack variable ξ_i is the smallest amount which can be added to $y_i(\theta_\star x_i + \theta_0)$ so that the total is at least one: thus for each i, either $y_i(\theta_\star x_i + \theta_0) \geq 1$ and $\xi_i = 0$ or $y_i(\theta_\star x_i + \theta_0) + \xi_i = 1$, and $\xi_i > 0$. A data point *exceeds the margin* if $\xi_i > 0$. A data point is misclassified by the classification boundary $H(\theta_\star, \theta_0)$ if and only if $\xi_i > 1$. A support vector machine still seeks the maximum margin classifier, making allowance for some data points to exceed the margin and even to be misclassified. Optimization problem (4.7) becomes

$$
\begin{aligned}
\text{minimize over } \theta_\star, \theta_0 \text{ and } \xi_1, \dots, \xi_n: &\quad \tfrac{1}{2}\|\theta_\star\|^2 + \gamma \sum_{i=1}^{n} \xi_i \\
\text{subject to, for all } i: &\quad y_i(\theta_\star x_i + \theta_0) \geq 1 - \xi_i \quad \text{and} \quad \xi_i \geq 0,
\end{aligned}
\tag{4.9}
$$

where $\gamma \geq 0$ is a tuning parameter. In this case, the support vectors are the training data points (x_i, y_i) which satisfy (4.7) with equality or for which $\xi_i > 0$.

SVM loss functions

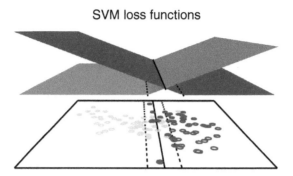

Figure 4.28   The loss functions $\max(0, 1 - Y(\theta_\star X + \theta_0))$ which are applied to the blue data (blue surface, class $Y = 1$) and the purple data (purple surface, class $Y = -1$) in the example of Figure 4.1. Training data which are support vectors are shown as solid dots, while the rest are shown as hollow dots, although this is partly obscured by the viewing angle—which dots are truly hollow and which are truly filled is more clearly seen in the lower-left-hand cell of Figure 4.29.

Optimization problem (4.9) has two goals: to maximize the margin (that is, to minimize $\|\theta_\star\|$) and to minimize a "risk" function of the training data, $\sum_{i=1}^{n} \xi_i$. These goals are to be met simultaneously, and their relative importance is determined by γ. The "loss" function

$$(X, Y) \mapsto \max(0, 1 - Y(\theta_\star X + \theta_0))$$

assigns a zero penalty to correctly classified data which are on the correct side of the classification boundary by distance at least $\frac{1}{\|\theta_\star\|}$. As the distance from correctly classified data to the boundary hyperplane goes from $\frac{1}{\|\theta_\star\|}$ to 0, the "loss" goes from 0 to 1, and as these data cross the boundary hyperplane and becomes misclassified, the "loss" increases from 1 proportionately with the distance to the boundary.[44] This is made explicit by rewriting (4.9) as

$$\text{minimize over } \theta_\star \text{ and } \theta_0: \quad \tfrac{1}{2}\|\theta_\star\|^2 + \gamma \sum_{i=1}^{n} \max(0, 1 - y_i(\theta_\star x_i + \theta_0)). \quad (4.10)$$

The loss function $\max(0, 1 - Y(\theta_\star X + \theta_0))$ is illustrated in Figure 4.28. In Figure 4.28, the left-hand dashed line drawn in the plane is $\{v : \theta_\star v + \theta_0 = 1\}$, the blue side of the margin: this line is where the blue surface representing the loss incurred by blue data changes from zero (to the left of the dashed line) to positive (to the right of the dashed line). The right-hand dashed line drawn in the plane is $\{v : \theta_\star v + \theta_0 = -1\}$, the purple side of the margin: this line is where the purple surface representing the loss incurred by purple data changes from positive (to the left

---

[44] Note that positive loss may be incurred for *correctly classified* training data.

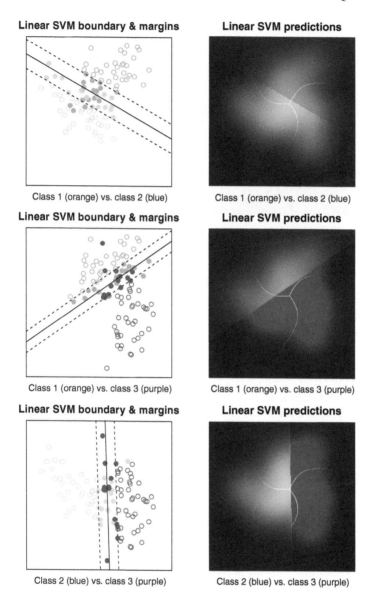

Figure 4.29   Three linear support vector machines, each trained on data of two classes. The left-hand cells show the separating hyperplane (solid lines), the margins (dashed lines), and the training data. Training data which are support vectors are shown as solid dots, while the rest are shown as hollow dots. The right-hand cells show the predictions made by the three support vector machines. All three support vector machines were trained using error penalty value $\gamma = 2.112$.

Linear SVM predictions   **Linear SVM predictions**

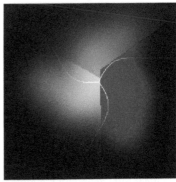

Figure 4.30   Classification decisions made using a linear support vector machine with error penalty values $\gamma = 2^{-8}$ (left cell) and $\gamma = 2.112$ (right cell), trained on the data of Figure 4.1. The value $\gamma = 2.112$ was selected as approximately optimal using leave-one-out cross-validation, described in Section 7.3, to estimate risk from the training data. These classifiers have estimated risks 0.568 and 0.221, respectively. Larger values of γ, up to 2^{16}, produced essentially the same classifications as those shown in the right-hand cell.

of the dashed line) to zero (to the right of the dashed line). The solid line drawn in the plane is $\{v : \theta_\star v + \theta_0 = 0\}$, the separating hyperplane (class boundary): the trained support vector machine predicts the blue class to the left of this line, and predicts the purple class to the right of this line. On the solid line, both blue and purple data incur one unit of loss. Due to the shape looking somewhat like open hinge, the loss function $\max(0, 1 - Y(\theta_\star X + \theta_0))$ is called *hinge loss*. Note that loss is incurred for any data point within the margin, that is, any point (X, Y) such that $-1 < \theta_\star X + \theta_0 < 1$, whether or not it is correctly classified (though misclassified data are penalized more than correctly classified data).

An approximately optimal value of γ is chosen by cross-validation or some other method of risk estimation—see Chapter 7. This is advisable even in the case of linearly separable classes. The effect of the penalty parameter γ is illustrated in Figure 4.30.

Support vector machines are applied to data of $C > 2$ classes by training multiple binary SVMs and combining their predictions. This is illustrated in Figure 4.29—detailed discussion is deferred to Section 6.1.

4.9.2   Kernelization

One way to use a simple classifier on hard-to-separate data is to map the features into a higher-dimensional space in such a way that the classes become more easily separated than in the original feature space. For example, using a linear classifier in

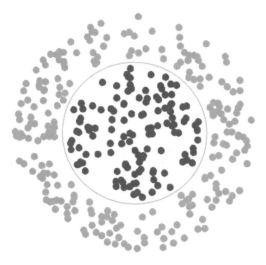

Figure 4.31   The two classes (orange and purple) in this dataset are not linearly separable in $\mathbb{R}^2$, though they are clearly separable (for example, the light gray ellipse is a class boundary which produces zero training error).

$\mathbb{R}^2$ to classify the data shown in Figure 4.31 seems like a bad idea. Consider, though, applying the map $\phi : \mathbb{R}^2 \to \mathbb{R}^3$, defined by $\phi(x) = \phi(x_1, x_2) = (x_1^2, \sqrt{2}x_1 x_2, x_2^2)$, to the data in Figure 4.31. The result is shown in Figure 4.32, where, by looking in the right direction, it can be seen that the classes have been made linearly separable in $\mathbb{R}^3$. The preimage in $\mathbb{R}^2$ of a linear classification boundary in $\mathbb{R}^3$ is an ellipse, shown in gray in Figure 4.31.

Exercise 4.17 *Name at least one very simple classifier which will perform well on the data in Figure 4.31 without any transformation of the data.*

A disadvantage of mapping data from $\mathbb{R}^{\text{small}}$ to $\mathbb{R}^{\text{big}}$ is that training a classifier can become computationally expensive in $\mathbb{R}^{\text{big}}$. In some cases, though, there is a trick to avoid this computational cost. If, for example, all of the information in the features $(x_i)_{i=1}^n$ which is needed to train the classifier is contained in the $n \times n$ matrix of inner products

$$\left(x_i^{\mathrm{T}} x_j\right)_{i,j=1}^n$$

(as in the case of support vector machines), then one need not compute $(\phi(x_i))_{i=1}^n$ but only the $n \times n$ matrix

$$\left(\phi(x_i)^{\mathrm{T}} \phi(x_j)\right)_{i,j=1}^n .$$

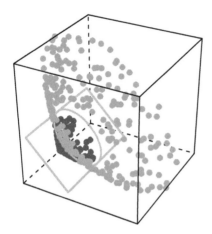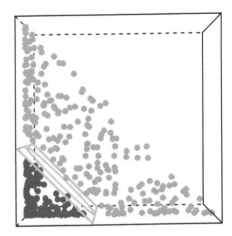

Figure 4.32   The data of Figure 4.31 have been mapped into a two-dimensional surface in $\mathbb{R}^3$ so that the classes are linearly separable: the right-hand cell shows that
the two classes can be separated by a plane. The light gray ellipse of Figure 4.31 is
the intersection of the surface containing the data with a class-separating plane in $\mathbb{R}^3$,
projected back into $\mathbb{R}^2$.

Furthermore, *we don't even need to know* ϕ, we merely need to construct a map
$K : \mathbb{R}^m \times \mathbb{R}^m \to \mathbb{R}$ such that there exists some phi with

$$K(x, w) = \phi(x)^{\mathrm{T}}\phi(w).$$

Conditions under which a bivariate function $K(x, w)$ has a decomposition as
$K(x, w) = \phi(x)^{\mathrm{T}}\phi(w)$ (where the dimension of the range of ϕ is perhaps countably
infinite) are given by Mercer's theorem[45] (Ash, 1965). Typically one specifies K and
replaces $x_i^{\mathrm{T}}x_j$ in (4.9) with $K(x_i, x_j)$. Commonly used kernels are:

$$\begin{array}{ll}
\text{polynomial} & K(x, w) = (\alpha\, x^{\mathrm{T}}w + \beta)^{\delta} \\
\text{sigmoid} & K(x, w) = \tanh(\alpha\, x^{\mathrm{T}}w + \beta) \\
\text{Gaussian or radial} & K(x, w) = \exp(-\alpha\, \|x - w\|^2).
\end{array}$$

Parameter values of these kernels are chosen by cross-validation or some other risk
estimation method.

---

[45] Mercer's theorem extends, to more general function spaces, the fact from linear algebra that a non-
negative definite symmetric matrix M has a decomposition as $M = Q \Lambda Q^{\mathrm{T}}$, where Q is the matrix of
eigenvectors of M and Λ is a diagonal matrix of the corresponding non-negative eigenvalues (a special
case of the spectral theorem (Strang, 1988)).

Radial SVM predictions   **Polynomial SVM predictions**

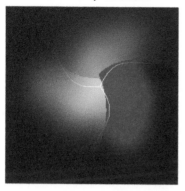 

Figure 4.33 Classification decisions made using a radial kernel (left cell, with $\gamma =$ 2.382 and $\alpha = 0.219$) and a polynomial kernel (right cell, with $\gamma = 1.073$, $\alpha = 0.677$, $\beta = 0.492$, and $\delta = 3.525$) support vector machine trained on the data of Figure 4.1. All parameters of these two classifiers were set to approximately optimal values using leave-one-out cross-validation, described in Section 7.3, to estimate risk from the training data (with optimization performed by simulated annealing and the Nelder–Mead algorithm, described in Chapter 10). These classifiers have estimated risks 0.201 and 0.208, respectively.

In terms of the estimated intercept parameter $\widehat{\theta}_0$ and estimated dual parameter $\widehat{\psi}$, the predicted class of a new feature vector X is

$$\text{sign}\left(\widehat{\theta}_0 + \sum_{\substack{i \,:\, (x_i, y_i) \text{ is a} \\ \text{support vector}}} \widehat{\psi}_i \, y_i \, K(x_i, X) \right).$$

Predictions made by support vector machines using a polynomial kernel and Gaussian kernel, trained on the data of Figure 4.1, are shown in Figure 4.33.

Exercise 4.18 *Show that the example illustrated in Figures 4.31 and 4.32 corresponds to the polynomial kernel with parameters $\alpha = 1$, $\beta = 0$, and $\delta = 2$. What values of α, β, and δ produce the linear kernel $K(x, w) = x^T w$?*

Exercise 4.19 *Show that for the polynomial kernel with integer parameter δ, if parameter $\beta \neq 0$, $K(x, w) = \phi(x)^T \phi(w)$ where ϕ is a function which maps $x = (x_1, \ldots, x_m)$ to a vector in the $\binom{m+\delta}{\delta}$-dimensional basis*

$$\left(x_1^{k_1} x_2^{k_2} \cdots x_m^{k_m} : k_1, \ldots, k_m \text{ are non-negative integers}, k_1 + \cdots + k_m \leq \delta \right).$$

Show that if parameter $\beta = 0$, then $K(x, w) = \phi(x)^{\mathrm{T}}\phi(w)$ where ϕ is a function which maps $x = (x_1, \ldots, x_m)$ to a vector in the $\binom{m+\delta-1}{\delta}$-dimensional basis

$$\left(x_1^{k_1} x_2^{k_2} \cdots x_m^{k_m} : k_1, \ldots, k_m \text{ are non-negative integers}, k_1 + \cdots + k_m = \delta \right).$$

Hint: *Use the multinomial theorem.*

Exercise 4.20 *Show that for the Gaussian kernel, $K(x, w) = \phi(x)^{\mathrm{T}}\phi(w)$ where ϕ is a function which maps $x = (x_1, \ldots, x_m)$ to a vector in the infinite-dimensional basis*

$$\left(x_1^{k_1} x_2^{k_2} \cdots x_m^{k_m} : k_1, \ldots, k_m \text{ are non-negative integers} \right).$$

4.9.3   Proximal Support Vector Machine Classifiers

It was observed empirically, some time in 1999 through 2001, that the minimization problem of SVMs (4.9) could be modified without changing classification performance, to

$$\text{minimize over } \theta_\star, \theta_0 \text{ and } \xi: \quad \tfrac{1}{2}\|\theta_\star\|^2 + \tfrac{1}{2}\theta_0^2 + \tfrac{1}{2}\gamma \sum_{i=1}^n \xi_i^2$$
$$\text{subject to, for all } i: \quad y_i(\theta_\star x_i + \theta_0) \geq 1 - \xi_i \quad . \tag{4.11}$$

The objective function has been made into a homogeneous quadratic function by adding $\tfrac{1}{2}\theta_0^2$ and changing the measure of the error vector from the 1-norm to the 2-norm. This makes the function strongly convex, which makes the quadratic programming problem easier to solve. Note that the condition $\xi \geq 0$ has been made superfluous by changing to the 2-norm: any negative ξ_i can be set to 0 while maintaining the inequalities and reducing the objective function.

A proximal support vector machine (PSVM) classifier, introduced by Fung and Mangasarian in 2001, is a further and more extreme modification of SVMs: the linear inequality constraints are changed to linear equations:

$$\text{minimize over } \theta_\star, \theta_0 \text{ and } \xi: \quad \tfrac{1}{2}\|\theta_\star\|^2 + \tfrac{1}{2}\theta_0^2 + \tfrac{1}{2}\gamma \sum_{i=1}^n \xi_i^2$$
$$\text{subject to, for all } i: \quad y_i(\theta_\star x_i + \theta_0) = 1 - \xi_i \quad . \tag{4.12}$$

It is very simple to fit a PSVM. After all, PSVM is solving a weighted least-squares regression problem, and the solution can be written down in closed form. Also, kernelization can be used with PSVMs just as in SVMs, as the dual problem still involves the data through inner products (Fung and Mangasarian, 2001).

Note that PSVMs differ from SVMs considerably in interpretation. The SVM constraint

$$y_i(\theta_\star x_i + \theta_0) \geq 1 - \xi_i$$

means "data in class ($+1$ or -1) lie *on or beyond* the hyperplane $\{v : \theta_\star v + \theta_0 = (+1 \text{ or } -1)\}$, except for some error." The PSVM constraint

$$y_i(\theta_\star x_i + \theta_0) = 1 - \xi_i$$

means "data in class ($+1$ or -1) lie *on* the hyperplane $\{v : \theta_\star v + \theta_0 = (+1 \text{ or } -1)\}$, except for some error." That is, a trained PSVM is approximating the data in the two classes by a pair of parallel hyperplanes. Thus PSVM is essentially a prototype method, where the class prototypes are not points, but hyperplanes. If kernelization is used, then "hyperplane" becomes "manifold" in this statement, and the parallelism between the two class prototypes exists in some higher-dimensional space.

The interpretation of PSVMs is made more explicit by rewriting (4.12) as

$$\text{minimize over } \theta_\star, \theta_0: \quad \tfrac{1}{2}\|\theta_\star\|^2 + \tfrac{1}{2}\theta_0^2 + \tfrac{1}{2}\gamma \sum_{i=1}^{n}(1 - y_i(\theta_\star x_i + \theta_0))^2 \quad (4.13)$$

The sum in (4.13) is the total squared-error loss incurred by simultaneously fitting the data in the two classes by the hyperplanes $\{v : \theta_\star v - \theta_0 = 1\}$ and $\{v : \theta_\star v - \theta_0 = -1\}$, while the other two terms penalize the size of the parameter vector $\theta = (\theta_0, \theta_\star)$. Viewed this way, PSVMs are a rediscovery of ridge regression (see Chapter 3).

4.10   Postscript: Example Problem Revisited

The result of fitting the models described in this Chapter (and also some models described in Chapter 6) to the example data of Figure 4.1 are summarized in Table 4.2 and Figure 4.34. It is interesting to note that while the Gaussian mixture model with three components per class is the correct model, in the sense that the training data truly were generated by such a model, it produced relatively poor predictive performance. Many find this result counter-intuitive at first: this was addressed in Section 4.4.3 and will be addressed further in Chapters 5 and 8.

It is absolutely not the purpose of Table 4.2 and Figure 4.34 to pass as evidence that any classification method is superior to any other on any dataset besides the one displayed in Figure 4.1. Nor was the dataset of Figure 4.1 designed to make any method appear favorably compared to any other. What Table 4.2 and Figure 4.34 show is that a range of different risks can be expected among classifiers trained on a given set of data, and that the relative performance of the methods may give some clue to the nature of the data. In this example, the classifiers of Chapter 4 fall naturally into two sets separated by a significant performance gap: those with risk 0.208 or below, and those with risk 0.220 or above. Seven of the eight classifiers with risk 0.220 or above produce class boundaries which are piecewise hyperplanes, and among these, performance tends to get worse when the hyperplanes are forced to be orthogonal to the coordinate axes. We might infer from this that whatever the class boundaries

Table 4.2   The risk of the methods described in this chapter as a solution to the example problem, estimated from 50,000 test points. Where applicable, tuning parameters (such as bandwidth or the number of nearest neighbors) were selected to minimize a computable risk estimate obtained from the training data.

Section	Method	Risk estimate	Standard error
4.1	Bayes classifier	0.191705	—
4.5	Learning vector quantization	0.195	0.0018
4.4	Kernel density estimation (product kernel)	0.199	0.0018
6.3	Bagged 1-nearest-neighbor	0.199	0.0018
4.9	Support vector machine (radial)	0.201	0.0018
4.7	Neural network*	0.201	0.0018
4.5	k-nearest-neighbor	0.202	0.0018
4.4	Kernel density estimation (Gaussian kernel)	0.203	0.0018
4.4	Quadratic discriminant analysis	0.204	0.0018
4.4	Two-component Gaussian mixture	0.205	0.0018
4.9	Support vector machine (polynomial)	0.208	0.0018
6.1	Ensemble of "bad" classifiers	0.210	0.0018
4.4	Naive Bayes	0.212	0.0018
4.6	Logistic regression	0.220	0.0019
6.5	Random forest	0.220	0.0019
4.9	Support vector machine (linear)	0.221	0.0019
6.3	Bagged stumps	0.221	0.0019
6.8	LR mixture of experts (bootstrapped stumps)	0.227	0.0019
4.4	Three-component Gaussian mixture	0.228	0.0019
4.4	Linear discriminant analysis	0.229	0.0019
6.8	LR stacking (bootstrapped stumps)	0.231	0.0019
4.8	Classification tree[†]	0.243	0.0019
6.4	Bumped 1-nearest-neighbor	0.245	0.0019
4.4	Histogram	0.260	0.0019
6.7	Arced stumps	0.262	0.0019
6.6	Boosted stumps	0.268	0.0019

*Cross-validation suggested that 2, 3, 4, or 5 neurons in the hidden layer would produce about the same risk. Among models of approximately equal estimated risk, one would naturally choose the simplest (as the most interpretable or the computationally cheapest to apply), which in this case means a neural network with two neurons in the hidden layer. The risk of this network, estimated from test data, was 0.201. The mean risk of these four networks is 0.218.

†This is the risk of a 15-leaf tree, which had minimal risk as estimated by leave-one-out cross-validation and so was selected as the optimal tree. A 5-leaf tree had significantly lower risk, 0.236, according to the test data.

Method   **Estimated risk**

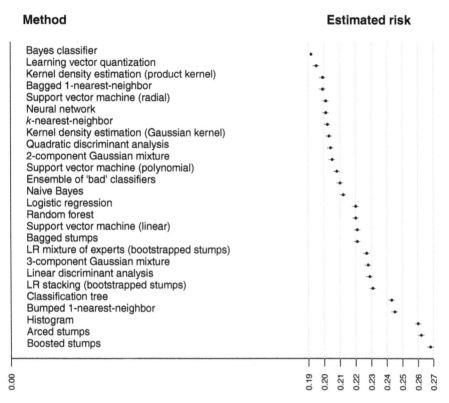

Figure 4.34   Graphical representation of the data in Table 4.2. For each method, estimated risk is plotted as a black dot, and red lines extend one standard error to each side.

may be, they are not well approximated by hyperplanes and in particular are not well approximated by hyperplanes orthogonal to the coordinate axes. Practically, we might decide not to focus future classification effort in this example on classification trees or histograms, and focus instead on methods which can learn curved class boundaries. Fitting classifiers to data is an exploratory process!

5

Bias–Variance Trade-off

A machine [classifier] with too much capacity [ability to fit training data exactly] is like a botanist with a photographic memory who, when presented with a new tree, concludes that it is not a tree because it has a different number of leaves from anything she has seen before; a machine with too little capacity is like the botanist's lazy brother, who declares that if it's green, then it's a tree. Neither can generalize well.

—Christopher J. C. Burges, *Data Mining and Knowledge Discovery*, 1998

Recall from Chapter 2 that an approximation method is a function which maps a training dataset S to an approximation $\widehat{f}_S$, and the risk of an approximation method is the expected loss with respect to the distribution of new data and of training datasets,

$$R = E_{S,X,Y}[L(Y,\widehat{f}_S(X))].$$

The risk of an approximation method decomposes in an informative way when squared-error loss is used. Specifically, under square-error loss, risk decomposes into a sum of three non-negative terms, one of which we can do nothing about and two of which we can affect. As we shall see in Chapter 6, viewing risk-minimization as minimization of the sum of two non-negative terms, and having useful interpretations of the two terms, strongly influences the design of approximation methods.

Various generalizations of this decomposition have been proposed for other loss functions in both regression and classification. While the author does not regard the issue of risk decomposition as definitively settled, intuitive understanding derived from what is known has been of unquestionable benefit to algorithm design.

5.1   Squared-Error Loss

In additive-noise regression problems, $Y = f(X) + E$ with $E[E] = 0$, so $E[Y|X] = f(X)$. In such settings, under squared-error loss, the risk decomposes as

$$\begin{aligned} R &= E_{S,X,Y}[(Y - \widehat{f}_S(X))^2] \\ &= E_{X,Y}[(Y - f(X))^2] + E_X[(f(X) - E_S[\widehat{f}_S(X)])^2] + E_X[\text{Var}_S\widehat{f}_S(X)] \end{aligned} \tag{5.1}$$

(Geman et al., 1992).

The three terms in this decomposition are worth description in words. The first,

$$E_{X,Y}[(Y - f(X))^2],$$

is the expected loss incurred when the predicted value at X is $f(X)$. Under squared-error loss, this is the minimum-risk prediction, so $f(X)$ is the *Bayes regressor* and the above term is the Bayes risk: in this context, it is called the *intrinsic risk* or the *irreducible risk*, indicating that this much risk is inherent in the problem. It is also $E_X[\text{Var}_{Y|X}[Y]]$. Note that it does not depend on any approximation of f.

The expression $E_S[\widehat{f}_S(x)] - f(x)$ is called the *bias*[1] of the approximation method (at x). The second term,

$$E_X[(f(X) - E_S[\widehat{f}_S(X)])^2],$$

is the expected value (with respect to the distribution of X) of the squared bias. This measures how close the average approximation, $E_S[\widehat{f}_S]$, is to the true function, f, on average with respect to the distribution of X.

The variance, $\text{Var}_S\widehat{f}_S(X)$, measures the average squared distance between a particular approximation, $\widehat{f}_S$, and the average approximation, $E_S[\widehat{f}_S]$. So the third term,

$$E_X[\text{Var}_S\widehat{f}_S(X)],$$

measures the average squared distance (with respect to the distribution of X) between approximations $\widehat{f}_S$ produced by the method and the average approximation, $E_S[\widehat{f}_S]$.

Exercise 5.1 *Prove (5.1), assuming that $E[Y|X] = f(X)$ and that the training set S is independent of the point (X, Y) at which prediction is made.*
Hint: *Write $Y - \widehat{f}_S(X)$ as*

$$Y - f(X) + f(X) - E_S[\widehat{f}_S(X)] + E_S[\widehat{f}_S(X)] - \widehat{f}_S(X)$$

and use additivity of the integral.

---

[1] Recall that in statistics, the *bias* of an estimator $\widehat{z}$ of a fixed quantity z is $E[\widehat{z}] - z$. The estimator is *unbiased* if its bias is zero.

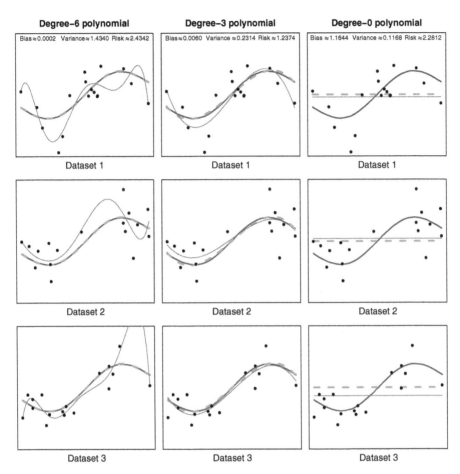

Figure 5.1   Bias and variance in regression. A function f approximated from three 15-element datasets using three different approximation methods. In each cell, the true function f is shown in blue, a training dataset S is shown in black, the estimate $\widehat{f}_S$ produced from the training data is shown as a thin gray line or curve, and the average estimate $E_S[\widehat{f}_S]$ produced by the method is shown in dashed orange. The left-hand cells illustrate a low-bias, high-variance method, the middle cells illustrate a relatively low-bias, low-variance method, and the right-hand cells illustrate a high-bias, low-variance method. The Bayes risk for this problem is 1.

The bias and variance of three different methods of approximating a real function f of a single real variable are illustrated in Figure 5.1. In the examples illustrated, the one-dimensional feature X is uniformly distributed in an interval, and $Y|(X = x)$ is drawn from a Gaussian distribution with mean $f(x)$ and unit variance (so the intrinsic risk with respect to squared-error loss is 1).

Each cell of Figure 5.1 shows four things: (1) the true function f, represented by a blue curve; (2) a specific 15-point dataset, represented by black dots; (3) the average approximation produced by one of the three methods, represented by a dashed orange curve[2]; (4) the specific approximation $\widehat{f}$ obtained by applying one of the three methods to the specific 15-point dataset shown, represented by a thin gray curve. Three distinct datasets are shown, repeated across rows of cells.

The left-hand three cells of Figure 5.1 show a method which approximates f by the least-squares fit of a degree-6 polynomial, that is, by performing linear regression on the expanded vector $(1, x, x^2, x^3, x^4, x^5, x^6)$. This method has high variance: each specific approximation (thin gray curve) is far from the average approximation (orange curve). It also has low bias: the average approximation (orange curve) is quite close to the true f (blue curve) in most places.

The center three cells of Figure 5.1 show a method which approximates f by the least-squares fit of a degree-3 polynomial, that is, by performing linear regression on the expanded $(1, x, x^2, x^3)$. This method has much lower variance and only slightly higher bias than a degree-6 polynomial, producing a much lower risk.

The right-hand three cells of Figure 5.1 show a method which approximates f by the least-squares fit of a degree-0 polynomial, that is, by performing linear regression on the constant vector (1). This produces a horizontal line intersecting the vertical axis at the mean response, $\frac{1}{n} \sum_{i=1}^{n} y_i$. This method has low variance: each specific approximation (thin gray line) is relatively close to the average approximation (orange line). It also has high bias: the average approximation (orange line) is far from the true f (blue curve) in most places.

The risk of most approximation methods generally decreases as the number of training data $|S|$ increases, and therefore the bias and variance of such methods depend on the number of training data. This is illustrated in the examples just described by using training datasets of different sizes. For each data size $|S| \in \{15, 150, 1500, 15000, 150000\}$, the examples were replicated independently 10000 times so that estimates of bias and variance could be computed. The results are shown in Table 5.1.

For squared-error loss, the *bias–variance trade-off* is the idea that minimizing risk requires minimizing the sum of the squared bias and the variance in (5.1),

$$E_X[(f(X) - E_S[\widehat{f}_S(X)])^2] + E_X[\text{Var}_S \widehat{f}_S(X)].$$

The importance of this has not always been recognized: in the early days of statistics, there was a great deal of emphasis on finding approximation methods with minimal variance, subject to having *zero* bias (that is, being *unbiased*). One can view ridge regression, described in Section 3.10, as an early method which exploited the bias–variance trade-off, reducing variance while increasing bias in order to produce lower-risk predictions.

---

[2] The average approximation shown is an estimate derived from 1000 random 15-point datasets simulated according to the model.

Table 5.1   The effect of data size on bias and variance in regression with squared-error loss, estimated by replicating the example described in this section $10\,000$ times for various data sizes $|S|$. Except for the case of the degree-6 polynomial fit to 15 data points, the variance is approximately proportional to $\frac{1}{|S|}$. Data size has far less effect on bias than on variance, and as data size increases, bias becomes the dominant contribution to the total risk.

$|S|$	Degree	Bayes risk	Bias	Variance	Total risk
15	0	1	1.164361	0.116805	2.281166
150	0	1	1.164361	0.014161	2.178523
1500	0	1	1.164361	0.001429	2.165790
15000	0	1	1.164361	0.000146	2.164507
150000	0	1	1.164361	0.000014	2.164375
15	3	1	0.006018	0.231417	1.237435
150	3	1	0.004459	0.026418	1.030877
1500	3	1	0.004427	0.002672	1.007099
15000	3	1	0.004427	0.000272	1.004700
150000	3	1	0.004427	0.000027	1.004454
15	6	1	0.000163	1.433968	2.434132
150	6	1	0.000029	0.045992	1.046022
1500	6	1	0.000019	0.004700	1.004719
15000	6	1	0.000019	0.000473	1.000492
150000	6	1	0.000019	0.000047	1.000065

5.2   Arbitrary Loss

The bias and variance of an approximation method extend *intuitively* to learning in general (either regression or classification) with an arbitrary loss function:

low bias means

- the average approximation is close to the truth[3];

high bias means

- the average approximation is far from the truth,
- the approximation method is not sufficiently flexible,
- individual approximations are not adequately adapted to the data;

---

[3] One of the difficulties of formalizing bias and variance is determining what "the average approximation" is when the range of f is a discrete, unordered set with no algebraic or geometric structure.

low variance means

- ○ each individual approximation is close to the average approximation,

- ○ individual approximations tend to be similar to one another,

- ○ the approximation method is "stable" with respect to which dataset (of all possible datasets) it is shown;

high variance means

- ○ individual approximations are often far from the average approximation,

- ○ individual approximations are quite different from one another,

- ○ the approximation method is very sensitive to which dataset it is shown.

For arbitrary loss, the *bias–variance trade-off* is the idea, motivated by (5.1), that finding a minimum-risk approximation method involves striking a balance between minimizing bias (and hence being right on average) and minimizing variance (and hence being stable with respect to variation in training datasets). An approximation method which performs poorly due to high variance is said to *over-fit* when presented with data. One which performs poorly due to high bias is said to *under-fit*.

Figure 5.2 illustrates bias and variance in the k-nearest-neighbors classifier, trained on three different 150-point datasets drawn from the data source described in Section 4.3 (the source of the running example of Chapter 4). Recall from Chapter 4 that the Bayes risk for this problem, with respect to 0–1 loss, is 0.191705.

Figure 5.2 shows 12 cells, arranged in four rows of three. The first three rows show three classifiers trained on three datasets. The first row shows the 1-NN, 9-NN, and 100-NN classifiers, each trained on one particular 150-point dataset drawn from the source described in Section 4.3. The second row shows the 1-NN, 9-NN, and 100-NN classifiers, each trained on another 150-point dataset drawn from the source described in Section 4.3. The third row shows the 1-NN, 9-NN, and 100-NN classifiers, each trained on yet another 150-point dataset drawn from the source described in Section 4.3. The fourth row of Figure 5.2 shows the most common prediction made by the 1-NN, 9-NN, and 100-NN classifiers, taken over 1000 independent 150-point datasets drawn from the source described in Section 4.3. These 1000 datasets were also used for risk estimation.

The left-most four cells of Figure 5.2 show the 1-nearest-neighbor classifier. This method has high variance: from cell to cell, the classifications made in the plane change considerably, particularly in the center of each cell. This method has low bias: the class boundary of the most common prediction is very close to the Bayes class boundary (white curve). The risk of this method is approximately 0.275 (standard deviation 0.017).

The center four cells of Figure 5.2 show the 9-nearest-neighbor classifier. This method has moderate variance: from cell to cell, the classifications made in the plane change, but not as much as those of the 1-nearest-neighbor classifier, particularly in

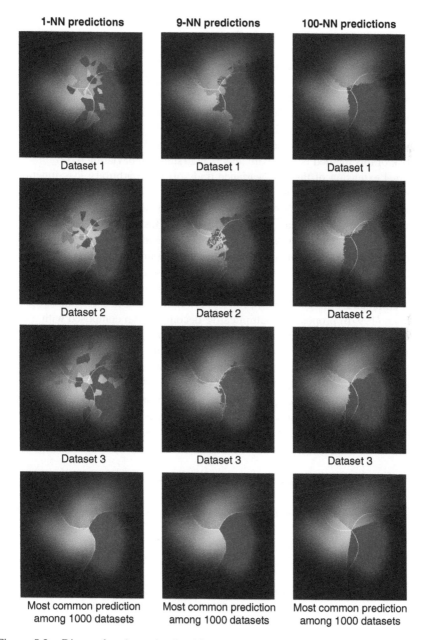

Figure 5.2   Bias and variance in classification. The 1-NN, 9-NN and 100-NN classifiers trained on datasets drawn from the running example distribution of Section 4.3. See the text for explanation.

the center of each cell. This method has moderate bias: the class boundary of the most common prediction is close to the Bayes class boundary (white curve) toward the center of the cell, but is not close toward the edges. The risk of this method is approximately 0.215 (standard deviation 0.010).

The right-most four cells of Figure 5.2 show the 100-nearest-neighbor classifier. This method has low variance: from cell to cell, the classifications made in the plane change hardly at all. This method has high bias: the class boundary of the most common prediction is quite far from the Bayes class boundary (white curve). In particular, the average class boundary is considerably less curved than the Bayes class boundary. The risk of this method is approximately 0.272 (standard deviation 0.047).[4]

Formal extension of the bias–variance trade-off to an arbitrary loss function, or just for classification with 0–1 loss, is an active area of research: see, for example, Kong and Dieterich (1995), Breiman (1996b), Kohavi and Wolpert (1996), Tibshirani (1996a), Friedman (1997b), James and Hastie (1997), Breiman (1998), Domingos (2000), James (2003), Efron (2004), and Le Borgne (2005). Most of these papers propose definitions of bias and variance for classification with 0–1 loss, though some also treat more general loss. Also, most of these papers decompose risk additively, into a sum of intrinsic risk plus bias plus variance (mirroring the form of (5.1)), although Domingos (1999) proposes a weighted additive decomposition, and Friedman (1997b) proposes a multiplicative decomposition composed with a Gaussian cumulative distribution function. It may be that formal extension of the bias–variance trade-off actually requires more terms than just intrinsic risk, bias, and variance: James considers this possibility in the case of symmetric loss functions.

The following extension of bias and variance to classification with 0–1 loss is from Breiman (1996b, 1998). Let $\hat{f}_S(X)$ denote a classification method which takes as input a training dataset S and a point X in feature space, and returns a class label (the predicted class at X). Let f_b denote the Bayes classifier, which in Exercise 4.2 was shown to be

$$f_b(X) = \text{argmax}_{c=1,\dots,C} \, P(Y = c | X).$$

Let P_S denote a probability distribution on training datasets of a given size, and let

$$\hat{f}_a(X) = \text{argmax}_{c=1,\dots,C} \, P_S(\hat{f}_S(X) = c)$$

---

[4] The astute reader will have noticed that the estimated risk of the 1-NN, 9-NN, and 100-NN approximation methods, respectively 0.275, 0.215, and 0.272, are higher than the risk of these classifiers when trained on the specific dataset used in Chapter 4, respectively 0.248, 0.203, and 0.247. Of the 1000 datasets drawn from the source described in Section 4.3, 5.4% produced a 1-NN classifier with estimated risk ≤ 0.248, 7.1% produced a 9-NN classifier with estimated risk ≤ 0.215, and 36.4% produced a 100-NN classifier with estimated risk ≤ 0.247. Thus it appears that the specific dataset used in Chapter 4 produces somewhat lower-risk classifiers than average. This property was not consciously arranged by the author.

be the class label most likely to be predicted at X with respect to the distribution on sets of training data. Looking ahead slightly to Chapter 7, one can think of $\widehat{f}_a(X)$ as arising from applying the classification method to many datasets drawn from P_S and letting the trained classifiers "vote" on the predicted class label at X. Breiman calls $\widehat{f}_a(X)$ the *aggregated classifier*.

Breiman defines a classification method to be *unbiased at* $x \in \mathcal{X}$ if $\widehat{f}_a(x) = f_b(x)$: that is, if the prediction made at x by the classification method is more likely to be the optimal (Bayes) prediction than it is to be any other single value. Breiman defines the *bias* and *variance* of a classification method under 0–1 loss as

$$\text{bias} = P_{X,Y}(f_b(X) = Y \text{ and } f_b(X) \neq \widehat{f}_a(X)) - E_S\left[P_{X,Y}(\widehat{f}_S(X) = Y \text{ and } f_b(X) \neq \widehat{f}_a(X))\right]$$

and

$$\text{var} = P_{X,Y}(f_b(X) = Y \text{ and } f_b(X) = \widehat{f}_a(X)) - E_S\left[P_{X,Y}(\widehat{f}_S(X) = Y \text{ and } f_b(X) = \widehat{f}_a(X))\right],$$

and shows that, under 0–1 loss, the risk of a classification method can be decomposed as

$$R = E_{S,X,Y}[L(Y,\widehat{f}_S(X))] = P_{X,Y}(f_b(X) \neq Y) + \text{bias} + \text{variance}. \tag{5.2}$$

The first term on the right-hand side is the irreducible error, the Bayes error rate.

Approximating Breiman's measures of bias and variance for the three k-nearest-neighbor classifiers illustrated in Figure 5.2, using the 1000 independent 150-point datasets drawn from the source described in Section 4.3, produces the following:

k	Intrinsic risk	Bias	Variance	Total risk
1	0.191705	0.00002	0.082	0.275
9	0.191705	0.00049	0.021	0.215
100	0.191705	0.021	0.058	0.272

It is curious that the variance does not decrease monotonically with k.

Exercise 5.2 *Prove (5.2).*

Exercise 5.3 *Show the following, using the above definitions of bias and variance for a classification method:*

(1) the Bayes classifier f_b has zero bias;

(2) f_b and $\widehat{f}_a$ have zero variance;

(3) more generally, any classification method has zero variance if the trained classifier does not depend on the data;

(4) bias and variance can be represented as

$$bias = \int_{\{x \in \mathcal{X}: f_b(x) \neq \hat{f}_a(x)\}} \left(E_{Y|X=x}\left[[f_b(x) = Y]\right] - E_{S,Y|X=x}\left[[\hat{f}_S(x) = Y]\right] \right) P_X(x)\,dx$$

and

$$variance = \int_{\{x \in \mathcal{X}: f_b(x) = \hat{f}_a(x)\}} \left(E_{Y|X=x}\left[[f_b(x) = Y]\right] - E_{S,Y|X=x}\left[[\hat{f}_S(x) = Y]\right] \right) P_X(x)\,dx$$

(5) the bias and variance are non-negative.

The point of the following exercise is that Breiman's definitions of bias and variance have an odd property, which is that they can exhibit a discontinuity when a classifier goes from being slightly more like the Bayes classifier than guessing class labels uniformly at random to being slightly less like the Bayes classifier than guessing class labels uniformly at random.

Exercise 5.4 *Let a (fictional) C-class classification problem be given such that the Bayes classifier is known, and let the noisy Bayes classifier be defined as follows. Given x, the noisy Bayes classifier randomly chooses either to predict the class predicted by the Bayes classifier (with probability γ) or it chooses its prediction uniformly at random from among the $C - 1$ classes not predicted by the Bayes classifier. That is,*

$$\hat{f}_S(x) \sim \text{Multinomial}\,(1, (p_1, \ldots, p_C)),$$

where, for $c = 1, \ldots, C$,

$$p_c = \begin{cases} \gamma & \text{if } f_b(x) = c \\ \frac{1-\gamma}{C-1} & \text{if } f_b(x) \neq c \end{cases}.$$

The random decisions are made once for each training set S and each input x, so while $\hat{f}_S(x)$ is randomly generated when it is trained, it is a deterministic function once it is trained. In terms of γ, C, and the Bayes risk, express the bias, variance, and risk of the noisy Bayes classifier, for any $\gamma \in [0, 1]$, $\gamma \neq \frac{1}{C}$, and any $C \geq 2$. Describe any discontinuities as γ changes continuously from one side of $\frac{1}{C}$ to the other.

6

Combining Classifiers

> For each individual among the many has a share of virtue and prudence, and when they meet together, they become in a manner one man, who has many feet, and hands, and senses; that is a figure of their mind and disposition. Hence the many are better judges than a single man of music and poetry; for some understand one part, and some another, and among them they understand the whole.
>
> —Aristotle, *Politics*, c. 350 BCE

The methods described in Chapters 3 and 4 produce regressors or classifiers which are not naturally decomposable into collections of smaller regressors or classifiers. As such, these regressors and classifiers are called *base learners* or *primitive learners*—although perhaps a more descriptive term would be *atomic learners*. This chapter introduces classification methods which combine base learners in various ways. The design of specific methods is usually based on an understanding of the bias–variance trade-off described in Chapter 5.

6.1 Ensembles

If one is willing to do the work to train L classifiers, of any type or types, one can get a new classifier by having the L classifiers "vote" as a committee. That is, one can classify a new data point as the class most commonly assigned to it by the individual trained classifiers. The voting may be weighted to favor preferred classifiers, or the votes of the individual classifiers may be used as inputs to another classification algorithm. Such techniques are called *ensemble methods*, or *committee methods*.

Machine Learning: a Concise Introduction, First Edition. Steven W. Knox.
© This publication is a US Government work and is in the public domain.
Published 2018 by John Wiley & Sons, Inc.
Companion Website: http://www.wiley.com/go/Knox/MachineLearning

Ensemble predictions

Figure 6.1   Predictions made by an ensemble of 20 bad classifiers (risk ≥ 0.220) constructed on the data of Section 4.3. Each of the 20 base learners votes with equal weight. The ensemble has risk 0.210.

An example of this type is illustrated in Figure 6.1. In Chapter 4, 36 classifiers were trained on the data of Section 4.3. The estimated risks of these classifiers, based on 50,000 test data, range from 0.195 (LVQ) to 0.665 (a one-leaf tree which always predicts the purple class). The author made an arbitrary choice to declare a classifier *bad* if its risk is at least 0.220. With this definition, there were 20 bad classifiers, representing every method in Chapter 4 except QDA and logistic regression. An ensemble composed of these 20 bad classifiers, all voting with equal weight, has risk 0.210, which is about 5.5 standard errors better than the risk of the best classifier in the ensemble.

A binary classifier can be applied to an arbitrary number of classes C by committee. One way to do this is to train a binary classifier to distinguish class c from the union of all other classes, for each class $c = 1, \ldots, C$, and to vote the resulting C binary classifiers in a committee. Another way to do this is to train a binary classifier to distinguish class c from class d, for all classes $1 \leq c < d \leq C$, and to vote the resulting $\binom{C}{2}$ binary classifiers in a committee.[1] An example is shown in Figure 6.2.

Committees of regressors combine continuous-valued predictions ("votes") of the base learners in some numerical way, such as computing the mean or using the individual votes as input to a linear function which is chosen to (approximately) minimize the risk of of the committee's predictions. This can be applied to classification when some or all of the base learners compute approximate probabilities of class membership,

$$(\widehat{P}(Y = 1 \mid X), \ldots, \widehat{P}(Y = C \mid X)),$$

---

[1] This is the method used to extend support vector machines to classification problems with $C \geq 3$ classes in the R library e1071, used in the example of Section 4.9.

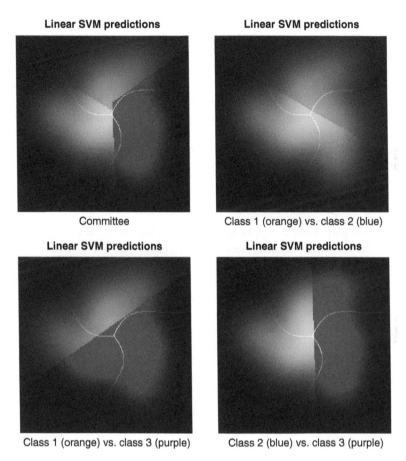

Figure 6.2   All trained support vector machines illustrated on the data of Section 4.3, which has $C = 3$ classes, were obtained by training $\binom{3}{2} = 3$ binary support vector machines. That is, support vector machines were trained to distinguish "orange vs. blue," "orange vs. purple," and "blue vs. purple," and then voted in a committee to produce a three-class classifier. The case of linear support vector machines is illustrated here: the upper-left cell, which is identical to the right-hand cell of Figure 4.30, shows the majority vote while the other three cells show the three binary support vector machines (these are shown in Figure 4.29).

by using a combined estimate of class probabilities to produce a single predicted class. If each of the classifiers under consideration compute approximate probabilities of class membership,

$$(\widehat{P}(Y = 1 \mid X), \dots, \widehat{P}(Y = C \mid X)),$$

then one can get a new classifier by making the minimum risk prediction based on a combined estimate of the class probabilities (such as the mean of the estimated class probabilities).

The observation that a combination of many poor statistical predictions might form a good prediction is quite old. In 1907, Francis Galton reported an analysis of 787 guesses in a contest to guess the dressed weight of an ox, based on observation of the ox while alive (Galton, 1907). Galton found that the median guess, 1207 pounds, was very close to the actual dressed weight of the ox (1198 pounds) in spite of the fact that the set of guesses displayed considerable variation (the inter-quartile range was [1162, 1236] pounds, and the range between the 5th and 95th percentiles was [1074, 1293] pounds). Each person casting a vote presumably had access to the same data—visual observation of the live ox in question—but varied in experience and expertise.[2]

6.2   Ensemble Design

An important part of the design of ensemble classifiers is the desire to control risk by controlling bias and variance. Because these concepts do not have widely agreed-upon formal definitions for classification and for general loss functions, as mentioned in Section 5.2, ensemble design depends partly on intuition and analogy with the bias–variance trade-off for squared-error loss.

Some ensemble design approaches may be arrived at by considering the risk, under squared-error loss, incurred when estimating a real parameter vector. Suppose $Z_1, \ldots, Z_L$ are estimators of an unknown real vector θ.[3] The lth estimator of θ has a bias, $\text{Bias}[Z_l] = \text{E}[Z_l] - \theta$, and a variance, $\text{Var}[Z_l]$.

Now consider combining the estimates $Z_1, \ldots, Z_L$ into a single ensemble estimator of θ by forming the sample mean,

$$\bar{Z} = \frac{1}{L} \sum_{l=1}^{L} Z_l.$$

The bias of $\bar{Z}$ for θ and the variance of $\bar{Z}$ are

$$\text{Bias}[\bar{Z}] = \frac{1}{L} \sum_{l=1}^{L} \text{Bias}[Z_l]$$

and

$$\text{Var}[\bar{Z}] = \frac{1}{L^2} \sum_{l=1}^{L} \text{Var}[Z_l] + \frac{1}{L^2} \sum_{l \neq k} \text{Cov}[Z_l, Z_k]$$

$$= \frac{1}{L^2} \sum_{l=1}^{L} \text{Var}[Z_l] + \frac{1}{L^2} \sum_{l \neq k} \text{Cor}[Z_l, Z_k] \sqrt{\text{Var}[Z_l]} \sqrt{\text{Var}[Z_k]}.$$

---

[2] Galton's purpose in this analysis was not frivolous: he was using the weight-guessing contest as a proxy for governing by democracy. In his words, "the average competitor was probably as well fitted for making a just estimate of the weight of the ox, as an average voter is of judging the merits of most political issues on which he votes, and the variety among the voters to judge justly was probably much the same in either case" (Galton, 1907). Compare with Aristotle (350 BCE).

[3] In this simple example, θ is unknown but fixed, so the intrinsic risk is zero.

Ensemble Design Approach A. The expressions for bias and variance show that if one can find a set of estimators $Z_1, \ldots, Z_L$ which:

(1) all have the same bias, β,

(2) all have the same variance, $\sigma^2 > 0$, and

(3) are all uncorrelated,

then the estimator $\bar{Z}$ has bias β and variance $\frac{\sigma^2}{L}$, and so has strictly smaller risk than any of the individual estimators. Thus one might produce a low-risk estimator $\bar{Z}$ of θ by constructing many high-risk estimators $Z_1, \ldots, Z_L$, provided that the individual high-risk estimators are uncorrelated and have low bias (but high variance).

Ensemble Design Approach B. The expressions for bias and variance also show that if one can find a set of estimators $Z_1, \ldots, Z_L$ which:

(1) have non-zero biases $\beta_1, \ldots, \beta_L$ which sum to zero, and

(2) all have the same variance, $\sigma^2 > 0$,

then the estimator $\bar{Z}$ has bias 0 and variance

$$\frac{\sigma^2}{L^2} \left(L + \sum_{l \neq k} \mathrm{Cor}[Z_l, Z_k] \right) \leq \sigma^2,$$

and so has strictly smaller risk than any of the individual estimators. Thus one might produce a low-risk estimator $\bar{Z}$ of θ by constructing many high-risk estimators $Z_1, \ldots, Z_L$, provided that the individual high-risk estimators have low variance (but have high biases which cancel each other out). While it is possible that $\mathrm{Var}[\bar{Z}] = \sigma^2$, such cases are pathological[4] and typically, in addition to the bias being zero, we would expect that $\mathrm{Var}[\bar{Z}] < \sigma^2$.

Exercise 6.1 *Consider a generalization of the sample average:* $Z = \sum_{l=1}^{L} c_l Z_l$, *where all the coefficients c_l are non-negative and $c_1 + \cdots + c_L = 1$. Assuming that $Z_1, \ldots, Z_L$ (1) all have the same bias, β, (2) have known, positive variances, $\sigma_1^2, \ldots, \sigma_L^2$, and (3) are all uncorrelated, find values of the coefficients $c_1, \ldots, c_L$ which minimize the risk of Z under squared-error loss.*

Exercise 6.2 *For each of five ensemble methods (bagging, random forests, boosting, arcing, and stacking, described in Sections 6.3, 6.5, 6.6, 6.7, and 6.8), state whether it resembles design approach A or design approach B (or both, or neither). For each of these ensemble methods, can you find choices of base learners and parameters (of the ensemble method or of the base learners) which make the method resemble approach A, and other choices which make the method resemble approach B?*

---

[4] If $\mathrm{Var}[\bar{Z}] = \sigma^2$ then $\mathrm{Cor}[Z_l, Z_k] = 1$ for all $1 \leq l \leq k \leq L$, which implies that every Z_l is an increasing linear function of every other Z_k (that is, for each pair (l, k) there are constants $a_{l,k} > 0$ and $b_{l,k}$ such that $Z_l = a_{l,k} Z_k + b_{l,k}$).

6.3   Bootstrap Aggregation (Bagging)

The bootstrap is a technique, due to Efron (1979), for generating new datasets with approximately the same (unknown) sampling distribution as a given dataset. A *bootstrap sample* of a dataset of size n is obtained by sampling the set with replacement n times. Thus a bootstrap sample of the set

$$\{(x_1, y_1), (x_2, y_2), (x_3, y_3), (x_4, y_4), (x_5, y_5), (x_6, y_6)\}$$

might be

$$\{(x_2, y_2), (x_4, y_4), (x_4, y_4), (x_5, y_5), (x_6, y_6), (x_6, y_6)\}.$$

Efron's original motivation for the bootstrap was to estimate the variance of statistical estimators.

Exercise 6.3 *Let $\rho > 0$. Show that if a dataset of size n is sampled independently with replacement ρn times, then the probability that any particular point in the dataset is excluded from the sample is $(1 - \frac{1}{n})^{\rho n}$. Show that*

$$\lim_{n \to \infty} \left(1 - \frac{1}{n}\right)^{\rho n} = e^{-\rho}.$$

Thus, the expected proportion of a dataset which is excluded from a given bootstrap sample is about $e^{-1} \approx 0.368$, and the expected proportion which is included is about $1 - e^{-1} \approx 0.632$.

Bagging, a portmanteau word meaning "bootstrap aggregation," is an ensemble technique due to Breiman (1996a). Bagging is a simple idea: choose a classification algorithm, draw L independent bootstrap samples of the training data (that is, draw L sets of size n independently from the training data, with replacement), train a classifier on each of the L sets, and then combine them in a committee.

The size of the bootstrap samples used in bagging need not be n, the number of training data. Instead, bootstrap samples of size ρn, for some real number $\rho > 0$, can be used (original bootstrapping corresponds to $\rho = 1$). In light of Chapter 5, one would expect that decreasing ρ would result in increasing both the variance and the bias of the base learners, while at the same time decreasing the correlation between any two base learners (because the expected proportion of training data common to two bootstrap samples of size ρn is about $(1 - e^{-\rho})^2$).

The effects of varying bootstrap sample size in bagged 1-nearest neighbor classifiers and bagged stumps,[5] trained on the data of Section 4.3, are shown in Figures 6.3 and 6.4. The top two cells of Figure 6.3 show classification decisions made by a 1-nearest-neighbor classifier and a stump, trained on all of the data of Section 4.3.

---

[5] Recall from Chapter 4 that a stump is a tree with only two leaf nodes.

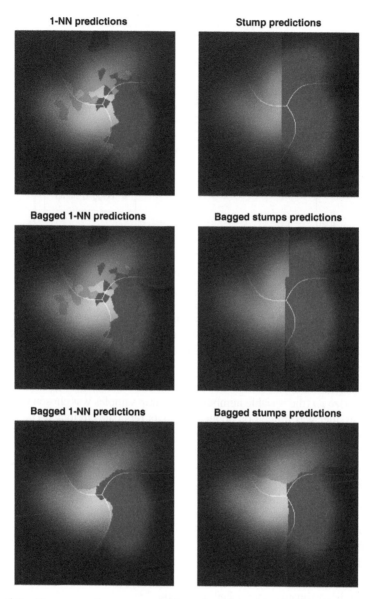

Figure 6.3   *Top row:* a 1-nearest-neighbor classifier (risk 0.247) and a stump (risk 0.423), trained on the data of Section 4.3. *Middle row:* bagged 1-nearest neighbor classifiers (risk 0.248) and bagged stumps (risk 0.419) trained on $L = 100$ bootstrap samples of size n. *Bottom row:* bagged 1-nearest neighbor classifiers trained on $L = \frac{100}{\rho}$ bootstrap samples of size ρn with $\rho = \frac{1}{8}$ (risk 0.199) and bagged stumps trained on $L = \frac{100}{\rho}$ bootstrap samples of size ρn with $\rho = \frac{1}{16}$ (risk 0.219). The bootstrap sample sizes in the bottom row were selected as approximately optimal using out-of-bag risk estimation, described in Section 7.3, to estimate risk from the training data.

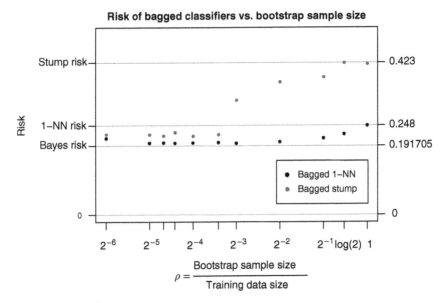

Figure 6.4   The risk of bagged 1-nearest-neighbor classifiers and bagged stumps trained on the data of Section 4.3, as a function of the size of the bootstrap samples. The horizontal axis is the ratio ρ of the bootstrap sample size to the total number of training data, n. For various values of ρ, a bagged classifier consisting of either 1-nearest-neighbor classifiers or stumps was constructed by drawing $\frac{100}{\rho}$ bootstrap samples of size ρn (the variable number of bootstrap samples was chosen so that each bagged classifier was trained on about $100\,n$ data replicates in total). The bootstrap sample size has a strong effect on the risk of the bagged classifier. In this example, since $n = 150$, choosing ρ much less than 2^{-6}, leads to bootstrap samples consisting of only one data point, and this results in an ensemble that predicts the same class at every point x.

The middle two cells show classification decisions made by bagged ensembles of 100 classifiers each, using bootstrap samples of size n. The bottom two cells show classification decisions made by bagged ensembles of $\frac{100}{\rho}$ classifiers each, using bootstrap samples of size ρn, for values of ρ chosen to be approximately optimal based on out-of-bag risk estimation (described in Section 7.3).

Visual comparison of the top and middle rows of Figure 6.3 shows that the bagged classifiers with sample size n perform nearly identically to their corresponding single base learners trained on all of the data. Figure 6.4 shows the effect of ρ on the risk of bagged 1-nearest-neighbor classifiers and bagged stumps. When $\rho = 1$, the risk of each bagged classifier is essentially the same as the risk of its respective base learner trained on all of the training data, as one would expect from the classification decisions shown in Figure 6.3. As ρ decreases from 1, the risk decreases—the author interprets this to mean that the increased bias and variance in the base learners is more than offset by the decreased correlation between them. When $\rho = 2^{-5}$, each base classifier is trained on five data points, and when $\rho = 2^{-6}$, each base classifier is trained on two data points[6], and even for these small bootstrap sample sizes this example shows no evidence of the risk going back up. For sufficiently small ρ, each bootstrap sample contains only one data point and each base learner predicts the class of the datum it was trained on (regardless of the input feature vector), so the bagged classifier predicts whichever class was most represented in the set of size-1 bootstrap samples (again, regardless of the input feature vector). The author interprets this to mean that increased bias and variance in the base learners have overwhelmed the decreased correlation between them.

Exercise 6.4 *Consider bagging the 1-nearest-neighbor classifier using L bootstrap samples, each of size ρn for some positive number ρ. Let X be a feature vector to be classified by the bagged classifier, and let (x, y) be the nearest training data point to X. Assuming n is large enough that the approximation $(1 - \frac{1}{n})^{\rho n} \approx e^{-\rho}$ of 6.3 can be used with negligible error, show that as $L \to \infty$, the probability that at least half of the bootstrap samples contain the training point (x, y) approaches 1 if and only if ρ is greater than $\log 2 \approx 0.693$. Conclude that a bagged 1-nearest-neighbor classifier will perform similarly to a single 1-nearest-neighbor classifier unless ρ is less than about $\log 2$.*

6.4   Bumping

Bumping, introduced in Tibshirani and Knight (1999), constructs bootstrap samples of the data, trains a classifier on each one, and then computes the training error of each classifier on the whole dataset. The classifier with the smallest overall training error is then used. This may be useful if a classifier is stuck at a sub-optimal fit due to a few misleading data points. Predictions made by a bumped 1-nearest-neighbor classifier trained on the data of Section 4.3 are shown in the upper-left cell of Figure 6.5. This bumped classifier was selected from the set of all base classifiers trained in production of Figure 6.4.

---

[6] In the training dataset for the running example of Section 4.3, no two data points have identical values in either the first feature or the second feature. Thus when training a classification tree on two data points of different classes, the root node can be split using either the first feature or the second feature in order to produce a zero-impurity tree with two leaves. From an impurity-minimization point of view, there is no reason to prefer splitting on the first feature over splitting on the second feature, but in this case the R function `rpart()` always chooses to split using the first feature. For these examples, features were permuted randomly when training any given tree with `rpart()`, so that choices between equally good splits were made uniformly at random.

Bumped 1-NN predictions   **Random forest predictions**

Boosted stump predictions   **Arced stump predictions**

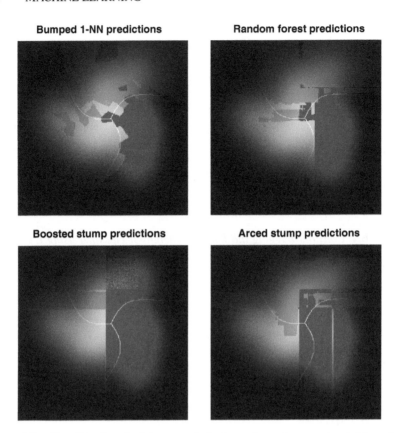

Figure 6.5   Classification decisions made by bumping a 1-nearest-neighbor classifier (upper left cell), applying a 1000-tree random forest (upper right cell), an ensemble of 1000 boosted stumps (lower left cell), and an ensemble of 1000 arced 1-nearest-
neighbor classifiers (lower right cell), trained on the data of Section 4.3. The bumped
classifier is a single 1-nearest-neighbor classifier chosen to have minimal out-of-bag
risk from the set of all base classifiers trained in the bagging experiments illustrated in
Figure 6.4. A *stump* is a classification tree constrained to have at most two leaf nodes.
The estimated risks of these classifiers are 0.245 for bumped 1-nearest-neighbor,
0.220 for the random forest, 0.268 for boosted stumps, and 0.262 for arced stumps.

6.5   Random Forests

Random forest classifiers are due to Breiman (2001a) and are a combination earlier
techniques with which he is associated, classification trees and bagging.[7] Omitting

---

[7] Ensembles of classification trees trained on random subsets of features had been considered earlier in
Ho (1995) and Dietterich (2000).

one detail, a random forest classifier is simply bagged trees: on L bootstrap samples of the data, trees are trained (grown to be over-fit, with no pruning) and then the trees vote in a committee. The omitted detail is that at each step in growing the tree, a random training decision is made: a small random sample of the m features (typically about $\sqrt{m}$ of them) are considered for the split rather than all m. The purpose of this is to reduce the correlation between pairs of trees in the forest.[8] Predictions made by a 1000-tree random forest trained on the data of Section 4.3 are shown in the upper-right cell of Figure 6.5.

Random forests are provably resistant to over-fitting in the sense that increasing the number of trees L without bound does not *cause* the random forest to be over-fit, in spite of the fact that the number of parameters needed to describe the forest goes to infinity.[9] Let $P_{(X,Y)}$ be the probability distribution from which data are drawn: it is assumed that the training data and all future data are drawn from this distribution. Let (X, Y) denote a random datum drawn from $P_{(X,Y)}$. One can show that under 0–1 loss the risk of a random forest with trees $T_1, \ldots, T_L$ is

$$R(T_1, \ldots, T_L) = P_{(X,Y)} \left(|\text{trees voting for class } Y| < \max_{c \neq Y} |\text{trees voting for class } c| \right).$$

Let P_F be the probability distribution used for generating random decisions when training the trees for a random forest. Breiman (2001a) has shown that as $L \to \infty$, the risk of a random forest with L trees approaches the probability that a new datum (X, Y) drawn from the data distribution $P_{(X,Y)}$ is misclassified by a random tree constructed on the training data using P_F to make random training decisions, that is,

$$R(T_1, \ldots, T_L)$$
$$\to P_{(X,Y)} \left(P_F (\text{a tree votes for class } Y) < \max_{c \neq Y} P_F (\text{a tree votes for class } c) \right),$$

with probability 1. Thus in practice there is no reason to worry about making L too large, except computational cost.

Breiman defined the *random forest proximity* of two data points (x_1, y_1) and (x_2, y_2) to be the proportion of trees in a random forest with the property that (x_1, y_1) and (x_2, y_2) are in the same terminal node (leaf). Random forest proximity can be useful for discovering clusters in data, particularly clusters within a given class.

Exercise 6.5 *Let* $L(d, c)$ *be an arbitrary loss function with the (very minimal) property that*

$$L(c, c) = 0 \quad \text{for all } c \quad \text{and} \quad L(d, c) > 0 \quad \text{for all } d \neq c.$$

---

[8] Other alternatives have been explored. For example, at each internal node, *completely random trees* use a random split of a feature selected at random (Liu et al., 2008), while *extremely randomized trees* select a random split for each of $\sqrt{m}$ features, and choose the optimal feature (Geurts et al., 2006). In this case, optimal means impurity-minimizing.

[9] This does *not* mean that any particular random forest is not over fit on any particular dataset!

Show that if each tree in a random forest is grown until all leaf nodes have zero impurity (that is, contain training data of only one class), then the actual values taken by the loss function have no effect on predictions made by the forest. Does the marginal distribution on classes $(P(Y = 1), \dots, P(Y = C))$ *have any effect, assuming* $P(Y = c) > 0$ *for all c?*

6.6   Boosting

Let real, non-negative *weights* $w_1, \dots, w_n$ be assigned to the training data, and let the loss incurred by misclassifying (x_i, y_i) as class d be $w_i L(y_i, d)$. Weight w_i reflects the relative importance of correctly classifying training datum (x_i, y_i).

Exercise 6.6 Open-Ended Challenge. *Modify each classification algorithm of Chapter 4 so that it is applicable to weighted data.* **Hint:** *If all of the weights* $w_1, \dots, w_n$ *are integers, then treat this as equivalent to a situation where data are unweighted, but datum (x_i, y_i) occurs in the training set w_i times. If all of the weights are rational, then the weights can be scaled up by an integer constant $\rho > 0$ such that $\rho w_1, \dots, \rho w_n$ are integers, and the loss function can be divided by ρ. A set of real weights can be handled as the limit of sets of rational weights.*

Boosting a classifier refers to an algorithm of the general type shown in Figure 6.6. A particular boosting algorithm is *AdaBoost* (short for "adaptive boosting") (Freund and Schapire, 1997; Schapire and Freund, 2012). The original AdaBoost algorithm was defined for $C = 2$ classes. Using 0–1 loss, AdaBoost is shown in Figure 6.7 (Friedman et al., 2000).

In Adaboost, if ever $\widehat{R}_l = 0$ then no reweighting occurs (because no training data are misclassified), and if training in step (2A) is deterministic (that is, does not involve a source of randomness external to the data) then $\widehat{f}_l = \widehat{f}_{l+1} = \dots = \widehat{f}_L$. These apparently perfect classifiers have infinite weight assigned to their votes, so AdaBoost

---

(1) initialize $w_1, \dots, w_n$ somehow (e.g., set all to 1).
(2) for $l = 1, \dots, L$,
    (2A) train classifier $\widehat{f}_l$ on the weighted training data.
    (2B) compute an estimate $\widehat{R}_l$ of the risk of $\widehat{f}_l$.
    (2C) 'boost' (increase) the weights of the training data misclassified by $\widehat{f}_l$.
(3) classify new data by voting classifiers $\widehat{f}_1, \dots, \widehat{f}_L$ in a committee: classifier $\widehat{f}_l$'s vote has high weight when its risk estimate $\widehat{R}_l$ is small, and vice versa.

Figure 6.6   A generic boosting algorithm.

---

(1) initialize $w_1 = \cdots = w_n = \frac{1}{n}$.
(2) for $l = 1, \ldots, L$,
    (2A) train classifier $\widehat{f}_l$ on the weighted training data.
    (2B) estimate the risk of $\widehat{f}_l$ by the error on the weighted training data,

$$\widehat{R}_l = \sum_{i=1}^{n} w_i \left[y_i \neq \widehat{f}_l(x_i) \right] = \text{sum of weights of the data misclassified by } \widehat{f}_l.$$

    (2C) for $i = 1, \ldots, n$, if $y_i \neq \widehat{f}_l(x_i)$ update w_i to the value $w_i \frac{1-\widehat{R}_l}{\widehat{R}_l}$.
    (2D) renormalize the weights so they sum to 1 .
(3) classify new data as

$$\text{argmax}_{c=1,\ldots,C} \sum_{l=1}^{L} \left[\widehat{f}_l(X) = c \right] \log \left(\frac{1 - \widehat{R}_l}{\widehat{R}_l} \right),$$

that is, the individual classifiers vote in a committee, and $\widehat{f}_l$ casts a vote with weight $\log \left(\frac{1-\widehat{R}_l}{\widehat{R}_l} \right)$.

Figure 6.7   The AdaBoost algorithm for 0–1 loss and $C = 2$ classes. Modifications for the case $C > 2$ are described in the text.

produces the same predictions as $\widehat{f}_l$. If $\widehat{R}_l$ is positive but very small, then $(1 - \widehat{R}_l)/\widehat{R}_l$ is large and the relatively few misclassified points are greatly up-weighted, causing $\widehat{f}_{l+1}$ to focus on classifying these points correctly. Also, classifier $\widehat{f}_l$ votes with relatively high weight. As long as $\widehat{R}_l < \frac{1}{2}$, the predictions made by $\widehat{f}_l$ are taken to be better than predicting by tossing a fair coin, and so misclassified points are up-weighted and $\widehat{f}_l$ votes with positive weight.

If ever $\widehat{R}_l = \frac{1}{2}$ then predictions by $\widehat{f}_l$ are taken to be equivalent to tossing a fair coin and weights are effectively not changed (raising again the possibility that $\widehat{f}_l = \widehat{f}_{l+1} = \cdots = \widehat{f}_L$). These perfectly useless classifiers have zero weight assigned to their votes.

If $\widehat{R}_l > \frac{1}{2}$, the predictions made by $\widehat{f}_l$ are taken to be *worse* than predictions made by tossing a fair coin. This does not mean that the classifier is useless, it merely has confused the meaning of the two class labels (or equivalently, $\widehat{f}_l$ is experiencing *opposite day* (Watterson, 1988)). Thus its votes have negative weight, which is to say positive weight assigned to the opposite vote. Misclassified points are down-weighted, because from the perspective of AdaBoost, it is useful to make a worse-than-coin-toss classifier even worse, as long as we know to reverse the predictions of the classifier by giving its votes negative weight. If ever $\widehat{R}_l = 1$ then the weights of all misclassified points are reduced to zero, and $\widehat{f}_l$ votes with infinite negative weight.

Exercise 6.7 *The AdaBoost algorithm can also be stated in a slightly different way from that shown in Figure 6.7. Specifically, step (2C) can be replaced by*

$(2C')$ *for $i = 1, \ldots, n$, if $y_i \neq \hat{f}_l(x_i)$ update weight w_i to the value $w_i \left(\frac{1-\hat{R}_l}{\hat{R}_l} \right)^{\frac{1}{2}}$, and*

if $y_i = \hat{f}_l(x_i)$ update weight w_i to the value $w_i \left(\frac{1-\hat{R}_l}{\hat{R}_l} \right)^{-\frac{1}{2}}$.

and step (3) can be replaced by

$(3')$ *classify new data as $argmax_{\{c=1,\ldots,C\}} \sum_{l=1}^{L} [\hat{f}_l(x_i) = c] \log \left(\frac{1-\hat{R}_l}{\hat{R}_l} \right)^{\frac{1}{2}}$.*

Show that this different statement of AdaBoost produces exactly the same ensemble of classifiers as the version shown in Figure 6.7.

Exercise 6.8 *In the lth iteration of the AdaBoost algorithm, illustrated in Figure 6.7 by steps (2A)-(2D), let $w_1, \ldots, w_n$ denote the weights in steps (2A) and (2B), and let $v_1, \ldots, v_n$ denote the updated weights in step (2D). That is,*

$$v_i = \begin{cases} c\, w_i & \text{if } y_i = \hat{f}_l(x_i) \\ c\, w_i \dfrac{1-\hat{R}_l}{\hat{R}_l} & \text{if } y_i \neq \hat{f}_l(x_i) \end{cases},$$

where c is chosen so that $v_1 + \cdots + v_n = 1$.

(A) Show that

$$c = \frac{1}{2(1 - \hat{R}_l)}$$

so step (2D) in AdaBoost is equivalent to dividing each weight by $2(1 - \hat{R}_l)$.

(B) Show that the new weights $v_1, \ldots, v_n$ make the classifier $\hat{f}_l(x_i)$ as bad as possible with respect to training risk, in the sense that

$$\sum_{i=1}^{n} v_i [y_i \neq \hat{f}_l(x_i)] = \frac{1}{2}.$$

AdaBoost was generalized to $C > 2$ classes by Zhu et al. (2009). Their generalized algorithm differs from the original only in the re-weighting applied to the weights of misclassified data in step (2C), which is

$$w_i \frac{1 - \hat{R}_l}{\hat{R}_l} (C - 1),$$

and the weight assigned to the vote of the lth classifier in step (3), which is

$$\log \left(\frac{1 - \hat{R}_l}{\hat{R}_l} (C - 1) \right).$$

As long as $\widehat{R}_l < \frac{C-1}{C}$, the interpretation and behavior of multiclass AdaBoost is the same as the original. If ever $\widehat{R}_l = \frac{C-1}{C}$, the predictions by $\widehat{f}_l$ are taken to be equivalent to rolling a fair C-sided die. Weights are effectively not changed in this case (raising the possibility that $\widehat{f}_l = \widehat{f}_{l+1} = \cdots = \widehat{f}_L$), and $\widehat{f}_l$ has zero weight assigned to its vote. If $\widehat{R}_l > \frac{C-1}{C}$ then generalized AdaBoost gives negative weight to votes by $\widehat{f}_l$ since $\widehat{f}_l$ makes worse predictions than a fair die roll, but notice that with $C > 2$ classes being frequently wrong does not mean that a classifier's predictions can be modified so that they are frequently right (as is the case when $C = 2$).

Predictions made by an ensemble consisting of 1000 stumps trained with three-class generalized AdaBoost on the data of Section 4.3 are shown in the lower-left cell of Figure 6.5.

6.7 Arcing

Arcing, which stands for *adaptive resampling and combining*, is similar to boosting. Instead of applying weights to data within a classification algorithm, arcing draws a new dataset on which to train a classifier at each step by sampling from the training data with replacement according to a changing probability distribution.

A particular arcing algorithm,[10] modeled on AdaBoost with 0–1 loss, is shown in Figure 6.8. In the terminology of Breiman (1996b), AdaBoost is *non-random arcing*.

Predictions made by an ensemble consisting of 1000 stumps trained with three-class generalized arcing on the data of Section 4.3 are shown in the lower-right cell of Figure 6.5.

6.8 Stacking and Mixture of Experts

Instead of casting votes as in a committee, the output of a set of trained classifiers (either predicted classes or estimated posterior distributions on the classes) can be used as input to another classifier. This is called *stacking* classifiers (Wolpert, 1992). When stacking, outputs of the trained classifiers are regarded as new features.

The left-hand cell of Figure 6.9 shows predictions made by a classification tree trained on the dataset

$$(z_1, y_1), \ldots, (z_{150}, y_{150})$$

where

$$z_i = (\widehat{f}_1(x_i), \ldots, \widehat{f}_L(x_i))$$

---

[10] In Breiman (1996b), this algorithm is called *arc-fs* in honor of Freund and Schapire, the creators of AdaBoost.

(1) initialize $p_1 = \cdots = p_n = \frac{1}{n}$.
(2) for $l = 1, \ldots, L$,
    (2A) draw a sample S_l from the training data according to $(p_1, \ldots, p_n)$.
    (2B) train classifier $\widehat{f}_l$ on S_l.
    (2C) estimate the risk of $\widehat{f}_l$ by the expected loss under $(p_1, \ldots, p_n)$,

$$\widehat{R}_l = \sum_{i=1}^{n} p_i \left[y_i \neq \widehat{f}_l(x_i) \right] .$$

    (2D) for $i = 1, \ldots, n$, if $y_i \neq \widehat{f}_l(x_i)$ update $p_i = p_i \frac{1 - \widehat{R}_l}{\widehat{R}_l}$.
    (2E) renormalize $(p_1, \ldots, p_n)$ so it sums to 1.
(3) classify new data as

$$\operatorname{argmax}_{c=1,\ldots,C} \sum_{l=1}^{L} \left[\widehat{f}_l(X) = c \right] \log \left(\frac{1 - \widehat{R}_l}{\widehat{R}_l} \right) ,$$

that is, the individual classifiers vote in a committee, and $\widehat{f}_l$ casts a vote with weight $\log \left(\frac{1 - \widehat{R}_l}{\widehat{R}_l} \right)$.

Figure 6.8   An arcing algorithm based on the AdaBoost algorithm for 0–1 loss and $C = 2$ classes. Modifications for the case $C > 2$ are described in the text of Section 6.6.

Figure 6.9   Predictions made by using the predictions of the 20 bad classifiers (risk ≥ 0.220) described in Section 6.1 as categorical features, and training a classification tree (left-hand cell), and predictions made by using the predictions of 100 stumps trained on "full size" (size-150) bootstrap samples of the training data, and training a logistic regression classifier (right-hand cell). The risk of the tree-stacked-on-bad-classifiers is 0.247 and the risk of logistic-regression-stacked-on-bootstrapped-stumps is 0.231.

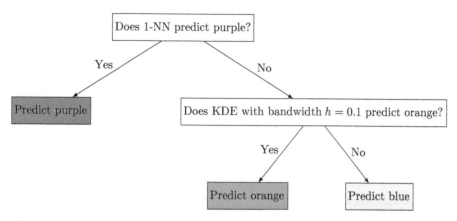

Figure 6.10   The classification tree which takes as input the class predictions of the 20 bad classifiers described in Section 6.1, and predicts a single class. The predictions made by this tree are shown in the left-hand cell of Figure 6.9.

and the base learners $\widehat{f}_1, \ldots, \widehat{f}_L$ are the bad classifiers described in Section 6.1 (so $L = 20$). The vectors $z_1, \ldots, z_n$ are regarded as categorical features for training the tree, since $\widehat{f}_l(x_i) \in \{\text{orange, blue, purple}\}$ for all l and x_i.

The classification tree stacked on 20 bad classifiers was grown and pruned as described in Chapter 4, with the cost-complexity parameter chosen to minimize the leave-one-out cross-validation estimate of risk described in Section 7.3. The tree has only three leaf nodes, and is shown in Figure 6.10. Two of the bad classifiers, the 1-nearest-neighbor classifier and the likelihood classifier based on kernel density estimation using bandwidth $h = 0.1$, are over-fit to the training data and have very low training risk, and as a result were identified by the classification tree as very good predictors of the class labels on the training data. The result is a stacked classifier which is very similar to its most over-fit base learners. The risk of the stacked classifier is 0.247, the risk of the 1-nearest-neighbor classifier is 0.248, and the risk of the likelihood classifier based on kernel density estimation using bandwidth $h = 0.1$ is 0.246. Visual comparison of predictions by these three classifiers (left-hand cell of Figure 6.9, upper-right cell of Figure 4.7, and upper-left cell of Figure 4.12) show that they are very similar.

The right-hand cell of Figure 6.9 shows predictions made by a logistic regression classifier trained on the dataset

$$(z_1, y_1), \ldots, (z_{150}, y_{150})$$

where

$$z_i = (\widehat{f}_1(x_i), \ldots, \widehat{f}_L(x_i))$$

and the base learners $\widehat{f}_1, \ldots, \widehat{f}_L$ are stumps trained on 100 full-size (size-150) bootstrap samples of the training data (so $L = 100$). As before, the vectors $z_1, \ldots, z_n$ are regarded as categorical features for training the logistic regression classifier.

Stacking logistic regression required two minor modifications from logistic regression as described in Section 4.6: dummy variables and parameter penalization. The predictions made by the L base learners are categorical features taking three possible values (orange, blue, or purple), and each of these categorical features was represented[11] by two binary dummy variables, described in Section 3.8. In terms of the dummy variables,

$$z_i = ([\widehat{f}_1(x_i) = \text{blue}], [\widehat{f}_1(x_i) = \text{purple}], \ldots, [\widehat{f}_L(x_i) = \text{blue}], [\widehat{f}_L(x_i) = \text{purple}])$$

is a $2L$-long binary vector: for $l = 1, \ldots, L$, the coordinates $(z_{i,2l-1}, z_{i,2l})$ are $(0,0)$ if $\widehat{f}_l(x_i) = \text{orange}$, $(1,0)$ if $\widehat{f}_l(x_i) = \text{blue}$, and $(0,1)$ if $\widehat{f}_l(x_i) = \text{purple}$. Since some of these dummy variables are highly correlated with one another, a quadratic penalty was placed on the non-intercept logistic regression parameters (compare this with ridge regression in Section 3.10). That is, the $C \times (m + 1)$ matrix of logistic regression model parameters

$$\theta = \begin{bmatrix} 0 & 0 & \cdots & 0 \\ \theta_{2,0} & \theta_{2,1} & \cdots & \theta_{2,m} \\ \theta_{3,0} & \theta_{3,1} & \cdots & \theta_{3,m} \end{bmatrix} = \begin{bmatrix} \theta_1 \\ \theta_2 \\ \theta_3 \end{bmatrix},$$

with $C = 3$ and $m = 2L = 200$ (the 100 base learners each have their class predictions represented by two binary dummy variables) is chosen to minimize

$$-\sum_{i=1}^{n} T(z_i, \theta_{y_i}) + \sum_{i=1}^{n} \log \left(\sum_{d=1}^{C} \exp(T(z_i, \theta_d)) \right) + \lambda \sum_{d=1}^{C} \sum_{j=1}^{m} \theta_{d,j}^2$$

(compare this with ridge regression in Section 3.10, and note that the intercept parameters $\theta_{d,0}$ are not penalized). The weight parameter λ applied to the quadratic penalty was selected to be approximately optimal using leave-one-out cross-validation, described in Section 7.3, to estimate the risk of the logistic regression classifier from the training data.

In stacking, the top-level classifier uses only the L base learner outputs: its input feature vectors are $z_1, \ldots, z_n$. If the top-level classifier uses both the L base learner outputs and also original features, so that its input feature vectors are $(x_1, z_1), \ldots, (x_n, z_n)$, then the resulting classifier is called a *mixture of experts* (Jacobs et al., 1991). Figure 6.11 shows predictions made by a logistic regression classifier trained on the data set

$$((x_1, z_1), y_1), \ldots, ((x_{150}, z_{150}), y_{150})$$

---

[11] The dummy variable representation of categorical features is handled automatically by the R function `multinom()`.

LR mixture of experts predictions

Figure 6.11   Predictions made by using the predictions of 100 stumps trained on "full size" (size-150) bootstrap samples of the training data, *and* the original feature vectors, and training a logistic regression classifier. The risk of the logistic regression mixture of experts is 0.227.

where each of $z_1, \ldots, z_{150}$ is the concatenated output of stumps trained on 100 full size (size-150) bootstrap samples of the training data, as described above.

Neural networks can be regarded as a type of stacking or a mixture of experts, depending on the specific network architecture. The neurons in the hidden layer immediately below the output layer can be thought of as base learners which are soft versions of binary classifiers. The classes learned by each of these binary classifiers do not necessarily correspond to any of the classes $1, \ldots, C$. Rather, they are *latent classes* which are extracted from the data and which are in some way pertinent to solving the overall classification problem (if the neural network does a good job). The continuous-valued "votes" of the base learners are combined by using logistic regression in the top layer of the network. In a neural network, the base learners are trained at the same time the logistic-regression output layer is trained, and the base learners are all trained in parallel in an inter-dependent way, in contrast with bagging (where base learners are trained independently in parallel) and boosting (where base learners are inter-dependent but trained sequentially).

7

Risk Estimation and Model Selection

Aesthetics and statistical accuracy might not be the same thing.
—Larry Wasserman, personal communication, 2001

The very fact that the representation is of such generality that it can always be made to fit the data exactly is considered an argument against it, not for it.
—Harold Jeffreys, Scientific Inference, 1931

In Chapter 2, we stated our goal to be finding an approximation $\widehat{f}$ of f with minimal risk $R(\widehat{f})$, the expected loss incurred when predicting values of response or class Y for new features X,

$$R(\widehat{f}) = E_{(X,Y)}[L(Y,\widehat{f}(X))].$$

In general, there is no way to compute risk exactly because the joint distribution of (X, Y) is unknown. The risk $R(\widehat{f})$ must be estimated from data, just as f must be.

This chapter describes several methods of estimating the risk of an approximation $\widehat{f}$ of f, and of selecting approximations with approximately minimal risk. Sections 7.1 through 7.5 describe methods of estimating risk. All of these methods have drawbacks as well as advantages, and these are discussed. Sections 7.6 through 7.9 describe model selection criteria which do not involve explicit risk estimation. Sections 7.10 and 7.11 contain general remarks about model selection.

Machine Learning: a Concise Introduction, First Edition. Steven W. Knox.
© This publication is a US Government work and is in the public domain.
Published 2018 by John Wiley & Sons, Inc.
Companion Website: http://www.wiley.com/go/Knox/MachineLearning

7.1 Risk Estimation via Training Data

Let $(x_1, y_1), \ldots, (x_n, y_n)$ be the data used to train an approximation $\hat{f}$ of f. In Chapter 2, the training risk was defined as the average loss incurred by using $\hat{f}(x_i)$ to predict the value of y_i on the training data,

$$\hat{R}_{\text{train}}(\hat{f}) = \frac{1}{n} \sum_{i=1}^{n} L(y_i, \hat{f}(x_i)).$$

Training risk is cheap to compute, but it tends to underestimate risk (that is, to be an *optimistic risk estimate*) because the data used to evaluate $\hat{f}$ are the same data used to compute $\hat{f}$ in the first place. As a result, overly complex models with very high variance, which approximate f very well near the training data but poorly away from the training data, tend to be chosen when selecting models to minimize training risk (an example of this phenomenon was suggested in Exercise 2.4).

Exercise 7.1 *Let $x_1, \ldots, x_n$ be distinct real numbers and for each i let $y_i = \theta_1 x_i + \theta_0 + e_i$, where $e_1, \ldots, e_n$ are independent, identically distributed draws from a $N(0, \sigma^2)$ distribution. The pairs $(x_1, y_1), \ldots, (x_n, y_n)$ are known. Unknown are θ_0, θ_1, σ^2, the e_i's and the fact that $f(x) = \theta_1 x + \theta_0$ is a linear function. Consider the sequence of approximations $\hat{f}_0, \hat{f}_1, \hat{f}_2, \ldots$ to f where $\hat{f}_d$ is a degree-d real polynomial which minimizes training risk with respect to squared-error loss. Show that, with probability one, $\hat{R}_{\text{train}}(\hat{f}_d)$ is a decreasing function of the degree d. Show that $\hat{R}_{\text{train}}(\hat{f}_d) = 0$ when $d \geq n - 1$. Explain these facts in terms of bias–variance trade-off.*

7.2 Risk Estimation via Validation or Test Data

The most accurate way to estimate the risk of an approximation $\hat{f}$ of f is by using data which have the same distribution as data to which $\hat{f}$ is to be applied in the future, but which have not been used to train $\hat{f}$. One way to obtain such *validation data* or *test data* is to remove it from the set of all available data before training any models.

7.2.1 Training, Validation, and Test Data

Let the set of all available data be partitioned randomly[1] into either two or three sets: a *training dataset* on which models are trained, a *validation dataset* which is used to

---

[1] It is important that each of the training, validation, and test sets be as much as possible like the future, unmarked data to which a trained classifier will be applied. To achieve this likeness, pure random sampling of the available data may be abandoned in favor of some form of *stratified sampling*. For example, stratified sampling based on the class label could be used to ensure that the proportion of classes among the training, validation, and test sets are as similar as possible. Stratified sampling is particularly important when there are rare classes or categorical features with rare values. Stratified sampling can be used any time data are randomly sampled or partitioned, for example in bagging (Section 6.3) or cross-validation (Section 7.3). Stratified sampling is not used when forming bootstrap samples in the

estimate the risk of trained models for the purpose of model selection, and perhaps also a *test dataset* which is used to estimate the risk of the best model found by the model selection process.

In some applications, an approximation $\hat{f}$ is considered worth implementing only if the risk, $R(\hat{f})$, can be shown to fall below a given threshold. Such applications require a test set in addition to a validation set. In other applications, the best approximation $\hat{f}$ will be used, at least on a trial basis, regardless of the risk, in which case only a validation set may be needed.

In what follows, let $(\tilde{x}_1, \tilde{y}_1), \ldots, (\tilde{x}_{\tilde{n}}, \tilde{y}_{\tilde{n}})$ denote validation data. It is assumed to be drawn independently from the same distribution as the training data but *it is not used to train any models* and, to the greatest extent possible, *it is excluded from exploratory data analysis*.[2] All remarks about validation data below also pertain to test data.

7.2.2   Risk Estimation

The *validation estimate* of the risk $R(\hat{f})$ of $\hat{f}$ is

$$\hat{R}_{\text{valid}}(\hat{f}) = \frac{1}{\tilde{n}} \sum_{i=1}^{\tilde{n}} L(\tilde{y}_i, \hat{f}(\tilde{x}_i)).$$

The validation estimate of risk is unbiased, since

$$E_{(\tilde{X}_1, \tilde{Y}_1), \ldots, (\tilde{X}_{\tilde{n}}, \tilde{Y}_{\tilde{n}})}[\hat{R}_{\text{valid}}(\hat{f})] = \frac{1}{\tilde{n}} \sum_{i=1}^{\tilde{n}} E_{(X,Y)}[L(Y, \hat{f}(X))] = R(\hat{f}).$$

Consequently, by the strong law of large numbers, $\hat{R}_{\text{valid}}(\hat{f}) \to R(\hat{f})$ with probability 1 as $\tilde{n} \to \infty$. By the central limit theorem, $\hat{R}_{\text{valid}}(\hat{f})$ is approximately normal-distributed under weak assumptions. This enables convenient testing of hypotheses about risk, provided the variance of the risk estimate can be estimated.

Exercise 7.2 *In the case of 0–1 loss, the risk (generalization error) of trained classifier $\hat{f}$ is*

$$R = probability\ that\ a\ new\ datum\ is\ misclassified\ by\ \hat{f}.$$

Show that under 0–1 loss, the validation estimate of risk is

$$\hat{R}_{\text{valid}}(\hat{f}) = proportion\ of\ validation\ data\ misclassified\ by\ \hat{f}.$$

---

original Breiman–Cutler implementation of random forests, and thus some trees in a random forest may be trained on samples which do not contain data of every class.

[2] If stratified sampling is used in the construction of the validation and test sets, then some exploratory data analysis has been done on these sets.

Exercise 7.3 *Use the fact that the variance of a sum of independent random variables is equal to the sum of the individual variances to show that*

$$\text{Var}_{(\tilde{X}_1, \tilde{Y}_1), \dots, (\tilde{X}_{\tilde{n}}, \tilde{Y}_{\tilde{n}})}[\widehat{R}_{\text{valid}}(\widehat{f})] = \frac{1}{\tilde{n}} \text{Var}_{(X,Y)}[L(Y, \widehat{f}(X))]$$
$$= \frac{1}{\tilde{n}} \left(E_{(X,Y)}[L(Y, \widehat{f}(X))^2] - R(\widehat{f})^2 \right).$$

Exercise 7.4 *Use result of Exercise 7.3 to show that if the range of* $L(c, d)$ *is* $[0, 1]$ *(that is, the loss is never more than one) then*

$$\text{Var}_{(\tilde{X}_1, \tilde{Y}_1), \dots, (\tilde{X}_{\tilde{n}}, \tilde{Y}_{\tilde{n}})}[\widehat{R}_{\text{valid}}(\widehat{f})] \leq \frac{1}{\tilde{n}} R(\widehat{f})(1 - R(\widehat{f}))$$

with equality if and only L *is 0–1 loss. Show that if the range of* $L(c, d)$ *is* $\{0\} \cup [1, \infty)$ *(that is, any non-zero loss is at least one) then*

$$\text{Var}_{(\tilde{X}_1, \tilde{Y}_1), \dots, (\tilde{X}_{\tilde{n}}, \tilde{Y}_{\tilde{n}})}[\widehat{R}_{\text{valid}}(\widehat{f})] \geq \frac{1}{\tilde{n}} R(\widehat{f})(1 - R(\widehat{f}))$$

with equality if and only L *is 0–1 loss.*

Exercises 7.3 and 7.4 lead to a simple plug-in estimator for the variance,

$$\widehat{\text{Var}}[\widehat{R}_{\text{valid}}(\widehat{f})] = \frac{1}{\tilde{n}} \left(\frac{1}{\tilde{n}} \sum_{i=1}^{\tilde{n}} L(\tilde{y}_i, \widehat{f}(\tilde{x}_i))^2 - \widehat{R}_{\text{valid}}(\widehat{f})^2 \right),$$

which in the case of 0–1 loss simplifies to

$$\widehat{\text{Var}}[\widehat{R}_{\text{valid}}(\widehat{f})] = \frac{1}{\tilde{n}} \widehat{R}_{\text{valid}}(\widehat{f})(1 - \widehat{R}_{\text{valid}}(\widehat{f})).$$

A consequence of Exercise 7.3 is that $\text{Var}_{(\tilde{X}_1, \tilde{Y}_1), \dots, (\tilde{X}_{\tilde{n}}, \tilde{Y}_{\tilde{n}})}[\widehat{R}_{\text{valid}}(\widehat{f})] \to 0$ as $\tilde{n} \to \infty$, provided that $\text{Var}_{(X,Y)}[L(Y, \widehat{f}(X))] < \infty$.

7.2.3   Size of Training, Validation, and Test Sets

Given a dataset of a certain size, how large should the training, validation, and test sets be? The answer depends balancing two (or three) competing demands. As more data are assigned to the validation set, the validation estimate of risk, $\widehat{R}_{\text{valid}}(\widehat{f})$, improves in the sense that the standard deviation of $\widehat{R}_{\text{valid}}(\widehat{f})$ goes to zero like $\tilde{n}^{-\frac{1}{2}}$ by Exercise 7.3. The same is true of the test set and the test estimate of risk. But as more data are assigned to the validation and test sets, fewer data are assigned to the training set, and one naturally expects the risk of trained approximation $\widehat{f}$ get worse as the number of training data decreases—though perhaps this effect is negligible if enough data remain in the training set.

Exercise 7.5 *In a given application where 0–1 loss is used, it is desired that the validation estimate of risk have standard deviation no more than σ. Find the minimum number $\tilde{n}$ of validation data needed to achieve this, assuming:*

(A) *expert opinion or a pilot study suggests the risk of any "reasonable" classifier will be no more than ρ, for some given number $\rho < \frac{1}{2}$;*

(B) *there is no knowledge of what the risk might be;*

(C) *as in (A), with $\rho = 0.25$ and $\sigma = 0.01$;*

(D) *Recommend a course of action in (C) if there are a total of 1800 data available.*

One occasionally encounters heuristic rules on the size of training, validation, and test sets, such as *use 70% of the data for training, 20% for validation, and 10% for testing* (or 60-20-20, or 50-30-20). The author advises that decisions about data be made to suit the applied goal of the data analysis, rather than by heuristics which may be unrelated to the applied goal.

7.2.4   Testing Hypotheses About Risk

The approximate normal distribution of the risk estimate $\widehat{R}_{\text{valid}}(\widehat{f})$ enables the construction of approximate confidence intervals for the true risk $R(\widehat{f})$ and hypothesis testing based upon such intervals. In addition to tests based on the asymptotic normality of the risk estimate, one can also use non-parametric tests.

Exercise 7.6 *Assume that the number $\tilde{n}$ of validation data is large enough that the validation estimate of risk, $\widehat{R}_{\text{valid}}(\widehat{f})$, can be thought of as normal-distributed with negligible error for any model $\widehat{f}$ under consideration. Given an observation of a random variable (the test statistic) $T \sim N(\mu, \sigma^2)$ and a fixed value ρ, a level-α one-sided Z-test of the null hypothesis*

$$H_0 : \mu \geq \rho$$

against the alternative hypothesis

$$H_a : \mu < \rho$$

works as follows: (1) let threshold τ be such that $P(U \leq \tau) = \alpha$, where $U \sim N(\rho, \sigma^2)$ (τ is the αth quantile of the $N(\rho, \sigma^2)$ distribution); (2) reject H_0 if $T < \tau$ and otherwise retain H_0.

(A) *Show that if the null hypothesis is true, then the probability of rejecting the null hypothesis is no more than α (this is what it means for the test have level α—see Chapter 12).*

(B) *Suppose that in a given application, a trained classifier $\widehat{f}$ will not be implemented unless there is evidence that $R(\widehat{f}) < \rho$, where ρ is a given threshold. Using $\widehat{R}_{\text{valid}}(\widehat{f})$ as a test statistic, construct a level-α one-sided Z-test of the null hypothesis $R(\widehat{f}) \geq \rho$ against the alternative hypothesis $R(\widehat{f}) < \rho$.*

(C) *Let $\widehat{f}_1$ and $\widehat{f}_2$ be two trained classifiers. Using a test statistic based on applying $\widehat{f}_1$ and $\widehat{f}_2$ to validation data, construct a level-α one-sided Z-test of the null hypothesis $R(\widehat{f}_2) \geq R(\widehat{f}_1)$ against the alternative hypothesis $R(\widehat{f}_2) < R(\widehat{f}_1)$.*

7.2.5   Example of Use of Training, Validation, and Test Sets

Say a classification dataset has been partitioned somehow into training, validation, and (perhaps) test sets and that, for concreteness of the example, we are determined to approximate f using a classification tree. We seek an approximately minimal-risk tree for making predictions and (perhaps) to estimate the risk of the optimal tree.

Recall from Section 4.8 that training a classification tree is a two-stage process: the first stage is to grow the tree by successively splitting the data until a tree is obtained which has zero, or nearly zero, training risk; the second stage is to prune the tree by finding a subtree of the tree grown in the first stage which minimizes the cost-complexity criterion,

$$\alpha \times \text{(number of leaf nodes)}$$

$$+ \sum_{\substack{\text{all leaf nodes } t}} \left(\min_{c=1,\ldots,C} \sum_{d=1}^{C} L(d, c)\widehat{P}(Y = d \mid X \in t) \right) \widehat{P}(X \in t).$$

Free, non-negative parameter α controls a penalty on the overall size of the tree: increasing α increases bias and decreases variance.

For simplicity, let us assume that all other aspects of tree-training described in Section 4.8 are fixed. The set of trees obtainable from any given set of training data, then, is a one-parameter family indexed by α, and searching for an approximately optimal tree corresponds to searching for an approximately optimal value of α. Intuitively, setting $\alpha = 0$ usually will result in a high-risk tree with very high variance and low bias. Increasing α from zero, we expect the risk of the tree which minimizes the cost-complexity criterion to decrease at first, then to reach some (not necessarily unique) minimum corresponding to the optimal bias–variance trade-off, and then to increase as the tree gets too much bias and too little variance. Eventually, for all α beyond some threshold, the tree which minimizes the cost-complexity criterion consists of only a single leaf node: this tree has high bias and low variance, and is usually high-risk.

An approximately optimal tree can be found in this way:[3]

(1) specify a finite set A of non-negative numbers to use as values of α;

(2) use the training data to compute, for each $\alpha \in A$, the tree $\widehat{f}_\alpha$ which minimizes the cost-complexity criterion;

(3) use the validation data to compute the validation estimate $\widehat{R}_{\text{valid}}(\widehat{f}_\alpha)$ of the risk of each tree $\widehat{f}_\alpha$;

(4) choose the tree $\widehat{f}_\alpha$ with minimal estimated risk $\widehat{R}_{\text{valid}}(\widehat{f}_\alpha)$.

The validation estimates of risk are *estimates*, so the criterion in step (4) is commonly replaced by

(4) choose the simplest tree $\widehat{f}_\alpha$ such that one cannot reject the hypothesis that it has minimal risk, of all trees considered.

Having found[4] an approximately optimal value $\widehat{\alpha}$ of α, the trained tree returned by this selection process is that corresponding to $\widehat{\alpha}$, trained either just on the training data or, so as not to waste data, on the training data and validation data combined. The test estimate of risk is then computed for this tree, if a test set has been created.

7.3   Cross-Validation

When data are not plentiful, an alternative to creating training and validation sets is *k-fold cross-validation*. In k-fold cross-validation, the data are partitioned randomly into k subsets of approximately equal size, $S = S_1 \cup \ldots \cup S_k$. Specifically, the k-fold cross-validation estimate of risk is the quantity $\widehat{R}_{\text{cv}}(\widehat{f})$ defined by the algorithm shown in Figure 7.1.

The expected value of the cross-validated risk estimate (taken with respect to the random partition π of S into k subsets *and* the distribution of the training data) is

$$E_{S,\pi}[\widehat{R}_{\text{cv}}(\widehat{f})] = \frac{1}{k} \sum_{i=1}^{k} E_{S,\pi}[\widehat{R}_i] \approx R(\widehat{f}_\star),$$

---

[3] Implementation of this procedure is given in detail in Section 14.15, using the R function rpart() and using cross-validation to estimate risk in step (3) rather than a separate validation set.

[4] Using, for example, one of the optimization algorithms of Chapter 10.

---

(1) for $i = 1, \ldots, k$

    (2) train predictor $\widehat{f}_i$ on data $S \setminus S_i$.

    (3) estimate the risk of $\widehat{f}_i$ using S_i as a validation set,

$$\widehat{R}_i = \frac{1}{|S_i|} \sum_{(x,y) \in S_i} L(y, \widehat{f}_i(x)) .$$

(4) estimate the risk of $\widehat{f}$ by the average of the individual risk estimates,

$$\widehat{R}_{cv}(\widehat{f}) = \frac{1}{k} \sum_{i=1}^{k} \widehat{R}_i .$$

Figure 7.1   An algorithm for k-fold cross-validation.

where $\widehat{f}_\star$ is the classifier trained on $\frac{k-1}{k} n$ data instead of n data. The variance is approximately

$$\text{Var}_{S,\pi}[\widehat{R}_{cv}(\widehat{f})] = \frac{1}{k^2} \left(\sum_{i=1}^{k} \text{Var}_{S,\pi}[\widehat{R}_i] + \sum_{\substack{i,j=1 \\ i \neq j}}^{k} \text{Cov}_{S,\pi}[\widehat{R}_i, \widehat{R}_j] \right)$$

$$\approx \left(\frac{1}{k} + \frac{k-1}{k} \text{Cor}_{S,\pi}[\widehat{R}_1, \widehat{R}_2] \right) \text{Var}_{S,\pi}[\widehat{R}_1]$$

The approximate equality is equality when all subsets S_i are exactly the same size. Considering S_1 as a validation set for f_1, of size approximately $\frac{n}{k}$, the result of Exercise 7.2 yields

$$\text{Var}_{S,\pi}[\widehat{R}_{cv}(\widehat{f})] \approx \left(\frac{1}{k} + \frac{k-1}{k} \text{Cor}_{S,\pi}[\widehat{R}_1, \widehat{R}_2] \right) \frac{1}{|S_1|} \left(E_{(X,Y)} \left[L(Y, \widehat{f}_1(X))^2 \right] - R(\widehat{f}_1)^2 \right)$$

$$\approx \left(\frac{1}{n} + \frac{k-1}{n} \text{Cor}_{S,\pi}[\widehat{R}_1, \widehat{R}_2] \right) \left(E_{(X,Y)} \left[L(Y, \widehat{f}_\star(X))^2 \right] - R(\widehat{f}_\star)^2 \right).$$

As shown above, the expected value of the cross-validated risk estimate, $\widehat{R}_{cv}(\widehat{f})$, is (approximately) the risk of approximating f using $\frac{k-1}{k} n$ training data. When k is small, $\frac{k-1}{k}$ is small and the expected value of $\widehat{R}_{cv}(\widehat{f})$ is the risk of training the approximation method on substantially fewer training data than are actually available. Since decreasing the amount of training data available to a given approximation method tends to produce higher-risk approximations,[5] $\widehat{R}_{cv}(\widehat{f})$ is generally biased toward over-estimating the risk of training $\widehat{f}$ on n data ($\widehat{R}_{cv}(\widehat{f})$ is a *pessimistic risk estimate*). When k is large (the extreme case, $k = n$, is called *leave-one-out cross-validation*), $\frac{k-1}{k}$ is close to one and so $\widehat{R}_{cv}(\widehat{f})$ is nearly unbiased. The correlation between pairs of risk estimates, for example $\widehat{R}_1$ and $\widehat{R}_2$, depends on k. When k is large, approximations $\widehat{f}_1$ and $\widehat{f}_2$ are trained on nearly the same data, and so $\widehat{R}_1$ and $\widehat{R}_2$ will in general be highly correlated: in the extreme case of leave-one-out cross-validation, the $(n-1)$-point datasets $S \setminus S_1$ and $S \setminus S_2$ used to train $\widehat{f}_1$ and $\widehat{f}_2$ have $n-2$ points in common. Thus when k is large, $\mathrm{Cor}[\widehat{R}_1, \widehat{R}_2]$ is relatively large. When k is small, approximations $\widehat{f}_1$ and $\widehat{f}_2$ are less correlated.

In computing the k-fold cross-validation estimate of risk, there is a bias–variance trade-off problem in choosing k. When k is small, the estimate has relatively high bias and low variance, and when k is large, it has relatively low bias but high variance. Both the bias and variance get smaller as n increases, but this is of not much help since, for large datasets, we would generally choose to estimate risk using a separate validation set. It seems that $k = 5$, $k = 10$, and $k = n$ are used most commonly in practice.[6]

7.4 Improvements on Cross-Validation

The inventor of the bootstrap proposed several ways to apply bootstrapping to risk estimation (Efron, 1983, 1986; Efron and Tibshirani, 1997). The general idea of these methods is to construct bootstrap samples of the training data, train a model on each bootstrap sample and apply the trained model to data not in the bootstrap sample on which it was trained, and average the resulting risk estimates (bootstrap samples are discussed in Section 6.3). In the words of Efron and Tibshirani (1997), "the bootstrap procedures are nothing more than smoothed versions of cross-validation, with some adjustments to correct for bias." The best of these, as determined by simulation studies in Efron and Tibshirani (1997), is the *.632+ bootstrap risk estimate*, which is computed as follows (the notation follows Efron and Tibshirani (1997)).

First, construct B independent bootstrap samples from the training data: Efron and Tibshirani (1997) recommend $B = 50$ samples and also discusses criteria for choosing B. Train a model $\widehat{f}_b$ on the bth bootstrap sample for $b \in \{1, \dots, B\}$. For $i \in \{1, \dots, n\}$, let $\mathcal{B}_i$ be the set of indices of bootstrap samples which do not contain training datum

---

(x_i, y_i), and let E_i be the average (over $b \in B_i$) loss incurred when using $\widehat{f}_b(x_i)$ in place of y_i:

$$
E_i = \begin{cases} 0 & \text{if } B_i = \emptyset \text{ (that is, if } (x_i, y_i) \text{ is in every} \\ & \text{bootstrap sample)} \\ |B_i|^{-1} \sum_{b \in B_i} L(y_i, \widehat{f}_b(x_i)) & \text{otherwise} \end{cases}
$$

Let the *leave-one-out bootstrap estimate of risk* be

$$
\widehat{\mathrm{Err}}^{(1)}(\widehat{f}) = \frac{1}{n} \sum_{i=1}^{n} E_i,
$$

the average loss incurred by predicting the class or response of a datum using bootstrap samples not containing the datum. Denote the training risk by $\widehat{R}_{\mathrm{train}}(\widehat{f})$ ($\widehat{f}$ with no subscript denotes a model trained on all of the training data, as usual). The *no-information risk* is the expected loss incurred, using $\widehat{f}$ to make predictions, when the input X and response or class label Y are independent, that is, when X is assumed to contain no information about Y, in the sense that the conditional distribution $P(Y \mid X)$ is the same as the marginal distribution $P(Y)$. The no-information risk is estimated by

$$
\widehat{\gamma}(\widehat{f}) = \frac{1}{n^2} \sum_{i=1}^{n} \sum_{j=1}^{n} L(y_i, \widehat{f}(x_j)),
$$

and it is a very pessimistic risk estimate indeed! Efron and Tibshirani define

$$
\widehat{\mathrm{Err}}^{(1)'}(\widehat{f}) = \min\left(\widehat{\mathrm{Err}}^{(1)}(\widehat{f}), \widehat{\gamma}(\widehat{f}) \right),
$$

which truncates the leave-one-out bootstrap risk estimate at the no-information risk estimate, and they define the *relative over-fitting rate* to be

$$
\widehat{R}' = \begin{cases} \dfrac{\widehat{\mathrm{Err}}^{(1)'}(\widehat{f}) - \widehat{R}_{\mathrm{train}}(\widehat{f})}{\widehat{\gamma}(\widehat{f}) - \widehat{R}_{\mathrm{train}}(\widehat{f})} & \text{if } \widehat{\mathrm{Err}}^{(1)'}(\widehat{f}) > \widehat{R}_{\mathrm{train}}(\widehat{f}) \\ & \text{(which implies } \widehat{\gamma}(\widehat{f}) > \widehat{R}_{\mathrm{train}}(\widehat{f})) \\ 0 & \text{otherwise} \end{cases}
$$

which takes values in $[0,1]$. The range in which any reasonable risk estimate must fall is taken to be the interval $[\widehat{R}_{\mathrm{train}}(\widehat{f}), \widehat{\gamma}(\widehat{f})]$, and $\widehat{R}'$ is the proportion of this range $\widehat{\mathrm{Err}}^{(1)'}(\widehat{f})$ covers, starting at optimism and moving in the direction of pessimism. If $\widehat{R}' = 1$, then $\widehat{\mathrm{Err}}^{(1)'}(\widehat{f}) \geq \widehat{\gamma}(\widehat{f}) > \widehat{R}_{\mathrm{train}}(\widehat{f})$, which means that the leave-one-out bootstrap estimate of risk is at least as pessimistic as the estimated no-information risk $\widehat{\gamma}(\widehat{f})$. If $\widehat{R}' = 0$, then the training estimate of risk is at least as pessimistic as the leave-one-out bootstrap estimate.

The *.632+ bootstrap risk estimate* is

$$\widehat{\text{Err}}^{(.632+)}(\hat{f}) = 0.368\,\widehat{R}_{\text{train}}(\hat{f}) + 0.632\,\widehat{\text{Err}}^{(1)'}(\hat{f})$$

$$+ \left(\widehat{\text{Err}}^{(1)'}(\hat{f}) - \widehat{R}_{\text{train}}(\hat{f}) \right) \underbrace{\frac{0.368 \times 0.632\,\widehat{R}'}{1 - 0.368\,\widehat{R}'}}_{\in[0,0.368]}.$$

Intuitively, the .632+ bootstrap risk estimate strikes a balance between an optimistic risk estimate (training risk) and one which tends to be pessimistic (the leave-one-out bootstrap estimate). The balance point is chosen based on how these two estimates disagree. The reader is directed to Efron (1983, 1986) and Efron and Tibshirani (1997) for discussion of bootstrap estimates of risk.

7.5 Out-of-Bag Risk Estimation

A classifier produced by bootstrap aggregation (bagging) of other base classifiers is called a *bagged classifier* (see Section 6.3). A random forest is a bagged classifier, for example. The risk of a bagged classifier can be estimated using the bootstrap samples already constructed in training.

Assuming that the bootstrap samples are of size n, each datum in a training set for a bagged classifier is used to train approximately proportion $1 - \frac{1}{e} \approx 0.632$ of the base classifiers. For these base classifiers, the datum is *in-bag* and for the remaining ones (which it is not used to train) it is *out-of-bag*: in the notation of Section 7.4, B_i indexes the bootstrap samples for which (x_i, y_i) is out-of-bag. The set of base classifiers for which a datum is out-of-bag, aggregated together into a committee classifier, is the *out-of-bag classifier* for that datum.

The *out-of-bag risk estimate* $\widehat{R}_{\text{oob}}(\hat{f})$ of a bagged classifier is

$$\widehat{R}_{\text{oob}}(\hat{f}) = \frac{1}{n} \sum_{i=1}^{n} L(y_i, \text{ most common class among } \{\hat{f}_b(x_i) : b \in B_i\}).$$

The out-of-bag risk estimate is generally biased high (Bylander, 2002) that is, $\widehat{R}_{\text{oob}}(\hat{f})$ tends to over estimate the risk of $\hat{f}$. At least in the case of random forests, experiments by the author indicate that the bias becomes small as the number of trees increases. The author has observed empirically that a simple estimate of the variance of $\widehat{R}_{\text{oob}}(\hat{f})$,

$$\frac{1}{n} \left(\frac{1}{n} \sum_{(d,c) \in C \times C} L(d,c)^2 N_{\text{oob}}(d,c) - \widehat{R}_{\text{oob}}(\hat{f})^2 \right)$$

where

$N_{\text{oob}}(d, c)$ = number of training data (x_i, d) such that the out-of-bag classifier
for x_i predicts c,

tends to be biased low.

7.6   Akaike's Information Criterion

In the case of parametric models which are trained by computing maximum likelihood estimates of parameters (for example, likelihood methods, logistic regression, and neural networks),

$$\widehat{\theta} = \text{argmax}_\theta P(y_1, \dots, y_n \mid x_1, \dots, x_n, \theta),$$

there is a computationally cheap method of choosing a model which has approximately minimal risk. This is by minimizing *Akaike's information criterion (AIC)*, which is

$$-2 \log P(y_1, \dots, y_n \mid x_1, \dots, x_n, \widehat{\theta}) + 2k,$$

where k is the number of coordinates in the parameter vector θ. Here and elsewhere, log is the natural logarithm. In literature and software, AIC is sometimes defined as the above expression multiplied by $\frac{1}{2}$, $-\frac{1}{2}$ or -1 (software users are advised to find out whether AIC is to maximized or minimized).

AIC decreases the better the model fits the observed data, and increases the more complex the model is, where complexity is measured by the number of parameters, k (that is, the number of coordinates in the parameter vector θ). Akaike derived his criterion by approximately minimizing risk with respect to squared-error loss in regression (Akaike, 1974). The term penalizing model complexity, $2k$, is derived from the expected improvement in $-2 \log P(Y \mid X, \theta)$ caused by including irrelevant parameters. Application of AIC has been extended to other contexts (Sakamoto et al., 1986).

Shortly after cross-validation and AIC were both developed, Stone showed that in the case of parametric models which are trained by computing maximum likelihood estimates of parameters, cross-validation and AIC will choose the same model as the data size $n \to \infty$ (Stone, 1977).

7.7   Schwartz's Bayesian Information Criterion

The *Bayesian information criterion (BIC)* is applicable in the same setting as AIC, and has a similar form: choose a model to minimize

$$-2 \log P(y_1, \dots, y_n \mid x_1, \dots, x_n, \widehat{\theta}) + k \log n.$$

Like AIC, BIC decreases the better the model fits the observed data, and increases the more complex the model is, where complexity is measured by the number of parameters, k. In literature and software, BIC is sometimes defined as the above expression multiplied by $\frac{1}{2}$, $-\frac{1}{2}$ or -1.

The idea behind BIC is this. Suppose there are L models under consideration, $M_1, \dots, M_L$, and that model M_i has a vector parameter θ_i of dimension k_i, and let

$P(M_i)$ and $P(\theta_i \mid M_i)$ denote prior distributions on the set of models and on the parameter space Θ_i of the ith model, respectively. Given data, $(x_1, y_1), \ldots, (x_n, y_n)$, the posterior probability of the ith model is

$$P(M_i \mid y_1, \ldots, y_n, x_1, \ldots, x_n) \propto P(M_i) \int_{\Theta_i} P(y_1, \ldots, y_n \mid x_1, \ldots, x_n, \theta_i, M_i) \, P(\theta_i \mid M_i) \, d\theta_i,$$

where the constant of proportionality, $P(y_1, \ldots, y_n)^{-1}$, is the same for all models. In Schwartz (1978), Schwartz proves that, under mild regularity conditions on the priors $P(\theta_i \mid M_i)$ and the likelihoods $P(y_1, \ldots, y_n \mid x_1, \ldots, x_n, \theta_i, M_i)$, the logarithm of the integral above is

$$\log P(y_1, \ldots, y_n \mid x_1, \ldots, x_n, \widehat{\theta}_i, M_i) - \frac{k_i}{2} \log n + (\text{a term bounded in } n),$$

where $\widehat{\theta}_i$ is the maximum likelihood estimate for θ_i. Thus, as $n \to \infty$, choosing the model with smallest BIC is equivalent to choosing the model with largest posterior probability.

Since selecting a model with maximal BIC is selecting a model with (approximately) maximal posterior probability, *BIC is a criterion for selecting a good explanatory model rather than a good predictive model.* BIC places a heavier penalty on the number of parameters than does AIC (provided models are trained on at least eight data points), so BIC chooses models no more complex, and usually simpler, than those chosen by AIC.

7.8   Rissanen's Minimum Description Length Criterion

The *minimum description length (MDL) criterion* is applicable more generally than AIC or BIC. The MDL criterion is to choose the model which minimizes

$$-\log_2 P(y_1, \ldots, y_n \mid x_1, \ldots, x_n, \theta) + \log_2^\star \left((\theta^T H \theta)^{\frac{k}{2}} \frac{\pi^{\frac{k}{2}}}{\Gamma\left(\frac{k}{2} + 1\right)} \right),$$

where $\log_2$ is the base-2 logarithm and θ is a k-long parameter vector. In the second term,

$$H = \left[\frac{\partial^2}{\partial \theta_i \partial \theta_j} - \log_2 P(y_1, \ldots, y_n \mid x_1, \ldots, x_n, \theta) \right]_{i,j=1}^{k}$$

is the Hessian of $-\log_2 P(y_1, \ldots, y_n \mid x_1, \ldots, x_n, \theta)$ as a function of θ, $\pi^{\frac{k}{2}}/\Gamma\left(\frac{k}{2} + 1\right)$ is the volume of a k-dimensional Euclidean unit ball, and for any positive number z,

$$\log_2^\star(z) = \log_2(z) + \log_2 \log_2(z) + \log_2 \log_2 \log_2(z) + \cdots$$

is a finite sum of all of the positive terms of the form $\log_2 \cdots \log_2(z)$. Note that the MDL criterion applies to selection of a value of parameter θ as well as model complexity k, unlike AIC and BIC, where θ is estimated by maximum likelihood.

The idea behind the MDL criterion is that the best model is one which simultaneously encodes the data efficiently while being itself efficient to encode. The first term in the MDL criterion, $-\log_2(P(y_1, \ldots, y_n \mid x_1, \ldots, x_n, \theta))$, is the number of bits required to represent the observed responses $y_1, \ldots, y_n$, given the model, parameter θ, and observed features $x_1, \ldots, x_n$. The second term in the MDL criterion, $\log_2^\star((\theta^T H \theta)^{\frac{k}{2}} \pi^{\frac{k}{2}} / \Gamma(\frac{k}{2} + 1))$, is the number of bits required to represent the model in an approximately optimal encoding of models constructed in Rissanen (1978). Like AIC and BIC, the MDL criterion decreases the better the model fits the observed data, and increases the more complex the model is, although in MDL, the complexity of a model is measured in the information-theoretic sense just described.

The MDL criterion is a practical criterion which builds on the idea of *Kolmogorov complexity*, which defines the complexity of a dataset to be the length of the shortest program which would cause a universal Turing machine to produce the dataset as output[7] (Cover and Thomas, 2006; Kolmogorov, 1968; Rissanen, 1978; Solomonoff, 1964a, 1964b). Since selecting a model with optimal MDL criterion is selecting a model which (approximately) provides the simplest representation of the data in an information-theoretic sense, *the MDL criterion is, like BIC, a criterion for selecting a good explanatory model rather than a good predictive model.*

7.9 R^2 and Adjusted R^2

In the standard regression setting with squared-error loss, training error times n is called the *residual sum of squares* (RSS) of a model,

$$\text{RSS} = \sum_{i=1}^{n} (y_i - \widehat{f}(x_i))^2 = \widehat{R}_{\text{train}}(\widehat{f}).$$

See Section 3.4. RSS is interpreted as the variability in the observed response *not* explained by the trained model $\widehat{f}$. The *total sum of squares* (TSS) is

$$\text{TSS} = \sum_{i=1}^{n} (y_i - \bar{y})^2 = \widehat{R}_{\text{train}}(\text{constant model } \widehat{f}(x) = \bar{y}),$$

where $\bar{y} = n^{-1} \sum_{i=1}^{n} y_i$ is the mean response in the data: it measures the overall variability in the observed response. RSS can be no more than TSS (under very mild

---

[7] Kolmogorov complexity is a literal, information-theoretic expression of the idea that the simplest explanation of a dataset is the best explanation (see Occam's Razor, Section 7.11). Also known as *Solomonoff complexity*, this measure of complexity is *non-computable* in the formal sense that there is no Turing machine which will input any set and output the set's complexity.

model assumptions) and the trained model predicts the observed response perfectly if and only if RSS $= 0$. The *model sum of squares* is

$$\text{MSS} = \sum_{i=1}^{n}(\hat{y}_i - \bar{y})^2.$$

The model sum of squares measures the overall variability of the fitted values about the mean observed response.

A commonly used measure of fit in regression is

$$R^2 = 1 - \frac{\text{RSS}}{\text{TSS}} = \frac{\text{MSS}}{\text{TSS}}.$$

It is interpreted as *the proportion of the variation in the response which is explained by the model.* When R^2 is close to 1, the model explains most of the variation in the data, and when R^2 is close to 0, the model explains very little. As stated in Exercise 3.6, R^2 is the square of the sample correlation between the vector of observed responses $(y_1, \dots, y_n)$ and the vector of fitted responses $(\hat{y}_1, \dots, \hat{y}_n)$.

As models become more complex, R^2 tends to increase (in fact, cannot decrease if the models are nested—see Exercise 7.1). After all, RSS is a decreasing function of the training error. This is compensated for in *adjusted R^2*,

$$R_{\text{adj}}^2 = 1 - \frac{n-1}{n-k}\frac{\text{RSS}}{\text{TSS}},$$

which penalizes model complexity (the number of parameters, k).[8] Note that when $k = m + 1$,

$$R_{\text{adj}}^2 = 1 - \frac{\frac{\text{RSS}}{n-m-1}}{\frac{\text{TSS}}{n-1}}$$

and, as seen in Chapter 3, $\frac{\text{TSS}}{n-1}$ is an unbiased estimate of $\text{Var}[Y]$ while $\frac{\text{RSS}}{n-m-1}$ is an unbiased estimate of $\text{Var}[E]$. The goal is to choose a model for which R_{adj}^2 is relatively large, ideally close to 1.

7.10 Stepwise Model Selection

Let $\{1, \dots, m\}$ index the set of all available features, let I denote a subset of this index set, and let $\hat{f}_I$ denote a classifier trained on the training data using exactly the features indexed by I (note that if I is empty then $\hat{f}_I$ predicts all data to be of the same

---

[8] In linear regression, it is customary to count the intercept parameter separately from the other parameters, since the usual model assumption is $f(x) = (1, x_1, \dots, x_m) \cdot (\theta_0, \theta_1, \dots, \theta_m)$. A linear regression model with m features has $k = m + 1$ parameters.

(1) initialize index set I somehow (for example, set $I = \emptyset$ or $I = \{1, \ldots, m\}$) and estimate $\mathrm{R}(\widehat{f}_I)$

(2) repeat until I does not change {

    (3) for each $i \in I$, let $J = I \setminus \{i\}$, train $\widehat{f}_J$ on J, and estimate $\mathrm{R}(\widehat{f}_J)$

    (4) for each $i \in \{1, \ldots, m\} \setminus I$, let $J = I \cup \{i\}$, train $\widehat{f}_J$ on J, and estimate $\mathrm{R}(\widehat{f}_J)$

    (5) replace I with $\operatorname{argmin}_{K \in \{I\} \cup \{\text{all } m \text{ subsets } J \atop \text{constructed in steps (2) and (3)}\}} \mathrm{R}(\widehat{f}_K)$

}

Figure 7.2   An algorithm for stepwise model selection.

class). *Stepwise model selection*, generically, refers to any kind of discrete optimization algorithm used to search the subsets of $\{1, \ldots, m\}$ to find a subset I for which the estimated risk of $\widehat{f}_I$ is minimal.[9] It also refers to the specific algorithm shown in Figure 7.2, which is a discrete form of gradient descent (see Section 10.1).

7.11 Occam's Razor

Occam's Razor is a principle which says (in the context of statistical models) that, given a set of statistical models, we ought to choose the simplest one which has sufficiently low risk, or the simplest one for which there is no more complex model with significantly lower risk. This principle is followed when simplicity of a model is considered a virtue. Reasons for preferring a simple model include:

- a simple model is easier to understand than a complex one and therefore is more likely to lead to insights about the data and to be understood—hence believed (Jeffreys, 1931) and applied—by those not involved with its construction;

- a simple model may be computationally less burdensome than a complex one, particularly when the complex model requires expensive-to-acquire features which are not used by the simple model.

However, *simple models do not necessarily make better predictions than complex ones*. To return to the quote at the start of the chapter, "aesthetics and statistical accuracy might not be the same thing."

---

[9] Typically, we can only hope to find local minima, although branch-and-bound algorithms for finding global minima have been proposed (Furnival and Wilson, 1974).

8

Consistency

> When you have data, you analyze the data. When you don't have data,
> you prove theorems.

By this point, the mathematically sophisticated reader may, upon consideration of all of the classification and regression methods presented in Chapters 3, 4, and 6, throw up his or her hands in frustration due to the feeling that such a wide array of different methods is a sign not of knowledge and understanding, but of ignorance. "Surely," such a reader might say, "there ought to be *one* method that solves all classification problems optimally, at least as the number of data, n, increases without bound?"

This short chapter answers that question in the affirmative, introducing the reader to a property of classification methods known as consistency. A classification method is *consistent* for a given classification problem if the risk of the trained classifier(s) it produces converges to the risk of the Bayes classifier for that problem as $n \to \infty$ (for some appropriate definition of convergence). A classification method is *universally consistent* if it is consistent with respect to all joint distributions $P(X, Y)$ on a given domain and range, $\mathcal{X} \times f(\mathcal{X})$.

The main results presented in this chapter are: there are classification methods which are known to be universally consistent; there is at least one classification method (random forests) which is widely used in practice and which is known to be not universally consistent; and (in the author's opinion) the behavior of a classification method on an arbitrary problem as $n \to \infty$ does not provide much useful insight about how to solve any particular applied problem. That said, the application-minded reader may skip this chapter without harm. The theory-minded reader can

Machine Learning: a Concise Introduction, First Edition. Steven W. Knox.
© This publication is a US Government work and is in the public domain.
Published 2018 by John Wiley & Sons, Inc.
Companion Website: http://www.wiley.com/go/Knox/MachineLearning

find proofs and other details, omitted in what follows, in Devroye et al. (1996), Biau et al. (2008), and Biau and Devroye (2010).

8.1   Convergence of Sequences of Random Variables

Let $Z_1, Z_2, \ldots$ denote an infinite sequence of real-valued random vectors, and let Z denote another real-valued random vector. The sequence $Z_1, Z_2, \ldots$ *converges in probability* to Z if, for any $\epsilon > 0$,

$$\lim_{n \to \infty} P(\|Z_n - Z\| > \epsilon) = 0.$$

Convergence in probability is denoted $Z_n \overset{P}{\to} Z$. The sequence $Z_1, Z_2, \ldots$ *converges almost surely* to Z (or *converges strongly* to Z, or *converges with probability 1* to Z) if

$$P\left(\lim_{n \to \infty} Z_n = Z\right) = 1.$$

Almost sure convergence is denoted $Z_n \overset{a.s.}{\to} Z$.[1]

8.2   Consistency for Parameter Estimation

Let z be a fixed but unknown quantity, and let $Z_1, Z_2, \ldots$ be a sequence of random variables which serve as estimates of z. The sequence of estimates $Z_1, Z_2, \ldots$ is *consistent for z* (respectively *strongly consistent for z*) if $Z_1, Z_2, \ldots$ converges in probability to z (respectively converges strongly to z).[2]

For example, consider the case that z is the mean of some distribution, that an unlimited sequence of data $W_1, W_2, \ldots$ are drawn independently from this distribution, and that, for each n, Z_n is the sample mean of the first n data, $Z_n = \frac{1}{n} \sum_{i=1}^{n} W_i$. In this case, the sequence $Z_1, Z_2, \ldots$ is both consistent and strongly consistent for z—these two facts are respectively known as the *weak law of large numbers* and the *strong law of large numbers*.[3]

---

[1] We shall not need it in what follows, but for completeness: the sequence $Z_1, Z_2, \ldots$ *converges in distribution* to Z (or *converges weakly* to Z) if the cumulative distribution function F_Z of Z is the pointwise limit of the cumulative distribution function F_{Z_n} of Z_n,

$$\lim_{n \to \infty} F_{Z_n}(x) = F_Z(x),$$

for all $x \in \mathbb{R}^m$ at which $F_Z(x)$ is continuous. Convergence in distribution is denoted $Z_n \rightsquigarrow Z$. If $Z_n \overset{P}{\to} Z$ then $Z_n \rightsquigarrow Z$.

[2] When discussing convergence, we do not distinguish between the constant z and the random variable which takes the value z with probability 1.

[3] Yes, the strong law is about strong convergence and the weak law is about convergence in probability, not weak convergence.

Under certain regularity conditions (see Ferguson (1996) or van der Vaart (2000)) maximum likelihood estimators of model parameters are both consistent and strongly consistent. In particular, in linear regression with independent, identically distributed Gaussian noise, the regression parameter estimate

$$\hat{\theta} = (\mathbf{x}^T\mathbf{x})^{-1}\mathbf{x}^T\mathbf{y},$$

obtained in Exercise 3.2 and Exercise 3.7 is strongly consistent for the true parameter θ when the data $(X_1, Y_1), (X_2, Y_2), \ldots$ are in fact generated by the linear model, that is, when $Y_i = (1, X_i)\theta + E_i$ where $E_1, E_2, \ldots$ are independent, identically distributed $N(0, \sigma^2)$.

8.3   Consistency for Prediction

Recall from Chapter 2 that an approximation method is a function which takes an observed dataset (of size n, say) as input and outputs an approximation of the true unknown function f which has produced class labels or continuous responses. The risk of an approximation method (trained on datasets of size n) is the expected loss incurred by drawing a random training set S of size n, constructing an approximation $\hat{f}_S$ of f from it and using $\hat{f}_S(X)$ in place of Y for new data (X, Y),

$$R_n = E_{(S,X,Y)}[L(Y, \hat{f}_S(X))] = E_S[E_{(X,Y)}[L(Y, \hat{f}_S(X))]] = E_S[R(\hat{f}_S)],$$

where $R(\hat{f}_S)$ is the risk of approximation $\hat{f}_S$. Recall from Section 4.1 that the Bayes risk is the minimum possible risk for any approximation method for data with a given joint distribution on (X, Y),

$$R_{Bayes} = E_X[\min_{c \in \{1,\ldots,C\}} E_{Y|X}[L(Y, c)]].$$

The Bayes risk is the risk of the Bayes classifier.

With respect to a given joint distribution $P(X, Y)$ *on* $\mathcal{X} \times f(\mathcal{X})$, as $n \to \infty$, a prediction method is a *consistent prediction method* (or a *weakly consistent prediction method*) if

$$R_n \to R_{Bayes}$$

(which implies $R(\hat{f}_S) \xrightarrow{P} R_{Bayes}$) and is a *strongly consistent prediction method* if

$$R(\hat{f}_S) \xrightarrow{a.s.} R_{Bayes}.$$

A prediction method is a *universally consistent prediction method* (respectively a *universally strongly consistent prediction method*) if it is consistent (respectively strongly consistent) with respect to all joint distributions on $\mathcal{X} \times f(\mathcal{X})$.

8.4   There Are Consistent and Universally Consistent Classifiers

Much is known about consistency and universal consistency in general and for various specific classification methods. We summarize it here for *binary* classifiers, following closely the book Devroye et al. (1996) and also the papers Biau et al. (2008) and Biau and Devroye (2010).

The *diameter of a set* $R \in \mathbb{R}^m$ is the supremum of the Euclidean distance between any two points in R,

$$\mathrm{diam}R = \sup_{(r,s)\in R\times R} \|r - s\|.$$

Theorem 8.1 Consistency of Partitioning Classifiers. *Let features* $X \in \mathbb{R}^m$. *Let a binary classification method operate by partitioning* $\mathbb{R}^m$ *into disjoint regions and, given any point* $x \in \mathbb{R}^m$, *under 0–1 loss, predicting the majority class of the training data in the region* $R(x)$ *containing* x *(with ties broken in a fixed but arbitrary way). The classification method is consistent for* $P(X, Y)$ *if, as* $n \to \infty$,

$$\mathrm{diam}R(X) \overset{P}{\to} 0$$

and

$$\textit{the number of training data in } R(X) \overset{P}{\to} \infty.$$

Histogram classifiers (Section 4.4.5) and classification trees (Section 4.8) are examples of classifiers to which this theorem applies.

A *cubic histogram* classifier is one which partitions $\mathbb{R}^m$ into cubes of side length h and, given any point $x \in \mathbb{R}^m$, predicts the majority class of the training data in cube $R(x)$ containing x, breaking ties in a fixed but arbitrary way. In the next theorem, which follows from Theorem 8.1, the bandwidth (side length) $h = h(n)$ is a function of the number n of training data.

Theorem 8.2 Universal Consistency of the Cubic Histogram Classifier. *The cubic histogram classifier is universally consistent if, as* $n \to \infty$, $h(n) \to 0$ *and* $n\,h(n)^m \to \infty$.

A *weighted average classifier* assigns a weight $w(x, x_i)$ to any point $x \in \mathbb{R}^m$ and any training point x_i, $i = 1, \dots, n$. At a point $x \in \mathbb{R}^m$, it predicts the class c such that the sum of the weights of that class is maximal, that is, it predicts

$$\mathrm{argmax}_{c\in\{1,\dots,C\}} \sum_{\substack{i = 1 \\ y_i = c}}^{n} w(x, x_i).$$

For example, the k-nearest-neighbor classifier is a weighted average classifier where

$$w(x, x_i) = \begin{cases} 1 & \text{if } x_i \text{ is one of the } k \text{ nearest training points to } x \\ 0 & \textit{else} \end{cases}.$$

Theorem 8.3 Consistency of the Weighted-Average Classifier (Stone). *Under the following three conditions on the distribution of* X *and weights* $w(X, x_i)$, $i = 1, \dots, n$, *the weighted-average classifier is consistent:*

(1) there is a constant α such that for every measurable[4] function g,

$$E[g(X)] < \infty \qquad \text{implies} \qquad E\left[\sum_{i=1}^{n} w(X, x_i) f(x_i)\right] < \alpha E[g(X)],$$

(2) for all ε > 0,

$$\lim_{n \to \infty} E\left[\sum_{i=1}^{n} w(X, x_i)[\|X - x_i\| > \epsilon]\right] = 0,$$

(3)
$$\lim_{n \to \infty} E\left[\max_{i=1,\ldots,n} w(X, x_i)\right] = 0.$$

Theorem 8.3 implies universal consistency of the k-nearest-neighbor classifier under certain conditions.

Theorem 8.4 Universal Consistency of the k-Nearest-Neighbor Classifier (Stone). *The k-nearest-neighbor classifier is universally consistent if, as $n \to \infty$, $k \to \infty$ and $\frac{k}{n} \to 0$.*

Likelihood methods based on parametric models are consistent, provided that the model assumption is correct and a consistent estimator of the model parameters is used.

Theorem 8.5 Consistency of Parametric Likelihood Classifiers with Plug-in Parameter Estimates. *Let $P(Y \mid X) = P(Y \mid X, \theta)$ be a continuous function of a feature vector X and a parameter vector θ. If $P(Y \mid X, \theta)$ is a continuous function of X and $\widehat{\theta}_n \overset{P}{\to} \theta$, then the likelihood classifier constructed from $P(Y \mid X, \widehat{\theta})$ is consistent.*

Some classifiers are known to be *not* universally consistent. For example, if k remains bounded away from ∞ or if $\frac{k}{n}$ remains bounded away from 0 as $n \to \infty$ then the k-nearest-neighbor classifier is not universally consistent (Devroye et al., 1996, Exercise 11.1). Random forests are also known to be not universally consistent, although there are bagged classifiers which are universally consistent Biau et al. (2008).

8.5 Convergence to Asymptopia Is Not Uniform and May Be Slow

The following two theorems should modulate any sense of euphoria caused by the preceding section. The first says that for every classification method and every

---

[4] This book has been written so that readers with and without a background in measure theory may benefit equally. This is a technical condition needed for the proof of the theorem, and the non-measure-theoretic reader may safely skip it without loss of appreciation of what is being developed here.

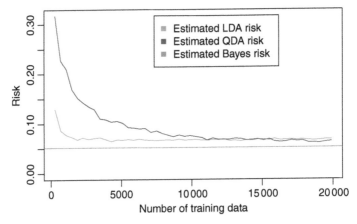

Figure 8.1   The risk of QDA and LDA binary classifiers, as functions of the size of the training data. The data were generated by drawing data of class 1 from one 100-dimensional Gaussian distribution and the data of class 2 from another with different mean and covariance. QDA is consistent for this problem and LDA is not.

data size, there is some joint distribution such that we are still arbitrarily far from Asymptopia. The second says that there is some joint distribution such that the approach to Asymptopia is arbitrarily slow.

Theorem 8.6 Every Method Fails Badly on Some Easy Problem (Devroye).
Under 0–1 loss, for any $\epsilon > 0$, any integer n and any binary classification method, there is a joint distribution on (X, Y) with Bayes risk 0 such that the risk of the method satisfies $R_n > \frac{1}{2} - \epsilon$.

Theorem 8.7 Convergence to Bayes Risk Can Be Arbitrarily Slow (Devroye). *Let $\frac{1}{16} \geq a_1 \geq a_2 \geq \ldots$ be any sequence of positive numbers converging to zero. Under 0–1 loss, for any sequence of binary classification methods applied to n training data, there is a joint distribution on (X, Y) with Bayes risk 0 such that the risk of the nth method satisfies $R_n > a_n$.*

Selecting a consistent classification method may not lead to a good classifier trained on limited data. Figure 8.1 shows QDA and LDA classifiers for a binary classification problem where QDA is the correct model (that is, the data of each class are drawn from a Gaussian, and the Gaussians have different covariance matrices). QDA is a consistent classifier in this case (Devroye et al., 1996, Theorem 16.1) and LDA is not, but LDA has the lower risk when the two are trained on fewer than 10,000 points. What is happening in Figure 8.1 is that QDA has higher variance and lower bias than LDA. The variance of QDA is reduced as the number of training data increase, but LDA wins the bias–variance trade-off for small data sizes.[5]

---

[5] The author is grateful to Mark Jacobson for this example.

9

Clustering

Do not assume that "clustering" methods are the best way to discover interesting groupings in the data; in our experience the visualization methods are often far more effective. There are many different clustering methods, often giving different answers, and so the danger of over-interpretation is high.

—W. N. Venables and B. D. Ripley, *Modern Applied Statistics with S-PLUS, Third Edition*, 2001

As described in Chapter 2, the goal of clustering is to learn an unknown, discrete-valued function f without observing its outputs. Since no observed outputs of f are available, no loss function which compares a predicted output to an observed output can be computed. As a result, clustering tends to be driven by algorithms and heuristics rather than by trying to minimize a meaningful measure of risk as is done in classification.

The clustering algorithms presented in this chapter naturally fall into two groups. Algorithms which are applicable when the observed data $x_1, \ldots, x_n$ are in $\mathbb{R}^m$ (for example, Gaussian mixture models, k-means, and mode-hunting in a density estimate) are presented first, and algorithms which are applicable more generally (for example, k-medoids and hierarchical methods) are presented later. Some clustering algorithms partition the data $x_1, \ldots, x_n$ into k distinct clusters—that is, they perform a *k-clustering* of the data—where k is a user-specified parameter of the algorithm. Other clustering algorithms perform k-clusterings for a range of k's, or for all $k = 1, \ldots, n$. Section 9.9 discusses methods for determining how many clusters are in a given dataset.

Machine Learning: a Concise Introduction, First Edition. Steven W. Knox.
© This publication is a US Government work and is in the public domain.
Published 2018 by John Wiley & Sons, Inc.
Companion Website: http://www.wiley.com/go/Knox/MachineLearning

9.1   Gaussian Mixture Models

Suppose that the data $x_1, \ldots, x_n$ are drawn from a Gaussian mixture model. That is, suppose the data are drawn from a distribution which has a density function $P(x)$ of the form

$$P(x) = \sum_{j=1}^{J} w_j \phi(x \mid \mu_j, \Sigma_j),$$

where $\phi(x \mid \mu, \Sigma)$ denotes a Gaussian density function with mean μ and covariance matrix Σ, $w_1, \ldots w_J$ are non-negative weights with $w_1 + \cdots + w_J = 1$, and $J > 0$ is the number of clusters presumed to be in the data. Gaussian mixture models are discussed in Section 4.4.3 in the context of likelihood-based classifiers. Fitting Gaussian mixture models (that is, estimating parameters $\mu_1, \ldots, \mu_J, \Sigma_1, \ldots, \Sigma_J, w_1, \ldots, w_J$ for a given value of J) is done by the expectation-maximization algorithm described in Section 10.7. Methods for selecting such models (that is, selecting J) are described in several sections of Chapter 7: see in particular the Bayesian Information Criterion (BIC) in Section 7.7.

A fitted Gaussian mixture model provides a "soft" or "fuzzy" clustering rule, expressed in terms of the *responsibility* γ_{ij} of mixture component j for datum x_i,

$$\gamma_{ij} = \frac{\widehat{w}_j \phi(x_i \mid \widehat{\mu}_j, \widehat{\Sigma}_j)}{\sum_{k=1}^{J} \widehat{w}_k \phi(x_i \mid \widehat{\mu}_k, \widehat{\Sigma}_k)}.$$

The fitted means $\widehat{\mu}_1, \ldots, \widehat{\mu}_J$ are the *cluster centers*. Two advantages of clustering with a Gaussian mixture model are that it provides a measure of certainty regarding which data points are assigned to clusters, and it is an interpretable, statistical model. A disadvantage is that the expectation-maximization algorithm tends to converge slowly, particularly when m is large and the covariance matrices Σ_j are unconstrained. Using other distributions in place of the Gaussian distribution may be useful in some situations: for example, using Student's t can provide robustness to outliers.

9.2   *k*-Means

The *k-means algorithm* begins with an initial set of putative cluster centers, $\widehat{\mu}_1, \ldots, \widehat{\mu}_k$ (obtained, for example, by randomly sampling the data $x_1, \ldots, x_n$ without replacement k times). The k-means algorithm then iterates the two steps shown in Figure 9.1. The algorithm terminates when the cluster assignments do not change between iterations.

The k-means algorithm approximates fitting a Gaussian mixture model, giving up the flexibility of the mixture model (soft cluster assignment and variable covariance matrices) in exchange for speed. Step (1) shown in Figure 9.1 is an approximation of the expectation-step in the expectation-maximization algorithm, and step (2) is

(1) Given a set of putative cluster centers $\widehat{\mu}_1, \ldots, \widehat{\mu}_k$, assign each datum to the cluster which has the nearest center: for $i = 1, \ldots, n$, datum x_i is assigned to cluster $\mathrm{argmin}_{j=1,\ldots,k} \| x_i - \widehat{\mu}_j \|$.

(2) Set the center of each cluster to be the mean of the data in the cluster: for $j = 1, \ldots, k$,

$$\widehat{\mu}_j = \frac{1}{\text{number of data in cluster } j} \sum_{x_i \in \text{ cluster } j} x_i.$$

Figure 9.1   The k-means clustering algorithm iterates two steps.

an approximation of the maximization-step (see Section 10.7). Geometrically, using the mean in step (2) implicitly ties the k-means algorithm to (squared) Euclidean distance. This is because the sample mean of a set of data S in $\mathbb{R}^m$ is the point z which minimizes the sum of squared deviations between z and every point in S. Thus step (2) is equivalent to

$$\widehat{\mu}_j = \mathrm{argmin}_{z \in \mathbb{R}^m} \sum_{x_i \in \text{ cluster } j} \| x_i - z \|^2.$$

9.3   Clustering by Mode-Hunting in a Density Estimate

Clustering data $x_1, \ldots, x_n$ can be identified with the problem of finding modes (local maxima) in the density function $P(x)$ of the unknown probability distribution on $\mathcal{X}$ from which the data were drawn (when taking this approach, the density function is assumed to exist). The density function $P(x)$ can be estimated in a variety of ways, either through parametric methods, such as Gaussian mixture models, or non-parametric methods, such as kernel density estimation: a variety of methods are described in Section 4.4 in the context of likelihood methods for classification. Modes in a density estimate $\widehat{P}(x)$ can be found by applying a numerical optimization algorithm from many starting points, and keeping track of the local maxima at which the algorithm terminates. An algorithm for clustering by mode-hunting in a density estimate is shown in Figure 9.2.

Clustering by mode-hunting can be sensitive to parameters of the optimization algorithm used, and it can also be expensive. Note that for the purpose of clustering, the propensity of an optimization algorithm to terminate in a local, rather than a global, optimum is a desirable feature: this affects the choice of optimizer and its parameters. Computational cost can be reduced by terminating the optimization algorithm early, combined with relaxing the criterion "distinct" in step (3).

(1) Given a set of data, $x_1, \ldots, x_n$, construct a density estimate $\widehat{P}(x)$.
(2) For $i = 1, \ldots, n$, apply a numerical optimization algorithm, initialized at x_i, to find an approximate local maximum m_i of $\widehat{P}(x)$.
(3) Let $\mu_1, \ldots, \mu_k$ be the distinct values in the set $\{m_1, \ldots, m_n\}$.
(4) For $j = 1, \ldots, k$, define cluster S_j as

$$S_j = \{x_i : \text{the optimizer starting at } x_i \text{ climbs to } \mu_j\},$$

and identify μ_j as the center of cluster S_j.

Figure 9.2   A generic mode-hunting clustering algorithm.

9.4   Using Classifiers to Cluster

"If you can classify, you can cluster"—or so one hears, occasionally. One way to interpret this statement is the following trick for using a binary classifier to construct a density estimate, which can then be used for clustering as in Section 9.3. Let data $x_1, \ldots, x_n$ be given, and let this unlabeled data all be labeled as class 1. Our goal is to estimate the density function for the distribution from which the data were drawn: we write this density function as $P(x \mid Y = 1)$.

The trick is to synthesize data $x_{n+1}, \ldots, x_{n+n^\star}$, which will all be labeled class 2, by drawing it randomly from a probability distribution with *known* density function $P(x \mid Y = 2)$. A binary classification algorithm is trained on the marked data

$$(x_1, 1), \ldots, (x_n, 1), (x_{n+1}, 2), \ldots, (x_{n+n^\star}, 2)$$

to produce an estimate of the posterior distribution of each class,[1]

$$(\widehat{P}(Y = 1 \mid X = x), \widehat{P}(Y = 2 \mid X = x))$$

which can be evaluated at any point $x \in \mathcal{X}$. Since

$$P(Y = 1 \mid X = x) = \frac{P(x \mid Y = 1) \, P(Y = 1)}{P(x)}$$

$$= \frac{P(x \mid Y = 1) P(Y = 1)}{P(x \mid Y = 1) P(Y = 1) + P(x \mid Y = 2) P(Y = 2)},$$

solving for $P(x \mid Y = 1)$ yields

$$P(x \mid Y = 1) = P(x \mid Y = 2) \frac{P(Y = 1 \mid X = x)}{P(Y = 2 \mid X = x)} \frac{P(Y = 2)}{P(Y = 1)}.$$

---

[1] Not every classifier estimates these class probabilities explicitly. For this purpose, it is necessary to use one that does.

The density for data of class 2 is known, the conditional probabilities of the class labels are estimated by the trained classifier, and the ratio of marginal probabilities of the class labels is $\frac{n^\star}{n}$ by construction. This produces the density estimate

$$\widehat{P}(x \mid Y = 1) = P(x \mid Y = 2) \frac{\widehat{P}(Y = 1 \mid X = x)}{\widehat{P}(Y = 2 \mid X = x)} \frac{n^\star}{n}.$$

9.5 Dissimilarity

Clustering requires an idea of something like distance between data. This often takes the form of a *dissimilarity measure*, which is a function $d : \mathcal{X} \times \mathcal{X} \to \mathbb{R}^+$ such that $d(x, x) = 0$ for all $x \in \mathcal{X}$ and $d(w, x) = d(x, w)$ for all $w, x \in \mathcal{X}$. For a particular dataset, the *dissimilarity matrix* is

$$[\, d(x_i, x_j)]_{i,j=1}^n,$$

an $n \times n$ symmetric matrix with zeros on the diagonal. Ideally the dissimilarity function will reflect something meaningful about the data, but it is often chosen for convenience. Common convenience choices of dissimilarity when $\mathcal{X} = \mathbb{R}^m$ are Euclidean and Manhattan distance on suitably scaled and transformed data—see Exercise 11.8.

Dissimilarity of data can be extended to dissimilarity of sets of data in a variety of ways. Three popular ways of measuring the dissimilarity of two subsets, S_1 and S_2, are:

single linkage	$d(S_1, S_2) = \min_{(x,y) \in S_1 \times S_2} d(x, y)$
complete linkage	$d(S_1, S_2) = \max_{(x,y) \in S_1 \times S_2} d(x, y)$
average linkage	$d(S_1, S_2) = \dfrac{1}{|S_1||S_2|} \displaystyle\sum_{(x,y) \in S_1 \times S_2} d(x, y)$

Some clustering algorithms, such as the hierarchical algorithms in Sections 9.7 and 9.8, make use of dissimilarity of clusters.

9.6 *k*-Medoids

The *k-medoids algorithm* is a generalization of *k*-means to an arbitrary dissimilarity function. It requires that the cluster centers be observed data. As in *k*-means, the *k*-medoids algorithm begins with an initial set of putative cluster centers, $\widehat{\mu}_1, \ldots, \widehat{\mu}_k$ (obtained, for example, by randomly sampling the data $x_1, \ldots, x_n$ without replacement k times). It then iterates the two steps shown in Figure 9.3. The algorithm terminates when the cluster assignments do not change between iterations.

---

(1) Given a set of putative cluster centers $\widehat{\mu}_1, \ldots, \widehat{\mu}_k$, assign each datum to the cluster which has the most similar center: for $i = 1, \ldots, n$, datum x_i is assigned to cluster $\operatorname{argmin}_{j=1,\ldots,k} d(x_i, \widehat{\mu}_j)$.

(2) Set the center of each cluster to be the datum it contains which minimizes the sum of dissimilarities to all other data in the cluster: for $j = 1, \ldots, k$,

$$\widehat{\mu}_j = \operatorname{argmin}_{x_i \in \text{ cluster } j} \sum_{w \in \text{ cluster } j} d(x_i, w) .$$

Figure 9.3   The k-medoids clustering algorithm iterates two steps.

The cluster centers found in step (2) are the *medoids* of the clusters. Generally, clustering by k-medoids is more expensive than clustering by k-means because finding the argmin in step (2) is computationally more intensive than computing a sample mean.

9.7   Agglomerative Hierarchical Clustering

Agglomerative hierarchical clustering constructs a k-clustering of the data for all $k = 1, \ldots, n$. It produces a *hierarchical clustering* in the sense that, for any $k < k'$, every cluster in the k'-clustering is contained in a unique cluster in the k-clustering. Agglomerative hierarchical clustering begins by considering all n data to be clusters of size one. It iteratively computes the dissimilarity of all pairs of clusters and merges two minimally dissimilar clusters, terminating when there is only one cluster, as shown in Figure 9.4.

---

(1) Initialize the set of clusters to be $\{S_1, \ldots, S_n\}$ where, for $i = 1, \ldots, n$, the ith cluster is the ith datum, $S_i = \{x_i\}$.

(2) Compute the dissimilarity between all pairs of clusters, that is, compute $d(S_i, S_j)$ for all $i < j$.

(3) While there is more than one cluster in the set of clusters:

  (4) Merge a pair of clusters which have minimal dissimilarity. Given indices $i' < j'$ such that

$$d(S_{i'}, S_{j'}) = \min_{i<j} d(S_i, S_j) ,$$

  set $S_{i'} = S_{i'} \cup S_{j'}$ and remove $S_{j'}$ from the set of clusters.

  (5) Compute the dissimilarity between the new cluster $S_{i'}$ and all other clusters in the set of clusters.

Figure 9.4   A generic agglomerative clustering algorithm.

It is sometimes useful to think of clustering algorithms in terms of graph algorithms. Suppose the dissimilarity function is bounded by some maximum value, which by re-scaling we can assume to be 1. Let the *similarity function* $s(w, x)$ be defined by $s(w, x) = 1 - d(w, x)$ and define the *similarity graph* of the data $x_1, \ldots, x_n$ as follows: each datum is a vertex; an edge joins vertices x_i and x_j if and only if $s(x_i, x_j) > 0$; and an edge joining x_i and x_j has weight $s(x_i, x_j)$. Thinking of data-clustering in terms of operations in the similarity graph can suggest computational methods which are very efficient when the graph is sparse, that is, when the number of edges, e, is much less than the maximum possible number of edges, $\binom{n}{2}$. For example, most of the work in agglomerative hierarchical clustering, when using the single-linkage criterion to measure the dissimilarity between clusters, can be done by finding a minimal spanning tree of the similarity graph. Efficient algorithms[2] can find a minimal spanning tree in $O(e \log(e))$ time, which can be much less than the $O(n^2)$ time required by a naive approach to single-linkage agglomerative hierarchical clustering when the graph is sparse.

9.8 Divisive Hierarchical Clustering

Similar to agglomerative hierarchical clustering, *divisive hierarchical clustering* constructs a k-clustering of the data for all $k = 1, \ldots, n$ such that, for any $k < k'$, every cluster in the k'-clustering is contained in a unique cluster in the k-clustering. Divisive hierarchical clustering begins by considering all data to belong to a single cluster and then iteratively splits clusters until all clusters have size one. A specific divisive hierarchical clustering algorithm, the DIANA algorithm of Kaufman and Rousseeuw (1990), is shown in Figure 9.5.

9.9 How Many Clusters Are There? Interpretation of Clustering

Determination of how many clusters are "really" in a dataset is a statistical inference, so it should be addressed using statistical models for the data. One way to approach this is by fitting Gaussian mixture models with different numbers of mixture components and selecting a model with maximal probability in an appropriate sense, either using an asymptotic approximation such as selecting a model with maximal Bayesian Information Criterion as described in Section 7.7, or using an explicit, fully Bayesian procedure and sampling from a posterior distribution on the number of clusters via reversible-jump Markov chain Monte Carlo (Green, 1995).[3]

---

[2] Kruskal's or Prim's algorithms, for example (Cormen et al., 2009).

[3] Markov chain Monte Carlo methods in general, and reversible-jump MCMC in particular, are outside the scope of this book.

(1) Initialize the set of clusters to be $\{S\}$ where $S = \{x_1, \ldots, x_n\}$ is all of the data.

(2) While any cluster contains more than one data point:

    (3) Find a cluster S which contains maximally dissimilar data,

$$S = \text{argmax}_{\text{all clusters } T} \max_{(w,x) \in T \times T} d(w, x) .$$

    (4) Find a datum $w \in S$ which is maximally different from the rest of S, remove this datum from S, and create a new one-point cluster, S':

$$w = \text{argmax}_{x \in S} \, d(x, S \setminus \{x\}) ,$$

$$S' = \{w\} , \quad \text{and} \quad S = S \setminus \{w\} .$$

    (5) While S contains more than one datum and at least one $x \in S$ satisfies $d(x, S \setminus \{x\}) > d(x, S')$, move a datum from S to S':

$$w = \text{argmax}_{x \in S : d(x, S \setminus \{x\}) > d(x, S')} \, d(x, S \setminus \{x\}) - d(x, S') ,$$

$$S' = S' \cup \{w\} , \quad \text{and} \quad S = S \setminus \{w\} .$$

Figure 9.5   The DIANA divisive clustering algorithm.

An extension of a statistical inferential method to a heuristic applicable to clustering, due to Sugar and James (2003), estimates the number of clusters in data as follows. For $k \in \{k_1, k_1 + 1, \ldots, k_2\}$, the data $x_1, \ldots, x_n$ are clustered with the k-means algorithm and the *distortion* is computed,

$$\widehat{d}_k = \frac{1}{mn} \sum_{i=1}^{n} \|x_i - \text{center of cluster which contains } x_i\|^2 .$$

The Sugar–James estimate of the number of clusters in the data is

$$\text{argmax}_{k \in \{k_1 + 1, \ldots, k_2\}} \widehat{d}_k^c - \widehat{d}_{k-1}^c ,$$

where c is a positive constant (Sugar and James (2003) recommend $c = \frac{m}{2}$).

Selecting a reasonable clustering from among a hierarchical set of clusterings is a well studied problem: see Gan et al. (2007), Chapter 17 for a survey. One method, based on a non-parametric statistical test, is as follows. A clustering of the data $x_1, \ldots, x_n$ partitions the set of all pairwise dissimilarities

$$\{d(x_i, x_j) : 1 \leq i < j \leq n\}$$

into two sets: dissimilarities between two items which are in the same cluster, and dissimilarities between two items which are in different clusters. Clusterings look meaningful to the (author's) eye when the inter-cluster pairwise item dissimilarities are generally lower than the intra-cluster pairwise item dissimilarities.

The Mann–Whitney test (Conover, 1999, Section 5.1), also known as the Wilcoxon test, is a non-parametric statistical test of the null hypothesis that two sets of numbers are drawn from the same one-dimensional probability distribution.[4] It is powerful against alternatives in which the distributions have different medians. One way to measure the quality of a clustering is the strength of evidence which the Mann–Whitney test statistic gives against the null hypothesis that the inter-cluster similarities and the intra-cluster similarities have the same distribution. More generally, a clustering of a set into k clusters partitions the set of pairwise item similarities into $k + 1$ sets: similarities between items in cluster 1, similarities between items in cluster 2, ..., similarities between items in cluster k and finally similarities between items which are in different clusters. The Kruskal–Wallis test[5] (Conover, 1999, Section 5.2) is a generalization of the Mann–Whitney test to the case of more than two sets. It tests the null hypothesis that the $k + 1$ sets of pairwise item similarities have the same distribution, and it is powerful against alternatives in which some of the $k + 1$ distributions have different medians.

9.10   An Impossibility Theorem

Clustering is sometimes perceived as a "squishy" subject due to the lack of an explicit, rigorous statement of a goal (compared to predictive modeling, where the goal of risk-minimization is relatively clear). Clustering can be the subject of rigorous, general statements: we close with a remarkable theorem due to Kleinberg (2002).

---

[4] Let $W_1, \dots, W_{n^\star}$ and $X_1, \dots, X_n$ be samples from two distributions. The Mann–Whitney statistic for testing the null hypothesis that the distributions are the same is

$$T_1 = \frac{\sum_{i=1}^{n^\star} R(W_i) - \frac{1}{2}n^\star(n + n^\star + 1)}{\sqrt{\frac{nn^\star}{(n + n^\star)(n + n^\star - 1)}\left(\sum_{i=1}^{n^\star} R(W_i)^2 + \sum_{j=1}^{n} R(X_j)^2\right) - \frac{nn^\star(n + n^\star + 1)^2}{4(n + n^\star - 1)}}}$$

where $R(Z)$ is the rank of Z in the concatenation $\{W_1, \dots, W_{n^\star}, X_1, \dots, X_n\}$ sorted into increasing order. If unique, the smallest of $W_1, \dots, W_{n^\star}, X_1, \dots, X_n$ has rank 1 and the largest has rank $n + n^\star$. In the case of ties, average ranks are used: see Conover (1999), Section 5.1 for details. The Mann–Whitney statistic T_1 is distributed approximately standard normal when n and $n^\star$ are large.

[5] For the historically curious: Joseph Kruskal (of Kruskal's algorithm), William Kruskal (of the Kruska–Wallis test) and, for good measure, Martin Kruskal (the inventor of surreal numbers) were brothers.

Kleinberg defines three properties of clustering algorithms, all of which seem desirable:

Scale-invariance: The output of the algorithm does not change when the dissimilarity matrix is scaled by a positive constant;

Richness: Given any partition of n data points, there is some $n \times n$ dissimilarity matrix which will cause the algorithm to produce that partition;

Consistency: Given a clustering of data produced by the algorithm, decreasing the dissimilarity between points in the same cluster and increasing the dissimilarity between points in different clusters and running the algorithm again will *not* cause the clusters to change.

He then proves three theorems:

Theorem 9.1 Kleinberg's Impossibility Theorem. *For $n \geq 2$, no clustering algorithm satisfies all three of these properties.*

Theorem 9.2 *For any two of these three properties, a stopping condition (which Kleinberg explicitly states) can be defined for single-linkage agglomerative clustering so that the resulting algorithm satisfies the two properties.*

Theorem 9.3 *A general class of centroid-based clustering algorithms, which includes both k-means and k-medoids and which trivially does not satisfy the richness property, also does not satisfy the consistency property.*

Critics have pointed out that Kleinberg's consistency property is not necessarily desirable, as Figure 9.6 shows.

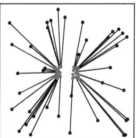

Figure 9.6   A two-dimensional dataset is shown in the left-hand cell. The center cell shows a function applied to the dataset, with the property that the distance between any two points in the image of the dataset (shown in red) is less than the distance between the corresponding two points in the original dataset (shown in black). The image of the dataset is shown in the right-hand cell. The function has transformed data apparently in one cluster to data apparently in two clusters, but no clustering algorithm which can detect this change is *consistent* in Kleinberg's sense.

10

Optimization

> I envy you your self-confidence and assurance, but I mistrust exceedingly
> the soundness of your judgment.
> —Alcon of Thrale in Edward E. Smith, *Second Stage Lensmen*, 1943

Many predictive modeling techniques of Chapter 4, and clustering methods of Chapter 9, require that certain numerical optimization problems be solved (at least approximately). This chapter presents several classes of optimization techniques.

The problem of optimization is, given a known[1] *objective function* $g : \mathbb{R}^m \to \mathbb{R}$, find a *minimizer*[2] $\omega^\star$ of g, defined by $g(\omega^\star) = \min_{\omega \in \mathbb{R}^m} g(\omega)$. The minimizer may be unique, or it may not. In some cases, the minimum value $g(\omega^\star)$ is of interest, but in the context of Chapters 4 and 9 we are usually more interested in the minimizer, $\omega^\star$.

All of the methods of this chapter are iterative: that is, they begin with an initial guess of the minimizer, ω^1, and for each iteration $t = 1, 2, 3, \ldots$, they construct a new approximation ω^{t+1}. The new approximation may or may not be better than the previous one. Typically, the methods are run until some upper bound on iterations is reached, or convergence in both the domain and range of g is detected, for example by both

$$\max_{i=1,\ldots,m} \left| \frac{\omega_i^{t+1} - \omega_i^t}{\omega_i^t} \right| \qquad \text{and} \qquad \left| \frac{g(\omega^{t+1}) - g(\omega^t)}{g(\omega^t)} \right|$$

---

[1] Objective function g, while known, may be a surrogate for another function we would like to optimize. For example, for a trained classifier $\hat{f}$ we may minimize an estimate of risk such as $\hat{R}_{valid}(\hat{f})$ or $\hat{R}_{cv}(\hat{f})$ but truly wish to minimize the risk $R(\hat{f})$.

[2] Maximization of g is equivalent to minimization of $-g$.

Machine Learning: a Concise Introduction, First Edition. Steven W. Knox.
© This publication is a US Government work and is in the public domain.
Published 2018 by John Wiley & Sons, Inc.
Companion Website: http://www.wiley.com/go/Knox/MachineLearning

falling below some preassigned thresholds. When the objective function is differentiable, there may also be a convergence criterion applied to a norm of the gradient, $\nabla g(\omega^t)$: for example, to the maximum absolute value of any coordinate,

$$\max_{i=1,\ldots,m} \left| \frac{\partial}{\partial \omega_i} g(\omega) \right| \Bigg|_{\omega=\omega^t}.$$

The domain of g is a continuum in this chapter, but many of the methods presented here have discrete-domain analogues.

10.1   Quasi-Newton Methods

10.1.1   Newton's Method for Finding Zeros

We begin with Newton's method for approximately finding zeros of a differentiable function $g : \mathbb{R} \to \mathbb{R}$. The goal is to find an $\omega^\star \in \mathbb{R}$ such that $g(\omega^\star) = 0$, starting from an initial and presumably incorrect guess ω^1 of such a point. From a current estimate, ω^t, Newton's method produces a new estimate,

$$\omega^{t+1} = \omega^t - \frac{g(\omega^t)}{g'(\omega^t)}.$$

The geometric motivation for updating the estimate this way is shown in Figure 10.1.

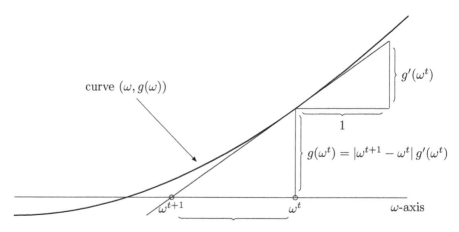

Figure 10.1   The geometry of Newton's method for finding zeros. From estimate ω^t on the ω-axis, move vertically to the point $(\omega^t, g(\omega^t))$ on the curve $(\omega, g(\omega))$, then leave $(\omega^t, g(\omega^t))$ on the ray tangent to the curve and toward the real line. The point at which the ray hits the ω-axis is the new estimate ω^{t+1}.

Newton's method does not always converge. Depending on the function g and the starting point ω_1, it may diverge to $\pm\infty$ or get stuck revisiting a finite set of points over and over in an infinite cycle.

10.1.2   Newton's Method for Optimization

Newton's method for optimizing a differentiable function g is to find a zero of the gradient of g. Let ∇g denote the gradient of g and let Hg denote the Hessian of g, and let a starting point $\omega^1 \in \mathbb{R}^m$ be given. From a current estimate, ω^t, Newton's method produces a new estimate,

$$\omega^{t+1} = \omega^t - \rho\,(Hg(\omega^t))^{-1}\,\nabla g(\omega^t),$$

where $\rho \in (0, 1]$ is a parameter (called the *learning rate*) which can be used to limit the step size.

Computation of the inverse Hessian, $(Hg(\omega^t))^{-1}$, can be expensive and can also be numerically unstable. Furthermore, away from a local minimum of g the Hessian $Hg(\omega^t)$ may not be positive definite, which means that there may be no point on the ray leaving ω^t in the direction of $-(Hg(\omega^t))^{-1}\,\nabla g(\omega^t)$ which has a value of g as small as $g(\omega^t)$. Heuristically, it is faster to perform more iterations of an approximate version of Newton's algorithm. Such methods are called *quasi-Newton methods*.

Exercise 10.1 *A matrix M is a* positive definite matrix *if M is symmetric and $x^{\mathrm{T}}Mx >$ 0 for all $x \in \mathbb{R}^m$, $x \neq 0$. Show that if M is positive definite and $\nabla g(\omega^t) \neq 0$, then taking a sufficiently small step from ω^t in the direction of $-M^{-1}\,\nabla g(\omega^t)$ results in a reduction of the value of g.* **Hints:** *(1) a sufficiently small step from ω^t in the direction of a vector v results in a reduction of the value of g if and only if the directional derivative of g at ω^t in the direction of v, $\nabla g(\omega^t) \cdot v$, is negative; (2) all positive definite matrices are invertible, and the inverse of a positive definite matrix is positive definite.*

10.1.3   Gradient Descent

The *gradient descent* algorithm is the result of approximating the Hessian $Hg(x)$ in Newton's method by the $m \times m$ identity matrix, so the update rule is

$$\omega^{t+1} = \omega^t - \rho\,\nabla g(\omega^t).$$

Gradient descent tends to be slow to converge when the starting point ω^1 is not near a zero of the gradient ∇g and when it encounters regions in the domain of g where $\|\nabla g\|$ is small but no zero of ∇g is nearby. Gradient descent (in its stochastic form— see Section 10.6.2) seems to be the *de facto* standard algorithm for training neural networks.

10.1.4   The BFGS Algorithm

The *Broyden-Fletcher-Goldfarb-Shanno (BFGS) algorithm* keeps a running approximation $\widehat{H}^t$ of $(Hg(\omega^t))^{-1}$, the inverse Hessian of g at ω^t. The initial value, $\widehat{H}^0$, is the $m \times m$ identity matrix. At each iteration, $\widehat{H}^t$ is updated by addition of three rank-1 matrices.[3] Specifically,

$$\widehat{H}^{t+1} = \widehat{H}^t + \frac{uu^{\mathrm{T}}}{t} - \frac{ww^{\mathrm{T}}}{s} + s\left(\frac{u}{t} - \frac{w}{s}\right)\left(\frac{u}{t} - \frac{w}{s}\right)^{\mathrm{T}},$$

where vectors u, v, and w, and scalars s and t are defined by

$$\begin{aligned} u &= \omega^{t+1} - \omega^t & s &= v^{\mathrm{T}}w = v^{\mathrm{T}}\widehat{H}^t v \\ v &= \nabla g(\omega^{t+1}) - \nabla g(\omega^t) & t &= u^{\mathrm{T}}v \\ w &= \widehat{H}^t v. \end{aligned}$$

Instead of moving ρ units in the direction of $\widehat{H}^t \nabla g(\omega^t)$, the BFGS algorithm performs a one-dimensional numerical minimization of g on the ray leaving ω^t in the direction of $\widehat{H}^t \nabla g(\omega^t)$. Furthermore, the update formula for $\widehat{H}^t$ is such that $\widehat{H}^t$ always remains positive definite,[4] so unless the algorithm has converged there is always a point on this ray with a lower value of g than ω^t.

BFGS is sometimes used for maximum-likelihood estimation (as in logistic regression in Section 4.6, for example). Upon convergence, it is tempting to use the last BFGS estimate of the inverse Hessian, $\widehat{H}^t$, to construct Gaussian confidence intervals for the true parameters, but BFGS may converge to an approximate local minimum *without* $\widehat{H}^t$ converging to a good estimate of the inverse Hessian evaluated at that minimum.

10.1.5   Modifications to Quasi-Newton Methods

Quasi-Newton methods are widely used, and through experimentation some modifications have been found to be generally useful. One of these modifications is to add *momentum*, which in gradient descent changes the update rule to

$$\omega^{t+1} = \omega^t - \rho \sum_{s=1}^{t} \eta^{t-s} \, \nabla g(\omega^s),$$

where $\eta \in [0, 1]$ is the *momentum parameter*. This is implemented by initializing a *momentum term* $v^1 = 0$ and iteratively updating

$$\begin{aligned} v^{t+1} &= \eta \, v^t + \nabla g(\omega^t) \\ \omega^{t+1} &= \omega^t - \rho \, v^{t+1}. \end{aligned}$$

---

[3] If g is quadratic, then $(Hg)^{-1}$ is constant and the BFGS update for $\widehat{H}^t$ ensures that $\widehat{H}^t$ converges to Hg^{-1} in m steps.

[4] Due to problems of numerical accuracy, care needs to be taken when programming that $\widehat{H}^t$ remains positive definite.

A second modification is to use an *adaptive learning rate*, that is, to allow parameter $\rho = \rho_i$ to change over time. One way to do this in gradient descent is the *bold driver* method,[5] which uses the update rule

(1) compute $z = \omega^t - \rho_t \nabla g(\omega^t)$.

(2) if $g(z) < g(\omega^t)$ set $\omega^{t+1} = z$ and set $\rho_{t+1} = c_1 \rho_t$.

(3) else set $\omega^{t+1} = \omega^t$ and set $\rho_{t+1} = c_2 \rho_t$.

Here, c_1 and c_2 are *adaptation parameters*, with $c_1 > 1$ and $c_2 < 1$. Typically $c_1 \in [1.01, 1.10]$ and $c_2 \approx 0.5$.

A third modification will be seen in Section 10.6.2.

10.1.6 Gradients for Logistic Regression and Neural Networks

The cost of computing the gradient ∇g of the objective function g can depend on multiple factors, such as dimension of the input space ($\mathbb{R}^m$, in this chapter), and whether computation of g involves accumulation of some quantity over a set of observed data. This is illustrated in the next two exercises by cases which arise when fitting a logistic regression model or single-hidden-layer neural network described in Chapter 4, where the objective function is the training estimate of risk with respect to cross-entropy loss.

Exercise 10.2 *Recall from Section 4.6 that a logistic regression classifier models the probability of each class label $c = 1, \ldots, C$, conditional on a feature vector X, as*

$$\widehat{P}(Y = c \mid X) = \frac{\exp(T(X, \theta_c))}{\sum_{d=1}^{C} \exp(T(X, \theta_d))},$$

where

$$T(X, \theta_c) = \theta_{c,0} + \sum_{j=1}^{m} \theta_{c,j} X_j$$

is a linear function of X and

$$\theta = \begin{bmatrix} \theta_1 \\ \theta_2 \\ \theta_3 \\ \vdots \\ \theta_C \end{bmatrix} = \begin{bmatrix} 0 & 0 & \cdots & 0 \\ \theta_{2,0} & \theta_{2,1} & \cdots & \theta_{2,m} \\ \theta_{3,0} & \theta_{3,1} & \cdots & \theta_{3,m} \\ \vdots & \vdots & & \vdots \\ \theta_{C,0} & \theta_{C,1} & \cdots & \theta_{C,m} \end{bmatrix}$$

---

[5] A bold driver is one whose speed increases exponentially until he or she is about to "drive off the road" ($g(z) > g(\omega^t)$), in which case the driver "stays on the road" ($\omega^{t+1} = \omega^t$) and continues at about half his or her previous speed (Battiti, 1989). Such drivers can be found in many places.

is a $C \times (m + 1)$ matrix of parameters with the top row constrained to be zero. Logistic regression models are often fit by finding a value of θ which (approximately) maximizes the likelihood of a set of observed data. By Exercise 4.11, this is equivalent to finding θ which minimizes the training risk with respect to cross-entropy loss,

$$\widehat{R}_{\text{train}} = -\sum_{i=1}^{n} T(x_i, \theta_{y_i}) + \sum_{i=1}^{n} \log \left(\sum_{d=1}^{C} \exp(T(x_i, \theta_d)) \right).$$

Show that, for $c = 1, \ldots, C$, the gradient of $\widehat{R}_{\text{train}}$ is given by

$$\frac{\partial}{\partial \theta_{c,0}} \widehat{R}_{\text{train}} = -\sum_{\substack{i=1 \\ y_i = c}}^{n} 1 + \sum_{i=1}^{n} \frac{\exp(T(x_i, \theta_c))}{\sum_{d=1}^{C} \exp(T(x_i, \theta_d))} = -\sum_{\substack{i=1 \\ y_i = c}}^{n} 1 + \sum_{i=1}^{n} \widehat{P}(Y = c \mid X = x_i)$$

and, for $j = 1, \ldots, m$,

$$\frac{\partial}{\partial \theta_{c,j}} \widehat{R}_{\text{train}} = -\sum_{\substack{i=1 \\ y_i = c}}^{n} x_{ij} + \sum_{i=1}^{n} x_{ij} \frac{\exp(T(x_i, \theta_c))}{\sum_{d=1}^{C} \exp(T(x_i, \theta_d))}$$

$$= -\sum_{\substack{i=1 \\ y_i = c}}^{n} x_{ij} + \sum_{i=1}^{n} x_{ij} \widehat{P}(Y = c \mid X = x_i).$$

Thus for any value of θ, computation of the gradient may be accomplished in one pass through the training data $(x_1, y_1), \ldots, (x_n, y_n)$, evaluating the summands and accumulating the sums shown.

Exercise 10.3 *Recall from Section 4.7 that a single-hidden-layer neural network models the probability of each class label $c = 1, \ldots, C$, conditional on a feature vector X, as*

$$\widehat{P}(Y = c \mid Z) = \frac{\exp(T(Z, \theta_c^{(2)}))}{\sum_{d=1}^{C} \exp(T(Z, \theta_d^{(2)}))},$$

where

$$T(Z, \theta_c^{(2)}) = \theta_{c,0}^{(2)} + \sum_{j=1}^{N} \theta_{c,j}^{(2)} Z_j$$

is a linear function of $Z = (Z_1, \ldots, Z_N)$ and, for $j = 1, \ldots, N$,

$$Z_j = \sigma \left(\theta_{j,0}^{(1)} + \sum_{k=1}^{m} \theta_{j,k}^{(1)} X_k \right)$$

is a composition of the sigmoid function $\sigma(v) = \frac{1}{1+e^{-v}}$ *with a linear function of X, and*

$$
\theta^{(2)} = \begin{bmatrix} \theta^{(2)}_1 \\ \theta^{(2)}_2 \\ \vdots \\ \theta^{(2)}_C \end{bmatrix} = \begin{bmatrix} \theta^{(2)}_{1,0} & \theta^{(2)}_{1,1} & \cdots & \theta^{(2)}_{1,N} \\ \theta^{(2)}_{2,0} & \theta^{(2)}_{2,1} & \cdots & \theta^{(2)}_{2,N} \\ \vdots & \vdots & & \vdots \\ \theta^{(2)}_{C,0} & \theta^{(2)}_{C,1} & \cdots & \theta^{(2)}_{C,N} \end{bmatrix} \quad and
$$

$$
\theta^{(1)} = \begin{bmatrix} \theta^{(1)}_1 \\ \theta^{(1)}_2 \\ \vdots \\ \theta^{(1)}_C \end{bmatrix} = \begin{bmatrix} \theta^{(1)}_{1,0} & \theta^{(1)}_{1,1} & \cdots & \theta^{(1)}_{1,m} \\ \theta^{(1)}_{2,0} & \theta^{(1)}_{2,1} & \cdots & \theta^{(1)}_{2,m} \\ \vdots & \vdots & & \vdots \\ \theta^{(1)}_{N,0} & \theta^{(1)}_{N,1} & \cdots & \theta^{(1)}_{N,m} \end{bmatrix}
$$

are respectively $C \times (N+1)$ *and* $N \times (m+1)$ *matrices of parameters. The training risk with respect to cross-entropy loss is*

$$
\widehat{R}_{\text{train}} = -\sum_{i=1}^n T(z_i, \theta^{(2)}_{y_i}) + \sum_{i=1}^n \log\left(\sum_{d=1}^C \exp\left(T(z_i, \theta^{(2)}_d) \right) \right),
$$

where, for $i = 1, \ldots, n$, z_i *represents the N-long vector*

$$
\left(\sigma\left(\theta^{(1)}_{j,0} + \sum_{k=1}^m \theta^{(1)}_{j,k} x_{ik} \right) \right)^N_{j=1}.
$$

Show that, for $c = 1, \ldots, C$, *the gradient of* $\widehat{R}_{\text{train}}$ *is given by*

$$
\frac{\partial}{\partial \theta^{(2)}_{c,0}} \widehat{R}_{\text{train}} = -\sum_{\substack{i=1 \\ y_i = c}}^n 1 + \sum_{i=1}^n \frac{\exp\left(T(z_i, \theta^{(2)}_c) \right)}{\sum_{d=1}^C \exp\left(T(z_i, \theta^{(2)}_d) \right)}
$$

$$
= -\sum_{\substack{i=1 \\ y_i = c}}^n 1 + \sum_{i=1}^n \widehat{P}(Y = c \mid Z = z_i)
$$

and, for $j = 1, \ldots, N$,

$$
\frac{\partial}{\partial \theta^{(2)}_{c,j}} \widehat{R}_{\text{train}} = -\sum_{\substack{i=1 \\ y_i = c}}^n z_{ij} + \sum_{i=1}^n z_{ij} \frac{\exp\left(T(z_i, \theta^{(2)}_c) \right)}{\sum_{d=1}^C \exp\left(T(z_i, \theta^{(2)}_d) \right)}
$$

$$
= -\sum_{\substack{i=1 \\ y_i = c}}^n z_{ij} + \sum_{i=1}^n z_{ij} \widehat{P}(Y = c \mid Z = z_i).
$$

and also, for $j = 1, \ldots, N$,

$$\frac{\partial}{\partial \theta_{j,0}^{(1)}} \widehat{R}_{\text{train}} = -\sum_{i=1}^{n} \theta_{y_i,j}^{(2)} z_{ij}(1 - z_{ij}) + \sum_{i=1}^{n} \frac{\sum_{d=1}^{C} \theta_{d,j}^{(2)} z_{ij}(1 - z_{ij}) \exp\left(T\left(z_i, \theta_d^{(2)}\right)\right)}{\sum_{d=1}^{C} \exp\left(T\left(z_i, \theta_d^{(2)}\right)\right)}$$

$$= -\sum_{i=1}^{n} \theta_{y_i,j}^{(2)} z_{ij}(1 - z_{ij}) + \sum_{i=1}^{n} \sum_{d=1}^{C} \theta_{d,j}^{(2)} z_{ij}(1 - z_{ij}) \widehat{P}(Y = d \mid Z = z_i)$$

and, for $k = 1, \ldots, m$,

$$\frac{\partial}{\partial \theta_{j,k}^{(1)}} \widehat{R}_{\text{train}} = -\sum_{i=1}^{n} \theta_{y_i,j}^{(2)} z_{ij}(1 - z_{ij}) x_{ik} + \sum_{i=1}^{n} \frac{\sum_{d=1}^{C} \theta_{d,j}^{(2)} z_{ij}(1 - z_{ij}) x_{ik} \exp\left(T\left(z_i, \theta_d^{(2)}\right)\right)}{\sum_{d=1}^{C} \exp\left(T\left(z_i, \theta_d^{(2)}\right)\right)}$$

$$= -\sum_{i=1}^{n} \theta_{y_i,j}^{(2)} z_{ij}(1 - z_{ij}) x_{ik} + \sum_{i=1}^{n} \sum_{d=1}^{C} \theta_{d,j}^{(2)} z_{ij}(1 - z_{ij}) x_{ik} \widehat{P}(Y = d \mid Z = z_i).$$

Thus for any value of $\theta^{(1)}$ and $\theta^{(2)}$, computation of the gradient may be accomplished in one pass through the training data $(x_1, y_1), \ldots, (x_n, y_n)$, evaluating the summands and accumulating the sums shown.

10.2   The Nelder–Mead Algorithm

The *Nelder–Mead algorithm* is useful for optimizing functions which are not differentiable (or where the derivative is too expensive or troublesome to compute).[6] It begins with the $m + 1$ vertices of a simplex in $\mathbb{R}^m$, with function g evaluated at each vertex.[7]

Each iteration of the algorithm is as illustrated in Figure 10.2. Moving along the ray from A to the midpoint of the opposite simplex facet can be interpreted as an approximation, given the available information, of a move in the direction of steepest descent.

The Nelder–Mead algorithm is sometimes called the "amoeba method" because the simplex oozes around $\mathbb{R}^m$, adapting its shape and size to the contours of the surface defined by g. Convergence is declared when $\frac{g(A)-g(C)}{|g(A)|+|g(C)|}$ falls below a given threshold.

---

[6] When confronted with an optimization problem, it is often good practice to start a simple optimizer running, starting at many randomly selected initial points, while one works on a more complex optimizer. The simple optimizer may find a good enough approximation to the optimum before implementation of the more complex optimizer is finished.

[7] In the author's implementation, the user provides a single point in $\mathbb{R}^m$ and a side length. The software constructs, as the starting point for the Nelder–Mead algorithm, a uniformly chosen random simplex in $\mathbb{R}^m$ with the given point at one vertex and all sides equal to the given length.

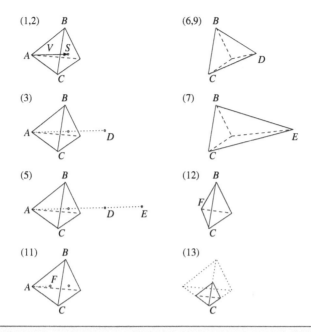

(1) let vertices A, B and C be such that $g(A)$ is the largest (worst), $g(B)$ is the second largest, and $g(C)$ is the smallest (best) value.

(2) let S be the centroid of the simplex facet not containing A, $S = \frac{1}{m} \sum_{\text{all vertices } v \neq A} v$, and let V be the vector from A to S, $V = S - A$.

(3) let point $D = A + 2V$ be the reflection of A through the centroid of the simplex facet not containing A.

(4) if($g(D) < g(C)$)

(5)   let $E = A + 3V$ be the point on ray $\overrightarrow{AD}$ which is half again as far from A as D is.

(6)   if($g(D) < g(E)$) replace vertex A with vertex D.

(7)   else replace vertex A with vertex E.

(8) else

(9)   if($g(D) < g(B)$) replace vertex A with vertex D.

(10)   else

(11)   let $F = A + \frac{1}{2}V$ be the point on the ray $\overrightarrow{AD}$ which is halfway to the simplex facet.

(12)   if($g(F) < g(A)$) replace vertex A with vertex F.

(13)   else move all vertices except C halfway to C along their edges to C, $v = v + \frac{1}{2}(C - v)$ for all vertices $v \neq C$.

Figure 10.2   The points evaluated and the operations performed on a simplex by one iteration of the Nelder–Mead algorithm.

10.3   Simulated Annealing

Simulated annealing is a random search strategy. Given the current state, ω^t, a new point w is drawn randomly from some probability distribution P, called the *proposal distribution*, which is part of the definition of the algorithm and usually depends on the current state. The decision whether to accept the proposed point w as the new state ω^{t+1} is also made randomly: the probability depends on $g(w)$, $g(\omega^t)$ and a positive parameter T, the *annealing temperature*, which decreases as the algorithm proceeds. Specifically, one step of a simulated annealing algorithm is

> (1) draw w from the proposal distribution $P(w \,|\, \omega^t)$.
>
> (2) draw a uniform(0,1)-distributed random variable u.
>
> (3) if $u < \min\left(1, e^{-\frac{g(w)-g(\omega^t)}{T}}\right)$ set $\omega^{t+1} = w$,
>
> (4) else set $\omega^{t+1} = \omega^t$.
>
> (5) reduce T.

Usually, T is reduced by multiplication by a constant close to but less than one (for example, 0.999) at each step.

Note that if $g(w) \leq g(\omega^t)$ then the proposed move is always accepted, meaning $\omega^{t+1} = w$. If, on the other hand, $g(w) > g(\omega^t)$ then the proposed move from ω^t to w is accepted with some positive probability, which depends on how much worse $g(w)$ is than $g(\omega^t)$. As the annealing temperature $T > 0$ decreases, the probability of accepting any given proposal w with $g(w) > g(\omega^t)$ decreases. Toward the beginning, simulated annealing is willing to move from a "good" point to a "bad" one, while later on it is reluctant to move to a "bad" point, essentially becoming a greedy random search. This makes simulated annealing a good search strategy when g has many local minima.

10.4   Genetic Algorithms

In a *genetic algorithm*, a point ω in the domain of g is called a *gene*. The algorithm acts iteratively on a set of genes, known as the *population*. Each gene ω has a property called *fitness*, which is a non-negative number that increases as $g(\omega)$ decreases:

$$\text{fitness}(\omega) = e^{-g(\omega)}$$

is a typical example. The algorithm requires two randomized functions: a *crossover map C* which takes a pair of genes and returns a new gene, and a *mutation map M* which takes a single gene and returns a new gene.

At the tth iteration, the current population S^t is used to produce a new population S^{t+1} as follows:

```
(1)  repeat some number of times:
(2)    draw distinct genes u and v from S^t with probability proportional to fitness:
       that is, u is drawn with probability  fitness(u)/∑_{w∈S^t} fitness(w) .
(3)    create the crossover of u and v, w = C(u,v).
(4)    create a mutation of the crossover, z = M(w).
(5)    insert the mutated crossover z into S^{t+1}.
```

Typically, the population size remains constant from one iteration (also known as a *generation*) to the next.

In some genetic algorithms, S^{t+1} may include unmutated crossovers of genes in S^t and S^{t+1} may include mutations of single genes drawn from S^t. Also, S^{t+1} may include genes directly copied from S^t, for example, by replacing S^{t+1} with the fittest elements of $S^t \cup S^{t+1}$.

The mutation map M is similar to a simulated annealing proposal distribution: given a gene ω, it draws a random gene from some distribution, typically with probability mass centered at ω in some sense. The defining characteristic of a genetic algorithm is the crossover map C, which creates a new gene by combining parts of the two other genes. For example, when the domain of g is $\mathbb{R}^m$, a crossover map applied to genes u and v could be defined as $C(u, v) = (w_1, \ldots, w_m)$, where each w_i is an independent, uniform random draw from the set $\{u_i, v_i\}$.

Genetic algorithms are most useful for minimizing functions which have a known (or suspected) structural relationship among the inputs which can be exploited by a well chosen crossover map. To give an unrealistically simple example, suppose the domain of g is $\mathbb{R}^6$ and

$$g(\omega) = \max(|\omega_1|, |\omega_2|, |\omega_3|) \times \max(|\omega_4|, |\omega_5|, |\omega_6|).$$

Here, if g is small then the first three coordinates or the last three coordinates are all small. A crossover map which exploits this property to propose new members of the population with potentially small values of g is

$$C(u, v) = \begin{cases} (u_1, u_2, u_3, v_4, v_5, v_6) & \text{if a fair coin toss comes up "heads"} \\ (v_1, v_2, v_3, u_4, u_5, u_6) & \text{otherwise} \end{cases}.$$

10.5   Particle Swarm Optimization

Particle swarm optimization algorithms are an outgrowth proposed in Kennedy and Eberhart (1995) of computer models for simulating the behavior of bird flocks, fish schools, and other group behavior. A *particle swarm* is a set of objects, each of which has the following properties:

(1) a *position p*, point in the domain of *g*;

(2) a *velocity v*, a vector in the domain of *g*;

(3) a *personal best point*, the minimizer of *g* among all positions which the particle has occupied in the past;

(4) the *global best point*, the minimizer of *g* among all positions which *any* particle has occupied in the past.

Particles' positions and velocities are initialized randomly (often in such a way that they are well dispersed in the domain of *g*).

At each iteration, each particle in the swarm is updated according to the rules:

$$p_{\text{new}} = p_{\text{current}} + v_{\text{current}}$$

and

$$v_{\text{new}} = k(v_{\text{current}} + c_1 U_1 (\text{personal best} - p_{\text{current}}) + c_2 U_2 (\text{global best} - p_{\text{current}})).$$

In the velocity update formula, k, c_1 and c_2 are universal positive constants and U_1 and U_2 are draws from a Uniform $(0, 1)$ distribution (drawn independently for each particle at each iteration). Particles' personal best points and the global best point are updated at each iteration.

The purpose of constants k, c_1 and c_2 are to control how "attracted" each particle is to its own personal best point and to the global best point. Constants c_1 and c_2 are respectively called the *cognitive parameter* and the *social parameter*, and constant k is the *constriction rate*. Based on simulation studies, Carlisle and Dozier (2000) recommend $c_1 = 2.8$, $c_2 = 1.3$, and $k = \dfrac{2}{|2-c_1-c_2-\sqrt{(c_1+c_2)(c_1+c_2-4)}|} \approx 0.7298$.

There are many variations of particle swarm optimizers. One common variation imposes a neighborhood structure on the particles, replacing the "global best" with a "neighborhood best." This means that information about the global best point found so far propagates slowly through the swarm, as it is passed from neighbor to neighbor in each iteration, which has the effect of making the swarm less aggressive and more robust. Other variations include multiple swarms which avoid each other and multiple types of particles in a swarm ("settlers" which refine estimates of local minima and "explorers" which search for new local minima). How to identify when a particle swarm has converged is an open question.

10.6   General Remarks on Optimization

10.6.1   Imperfectly Known Objective Functions

In machine learning it is usually the case that the objective function g we truly wish to optimize is not computable, and therefore we are reduced to optimizing an approximation or estimate, $\hat{g}$, of the ideal objective function g. Uncertainty in the estimate $\widehat{g}$ of g can lead to a new halting criterion for iterative optimization algorithms: *halt if the algorithm can't tell whether it is really improving.*

Let a training dataset be given, let a classification method be specified, and let θ be a vector of both model parameters and tuning parameters which control the method's behavior: in classification trees, for example, θ could include the cost-complexity parameter, while in a neural network θ could encode the number of hidden layers and the number of neurons in each hidden layer as well as the parameters of the neurons.[8] Training the classifier defines a function $\theta \mapsto \widehat{f}_\theta$, and the optimal value of θ is that which minimizes the risk of the trained classifier. That is, the objective function g is

$$g(\theta) = R(\widehat{f}_\theta) = E_{(X,Y)}[L(Y,\widehat{f}_\theta(X))].$$

The true risk of the trained classifier is not computable (because it depends on the unknown probability distribution $P(X, Y)$), so an estimate must be used instead. For example, if a validation dataset is available (see Chapter 7), parameter θ can be sought to minimize the validation estimate of risk. This provides a surrogate objective function $\widehat{g}$,

$$\widehat{g}(\theta) = \widehat{R}_{\text{valid}}(\widehat{f}_\theta) = \frac{1}{\tilde{n}} \sum_{i=1}^{\tilde{n}} L(\tilde{y}_i, \widehat{f}_\theta(\tilde{x}_i)).$$

The surrogate objective function $\widehat{g}$ is derived from data, and hence is random with mean and variance (and variance estimators) as described in Section 7.2.2.

Exercise 10.4 *Assume that the number $\tilde{n}$ of validation data is large enough that $\widehat{g}(\theta) = \widehat{R}_{\text{valid}}(\widehat{f}_\theta)$, can be thought of as normal-distributed with negligible error for any value of θ under consideration. Describe a halting criterion for an iterative optimization algorithm $\theta_1, \theta_2, \ldots$ based on a level-α statistical test of the null hypothesis that $g(\theta_{i+1}) \geq g(\theta_i)$ using the validation estimate $\widehat{g}$ for g. If a maximum number I of iterations is fixed in advance, explain how Bonferroni correction, described in Chapter 12, can be used so that the probability of any false rejection of the null is bounded by α.* **Hint:** *See part (C) of Exercise 7.5 for the test, and see Exercise 12.7 for the development of Bonferroni's method.*

10.6.2   Objective Functions Which Are Sums

In some cases, the objective function g to be optimized (or a surrogate, $\widehat{g}$) is naturally expressed as a sum. For example, some classifiers are trained by explicitly minimizing a training or validation estimate of risk, in which case

$$\widehat{g}(\theta) = \frac{1}{n} \sum_{i=1}^{n} L(y_i, \widehat{f}_\theta(x_i))$$

---

[8] Parameter θ encodes *any* choice over which the user wishes to optimize. In addition to those mentioned above, θ could include the node impurity criterion and halting condition for classification trees, or the inter-neuron connectivity or seed value for random initialization in a neural network.

or

$$\widehat{g}(\theta) = \frac{1}{\tilde{n}} \sum_{i=1}^{\tilde{n}} L(\tilde{y}_i, \widehat{f}_\theta(\tilde{x}_i)).$$

Some classifiers are trained by maximizing a log-likelihood function[9] for independent data, in which case

$$g(\theta) = - \sum_{i=1}^{n} \log P(y_i \mid X = x_i, \theta).$$

Ignoring the distinction between whether the objective function is the ideal one or a surrogate, in both of the above cases the objective function is a sum over data, with the ith summand depending only on the parameter θ and the ith datum. The same is also true of the gradient, thus:

$$g(\theta) = \sum_{i=1}^{n} g(x_i, y_i, \theta) \qquad \text{and} \qquad \nabla g(\theta) = \sum_{i=1}^{n} \nabla g(x_i, y_i, \theta).$$

When the number of data n is large, g and ∇g can be expensive to compute, and even more so if the number of parameters k is large. One response to this situation, when using quasi-Newton optimization methods, is to approximate ∇g by computing it only on a random sample of the data,

$$\nabla g(\theta) \approx \sum_{i \in S} \nabla g(x_i, y_i, \theta),$$

where S is a small sample drawn randomly from $\{1, \ldots, n\}$. In the most extreme case, the random sample is a single data point: *stochastic gradient descent* is the gradient descent algorithm with $\nabla g(\theta)$ approximated by $\nabla g(x_i, y_i, \theta)$ computed for a single point (x_i, y_i), which is drawn uniformly at random from the data at each iteration of the algorithm.[10]

10.6.3   Optimization from Multiple Starting Points

Heuristically, it is good practice to start optimization algorithms from multiple points. Indeed for a given total amount of work, many applications of a simple optimization algorithm from different starting points may (in the aggregate) find a better optimum than a sophisticated algorithm starting from only one point. Some algorithms incorporate this heuristic explicitly: there are particle swarms with "explorer" and "settler" particles, and genetic algorithms with the population divided into "islands" which interbreed only when a fluctuating "sea level" is sufficiently low.

---

[9] In sections 4.6 and 4.7, it was seen that for training logistic regression and neural network classifiers with cross-entropy loss, minimizing training risk and maximizing likelihood are equivalent.

[10] Stochastic gradient descent may sample points from the data without replacement until all the data have been used (so all data are used exactly once in the first n iterations), and then begin anew for the next n iterations, and so on.

10.7   The Expectation-Maximization Algorithm

10.7.1   The General Algorithm

In some applications, important data are missing. One example of this, which we shall examine in detail, is the fitting of a Gaussian mixture model when the available data are points $x_1, \ldots, x_n \in \mathbb{R}^m$ *without* any accompanying information about which points were drawn from which mixture component of the distribution. In this section we will denote observed (or observable) data by X, and unobserved (or hidden, or latent) data by Z.

Let a statistical model be given for observable data X and hidden data Z, parametrized by θ. The likelihood is $P(X, Z \mid \theta)$, and a maximum likelihood estimate $\hat{\theta}$ for θ is desired. Ideally, this would be obtained by marginalizing out—that is, averaging over—the distribution of the hidden data Z (which presumably depends on θ), selecting a value of θ which maximizes the marginal distribution of the observed data, $P(X \mid \theta)$:

$$\hat{\theta} = \mathrm{argmax}_\theta \, P(X \mid \theta) = \mathrm{argmax}_\theta \int P(X, z \mid \theta) \, dz. \qquad (10.1)$$

In the language of optimization, we seek θ to minimize the objective function $g(\theta) = -P(x_1, \ldots, x_n \mid \theta)$ for some observed data $x_1, \ldots, x_n$. The integral in (10.1) is often too hard to deal with, leading to an objective function which is not computable.

In response to this situation, Dempster et al. (1977) developed the *expectation-maximization (EM) algorithm*, an iterative algorithm for approximating $\hat{\theta}$. Given observed data $x_1, \ldots, x_n$ and an initial value $\hat{\theta}^0$, the EM algorithm repeats the following two steps until convergence is declared:

---

(1) compute $\mathrm{E}_{Z \mid x, \hat{\theta}^t} [\log P(x, Z \mid \theta)]$, a function of θ (the ''expectation'' step);

(2) compute $\hat{\theta}^{(t+1)} = \mathrm{argmax}_\theta \mathrm{E}_{Z \mid x, \hat{\theta}^t} [\log P(x, Z \mid \theta)]$ (the ''maximization'' step).

The expectation step looks daunting, but it really involves computing parameters which describe a state of knowledge or belief at the tth iteration about the hidden data Z.

10.7.2   EM Climbs the Marginal Likelihood of the Observations

It is remarkable (so we make this remark) that at any iteration of the EM algorithm, the marginal likelihood of the observed data satisfies

$$P(X \mid \hat{\theta}^{(t+1)}) \geq P(X \mid \hat{\theta}^t).$$

The reason for this is as follows. For any value of θ, x, and z, the joint density for the observed and unobserved data can be factored as

$$P(X = x, Z = z \mid \theta) = P(Z = z \mid \theta, X = x) P(X = x \mid \theta).$$

Taking logs, this becomes

$$\log P(X = x \mid \theta) = \log P(X = x, Z = z \mid \theta) - \log P(Z = z \mid \theta, X = x). \quad (10.2)$$

Since equation (10.2) holds for all values z of the hidden variables, both sides can be integrated with respect to *any* distribution on the hidden variables and still have equality. In particular, we can pick some value $\tilde{\theta}$ of θ and integrate both sides of (10.2) with respect to the distribution it induces on the hidden data, $P(Z \mid \tilde{\theta}, X = x)$. This yields

$$\log P(X = x \mid \theta) = E_{Z \mid \tilde{\theta}, X=x}[\log P(X = x \mid \theta)]$$
$$= E_{Z \mid \tilde{\theta}, X=x}[\log P(X = x, Z \mid \theta)] - E_{Z \mid \tilde{\theta}, X=x}[\log P(Z \mid \theta, X = x)].$$
$$(10.3)$$

Consider the second term on the right-hand side of (10.3). The following sequence of exercises shows that, as a function of θ,

$$E_{Z \mid \tilde{\theta}, X=x}[\log P(Z \mid \theta, X = x)] \quad (10.4)$$

is maximal when $\theta = \tilde{\theta}$.

Exercise 10.5 Jensen's Inequality. *A function $g : \mathbb{R} \to \mathbb{R}$ is a concave function if for any $x, y \in \mathbb{R}$ and any $t \in [0, 1]$, $g(tx + (1 - t)y) \geq tg(x) + (1 - t)g(y)$, and is a strictly concave function if $g(tx + (1 - t)y) > tg(x) + (1 - t)g(y)$. Equivalently, g is concave if, at each point x, there is a line through the point $(x, g(x))$ such that the curve parametrized by $(y, g(y))$ is always on or below the line. This is called a supporting line of the curve at x. Put this way, g is strictly concave if, at each point x, there is a line through the point $(x, g(x))$ such that the curve parametrized by $(y, g(y))$ is below the line, touching the line only at the point $(x, g(x))$. These definitions are illustrated in Figure 10.3. Show that for a real random variable X, and a concave function g,*

$$E[g(X)] \leq g(E[X]).$$

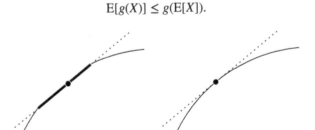

Figure 10.3   A concave function (left) and a strictly concave function (right). For each curve, a dashed supporting line is shown at a point $(x, g(x))$. For the strictly concave function, the supporting line intersects the curve at only this point, while for the concave function, the line may intersect the curve elsewhere (shown in bold).

Show that if g is strictly concave, then $E[g(X)] = g(E[X])$ *if and only if* $P(X = c) = 1$ *for some constant c.* **Hint:** *Let* $\alpha = E[X]$, *consider a line with equation* $g(\alpha) + s(y - \alpha)$ *which lies above the curve* $(y, g(y))$, *and integrate both sides of an inequality.*

Exercise 10.6 The Shannon–Kolmogorov Information Inequality.[11] *Let P_0 and P_1 be probability densities on some set S and let X have the distribution with density P_0. Show that*

$$E\left[\log\left(\frac{P_0(X)}{P_1(X)}\right)\right] = \int_S \log\left(\frac{P_0(x)}{P_1(x)}\right) P_0(x)\, dx \geq 0,$$

with equality if and only if $P(P_0(X) = P_1(X)) = 1$. **Hint:** *Use Jensen's inequality, the fact that log is strictly concave on the positive real line, and the fact that densities integrate to 1.*

Exercise 10.7 *Apply the Shannon–Kolmogorov information inequality to show that for all θ,*

$$E_{Z\mid\tilde{\theta},X=x}[\log P(Z \mid \theta, X = x)] \leq E_{Z\mid\tilde{\theta},X=x}[\log P(Z \mid \tilde{\theta}, X = x)]. \qquad (10.5)$$

Now consider the first term on the right-hand side of (10.3). If θ and $\tilde{\theta}$ are any two values such that

$$E_{Z\mid\tilde{\theta},X=x}[\log P(X = x, Z \mid \tilde{\theta})] \leq E_{Z\mid\tilde{\theta},X=x}[\log P(X = x, Z \mid \theta)] \qquad (10.6)$$

(for example, if θ is a maximizer of $E_{Z\mid\tilde{\theta},X=x}[\log P(X = x, Z \mid \theta)]$), then inserting (10.5) and (10.6) into (10.3) makes the positive term no smaller (generally bigger) and the negative no bigger (generally smaller), yielding

$$\log P(X = x \mid \theta) \geq \log P(X = x \mid \tilde{\theta}).$$

---

[11] The Kullback–Leibler information between two discrete probability distributions was introduced in Exercise 2.1. The Kullback–Leibler information between two distributions with densities P_0 and P_1 is $E[\log(\frac{P_0(X)}{P_1(X)})]$, where P_0 is the density of the distribution of X. The Shannon–Kolmogorov information inequality states that the Kullback–Leibler information between two distributions is non-negative, and positive unless $P(P_0(X) = P_1(X)) = 1$. The Shannon–Kolmogorov information inequality can be used to prove that certain well known distributions have a maximum entropy property. Assuming that distributions have densities in parts (1)–(3),

(1) of all distributions on $S = (-\infty, \infty)$ with mean μ and variance σ^2, the Gaussian distribution has maximum entropy;

(2) of all distributions on $S = (0, \infty)$ with mean μ, the exponential distribution has maximum entropy;

(3) of all distributions on $S = [a, b]$, the uniform distribution has maximum entropy;

(4) of all distributions on $S = \{1, 2, 3, ...\}$ with mean μ, the geometric distribution has maximum entropy.

In actual implementation, $\tilde{\theta} = \widehat{\theta}^t$ and $\widehat{\theta}^{t+1}$ is set to the maximizer of $E_{Z \mid \tilde{\theta}, X=x}[\log P(X = x, Z \mid \theta)]$.

Thus the EM algorithm results in a sequence of parameter estimates $\widehat{\theta}^0, \widehat{\theta}^1, \widehat{\theta}^2, \ldots$ for which $P(X = x \mid \widehat{\theta}^0), P(X = x \mid \widehat{\theta}^1), P(X = x \mid \widehat{\theta}^2), \ldots$ is non-decreasing (and in fact is increasing unless equality holds in both (10.4) and (10.6)). Furthermore, we need not actually maximize the expected log-likelihood in step (2) of EM (the M-step): it is sufficient to merely find a new parameter $\widehat{\theta}^{(t+1)}$ which produces a greater expected log-likelihood than the current parameter, $\widehat{\theta}^t$. Algorithms which improve but do not maximize the log-likelihood in step (2) are called *generalized EM algorithms*.

10.7.3   Example—Fitting a Gaussian Mixture Model Via EM

The EM algorithm is illustrated by providing technical details omitted in Section 4.4.3 and Section 9.2. Let $x_1, \ldots, x_n$ be independent draws from a Gaussian mixture with J components. For each i, the density at x_i is

$$P(x_i \mid \theta) = \sum_{j=1}^{J} w_j \, \phi(x_i \mid \mu_j, \Sigma_j),$$

where $\phi(x \mid \mu, \Sigma)$ denotes a Gaussian density function with mean μ and covariance matrix Σ, $w_1, \ldots, w_J$ are non-negative weights which sum to 1 and

$$\theta = (w_1, \ldots, w_J, \mu_1, \ldots, \mu_J, \Sigma_1, \ldots, \Sigma_J)$$

is a shorthand for all of the parameters. For $i = 1, \ldots, n$, define $z_i \in \{1, \ldots, J\}$ to be the label of the mixture component from which x_i was drawn. One can think of the data as generated this way:

```
(1)  for i = 1,...,n ,
(2)      draw z_i from {1,...,J} with probability distribution w_1,...,w_J .
(3)      draw x_i from N(μ_{z_i}, Σ_{z_i}) .
```

If $z_1, \ldots, z_n$ are known then it is easy to compute the maximum likelihood estimate of θ. The log-likelihood can be written as

$$\log P(x_1, \ldots, x_n, z_1, \ldots, z_n \mid \theta) = \sum_{i=1}^{n} \log \left(w_{z_i} \, \phi(x_i \mid \mu_{z_i}, \Sigma_{z_i}) \right)$$

$$= \sum_{j=1}^{J} \left(\sum_{\substack{i=1 \\ z_i = j}}^{n} \log(w_j \, \phi(x_i \mid \mu_j, \Sigma_j)) \right).$$

and each term in the right-hand sum over j can be maximized separately.

Exercise 10.8 *Show that the maximum likelihood estimates of the parameters are:*

$$\widehat{w}_j = \frac{|\{i : z_i = j\}|}{n}, \qquad \widehat{\mu}_j = \frac{1}{|\{i : z_i = j\}|} \sum_{i:z_i=j} x_i$$

and

$$\widehat{\Sigma}_j = \frac{1}{|\{i : z_i = j\}|} \sum_{i:z_i=j} (x - \widehat{\mu}_j)(x - \widehat{\mu}_j)^{\mathrm{T}}.$$

Hint: *Don't forget to put in a Lagrange multiplier term to capture the constraint* $w_1 + \cdots + w_J = 1$.

If $z_1, \ldots, z_n$ are unknown, an approximate maximizer of the marginal log-likelihood,

$$\log P(x_1, \ldots, x_n \mid \theta) = \sum_{i=1}^{n} \log P(x_i \mid \theta) = \sum_{i=1}^{n} \log \left(\sum_{j=1}^{J} w_j \, \phi(x_i \mid \mu_j, \Sigma_j) \right),$$

can be found by the Expectation-Maximization (EM) algorithm.

10.7.4   Example—The Expectation Step

Theoretically, the point of the expectation step is to obtain the expected value of the joint log-likelihood of X and Z with respect to the distribution on $Z_1, \ldots, Z_n$ induced by the current estimate $\widehat{\theta}^t$ for θ. Specifically,

$$E_{(Z_1,\ldots,Z_n) \mid (x_1,\ldots,x_n), \widehat{\theta}^t} \; [\log P(x_1, \ldots, x_n, Z_1, \ldots, Z_n \mid \theta)]$$

$$= E_{(Z_1,\ldots,Z_n) \mid (x_1,\ldots,x_n), \widehat{\theta}^t} \left[\sum_{i=1}^{n} \log \left(w_{Z_i} \, \phi(x_i \mid \mu_{Z_i}, \Sigma_{Z_i}) \right) \right]$$

$$= \sum_{i=1}^{n} E_{Z_i \mid x_i, \widehat{\theta}^t} \left[\log \left(w_{Z_i} \, \phi(x_i \mid \mu_{Z_i}, \Sigma_{Z_i}) \right) \right]$$

$$= \sum_{i=1}^{n} \sum_{j=1}^{J} P(Z_i = j \mid \widehat{\theta}^t, x_i) \, \log(w_j \, \phi(x_i \mid \mu_j, \Sigma_j))$$

$$= \sum_{i=1}^{n} \sum_{j=1}^{J} \gamma_{ij}^t \, \log(w_j \, \phi(x_i \mid \mu_j, \Sigma_j)). \tag{10.7}$$

The last step introduces the short-hand notation

$$\gamma_{ij}^t = P(Z_i = j \mid \widehat{\theta}^t, x_i).$$

Probability γ_{ij}^t is called the *responsibility* of mixture component j for data x_i at iteration t, and it expresses "what is known so far" about the hidden states $Z_1, \ldots, Z_n$. The responsibilities can be computed using Bayes' theorem, since

$$\gamma_{ij}^t \propto P(Z_i = j \mid \hat{\theta}^t) \times P(x_i \mid \hat{\theta}^t, Z_i = j) = \hat{w}_j^t \, \phi(x_i \mid \hat{\mu}_j^t, \hat{\Sigma}_j^t).$$

The constant of proportionality comes from the fact that $\gamma_{i1}^t + \cdots + \gamma_{iJ}^t = 1$, so

$$\gamma_{ij}^t = \frac{\hat{w}_j^t \, \phi(x_i \mid \hat{\mu}_j^t, \hat{\Sigma}_j^t)}{\displaystyle\sum_{k=1}^{J} \hat{w}_k^t \, \phi(x_i \mid \hat{\mu}_k^t, \hat{\Sigma}_k^t)}.$$

Thus

$$E_{(Z_1,\ldots,Z_n) \mid (x_1,\ldots,x_n), \hat{\theta}^t} \, [\log P(x_1, \ldots, x_n, Z_1, \ldots, Z_n \mid \theta)]$$

$$= \sum_{i=1}^{n} \sum_{j=1}^{J} \frac{\hat{w}_j^t \, \phi(x_i \mid \hat{\mu}_j^t, \hat{\Sigma}_j^t)}{\displaystyle\sum_{k=1}^{J} \hat{w}_k^t \, \phi(x_i \mid \hat{\mu}_k^t, \hat{\Sigma}_k^t)} \, \log(w_j \, \phi(x_i \mid \mu_j, \Sigma_j)),$$

and the right-hand side is a function of θ (all other quantities, $\hat{\theta}^t$ and $x_1 \ldots, x_n$, being known).

10.7.5 Example—The Maximization Step

The purpose of the maximization step is to compute the parameter $\hat{\theta}^{t+1}$ which maximizes the expected log-likelihood (10.7) which was computed in the expectation step.

Exercise 10.9 *Modify the solution to Exercise 10.8 to show that the maximizer of (10.7) is the value $\hat{\theta}^{t+1}$ defined by*

$$\hat{w}_j^{t+1} = \frac{\sum_{i=1}^{n} \gamma_{ij}^t}{n}, \qquad \hat{\mu}_j^{t+1} = \frac{\sum_{i=1}^{n} \gamma_{ij}^t \, x_i}{\sum_{i=1}^{n} \gamma_{ij}^t}$$

and

$$\hat{\Sigma}_j^{t+1} = \frac{\sum_{i=1}^{n} \gamma_{ij}^t \left(x_i - \hat{\mu}_j^{t+1}\right)\left(x_i - \hat{\mu}_j^{t+1}\right)^{\mathsf{T}}}{\sum_{i=1}^{n} \gamma_{ij}^t}.$$

for $j = 1, \ldots, J$. **Hint:** *See the hints for Exercise 4.5 and Exercise 10.8.*

From a computational or algorithmic point of view, the purpose of the expectation step is to compute all of the γ_{ij}^t's from $\hat{\theta}^t$, while the purpose of the maximization step is to compute $\hat{\theta}^{t+1}$ from the γ_{ij}^t's.

11

High-Dimensional Data

> By lumping all these choices together, we "reduce" the problem to a classical problem of determining the maximum of a given function. ...
>
> There are, however, some details to consider. In the first place, the effective analytic solution of a large number of even simple equations as, for example, linear equations, is a difficult affair. Lowering our sights, even a computational solution usually has a number of difficulties of both gross and subtle nature. Consequently, the determination of this maximum is quite definitely not routine when the number of variables is large.
>
> All this may be subsumed under the heading "the curse of dimensionality." Since this is a curse which has hung over the head of the physicist and astronomer for many a year, there is no need to feel discouraged about the possibility of obtaining significant results despite it.
>
> —Richard E. Bellman, *Dynamic Programming*, 1957

Although it was originally defined in the context of numerical equation-solving and optimization (in the quote above), the *curse of dimensionality* now serves as a catch-all term describing difficulties which arise when the number of features, m, is large. This chapter focuses on a major source of difficulty for the design and application of machine learning algorithms: the fact that high-dimensional Euclidean space has properties which conflict with intuition obtained from two- and three-dimensional Euclidean space. In particular, three-dimensional intuition about the set of points approximately a given distance away from a given point can be quite misleading because of the changing relationship between distance and volume as the dimension of Euclidean space increases.

Machine Learning: a Concise Introduction, First Edition. Steven W. Knox.
© This publication is a US Government work and is in the public domain.
Published 2018 by John Wiley & Sons, Inc.
Companion Website: http://www.wiley.com/go/Knox/MachineLearning

Approaches to dealing with the curse of dimensionality fall roughly into two categories. First, there is searching for explicit or implicit mappings of a high-dimensional feature space into a lower dimensional space such that useful information for solving a given learning problem is preserved. Methods for this approach may be as simple as linear projection, or as complex as deep autoencoders. Second, there are methods which view high-dimensional data as a bias–variance problem, and introduce bias into estimates of model parameters (typically by forcing them to be smaller in absolute value than they would be otherwise) in order to reduce variance and produce a lower-risk approximation $\hat{f}$. Such methods, encountered in specific instances in Chapters 3 and 4, are discussed in more detail and generality in this chapter.

11.1   The Curse of Dimensionality

This section illustrates the curse of dimensionality with some examples, leaving theoretical results to the exercises. A *ball* in $\mathbb{R}^m$ is the set of points no more than some given distance from a given point, that is, a ball is

$$\{x \in \mathbb{R}^m : \|x - c\| \leq r\}$$

for some center $c \in \mathbb{R}^m$ and positive radius r. For future reference, volume and surface area of an m-dimensional ball of radius r are respectively

$$V(m, r) = \frac{\pi^{\frac{m}{2}} r^m}{\Gamma\left(\frac{m}{2} + 1\right)} \quad \text{and} \quad S(m, r) = \frac{\pi^{\frac{m}{2}} m r^{m-1}}{\Gamma\left(\frac{m}{2} + 1\right)} = \frac{2 \pi^{\frac{m}{2}} r^{m-1}}{\Gamma\left(\frac{m}{2}\right)},$$

where $\Gamma(z) = \int_0^\infty t^{z-1} e^{-t} dt$ is the gamma function, the usual generalization of factorial: $\Gamma(z + 1) = z!$ for integer $z \geq 0$. For our purposes, there is nothing special about a sphere: it is merely an analytically tractable stand-in for an m-dimensional "blob" in $\mathbb{R}^m$.

Consider a *spherical shell* S consisting of all points in a ball which are within a given distance $\delta < 1$ from the boundary (equivalently, S is a unit ball with a concentric radius-$(1 - \delta)$ ball removed):

$$S = \{x \in \mathbb{R}^m : 1 - \delta < \|x - c\| \leq 1\}$$
$$= \{x \in \mathbb{R}^m : \|x - c\| \leq 1\} \setminus \{x \in \mathbb{R}^m : \|x - c\| \leq 1 - \delta\}.$$

How big does the distance δ need to be so that the volume of the spherical shell is a given proportion of the volume of the sphere—for specificity, say, 90% of the volume? The answer is whatever value of δ satisfies

$$V(m, 1) - V(m, 1 - \delta) = 0.90 \times V(m, 1),$$

Figure 11.1   In $\mathbb{R}^1$, 90% of the volume of a unit sphere lies within a distance of 0.90 units of its boundary (left). In $\mathbb{R}^2$, 90% of the volume of a unit sphere lies within a distance of about 0.68 units of its boundary (center). In $\mathbb{R}^3$, 90% of the volume of a unit sphere lies within a distance of about 0.54 units of its boundary (right).

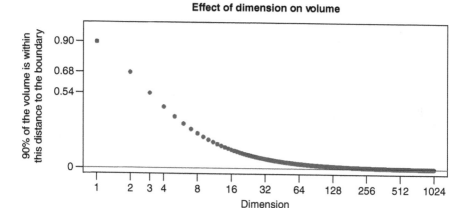

Figure 11.2   In $\mathbb{R}^m$, 90% of the volume of a unit sphere lies within a distance of $1 - (1 - 0.90)^{\frac{1}{m}}$ units of its boundary, and this distance goes rapidly to zero as m increases.

which is

$$\delta = 1 - (1 - 0.90)^{\frac{1}{m}}.$$

This value of δ is shown for various dimensions m in Figures 11.1 and 11.2. As the dimension becomes large, the radius of the "smaller" concentric ball removed grows to be nearly that of the original ball, as shown in Figure 11.2. What this means is that *nearly all the points in a high-dimensional ball are nearly on the boundary.*[1]

---

[1] Throughout this chapter, the term "nearly" is intended to have only intuitive, rather than technical, meaning.

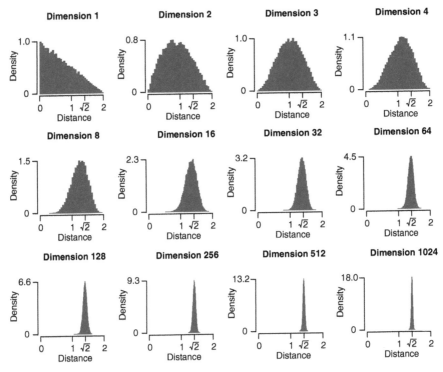

Figure 11.3   The distribution of distance between pairs of points drawn uniformly from a unit ball, in various dimensions. Each histogram was obtained from a sample of 20,000 pairs of points.

The distribution of the distance between pairs of points chosen uniformly at random from a unit ball is shown in Figure 11.3 (each cell is a histogram derived from 20,000 randomly drawn pairs). Note that as the dimension increases, the distribution becomes quite concentrated around a single value ($\sqrt{2}$). What this means is that *nearly all pairs of points in a high-dimensional ball are nearly equidistant from each other.*

The curse of dimensionality can negatively affect machine learning techniques which depend on distance. For example, consider the following binary classification problem. Feature vectors are points drawn uniformly from the m-dimensional unit sphere centered at the origin, and a hyperplane H is given, passing through the center of the sphere. Data falling on one side of H are defined to be class 1, while data falling in or on the other side of H are defined to be class 2. The Bayes error rate is zero.

Figure 11.4 shows how the curse of dimensionality wrecks the performance of the 1-nearest-neighbor classification method on this problem relative to the performance of logistic regression and a linear support vector machine. Each point in the figure corresponds to training one of these classifiers on 10,000 training data and reporting

Effect of dimension on risk of 1–NN classifier

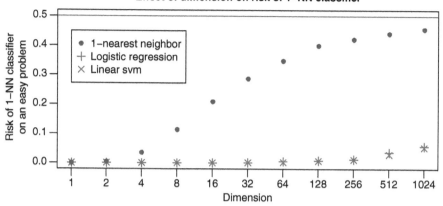

Figure 11.4   The effect of dimension on the 1-nearest-neighbor classifier using Euclidean distance, compared to logistic regression and a linear support vector machine, on a binary classification problem with zero Bayes risk and a linear class boundary. The risk of the 1-nearest-neighbor classifier rapidly increases with dimension, because the information contained in the distance between points decreases. The horizontal gray line shows the maximum possible risk under 0–1 loss.

the test error, estimated by using 10,000 test data.[2] As the dimension increases, the risk of the 1-nearest-neighbor classifier rapidly increases toward one-half (shown as a gray horizontal line), the maximum possible risk under 0–1 loss.[3] This is not surprising: since nearly all pairs of points are nearly equidistant, the distance between any pair of points provides little information about the points. The two linear classifiers are less affected by increasing dimension.

By symmetry, if X and Y are independent, uniformly distributed points in the unit ball or sphere then the distribution of $X^T Y$ is the same as the distribution of $\|Y\| X_1$, the length of Y times the first coordinate of X (the dot product of X with the first standard basis vector). Thus by Exercises 11.2, 11.3, and 11.4 below, if X and Y are independent and uniform in the ball then

$$E[X \cdot Y] = 0 \quad \text{and} \quad \text{Var}[X \cdot Y] = E[X_1^2]E[\|Y\|^2] - E[X_1]^2 E[\|Y\|]^2 = \frac{1}{m+2} \frac{m}{m+2}$$

and if X and Y are independent and uniform in the sphere then

$$E[X \cdot Y] = 0 \quad \text{and} \quad \text{Var}[X \cdot Y] = \frac{1}{m+1}.$$

---

[2] The specific hyperplane defining the problem should be irrelevant here, but for reference it is $H = \{x \in \mathbb{R}^m : x \cdot (1, \ldots, 1) = 0\}$.

[3] As before, if a trained binary classifier had risk strictly greater than one-half, we would obtain a classifier with risk less than one-half by reversing the class labels it predicts.

In this sense, *nearly all vectors in a high-dimensional ball or sphere centered at the origin are nearly orthogonal to any given vector.*

Exercise 11.1 *Determine the proportion ρ of the radius r of an m-dimensional ball such that proportion v of the volume is within ρr of the boundary.*

Exercise 11.2 *Consider just the first coordinate, X_1, of a uniformly distributed random point X in the unit ball $\{x \in \mathbb{R}^m : \|x\| \le 1\}$. Show that the density of X_1 at a point $x_1 \in [-1, 1]$ is proportional to*

$$V\left(m - 1, \sqrt{1 - x_1^2}\right) \propto \left(1 - x_1^2\right)^{\frac{m-1}{2}}.$$

Show that

$$E[X_1] = 0 \quad and \quad \mathrm{Var}[X_1] = \frac{1}{m + 2}.$$

Show that X_1 has the distribution of $N \times W^{\frac{1}{2}}$, where the sign N is uniformly distributed on the set $\{-1, 1\}$,

$$W \sim \mathrm{Beta}\left(\frac{1}{2}, \frac{m + 1}{2}\right),$$

and N and W are independent. **Hint:** *The variance can be obtained by integration by parts, but there is an easier way. Consider the distribution function $P(X_1^2 \le x)$ for $x \in [0, 1]$.*

Exercise 11.3 *Consider just the first coordinate, X_1, of a uniformly distributed random point X in the unit sphere $\{x \in \mathbb{R}^m : \|x\| = 1\}$. Show that the density of X_1 at a point $x_1 \in [-1, 1]$ is proportional to*

$$S\left(m - 1, \sqrt{1 - x_1^2}\right) \propto \left(1 - x_1^2\right)^{\frac{m-2}{2}}.$$

Show that

$$E[X_1] = 0 \quad and \quad \mathrm{Var}[X_1] = \frac{1}{m + 1}.$$

Show that X_1 has the distribution of $N \times W^{\frac{1}{2}}$, where the sign N is uniformly distributed on the set $\{-1, 1\}$,

$$W \sim \mathrm{Beta}\left(\frac{1}{2}, \frac{m}{2}\right),$$

and N and W are independent. **Hint:** *See the hint for Exercise 11.2. Note that X_1 is both the dot product of X with the first standard basis vector and also the cosine of the angle between these vectors.*

Note that by symmetry, Exercise 11.2 gives the distribution of the dot product of a uniformly distributed random point in the unit ball $\{x \in \mathbb{R}^m : \|x\| \le 1\}$ and any given unit vector (in the exercise, the ball was rotated so that the given unit vector is $(1, 0, \ldots, 0)$). Similarly, Exercise 11.3 gives the distribution of the dot product of a uniformly distributed random point in the unit sphere $\{x \in \mathbb{R}^m : \|x\| = 1\}$ and any given unit vector. Both of these distributions are symmetric about zero (and therefore have expected value zero) and have variances which approach zero as $m \to \infty$. Thus for large m, for any vector v, the vector from the origin to a uniform random point in the ball or sphere is likely to be nearly orthogonal to v.

Exercise 11.4 *What is the distribution of the distance between a random point uniformly distributed in a unit ball and the center of the ball? What is the distribution of the squared distance?*

Exercise 11.5 *Let X and Y be independent and uniformly distributed in the unit ball. Show that*

$$E[X \cdot Y] = 0, \quad \lim_{m \to \infty} \mathrm{Var}[X \cdot Y] = 0,$$

$$\lim_{m \to \infty} E\left[\|X - Y\|^2\right] = 2, \quad and \quad \lim_{m \to \infty} \mathrm{Var}\left[\|X - Y\|^2\right] = 0.$$

Since the function $z \to \sqrt{z}$ is continuous for positive z, it follows that[4]

$$\lim_{m \to \infty} E[\|X - Y\|] = \sqrt{2} \ and \ \lim_{m \to \infty} \mathrm{Var}[\|X - Y\|] = 0,$$

which explains why the distributions shown in Figure 11.3 become concentrated about $\sqrt{2}$ as m increases. **Hint:** *Use facts about $\|X\|$, $\|Y\|$ and $X \cdot Y$ established in other exercises, and $\|X - Y\|^2 = \|X\|^2 + \|Y\|^2 - 2X \cdot Y$.*

Exercise 11.6 *Show that if X and Y are independent, uniformly distributed points in the non-negative orthant[5] of either the unit ball or the unit sphere then $E[X \cdot Y] \to \frac{2}{\pi} \approx 0.63662$ as $m \to \infty$. Conclude that the expected squared distance from X to Y approaches $2(1 - \frac{2}{\pi}) \approx 0.72676$ as $m \to \infty$ for both the sphere and the ball.* **Hint:** *Use Exercises 11.2, 11.3, and 11.4. Also, two facts about the Gamma function may be useful: $\lim_{x \to \infty} \frac{\Gamma(x+a)}{\Gamma(x)x^a} = 1$ and $\Gamma(\frac{1}{2}) = \sqrt{\pi}$.*

Exercise 11.7 *Let C be the m-dimensional cube with vertices at $(\pm 1, \pm 1, \ldots, \pm 1)$, and let a sphere of radius $\frac{1}{2}$ be centered at each of the 2^m points of the form $(\pm\frac{1}{2}, \pm\frac{1}{2}, \ldots, \pm\frac{1}{2})$. Each sphere is tangent to the surface of the cube at m points and is tangent to m other spheres. Let S be the sphere which is centered at the origin and*

---

[4] This statement uses facts about convergence of random variables here which the reader may not have encountered—see Ferguson (1996, Chapters 1–3) for full justification.
[5] The *non-negative orthant* of $\mathbb{R}^m$ (or any subset thereof) is the subset with all non-negative coordinates.

tangent to all 2^m other spheres. Sphere S is shown in bold in the figure, which illustrates the case $m = 2$. Determine the radius of S, and find the smallest dimension m such that S contains a point outside of C (Hamming, 1995).

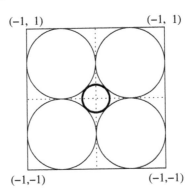

Exercise 11.8 *The Minkowski distance with parameter $p \in (0, \infty]$, or l_p distance, between two m-long vectors is*

$$d_p(x, y) = \left(\sum_{i=1}^{m} |x_i - y_i|^p \right)^{\frac{1}{p}}$$

for $p < \infty$ and

$$d_\infty(x, y) = \max_{i=1,\ldots,m} |x_i - y_i|.$$

Euclidean distance corresponds to $p = 2$. Distance d_1 is called Manhattan distance or taxicab distance, and d_∞ is called Chebyshev distance. Show that when $p = \infty$, the "ball" centered at $c \in \mathbb{R}^m$ with radius r is the cube

$$\{ x \in \mathbb{R}^m : |x_i - c_i| \leq r \text{ for all } i = 1, \ldots, m \}$$

(the volume and surface area of this ball are $(2r)^m$ and $2m(2r)^{m-1}$, respectively). Show that when $p = 1$, the "ball" centered at c with radius r is the cross-polytope (the m-dimensional generalization of a regular octahedron)

$$\{ x \in \mathbb{R}^m : (x - c) \cdot (\pm 1, \ldots, \pm 1) \leq r \}.$$

(the volume and surface area of this ball are $\frac{1}{m!}(2r)^m$ and $\frac{2}{(m-1)!}(2r)^{m-1}$, respectively). Two-dimensional spheres in l_p are shown for various values of p:

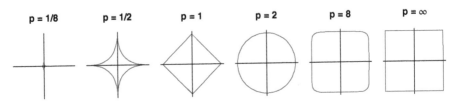

Exercise 11.9 Open-Ended Challenge. *How do the observations of this section change if l_2 distance is replaced by l_1 or l_∞ distance?*

11.2   Two Running Examples

In what follows it will be useful to have examples for illustrative purposes. As in Chapter 4, we introduce the examples here and then refer to them in the rest of the chapter.

11.2.1   Example 1: Equilateral Simplex

The *simplex dataset* consists of 650 points $x_1, \ldots, x_{650}$ in $\mathbb{R}^{64}$, and was constructed as follows. An equilateral, 64-dimensional simplex with side length 1 was specified, and its 65 vertices labeled $v_1, \ldots, v_{65}$. Then for each $i \in \{1, \ldots, 650\}$, an index j was drawn uniformly at random from the set $\{1, \ldots, 65\}$, and x_i was drawn from a Gaussian distribution with mean v_j and covariance matrix equal to the identity matrix scaled by 10^{-5}. This dataset contains 65 tight clusters, all approximately equidistant from one another and approximately the same size (the clusters vary in size from 4 to 19 data points). In plots, data points will be colored according to membership in one of the 65 clusters, which is known due to the way the data are generated.

The methods of Section 11.3 will be applied to either the 64-dimensional vectors of this dataset, or to the dissimilarity between vectors, as measured by Euclidean distance. This dataset is a difficult case for dimension-reduction because, while it has identifiable structure in the form of tight clusters, the structure is not low-dimensional.

11.2.2   Example 2: Text

The *text dataset* is obtained from this book itself.[6] This book can be decomposed into 130 small documents: 110 numbered chapter sections, 13 chapter introductions (considered as "Section 0" of each chapter), plus Chapter 1 (which has no sections), four appendices (labeled A through D), a preface (labeled P, and including the organization and acknowledgements), and a list of references (labeled R). Each of these is contained in a computer file written in the TeX typesetting language.[7] In plots, sections will be colored by chapter.

A feature vector was constructed for each of the 130 files by counting the occurrences of the terms in each file. A *character N-gram* is any sequence of N consecutive characters, including whitespace characters. For example, the first ten five-grams of this sentence, allowing overlaps, are

"For␣e", "or␣ex", "r␣exa", "␣exam", "examp", "xampl", "ample", "mple,",
"ple,␣", and "le,␣t",

---

[6] Where convenient, references to this book may actually refer to a nearly identical, earlier draft—otherwise, the book might never be finished!

[7] The TeX files have been modified slightly. For example, all characters were converted to lowercase, and punctuation, TeX comments, and extraneous white space characters were removed.

where the symbol "␣" stands for a single space character. In this example, a *term* is any five-gram, allowing overlaps as above, which occurs in this book. This book contains 61,190 distinct terms, the six most common being, in order, "␣the␣" (which occurs 6429 times), "tion␣" (2876), "␣and␣" (2145), "param" (1784), "regre" (1706), and "class" (1573)—the high frequency of the terms "param" and "regre" is due, in part, to the author's use of the TEX macro \regreparam to typeset the symbol θ.

The occurrences of each term in each file are counted, producing a 61,190-long *term-frequency (TF)* vector. The term-frequency vector can be treated as a numeric feature vector describing each file. It is generally useful to weight the coordinates of this vector so that terms which occur in most files (for example, "␣the␣" occurs in all 130 sections of this book, "␣and␣" occurs in 126, and "␣data" occurs in 110) are suppressed and terms which occur in relatively few files (for example, "eigen" occurs in only five sections of this book) are enhanced. One way to accomplish this is to count the number of sections in which each term occurs (since the terms are precisely those N-grams which occur in the book, each term occurs in at least one section) and weight each term inversely to the number of sections. This is typically done on a logarithmic scale, so that the feature vector associated with each section S of the book is

$$\left(\left(\begin{array}{c} \text{number of times term } t \\ \text{occurs in document } S \end{array}\right) \times \log\left(\frac{\text{total number of documents}}{\text{number of documents in which term } t \text{ occurs}}\right)\right)_{\text{all terms } t}.$$

This is called the *term-frequency inverse-document-frequency (TF-IDF)* vector associated with section S. TF-IDF vectors are usually scaled so that they are unit vectors. In many applications, the set of terms is much larger than the set of terms occurring in any particular document, in which case most coordinates of the resulting TF-IDF vectors are equal to zero.

Let $x_1, \ldots, x_n$ denote the TF-IDF vectors for the $n = 130$ sections of the book. One commonly used way to measure the similarity between these vectors is *cosine similarity*,

$$s(w, x) = \cos \angle wx = \frac{w}{\|w\|} \cdot \frac{x}{\|x\|}.$$

When vectors w and x have all non-negative coordinates, as is the case for TF-IDF vectors, $s(w, x) \in [0, 1]$. When the cosine similarity of two TF-IDF vectors is large, it generally means that some relatively rare terms occur relatively frequently in both documents.

The methods of Section 11.3 will be applied to either the 61,190-dimensional TF-IDF vectors of this dataset (normalized to be unit vectors), or to the dissimilarity between vectors, as measured by cosine dissimilarity (that is, one minus the cosine similarity). The dissimilarity between sections of this book are shown in Figure 11.5.

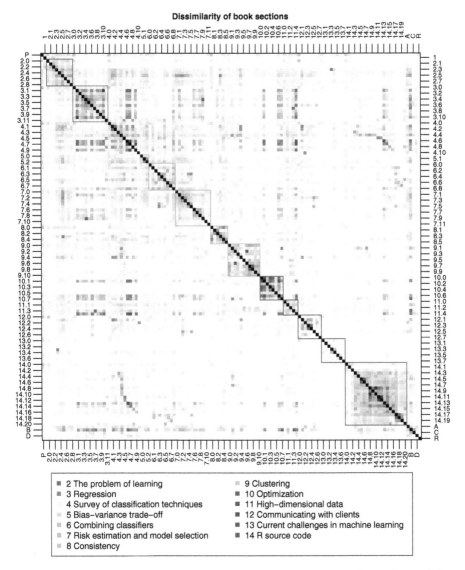

Dissimilarity of book sections

■ 2 The problem of learning	▨ 9 Clustering
■ 3 Regression	■ 10 Optimization
4 Survey of classification techniques	■ 11 High-dimensional data
▨ 5 Bias-variance trade-off	■ 12 Communicating with clients
▨ 6 Combining classifiers	■ 13 Current challenges in machine learning
▨ 7 Risk estimation and model selection	■ 14 R source code
▨ 8 Consistency	

Figure 11.5   The matrix of pairwise dissimilarities between the 130 sections of this book, as measured by the cosine similarity between the corresponding TF-IDF vectors computed from 5-grams. The dissimilarity is shown in grayscale, and ranges from zero (black) to one (white).

11.3   Reducing Dimension While Preserving Information

This section presents various approaches to finding a k-dimensional, approximate representation $\hat{x}_1, \ldots, \hat{x}_n \in \mathbb{R}^k$ of an observed set of m-dimensional feature vectors $x_1, \ldots, x_n \in \mathbb{R}^m$, where $k < m$. There are several reasons one might wish to do this: because not all m features carry information relevant to a given problem, and a smaller, more informative feature space is desired; because certain algorithms are perceived to offer better performance (lower-risk predictions, lower computational cost, or both) working in a lower-dimensional space; or for exploratory plots of the data (in which case the values $k = 1$, $k = 2$, and $k = 3$ are of particular interest).

Each approach is distinguished by a set of criteria defining a "good" low-dimensional representation of $x_1, \ldots, x_n$, and a method of finding an optimal (or approximately optimal) representation with respect to its criteria. Some approaches (principal component analysis, linear multidimensional scaling, projection pursuit, autoencoders) construct explicit maps $\mathbb{R}^m \to \mathbb{R}^k$ which can be applied to as-yet-unobserved data, while others (stress-minimizing multidimensional scaling, manifold learning, clustering) work only on the data given. Some approaches (multidimensional scaling, manifold learning) depend only on a matrix of dissimilarities between feature vectors, and thus generalize to the case where only these dissimilarities are given, in which case the goal is to find a set of n points in $\mathbb{R}^k$ whose interpoint Euclidean distances approximate the given dissimilarities.

11.3.1   The Geometry of Means and Covariances of Real Features

When all features are real, the observed feature vectors can be expressed in the rows of a $n \times m$ matrix[8]

$$\mathbf{X} = \begin{bmatrix} x_{11} & x_{12} & \cdots & x_{1m} \\ x_{21} & x_{22} & \cdots & x_{2m} \\ \vdots & \vdots & & \vdots \\ x_{n1} & x_{n2} & \cdots & x_{nm} \end{bmatrix} = \begin{bmatrix} x_1 \\ x_2 \\ \vdots \\ x_n \end{bmatrix}.$$

---

[8] In Chapter 3 and Sections 4.6 and 4.7, it was convenient within the context of linear models to use the symbol $\mathbf{X}$ to represent this matrix with a column of all 1's adjoined to it,

$$\mathbf{X} = \begin{bmatrix} 1 & x_{11} & x_{12} & \cdots & x_{1m} \\ 1 & x_{21} & x_{22} & \cdots & x_{2m} \\ \vdots & \vdots & \vdots & & \vdots \\ 1 & x_{n1} & x_{n2} & \cdots & x_{nm} \end{bmatrix}.$$

In this chapter, $\mathbf{X}$ does not have a column of all 1's adjoined to the features.

We follow the convention of treating all vectors—including the feature vectors $x_1, \ldots, x_n$—as column vectors, although $x_1, \ldots, x_n$ are represented as the rows of $\mathbf{X}$. Sometimes it is convenient to have the data translated so that the mean feature vector is at the origin, and sometimes it is convenient to have the data rotated so that the features are uncorrelated. This can be done by matrix operations on $\mathbf{X}$ as follows.

Let the sample mean and the sample covariance matrix of feature vectors $x_1, \ldots, x_n$ (the rows of $\mathbf{X}$) be denoted respectively by

$$\bar{x} = \frac{1}{n} \sum_{i=1}^{n} x_i \quad \text{and} \quad \mathbf{S} = \frac{1}{n} \sum_{i=1}^{n} (x_i - \bar{x})(x_i - \bar{x})^{\mathrm{T}} = \frac{1}{n} \mathbf{X}^{\mathrm{T}} \mathbf{X} - \bar{x}\bar{x}^{\mathrm{T}}.$$

Translating the data so that the mean feature vector is at the origin is equivalent to subtracting $\bar{x}$ from each row of $\mathbf{X}$, and data which have been so translated are said to be *centered*. One way to center data is by multiplying $\mathbf{X}$ on the left[9] by the $n \times n$ *centering matrix*

$$\mathbf{H} = \mathbf{I} - \frac{1}{n} \begin{bmatrix} 1 \\ 1 \\ \vdots \\ 1 \end{bmatrix} [1, \ldots, 1] = \begin{bmatrix} 1 - \dfrac{1}{n} & -\dfrac{1}{n} & \cdots & -\dfrac{1}{n} \\ -\dfrac{1}{n} & 1 - \dfrac{1}{n} & \cdots & -\dfrac{1}{n} \\ \vdots & \vdots & \ddots & \vdots \\ -\dfrac{1}{n} & -\dfrac{1}{n} & \cdots & 1 - \dfrac{1}{n} \end{bmatrix}.$$

The following exercise says that if a dataset is represented by the rows of $\mathbf{X}$, then the centered dataset is represented by the rows of $\mathbf{HX}$.

Exercise 11.10 *Show that matrix* $\mathbf{HX}$ *is equal to matrix* $\mathbf{X}$ *with* $\bar{x}$ *subtracted from each row. Show that* $\mathbf{H}^2 = \mathbf{H}$. *Show that the sample covariance matrix of* $\mathbf{X}$ *and of* $\mathbf{HX}$ *is*

$$\mathbf{S} = \frac{1}{n} (\mathbf{HX})^{\mathrm{T}} (\mathbf{HX}) = \frac{1}{n} \mathbf{X}^{\mathrm{T}} \mathbf{HX}.$$

The sample covariance matrix $\mathbf{S}$ is non-negative definite, so it can be represented as

$$\mathbf{S} = \mathbf{Q} \Lambda \mathbf{Q}^{\mathrm{T}},$$

---

[9] Geometrically, left multiplication by $\mathbf{H}$ projects a column vector $z \in \mathbb{R}^m$ into the $(m - 1)$-dimensional subspace $\{x \in \mathbb{R}^m : x \cdot (1, \ldots, 1) = 0\}$. Forming the product $\mathbf{HX}$ is *not* how one would compute the translated version of $\mathbf{X}$.

where $\Lambda = \mathrm{diag}(\lambda_1, \lambda_2, \ldots, \lambda_m)$ and $\lambda_1 \geq \lambda_2 \geq \cdots \geq \lambda_m \geq 0$ are the eigenvalues of $\mathbf{S}$ written in non-increasing order,[10] and where $\mathbf{Q}$ is an $m \times m$ orthogonal matrix[11] whose columns are the corresponding eigenvectors. Rotating the centered data so that the features are uncorrelated is accomplished by multiplying $\mathbf{HX}$ on the right by $\mathbf{Q}$. Feature vectors which have been translated so that the mean feature vector is at the origin and rotated so that the features are uncorrelated are said to be *centered and decorrelated*.

Exercise 11.11 *Show that the sample covariance matrix of* $\mathbf{HXQ}$ *is the diagonal matrix* Λ.

This process can be taken one step further: the rows of $\mathbf{HXQ\Lambda}^{-\frac{1}{2}}$ have sample mean zero and sample covariance matrix equal to the identity matrix. Feature vectors which have been translated, rotated, and scaled this way are said to be *sphered*.

11.3.2 Principal Component Analysis

The goal of *principal component analysis (PCA)* is to find a linear projection of n centered data points in $\mathbb{R}^m$ into $\mathbb{R}^k$, $k < m$, which preserves as much information as possible, where information is measured in terms of variance. Given a centered dataset represented by the rows of $\mathbf{HX}$, a linear map $\mathbb{R}^m \to \mathbb{R}^k$, represented by an $m \times k$ matrix $\mathbf{W} = [W_1, \ldots, W_k]$, is sought such that:

(1) the columns $W_1, \ldots, W_k$ are mutually orthogonal unit vectors;

(2) $\mathrm{SVar}[\mathbf{HX}W_1] \geq \mathrm{SVar}[\mathbf{HX}z]$ for all unit vectors $z \in \mathbb{R}^m$, that is,

$$W_1 = \operatorname*{argmax}_{z \in \mathbb{R}^m \,:\, \|z\|=1} \mathrm{SVar}[\mathbf{HX}z] \; ;$$

(3) for $j = 2, \ldots, k$, $\mathrm{SVar}[\mathbf{HX}W_j] \geq \mathrm{SVar}[\mathbf{HX}z]$ for all unit vectors $z \in \mathbb{R}^m$ such that $\mathbf{HX}z$ is uncorrelated with all of $\mathbf{HX}W_1, \ldots, \mathbf{HX}W_{j-1}$, that is,

$$W_j = \operatorname*{argmax}_{\substack{z \in \mathbb{R}^m \,:\, \|z\|=1, \\ \mathrm{SCor}[\mathbf{HX}W_1,\, \mathbf{HX}z]=0, \\ \cdots \\ \mathrm{SCor}[\mathbf{HX}W_{j-1},\, \mathbf{HX}z]=0}} \mathrm{SVar}[\mathbf{HX}z].$$

where $\mathrm{SVar}[\cdot]$ and $\mathrm{SCor}[\cdot, \cdot]$ represent the sample variance and correlation, respectively. In words, the *first principal component* W_1 is a unit vector in $\mathbb{R}^m$ pointing in the direction in which the data have maximal variance. The *second principal component*

---

[10] The eigenvalues of a real, symmetric matrix are all real.

[11] An *orthogonal matrix* $\mathbf{Q}$ is one which satisfies $\mathbf{Q}^{-1} = \mathbf{Q}^{\mathrm{T}}$, that is, $\mathbf{Q}^{\mathrm{T}}\mathbf{Q} = \mathbf{Q}\mathbf{Q}^{\mathrm{T}} = \mathbf{I}$. Geometrically, multiplication by $\mathbf{Q}$ performs a rotation and/or reflection of one basis onto another.

W_2 is a unit vector in $\mathbb{R}^m$, constrained to be orthogonal to the first principal component, pointing in the direction in which the data have maximal variance. And so on: the *jth principal component* W_j is a unit vector in $\mathbb{R}^m$, constrained to be orthogonal to all of the first $j - 1$ principal components, pointing in the direction in which the data have maximal variance. The rows of the $n \times k$ matrix $\mathbf{HXW}$ are the n feature vectors (data points) projected onto their first k principal components.

Exercise 11.12 *Show that the $m \times k$ matrix $[Q_1, \ldots, Q_k]$ formed by taking the first k columns of $\mathbf{Q}$ satisfies properties (1), (2), and (3), so the first k columns of $\mathbf{HXQ}$ are $x_1, \ldots, x_n$ projected onto their first k principal components.*

Exercise 11.12 states that principle component analysis is the same as translating a dataset to the origin, rotating it to decorrelate the features, and taking the first k decorrelated features. This means that computationally, the projection of the data onto the first k principal components is the same as finding the k largest eigenvalues of the covariance matrix $\mathbf{S}$ and their corresponding eigenvectors. It also means that the variance of the data projected onto the ith principal component is λ_i, the ith largest eigenvalue of $\mathbf{S}$. The results of applying PCA to the simplex dataset to produce a two-dimensional representation is shown in the left-hand cell of Figure 11.6.

The choice of k is usually made heuristically, balancing the need in any given application for k to be small against the need to preserve information in the data. The *proportion of total variation* preserved in projecting data onto its first k principal components is defined as

$$\frac{\sum_{i=1}^k \lambda_i}{\sum_{i=1}^m \lambda_i} = \frac{\sum_{i=1}^k \lambda_i}{\mathrm{tr}(\mathbf{S})} \in [0, 1]. \tag{11.1}$$

In the context of PCA, the columns $Q_1, \ldots, Q_k$ of $\mathbf{Q}$ are called *loading vectors*. The loading vectors can sometimes be interpreted to gain insight into the sources of variance in the data. For example, one might find that most of the coordinates of the first loading vector Q_1 are negligibly small relative to a few of the coordinates. Ignoring what is negligibly small, the first principal component can be viewed as a linear combination of a few of the original features, with weights given according to the non-negligible coordinates of Q_1. Depending on the application, this particular combination of the features may be found to be meaningful. Similarly for Q_2, and so on.

11.3.3   Working in "Dissimilarity Space"

A *dissimilarity measure* on feature space $\mathcal{X}$ is a function $d : \mathcal{X} \times \mathcal{X} \to \mathbb{R}^+$ such that $d(x, x) = 0$ for all $x \in \mathcal{X}$ and $d(w, x) = d(x, w)$ for all $w, x \in \mathcal{X}$. The value $d(w, x)$ is interpreted as the dissimilarity of two feature vectors w and x. In general, $d(w, x)$ need not satisfy a triangle inequality, although commonly used dissimilarity measures on $\mathbb{R}^m$ often do, such as the family of metrics defined in Exercise 11.8. Construction of

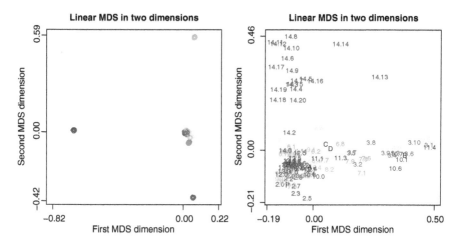

Figure 11.6   Linear MDS applied to the simplex dataset (left cell) and the text dataset with TF-IDF (right cell) of Section 11.2. In the simplex dataset, linear MDS (which in this case is equivalent to PCA) has separated the single largest cluster, of size 19, from the rest of the data on the first principal axis (horizontal). It has separated the two second-largest clusters, each of size 16, from each other and the rest of the data on the second principal axis (vertical). Linear MDS has preserved the fact that these three clusters are approximately equidistant from each other, at the cost of collapsing the other 62 clusters together. The two-dimensional linear MDS representation of the simplex data has preserved 5.4% of the total variation (11.1). In the text dataset, linear MDS has separated most of Chapter 3 (regression) and parts of Chapters 4 (logistic regression, neural networks, and support vector machines), 10 (quasi-Newton methods, general remarks, and EM), and 11 (model regularization) from the rest of the book on the first principal axis (horizontal). It has separated most of Chapter 14 (R code) from the rest of the book on the second principal axis (vertical). The two-dimensional linear MDS representation of the text data has preserved 10.3% of the dissimilarity matrix (11.2).

a good dissimilarity measure for any particular application is something of an art: some specific measures and their motivation will be discussed later in this chapter.[12]

A dissimilarity measure allows one to apply certain techniques without further regard for the structure of the feature space $\mathcal{X}$.[13] For example, the hierarchical and k-medoid clustering algorithms described in Chapter 9, and the k-nearest-neighbor

---

[12] It is often useful computationally to have $d(w, x)$ be equal to zero for most pairs of observed feature vectors w and x, and to have all of the non-zero $d(w, x)$ values be obtainable without doing $O(n^2)$ work.

[13] It is to be hoped that the structure of $\mathcal{X}$ which is relevant to the application at hand is expressed in the dissimilarity measure!

and nearest-cluster classifiers described in Chapter 4, can be applied given only the matrix of dissimilarity values

$$\mathbf{D} = [d(x_i, x_j)]_{i,j=1}^n.$$

11.3.4   Linear Multidimensional Scaling

Multidimensional scaling (MDS) is a family of techniques for moving from dissimilarity space to real feature space $\mathbb{R}^k$. Suppose there are objects $o_1, \ldots, o_n$ (which may or may not be represented by vectors in some feature space) and a matrix of pairwise dissimilarities between the objects is given,

$$\mathbf{D} = [d(o_i, o_j)]_{i,j=1}^n.$$

Given a value of k, multidimensional scaling attempts to construct a set of n points, $\hat{x}_1, \ldots, \hat{x}_n \in \mathbb{R}^k$, with the property that the matrix of Euclidean distances between the points,

$$[d_2(\hat{x}_i, \hat{x}_j)]_{i,j=1}^n,$$

is close to the dissimilarity matrix $\mathbf{D}$ in some user-specified sense. The points $\hat{x}_1, \ldots, \hat{x}_n$ are then used as surrogates for the objects $o_1, \ldots, o_n$, and the coordinates of the $\hat{x}_i$'s are interpreted as *latent features* of the objects.[14] This section presents the original, linear multidimensional scaling algorithm. A different approach is presented in Section 11.3.6.

We begin with the geometric motivation for a definition. Suppose that dissimilarity matrix $\mathbf{D}$ actually arose as the matrix of pairwise Euclidean distances between points in $\mathbb{R}^m$: that is, suppose the objects $o_1, \ldots, o_n$ correspond to points $x_1, \ldots, x_n \in \mathbb{R}^m$ and that $\mathbf{D}_{i,j} = d(o_i, o_j) = d_2(x_i, x_j)$ for all i and j. Then for all i and j,

$$\mathbf{D}_{i,j}^2 = d(o_i, o_j)^2 = (x_i - x_j)^T (x_i - x_j) = x_i^T x_i + x_j^T x_j - 2x_i^T x_j,$$

which means that the matrix of distances $\mathbf{D}$ can be obtained from the matrix of inner products $[x_i^T x_j]_{i,j=1}^n$. Since the distances between points $x_1, \ldots, x_n$ are translation invariant, $\mathbf{D}$ can also be obtained from the matrix of inner products of the x_i's after they have been centered. Thus $\mathbf{D}$ can be obtained from the matrix

$$\mathbf{B} = [(x_i - \bar{x})(x_j - \bar{x})^T]_{i,j=1}^n = \mathbf{HX}(\mathbf{HX})^T.$$

Furthermore, the matrix $\mathbf{B}$ of inner products can be obtained directly from the matrix of distances.

---

[14] The motivation for creating MDS was to enable the discovery of latent features in psychological data originally obtained as a matrix of dissimilarities (Torgerson, 1952).

Exercise 11.13 *Show that in the above,* $\mathbf{B} = \mathbf{HAH}$*, where*

$$\mathbf{A} = \left[-\frac{1}{2} d_2(x_i, x_j)^2 \right]_{i,j=1}^n$$

and $\mathbf{H}$ *is the centering matrix.*

This observation motivates a general definition. Given *any* dissimilarity matrix $\mathbf{D} = [d(o_i, o_j)]_{i,j=1}^n$ (not just a Euclidean distance matrix), define matrices $\mathbf{A}$ and $\mathbf{B}$ by

$$\mathbf{A} = \left[-\frac{1}{2} d(o_i, o_j)^2 \right]_{i,j=1}^n \quad \text{and} \quad \mathbf{B} = \mathbf{HAH}.$$

Theorem 11.1 A Property of Euclidean Distance (Young and Householder). *A necessary and sufficient condition for* $\mathbf{D}$ *to be the pairwise distances of a set of points in Euclidean space is that the matrix* $\mathbf{B}$ *be non-negative definite, and in this case the set of points is unique apart from a rigid motion.*

Linear multidimensional scaling is the result of treating the matrix $\mathbf{B}$ as if it is a matrix of inner products of n points in $\mathbb{R}^k$, for some value of k. Since $\mathbf{B}$ is real and symmetric, it has an eigendecomposition

$$\mathbf{B} = \mathbf{Q \Lambda Q}^\mathsf{T},$$

where $\mathbf{\Lambda} = \text{diag}(\lambda_1, \lambda_2, \ldots, \lambda_m)$ and $\lambda_1 \geq \lambda_2 \geq \cdots \geq \lambda_m$ are the eigenvalues of $\mathbf{B}$ written in non-increasing order. It is possible that some of the eigenvalues are negative: in fact, at least one of the eigenvalues must be negative unless $\mathbf{D}$ is Euclidean by Theorem 11.1. If fewer than k of the eigenvalues are positive, linear MDS cannot construct a k-dimensional realization. If at least k of the eigenvalues are positive, linear MDS can construct a k-dimensional realization: it consists of the rows of the $n \times k$ matrix

$$\hat{\mathbf{X}} = [Q_1, \ldots, Q_k] \, \text{diag}\left(\lambda_1^{\frac{1}{2}}, \ldots, \lambda_k^{\frac{1}{2}} \right).$$

Two generalizations of the proportion of total variation (11.1), both interpreted as "the proportion of the dissimilarity matrix explained" by a k-dimensional representation, are (Mardia et al., 1979):

$$\frac{\sum_{i=1}^k |\lambda_i|}{\sum_{i=1}^m |\lambda_i|} \tag{11.2}$$

and

$$\frac{\sum_{i=1}^k \lambda_i^2}{\sum_{i=1}^m \lambda_i^2}.$$

We shall use (11.2) in the examples which follow.

When it exists, the k-dimensional dataset returned by linear MDS is optimal with respect to two criteria, expressed in terms of the matrix of pairwise Euclidean distances between rows of $\hat{\mathbf{X}}$,

$$\hat{\mathbf{D}} = \left[d_2(\hat{x}_i, \hat{x}_j)\right]_{i,j=1}^n,$$

and the corresponding matrix of inner products,

$$\hat{\mathbf{B}} = \mathbf{H}\hat{\mathbf{X}}(\mathbf{H}\hat{\mathbf{X}})^\mathsf{T} = \mathbf{H}\left[-\frac{1}{2}d_2(\hat{x}_i, \hat{x}_j)^2\right]_{i,j=1}^n \mathbf{H}.$$

The optimality criteria are stated in terms of distance with respect to the Frobenius norm. The *Frobenius norm* of an $n \times m$ real matrix $\mathbf{M}$ is its Euclidean length, considered as an nm-long vector:

$$\|\mathbf{M}\|_F = \left(\sum_{i=1}^n \sum_{j=1}^m \mathbf{M}_{ij}^2\right)^{\frac{1}{2}}.$$

Theorem 11.2 Constrained Optimality Criterion of Linear MDS. *If dissimilarity matrix $\mathbf{D}$ is the matrix of Euclidean distances between the rows of $\mathbf{X}$, then the linear MDS realization minimizes $\|\mathbf{D} - \hat{\mathbf{D}}\|_F$ over all configurations of n points in $\mathbb{R}^k$ obtained by a projection of $\mathbf{X}$ into $\mathbb{R}^k$.*

Theorem 11.3 Global Optimality Criterion of Linear MDS. *The linear MDS realization minimizes $\|\mathbf{B} - \hat{\mathbf{B}}\|_F$ over all configurations of n points in $\mathbb{R}^k$.*

Note that in Theorem 11.3, the matrix $\hat{\mathbf{B}}$ is a matrix of inner products, but the matrix $\mathbf{B}$ need not be (because the matrix $\mathbf{D}$ need not be a matrix of Euclidean distances among some set of points).

11.3.5 The Singular Value Decomposition and Low-Rank Approximation

When the dissimilarity matrix $\mathbf{D}$ arises as the Euclidean distances between points $x_1, \ldots, x_n \in \mathbb{R}^m$, PCA and linear MDS are exactly the same thing. This can be shown by using a low-rank (as opposed to low-dimension) approximation of the centered data matrix $\mathbf{HX}$ obtained from its singular value decomposition.

The *singular value decomposition (SVD)* of an $n \times m$ matrix $\mathbf{M}$ is defined as

$$\mathbf{M} = \mathbf{U}\boldsymbol{\Sigma}\mathbf{V}^\mathsf{T}$$

where $\mathbf{U}$ is an $n \times n$ orthogonal matrix, $\mathbf{V}$ is an $m \times m$ orthogonal matrix, and $\boldsymbol{\Sigma}$ is an $n \times m$ diagonal matrix with diagonal entries $\sigma_1 \geq \sigma_2 \geq \cdots \geq \sigma_{\min(n,m)} \geq 0$. The diagonal entries of $\boldsymbol{\Sigma}$ are the *singular values* of the matrix $\mathbf{M}$, the columns of $\mathbf{U}$ are the *left singular vectors* of $\mathbf{M}$, and the columns of $\mathbf{V}$ (the rows of $\mathbf{V}^\mathsf{T}$) are the *right singular vectors* of $\mathbf{M}$.

Theorem 11.4 Existence of the SVD. *Every real matrix has a singular value decomposition.*

The SVD can be used to construct low-rank approximations of a matrix which are optimal with in the sense of distance with respect to the Frobenius norm.

Theorem 11.5 Optimality Criterion of the SVD (Eckhart-Young). *Let* $\mathbf{M}$ *be an* $n \times m$ *matrix with SVD* $\mathbf{M} = \mathbf{U}\mathbf{\Sigma}\mathbf{V}^{\mathrm{T}}$ *and let* $k \leq \mathrm{rank}(\mathbf{M})$. *Among all* $n \times m$ *matrices* $\mathbf{Z}$ *of rank* k, $\|\mathbf{M} - \mathbf{Z}\|_F$ *is minimized by the matrix*

$$\mathbf{Z} = [U_1, \dots, U_k] \begin{bmatrix} \sigma_1 & & & \\ & \sigma_2 & & \\ & & \ddots & \\ & & & \sigma_k \end{bmatrix} [V_1, \dots, V_k]^{\mathrm{T}}.$$

where $U_1, \dots, U_k$ *are the first* k *columns of* $\mathbf{U}$, $V_1, \dots, V_k$ *are the first* k *columns of* $\mathbf{V}$, *and the matrix in the middle is* $\mathrm{diag}(\sigma_1, \dots, \sigma_k)$. *The optimal matrix* $\mathbf{Z}$ *is uniquely defined if* $\sigma_k > \sigma_{k+1}$.

For an arbitrary matrix $\mathbf{M}$, the eigendecomposition of both $\mathbf{M}\mathbf{M}^{\mathrm{T}}$ and $\mathbf{M}^{\mathrm{T}}\mathbf{M}$ can be obtained from the singular value decomposition of $\mathbf{M}$:

$$\mathbf{M}\mathbf{M}^{\mathrm{T}} = \mathbf{U}\left(\mathbf{\Sigma}\mathbf{\Sigma}^{\mathrm{T}}\right)\mathbf{U}^{\mathrm{T}} \text{ and } \mathbf{M}^{\mathrm{T}}\mathbf{M} = \mathbf{V}\left(\mathbf{\Sigma}\mathbf{\Sigma}^{\mathrm{T}}\right)\mathbf{V}^{\mathrm{T}}$$

are the eigendecompositions of the respective matrices. In particular, the eigenvalues of $\mathbf{M}\mathbf{M}^{\mathrm{T}}$ are $\sigma_1^2 \geq \sigma_2^2 \geq \cdots \geq \sigma_{\min(n,m)}^2 \geq 0$, plus $n - m$ additional zero eigenvalues if $n > m$, and the eigenvalues of $\mathbf{M}^{\mathrm{T}}\mathbf{M}$ are $\sigma_1^2 \geq \sigma_2^2 \geq \cdots \geq \sigma_{\min(n,m)}^2 \geq 0$, plus $m - n$ additional zero eigenvalues if $m > n$.

Exercise 11.14 *Let* $\mathbf{X}$ *be an* $n \times m$ *matrix whose rows represent* n *feature vectors in* $\mathbb{R}^m$. *Let* $\mathbf{H}\mathbf{X}$ *be the matrix of centered feature vectors and let* $\mathbf{H}\mathbf{X} = \mathbf{U}\mathbf{\Sigma}\mathbf{V}^{\mathrm{T}}$ *be the singular value decomposition of* $\mathbf{H}\mathbf{X}$.

 (1) Show that projection of $\mathbf{H}\mathbf{X}$ *onto its first* k *principal components is the first* k *columns of* $\mathbf{H}\mathbf{X}\mathbf{V}$.

 (2) Show that linear multidimensional scaling constructs the first k *columns of* $\mathbf{U}\mathbf{\Sigma}$.

 (3) Show that these are the same.

Exercise 11.14 shows that when principal component analysis is applicable, linear multidimensional scaling on the matrix of Euclidean distances is also applicable and produces the same k-dimensional realization as PCA. Multidimensional scaling, however, is applicable more generally than PCA since MDS only requires a dissimilarity matrix, and the dissimilarity matrix can be non-Euclidean. The results of applying linear MDS to find two-dimensional realizations of the simplex and text datasets are shown in Figure 11.6.

11.3.6   Stress-Minimizing Multidimensional Scaling

Another way to approach multidimensional scaling is by approximate numerical solution of an optimization problem. Given a configuration of points $\hat{x}_1, \ldots, \hat{x}_n \in \mathbb{R}^k$, let

$$\hat{\mathbf{D}} = [d_2(\hat{x}_i, \hat{x}_j)]_{i,j=1}^n$$

be the matrix of interpoint Euclidean distances. Given a target dissimilarity matrix $\mathbf{D}$, the closeness of $\hat{\mathbf{D}}$ to $\mathbf{D}$ is measured by an objective function, which in this context is called a *stress function*: for example, the Frobenius distance from $\hat{\mathbf{D}}$ to $\mathbf{D}$, $\|\mathbf{D} - \hat{\mathbf{D}}\|_F$. Starting from an initial configuration of points, an optimization algorithm from Chapter 10 can be used to find an approximately optimal configuration in the sense of minimizing the stress between $\hat{\mathbf{D}}$ and $\mathbf{D}$. There are many variations of stress-minimizing MDS: interpoint distances need not be Euclidean and the stress function need not be Frobenius distance.

Given a high-dimensional dataset $x_1, \ldots, x_n \in \mathbb{R}^m$, configurations of points in $\mathbb{R}^k$ whose interpoint distances are close to the interpoint distances between $x_1, \ldots, x_n$ are found by both stress-minimizing MDS and PCA (or linear MDS, which is the same thing in this case). One difference between the methods is that PCA constructs a function from $\mathbb{R}^m \to \mathbb{R}^k$ while stress-minimizing MDS does not. A consequence of this is that new data $x_{n+1}, \ldots$ can be mapped into a k-dimensional realization by the function found by PCA, while this cannot be done with stress-minimizing MDS. Thus one criterion for choosing between the two methods is whether an application requires that as-yet-unobserved data be mapped onto an existing low-dimensional realization of observed data. The results of applying stress-minimizing MDS to find two-dimensional realizations of the simplex and text datasets are shown in Figure 11.7.

11.3.7   Projection Pursuit

Principal component analysis finds a linear projection of n data points in $\mathbb{R}^m$ into $\mathbb{R}^k$, $k < m$, which is optimal with respect to the criteria listed in (1), (2), and (3) of Section 11.3.2, and computation of this optimum is achieved by computation of the singular value decomposition of the centered data matrix $\mathbf{HX}$. As an alternative, one could retain the idea of linear projection, but replace (1), (2), and (3) with any set of criteria and use the methods of Chapter 10 to search for the best representation of a dataset with respect to the given criteria. Such approaches are called *projection pursuit*.

This section describes one of the earliest approaches to projection pursuit. Based on observation of human interaction with high-dimensional datasets, Friedman and Tukey (1974, p. 882) proposed a criterion which rewards projections that "produce many very small interpoint distances while, at the same time, maintaining the overall spread of the data." Let $\mathbf{M} = [M_1, \ldots, M_k]$ be an $m \times k$ matrix whose columns are constrained to be unit vectors and mutually orthogonal, so that multiplication on the

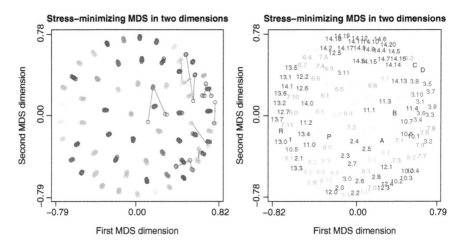

Figure 11.7   Stress-minimizing MDS applied to the simplex dataset (left cell) and the text dataset (right cell) of Section 11.2. In the simplex dataset, stress-minimizing MDS has separated all 65 clusters from one another, and has fragmented eight clusters (cluster fragments are connected by gray line segments). In the text dataset, stress-minimizing MDS has kept most of the chapters mostly together, exceptions being Chapter 4 (classification), Chapter 6 (ensembles), Chapter 8 (consistency), and Chapter 12 (communications), which are relatively diffuse.

right by $\mathbf{M}$ performs a linear projection of $\mathbb{R}^m$ into $\mathbb{R}^k$. The projection pursuit realization $\hat{x}_1, \ldots, \hat{x}_n$ will be the rows of the matrix $\hat{\mathbf{X}} = \mathbf{XM}$. Let three tuning parameters be given: $p \in [0, \frac{1}{2})$, $R > 0$, and a function $\psi : [0, \infty) \to [0, \infty)$ which decreases monotonically to zero on $[0, R]$ and is identically zero on $[R, \infty)$. Friedman and Tukey proposed the objective function

$$\delta(\mathbf{M}) \prod_{j=1}^{k} \sigma(\mathbf{M}_j),$$

where $\delta(\mathbf{M})$ measures "local density" of projected data $\hat{\mathbf{X}} = \mathbf{XM}$,

$$\delta(\mathbf{M}) = \sum_{i,j=1}^{n} \psi(d_2(\hat{x}_i, \hat{x}_j)),$$

and $\sigma(\mathbf{M}_j)$ measures the "spread" of the one-dimensional projected data $\hat{\mathbf{X}}_j = \mathbf{XM}_j$ by a trimmed standard deviation: $\sigma(\mathbf{M}_j)$ is the standard deviation of the set of numbers formed by sorting the coordinates of $\hat{\mathbf{X}}_j$ and deleting the pn smallest and pn largest. The factor $\delta(\mathbf{M})$ is large when data are concentrated locally, while the factor

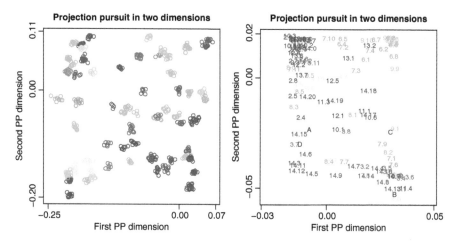

Figure 11.8   Projection pursuit applied to the simplex dataset (left cell, with tuning parameters $p = 0.1$, $R = 10$, and $\psi(r) = 1 - \frac{r}{R}$) and the text dataset (right cell, with tuning parameters $p = 0.1$, $R = 0.1$, and $\psi(r) = 1 - \frac{r}{R}$) of Section 11.2. In the simplex dataset, projection pursuit has separated some of the clusters and achieved a fairly uniform spread of the data in both the horizontal and vertical directions. In the text dataset, projection pursuit has put Chapters 6 and 9 mostly in the upper-right corner, Chapter 14 mostly along the bottom side, and Chapters 2, 10, 12, and 13 in the upper-left corner.

$\sigma(\mathbf{M}_j)$ is large when the data are spread out in the jth direction. The results of applying Friedman–Tukey projection pursuit to the simplex and text datasets is shown in Figure 11.8.

11.3.8   Feature Selection

Feature selection is a projection of feature space onto a subspace consisting certain coordinates, and the process of searching for a set of features which produce a low-risk model can be viewed as a particular form of projection pursuit. Given a risk estimate or model selection criterion from Chapter 7–or any other model selection criterion—feature selection seeks a subset of the features $\{i_1, i_2, \ldots, i_k\} \subseteq \{1, \ldots, m\}$ such that a model trained on that subset of features,

$$\begin{bmatrix} x_{1i_1} & x_{1i_2} & \cdots & x_{1i_k} \\ x_{2i_1} & x_{2i_2} & \cdots & x_{2i_k} \\ \vdots & \vdots & & \vdots \\ x_{ni_1} & x_{ni_2} & \cdots & x_{ni_k} \end{bmatrix},$$

optimizes the criterion. This can be done by discrete optimization, using a discrete analogue of methods described in Chapter 10 or stepwise feature selection described in Section 7.10.

11.3.9 Clustering

Application of a clustering algorithm to any dataset can viewed as a "projection" of m-dimensional features onto a single categorical variable (the cluster labels assigned to the feature vectors). Different clusterings—obtained by changing the algorithms, parameters, or raw features used—give different categorical variables.

11.3.10 Manifold Learning

Sometimes multidimensional scaling is preceded by a step in which a given dissimilarity matrix

$$\mathbf{D} = [d(o_i, o_j)]_{i,j=1}^{n}$$

is replaced by another dissimilarity matrix

$$\mathbf{D'} = [d'(o_i, o_j)]_{i,j=1}^{n},$$

where dissimilarity measure d' is constructed from measure d, but d' is thought to represent information about the objects $o_1, \ldots, o_n$ better than d. This situation arises when data in $\mathbb{R}^m$ lie in (or approximately in) a manifold[15] of lower dimension than m, and dissimilarity measure d is Euclidean distance in $\mathbb{R}^m$. In this case, a dissimilarity measure d' which respects the geometry of the manifold might be preferred to d, since curvature of the manifold in $\mathbb{R}^m$ might lead points which are far apart with respect to d' to be close to one another with respect to d. The problem of recovering the manifold distance d' is called *manifold learning*.

Several manifold methods approach the problem by constructing a weighted *nearest neighbors graph* from the data and producing a new distance d' from path weights in the graph. These will be illustrated by a particular method, due to Tenenbaum et al. (2000), known as *isomap* (short for "isometric feature mapping"). Two data objects o_i and o_j are said to be neighbors if the distance $d(o_i, o_j) < \epsilon$ for some given threshold $\epsilon > 0$, or, in an alternative approach, o_i and o_j are neighbors if o_i is one of the k closest data to o_j—or vice versa—for a given parameter $k \geq 1$. Each datum corresponds to a *vertex* of the graph, and the pair of vertices corresponding (o_i, o_j) is connected by an *edge* of the graph if and only if o_i and o_j are neighbors. If an edge corresponding to the pair (o_i, o_j) is in the graph, it is assigned an *edge weight* of $d(o_i, o_j)$. The distance between o_i and o_j within the (presumed) manifold is approximated by the

---

[15] For clarity, we omit the actual definition of a manifold.

lowest-weight path (sequence of edges) in the graph which connects the vertex corresponding to o_i to the vertex corresponding to o_j.[16]

This is illustrated in Figure 11.9 using a variation of the simplex dataset of Section 11.2. The *simplex-edges dataset* consists of 1000 points $x_1, \ldots, x_{1000}$ in $\mathbb{R}^{64}$, and was constructed as follows. An equilateral, 64-dimensional simplex with side length 1 was specified, and its 65 vertices labeled $v_1, \ldots, v_{65}$. For each $i \in \{1, \ldots, 1000\}$, an index j was drawn uniformly at random from the set $\{1, \ldots, 64\}$, and x_i was drawn uniformly at random from the edge of the simplex $[v_j, v_{j+1}]$. This dataset lies within a simple polygonal path through the edges of the simplex, which we will think of as a one-dimensional manifold (perhaps imagining that the corners of the path have been slightly rounded). In Figure 11.9, data points are colored so that data on each edge is the same color, and the colors corresponding to the edges form a rainbow as the polygonal arc is traced from v_1 to v_{65}.

The top three cells of Figure 11.9 illustrate the matrix of Euclidean distances between all pairs of points in the simplex-edges dataset, the matrix of true geodesic distance within the manifold, and the matrix of approximate geodesic distances obtained from the isomap algorithm (using the k-nearest-neighbors graph with $k = 13$, the smallest value which resulted in a connected graph). The center two cells show the result of applying one-dimensional linear MDS the Euclidean (left) and approximate geodesic (right) distance matrices, with vertical jitter added for clarity: one-dimensional linear MDS has preserved 3.0% of the Euclidean distance matrix and 99.3% of the approximate geodesic distance matrix, as measured by (11.2). The bottom two cells show the result of applying two-dimensional linear MDS the Euclidean (left) and approximate geodesic (right) distance matrices: two-dimensional linear MDS has preserved 5.9% of the Euclidean distance matrix and 99.5% of the approximate geodesic distance matrix. Working from the Euclidean distance matrix, the first MDS dimension separates a set of edges with a relatively large number of data (colored purple) from a set of edges with a relatively small number of data (colored orange through yellow-green). Working from the approximate geodesic distance matrix, the first MDS dimension has essentially recovered the order of the points along the manifold (isomap plus linear MDS has correctly recovered the fact that the data approximately lie on a one-dimensional manifold in $\mathbb{R}^{64}$).

The isomap algorithm was applied to the matrix of TF-IDF cosine dissimilarities between all points in the text dataset (using the k-nearest-neighbors graph with $k = 2$, the smallest value which resulted in a connected graph), and a two-dimensional linear MDS representation of the resulting approximate geodesic distance matrix is shown

---

[16] The weight of the lowest-weight path between every pair of vertices can be computed in $O(n^3)$ time using the Floyd–Warshall algorithm. Dijkstra's algorithm may be more efficient if the nearest-neighbor graph is sufficiently sparse, that is, has sufficiently few edges compared to the number of vertices. It may be that the nearest neighbors graph contains vertices which are not connected by any sequence of edges, in which case the distance d' between these edges is set to $+\infty$ (or, for practical purposes, a very large number).

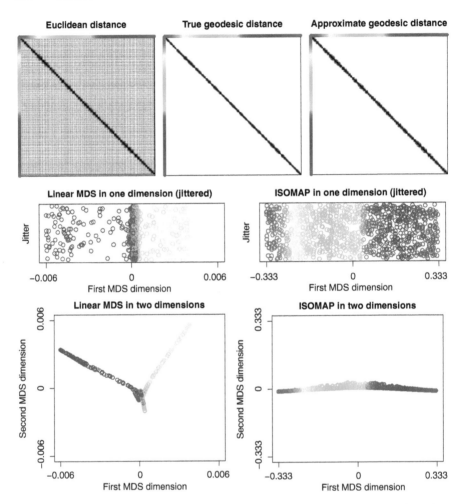

Figure 11.9   The isomap manifold learning algorithm applied to the simplex-edges dataset. The top three cells show distances between all pairs of points in the dataset, with the points in order along the one-dimensional manifold (points are colored to make a rainbow along the manifold). The center two cells show the result of applying one-dimensional linear MDS to the Euclidean (left) and approximate geodesic (right) distance matrices, with vertical jitter added for clarity. The bottom two cells show the result of applying two-dimensional linear MDS the Euclidean (left) and approximate geodesic (right) distance matrices. Further analysis is given in the text.

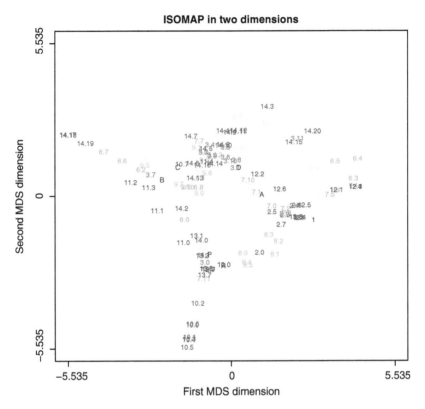

Figure 11.10   A two-dimensional linear MDS representation of the approximate geodesic distances recovered by the isomap manifold learning algorithm applied to the text dataset. The strand to the left of the central ring contains sections of Chapter 6 (ensemble design, boosting, and arcing) together with corresponding sections of Chapter 14 (R code for bagging, boosting, and arcing). The "fuzz" at the top of the ring also contains sections of Chapter 4 (classification) near corresponding sections of Chapter 14 (R code). The strand below the central ring shows Chapter 10 (optimization) separated from the rest of the book.

in Figure 11.10. In this case, two-dimensional linear MDS has preserved 34.8% of the approximate geodesic distance matrix, as measured by (11.2).

11.3.11   Autoencoders

This section describes a rather clever idea for training deep neural networks which has led to a way of finding useful lower-dimensional representations of high-dimensional data. Originating with the work of Hinton and Salakhutdinov (2006), it has led to the dramatic increase in research and application of neural networks since about 2007.

Suppose that feature space $\mathcal{X} = [0, 1]^m$. This may occur naturally, or it may occur by transforming real feature space in some way.[17] Consider a single-hidden-layer neural network, where the output layer T consists of m nodes, and both the output layer T and the N-node hidden layer Z consist of neurons (this is slightly different from the networks in Section 4.7, where the output layer consisted of linear functions). In the notation of Section 4.7,

$$Z = \sigma\left(\theta_0^{(1)} + \theta_\star^{(1)} X\right) \in [0, 1]^N$$

and

$$T = \sigma\left(\theta_0^{(2)} + \theta_\star^{(2)} Z\right) = \sigma\left(\theta_0^{(2)} + \theta_\star^{(2)} \sigma\left(\theta_0^{(1)} + \theta_\star^{(1)} X\right)\right) \in [0, 1]^m.$$

The neural network is a map $\mathcal{X} \to \mathcal{X}$.

Observing that first layer's matrix of parameters $\theta_\star^{(1)}$ is $N \times m$ and the second layer's matrix of parameters $\theta_\star^{(2)}$ is $m \times N$, the following constraint can be placed on the parameters:

$$\theta_\star^{(2)} = \theta_\star^{(1)\mathrm{T}}.$$

The other parameters, $\theta_0^{(1)}$ and $\theta_0^{(2)}$, are unconstrained. Thus the free parameters of this neural network are the full matrix $\theta^{(1)}$ and the m-long vector $\theta_0^{(2)}$.

Let d be any dissimilarity measure on elements of $\mathcal{X}$.[18] A *single-hidden-layer autoencoder* is a neural network of the type just described, with the parameters chosen to make the outputs match the inputs as closely as possible, with respect to the dissimilarity measure d, on a given dataset. That is, the free parameters $\theta^{(1)}$ and $\theta_0^{(2)}$ are chosen to minimize

$$\sum_{i=1}^{n} d(x_i, T(x_i)).$$

In other words, the network is trained to approximate the identity function at the training data $x_1, \ldots, x_n$ (and presumably also nearby the training data). A single-hidden-layer autoencoder is illustrated in Figure 11.11.

Using the estimated parameters $\widehat{\theta}^{(1)}$, a set of intermediate vectors $z_1, \ldots, z_n \in [0, 1]^N$ is computed from the set of input vectors $x_1, \ldots, x_n \in [0, 1]^m$,

$$z_i = \sigma\left(\widehat{\theta}_0^{(1)} + \widehat{\theta}_\star^{(1)} x_i\right) \quad \text{for } i = 1, \ldots, n.$$

---

[17] For example, by centering and decorrelating a set of feature vectors, and then, coordinatewise, replacing each value $x_{i,j}$ with the probability that a standard normal random variable exceeds $x_{i,j}$.

[18] In this context, d is typically chosen to be squared Euclidean distance for computational convenience.

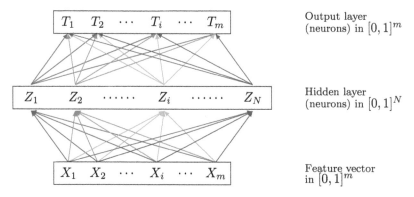

Figure 11.11   A single-hidden-layer autoencoder. The N-long hidden layer is $Z = \sigma(\theta_0^{(1)} + \theta_\star^{(1)}X)$ and the m-long top layer is $T = \sigma(\theta_0^{(2)} + \theta_\star^{(2)}Z)$. Values for parameter matrices $\theta^{(1)}$ and $\theta^{(2)}$ are sought which minimize $\sum_{i=1}^{n} d(x_i, T(x_i))$ subject to the constraint $\theta_\star^{(2)} = (\theta_\star^{(1)})^{\mathrm{T}}$, where d is some dissimilarity measure on feature space.

The N-long vectors $z_1, \ldots, z_n$ represent the state of the hidden layer Z when the m-long observed feature vectors $x_1, \ldots, x_n$ are fed through the network. A new single-hidden-layer autoencoder can be trained on the intermediate vectors $z_1, \ldots, z_n$.

This process can be iterated k times, according to the steps shown in Figure 11.12. The result, when $k > 1$, is called a *deep autoencoder* and is illustrated in Figure 11.13. The deep autoencoder has hidden layers $Z^{(1)}, Z^{(2)}, \ldots, Z^{(k-1)}, Z^{(k)}, Z^{(k+1)}, \ldots, Z^{(2k-1)}$

---

(1) For $i = 1, \ldots, n$, set $z_i^{(0)} = x_i$.

(2) For $j = 1, \ldots, k$:

(3)   train a single-hidden-layer autoencoder with $N^{(j)}$ hidden states on $z_1^{(j-1)}, \ldots, z_n^{(j-1)}$, learning parameters $\theta^{(j)}$ and $\theta^{(2k-j)}$, subject to the constraint $\theta_\star^{(2k-j)} = (\theta_\star^{(j)})^T$;

(4)   for $i = 1, \ldots, n$, set $z_i^{(j)} = \sigma(\widehat{\theta}_0^{(j)} + \widehat{\theta}_\star^{(j)} z_i^{(j-1)})$.

(5) Interpret $\theta^{(1)}, \ldots, \theta^{(2k)}$ as the parameters of a neural network with $2k - 1$ hidden layers. The numbers of states in the hidden layers are $N^{(1)}, N^{(2)}, \ldots, N^{(k-1)}, N^{(k)}, N^{(k-1)}, \ldots, N^{(2)}, N^{(1)}$.

(6) Train the entire $(2k - 1)$-hidden-layer network as an autoencoder, minimzing $\sum_{i=1}^{n} d(x_i, T(x_i))$, without contraints on the parameters, using $\widehat{\theta}^{(1)}, \ldots, \widehat{\theta}^{(2k)}$ from steps (2-4) as an initial state.

Figure 11.12   Iteration of a single-hidden-layer autoencoder to train a deep autoencoder.

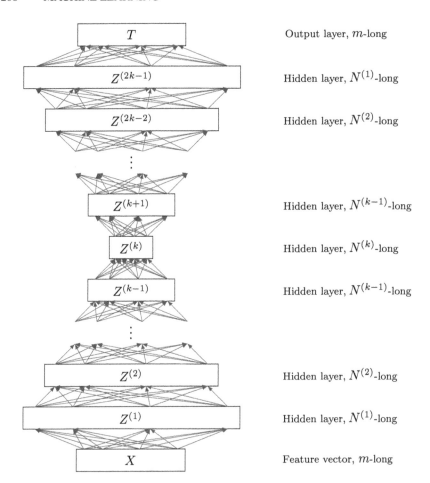

Figure 11.13 A $(2k-1)$-hidden-layer "deep" autoencoder. First, parameter matrices $\theta^{(j)}$ and $\theta^{(2k-j)}$ are obtained sequentially for $j = 1, \ldots, k$, by training a single-hidden-layer autoencoder on $Z^{(j-1)}$ (where $Z^{(0)} = X$). Using the resulting parameters as an initial state, values for parameter matrices $\theta^{(1)}, \ldots, \theta^{(2k)}$ are sought which minimize $\sum_{i=1}^{n} d(x_i, T(x_i))$, without constraints, where d is a given dissimilarity measure on feature space. The resulting function $[0, 1]^m \to [0, 1]^{N^{(k)}}$ given by $X \mapsto Z^{(k)}$ yields a lower-dimensional representation of feature space when $N^{(k)} < m$.

of respective lengths $N^{(1)}, N^{(2)}, \ldots, N^{(k-1)}, N^{(k)}, N^{(k-1)}, \ldots, N^{(2)}, N^{(1)}$—the symmetry is a natural result of the iterative process, due to hidden layers $Z^{(j)}$ and $Z^{(2k-j)}$ being constructed at the jth iteration. Typically $N^{(1)} > m$ ($N^{(1)} \approx 2m$ is a popular choice) and $N^{(1)} \geq N^{(2)} \geq \ldots \geq N^{(k)}$, with $N^{(k)} \ll m$.

Having trained a deep autoencoder, the map $[0, 1]^m \rightarrow [0, 1]^{N^{(k)}}$ given by $X \mapsto Z^{(k)}$ can be viewed as a lower-dimensional representation of feature space $\mathcal{X} = [0, 1]^m$. If, overall, the deep autoencoder does a good job at minimizing its objective function,

$$\sum_{i=1}^{n} d(x_i, T(x_i)),$$

then the set of intermediate states $z_1^{(k)}, \dots, z_n^{(k)} \in [0, 1]^{N^{(k)}}$, which constitutes an $N^{(k)}$-dimensional representation of the data $x_1, \dots, x_n$, must contain sufficient information about these original feature vectors to nearly reconstruct them (at least, as far as dissimilarity measure d can tell) via the map $[0, 1]^{N^{(k)}} \rightarrow [0, 1]^m$ given by $Z^{(k)} \mapsto T$. Approximate reconstruction of the original feature vectors in this sense (essentially, compression) is the criterion which can be viewed as motivating deep autoencoders.

Deep autoencoders were originally developed to enable the training of *deep neural networks* (networks with many hidden layers) as follows. To construct a neural network with k hidden layers, first a $(2k - 1)$-hidden-layer autoencoder is constructed. The top $k - 1$ hidden layers, $Z^{(k+1)}, \dots, Z^{(2k)}$, are discarded and the bottom k hidden layers, $Z^{(1)}, \dots, Z^{(k)}$, are retained. A new, linear output layer T with C nodes is added above the hidden layer $Z^{(k)}$ and, using the trained autoencoder parameters $\widehat{\theta}^{(1)}, \dots, \widehat{\theta}^{(k)}$ as an initial state, the entire network is trained as in Section 4.7.[19] A deep neural network is illustrated in Figure 11.14. Of course, one can use marked training data $(x_1, y_1), \dots, (x_n, y_n)$ to train any classifier on the (marked) transformed feature vectors $(z_1^{(k)}, y_1), \dots, (z_n^{(k)}, y_n)$, and one can iteratively adapt parameters $\widehat{\theta}^{(1)}, \dots, \widehat{\theta}^{(k)}$ to optimize the performance of any classifier.

11.4   Model Regularization

In the context of fitting predictive models to high-dimensional data, one can first find a low-dimensional representation of the data using one of the methods described in Section 11.3 and then fit a predictive model to the low-dimensional representation of the data. Alternatively, one can design methods of predictive modeling which are biased toward producing models which use a small subset of the features. This is done by simultaneously maximizing a measure of model quality (usually maximizing a likelihood function or minimizing some estimate of risk) and minimizing a measure

---

[19] Only at the this last step is marked training data $(x_1, y_1), \dots, (x_n, y_n)$ required. The set of feature vectors used to construct the deep autoencoder may or may not be marked, and may or may not be the set of feature vectors used to train the final deep neural network for classification. The case where the autoencoder and the neural network are trained on different feature vectors is an example of *transfer learning*.

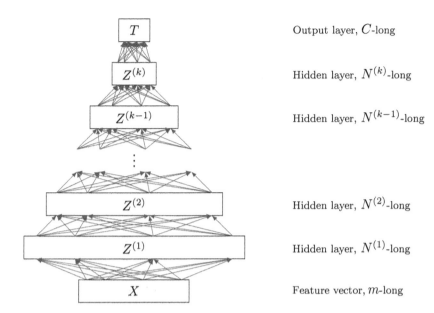

Figure 11.14   A k-hidden-layer neural network, constructed by discarding the top $(k-1)$ hidden layers from the autoencoder of Figure 11.13 and adding a C-node linear output layer. Using the parameter values from the autoencoder as an initial state, the network is trained as described in Section 4.7.

of model complexity, where the measure of model complexity is associated with the number of features actually used by the model.[20] This is known variously as *model regularization, parameter penalization*, or *shrinkage*.

The principal tool in model regularization is the addition of a penalty function of the model parameters θ to the objective function describing what makes a modeling technique "good." In the most general case, a *penalty function* of θ is a function which takes a minimum on some set Ω, and increases as θ moves away from Ω. Intuitively, Ω represents a set of "default" values of θ, and the penalty function describes one's willingness (or unwillingness) to accept values of θ outside of Ω in the face of evidence derived from data. Explicit connection between penalty functions and prior belief about θ will be made in Section 11.4.2.

---

[20] We have seen such methods before, in Chapter 3 (ridge regression, lasso), Chapter 4 (classification trees, support vector machines), and Chapter 7 (AIC, BIC). Except for AIC and BIC, these methods have not explicitly linked model complexity to the number of features used by the model.

Consider the case of least-squares linear regression, described in Chapter 3. Using the squared-error loss function, parameters are chosen to minimize a training estimate of risk,

$$\hat{\theta} = \mathrm{argmin}_\theta \sum_{i=1}^{n} \left(y_i - (1, x_{i1}, \ldots, x_{im})(\theta_0, \theta_1, \ldots, \theta_m)^\mathrm{T} \right)^2 .$$

In Exercise 3.7 the goal was to show that, in the case of $N\left(0, \sigma^2\right)$-distributed residuals, choosing θ to minimize the sum of squared errors is the same as choosing θ to maximize the likelihood of the data. A penalty function commonly applied to a parameter vector $\theta = (\theta_0, \theta_1, \ldots, \theta_m)$ is

$$\sum_{i=1}^{m} |\theta_i|^p$$

for some constant $p > 0$. In this penalty function, no penalty is applied to the intercept term θ_0, while all other parameters are penalized increasingly as they grow large in absolute value: the penalty function is minimal on the set $\Omega = \{(r, 0, \ldots, 0) : r \in \mathbb{R}\}$. Using this penalty function, *penalized least-squares regression* chooses parameters which minimize a weighted sum of the training risk and the penalty function,

$$\hat{\theta} = \mathrm{argmin}_\theta \left(\sum_{i=1}^{n} \left(y_i - (1, x_{i1}, \ldots, x_{im})(\theta_0, \theta_1, \ldots, \theta_m)^\mathrm{T} \right)^2 + \lambda \sum_{i=1}^{m} |\theta_i|^p \right), \quad (11.3)$$

where weight parameter λ is chosen to minimize the estimated risk of the penalized model.

In logistic regression, parameters are chosen to maximize the log-likelihood of the data

$$\sum_{i=1}^{n} \log P(y_i \mid X = x_i) = \sum_{i=1}^{n} T(x_i, \theta_{y_i}) - \sum_{i=1}^{n} \log \left(\sum_{d=1}^{C} \exp(T(x_i, \theta_d)) \right),$$

which corresponds to the case where, for each i, Y_i is drawn from the multinomial distribution on $\{1, \ldots, C\}$ with probabilities $(P(Y = 1 \mid X = x_i), \ldots, P(Y = C \mid X = x_i))$. In Exercise 4.11 the goal was to show that choosing θ to maximize this likelihood function is the same as choosing θ to minimize the training estimate of risk with respect to cross-entropy loss. Using the same penalty function as above, *penalized logistic regression* chooses parameters which minimize a weighted sum of the training risk and the penalty function,

$$\hat{\theta} = \mathrm{argmin}_\theta \left(-\sum_{i=1}^{n} \log P(y_i \mid X = x_i) + \lambda \sum_{i=1}^{m} |\theta_i|^p \right), \quad (11.4)$$

where weight parameter λ is chosen to minimize the estimated risk of the penalized model.

11.4.1   Duality and the Geometry of Parameter Penalization

In some cases there is a useful duality between optimization of a penalized function with no constraints and optimization of an unpenalized function with inequality constraints. For example, for any given $p \geq 1$ and $\lambda \geq 0$, parameter estimation in penalized least-squares regression is performed by solving the unconstrained optimization problem

$$\text{minimize over } \theta: \quad \sum_{i=1}^{n} \left(y_i - (1, x_{i1}, \dots, x_{im})(\theta_0, \theta_1, \dots, \theta_m)^{\mathsf{T}} \right)^2 + \lambda \sum_{i=1}^{m} |\theta_i|^p,$$

which is equivalent to the constrained optimization problem

$$\text{minimize over } \theta: \quad \sum_{i=1}^{n} \left(y_i - (1, x_{i1}, \dots, x_{im})(\theta_0, \theta_1, \dots, \theta_m)^{\mathsf{T}} \right)^2$$
$$\text{subject to:} \quad \sum_{i=1}^{m} |\theta_i|^p \leq c$$

The upper bound c in the constrained problem depends on the penalty parameter λ in the unconstrained problem. A similar example appears in Section 4.9, in the context of support vector machines.

Exercise 11.15 *Let g and h be two real-valued functions of a vector θ.*

(A) Let λ be given, and let $\widehat{\theta}$ be a solution to the unconstrained optimization problem

$$\text{minimize over } \theta: \quad g(\theta) + \lambda\, h(\theta).$$

Let $c_\lambda = h(\widehat{\theta})$. Show that $\widehat{\theta}$ is a solution to the constrained optimization problem

$$\text{minimize over } \theta: \quad g(\theta)$$
$$\text{subject to:} \quad h(\theta) \leq c_\lambda.$$

Hint: *Suppose there is a solution $\tilde{\theta}$ to the constrained problem such that $g(\tilde{\theta}) < g(\widehat{\theta})$ and get a contradiction.*

(B) Assume that g and h are convex and differentiable. Let c be given, and let $\widehat{\theta}$ be a solution to the constrained optimization problem

$$\text{minimize over } \theta: \quad g(\theta)$$
$$\text{subject to:} \quad h(\theta) \leq c.$$

If $h(\widehat{\theta}) < c$, let $\lambda_c = 0$, and if $h(\widehat{\theta}) = c$, let $\lambda_c \geq 0$ satisfy $\nabla g(\widehat{\theta}) = -\lambda_c \nabla h(\widehat{\theta})$. Show that $\widehat{\theta}$ is a solution to the unconstrained optimization problem

$$\text{minimize over } \theta: \quad g(\theta) + \lambda_c\, h(\theta).$$

Hint: $\nabla g(\widehat{\theta}) = \lambda \nabla h(\widehat{\theta})$ *for some λ—this follows from a Lagrange multiplier argument, and the condition $\lambda < 0$ follows from convexity of g; a nonnegative linear combination of convex functions is convex; any local minimum of a convex function is a global minimum.*

There are various conditions under which two forms of an optimization problem—one penalized and unconstrained, the other constrained and unpenalized—are equivalent to each other or nearly equivalent to each other (in the latter case there is said to be a positive *duality gap*). We do not concern ourselves with stating these conditions precisely, as the geometric insight gained from the duality has proved useful even in cases where the duality is not formally justified. This geometric insight is presented in Figure 11.15.

11.4.2   Parameter Penalization as Prior Information

In cases where the measure of model quality is given by a log-likelihood function, as in the cases of least-squares regression and logistic regression mentioned above, adding a penalty term can be viewed as adding prior information about the model parameters. In these specific examples, (11.3) and (11.4) can be viewed as explicitly choosing a value of the parameters θ which maximizes the density function of a posterior distribution on the parameter θ induced by the data and a prior distribution. Figure 11.16 shows four prior distributions which correspond to the four penalty functions shown in Figure 11.15.

Exercise 11.16 *In the case of least-squares linear regression with additive, independent Gaussian errors, where $Y = (1, X)\theta^{\mathrm{T}} + E$ and $E \sim \mathrm{N}\left(0, \sigma^2\right)$, the likelihood function is*

$$P(Y \mid X, \theta, \sigma^2) = \frac{1}{\sqrt{2\pi}\sigma} \exp\left(-\frac{1}{2\sigma^2}(Y - (1, X)\theta^{\mathrm{T}})^2\right).$$

Show that, given independent, identically distributed data $(x_1, y_1), \ldots, (x_n, y_n)$, the parameter value

$$\widehat{\theta} = \mathrm{argmin}_\theta \left(\sum_{i=1}^n \left(y_i - (1, x_{i1}, \ldots, x_{im})(\theta_0, \theta_1, \ldots, \theta_m)^{\mathrm{T}}\right)^2 + \lambda \sum_{i=1}^m |\theta_i|^p\right)$$

is the value which maximizes the posterior density $P(\theta \mid Y, X, \sigma^2, \lambda, p)$ when the prior distribution on $(\theta_1, \ldots, \theta_m)$ has density

$$P(\theta \mid \sigma^2, \lambda, p) \propto \exp\left(-\frac{\lambda}{2\sigma^2}\sum_{j=1}^m |\theta_j|^p\right).$$

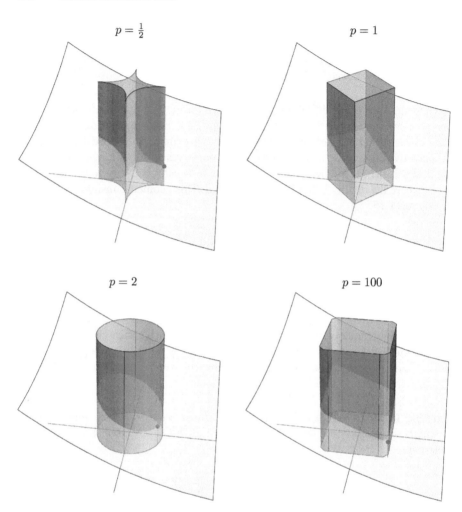

Figure 11.15   How a penalty function of the form $\sum_{i=1}^{m} |\theta_i|^p$ influences the sparsity of a model. Each surface shows the minimum (red dot) of a function of the variables (θ_1, θ_2) (blue surface) subject to the constraint $|\theta_1|^p + |\theta_2|^p \leq c$ (pink cylinder), for $p = \frac{1}{2}, 1, 2$, and 100. When p is small, the constraint region is "pointy" along the coordinate axes, resulting in a tendency for the minimizing value of (θ_1, θ_2) to occur where one of the coordinates of θ is zero (in higher dimensions, where most of the coordinates of θ are zero). When p is large, the constraint region is "pointy" along the lines $|\theta_1| = |\theta_2|$, resulting in a tendency for the minimizing value of (θ_1, θ_2) to occur where $|\theta_1| \approx |\theta_2|$ (in higher dimensions, where most of the coordinates of θ are approximately equal in magnitude).

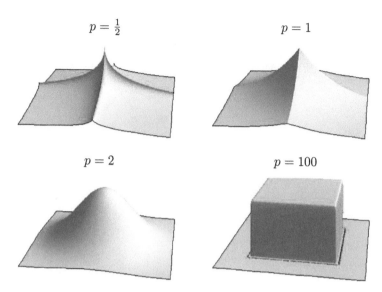

Figure 11.16   How a penalty function of the form $\sum_{i=1}^{m} |\theta_i|^p$ influences the sparsity of a model. Each surface shows the prior distribution on (θ_1, θ_2) corresponding to the penalty function $|\theta_1|^p + |\theta_2|^p$, for $p = \frac{1}{2}, 1, 2$, and 100. Each surface has a unique global maximum at the origin, $(\theta_1, \theta_2) = (0, 0)$. When p is small, the prior distribution strongly favors parameters which are exactly equal to zero.

When $p = 2$, the prior distribution is an m-dimensional Gaussian distribution, $\theta \sim N(0, \frac{\sigma^2}{\lambda} I)$. When $p = 1$, the prior distribution is an m-dimensional generalization of a Laplace distribution.

   In Exercise 11.15, the weight parameter λ has an explicit meaning: up to a constant, it is the reciprocal of the variance (the *precision*) of the prior distribution for θ.

12

Communication with Clients

If they fail to understand that we bring them mathematically infallible happiness, it will be our duty to compel them to be happy. But before resorting to arms, we shall try the power of words.
—The One State Gazette in Yevgeny Zamyatin, *We*, 1924

Many true statements are too long to fit on a slide, but this does not mean we should abbreviate the truth to make the words fit.
—Edward R. Tufte, *The Cognitive Style of PowerPoint*, 2005

For a successful technology, reality must take precedence over public relations, for Nature cannot be fooled.
—Richard Feynman, *What Do You Care What Other People Think?* 2001

The combination of some data and an aching desire for an answer does not ensure that a reasonable answer can be extracted from a given body of data.
—John Tukey, *Sunset Salvo*, 1986

I have not the pleasure of understanding you. Of what are you talking?
—Mr. Bennet in Jane Austen, *Pride and Prejudice*, 1813

In order to produce a real-world effect, a machine learning practitioner typically works with clients or collaborators in the one or more of the natural, social, or

Machine Learning: a Concise Introduction, First Edition. Steven W. Knox.
© This publication is a US Government work and is in the public domain.
Published 2018 by John Wiley & Sons, Inc.
Companion Website: http://www.wiley.com/go/Knox/MachineLearning

computer sciences. It is therefore beneficial to the machine learning practitioner to be able to communicate with people working in these fields. Indeed, it is the author's view that it is more necessary for the machine learning practitioner to speak the language of his or her scientific clients than vice versa—we must meet them more than halfway.

12.1   Binary Classification and Hypothesis Testing

We begin with a review of two frameworks for making binary decisions based on data. In binary classification, for each feature vector X we must decide between two actions based on the value of an approximated function $\widehat{f}(X)$. Either we predict that X belongs to class 1 (because $\widehat{f}(X) = 1$) or we predict that X belongs to class 2 (because $\widehat{f}(X) = 2$).

Similarly, when performing a hypothesis test, for each feature vector X we must decide between two actions based on the value of a *test statistic*[1] $S(X)$, and a *rejection region R* (a subset of the range of S). Either we reject a null hypothesis H_0 in favor of an alternative hypothesis H_a (because $S(X) \in R$) or we retain the null hypothesis (because $S(X) \notin R$).

These two frameworks can be unified by considering the Bayes classifier, provided that we identify class 1 with H_0 and class 2 with H_a.[2] In classification (particularly Chapters 2 and 4), we have been concerned with making the minimum risk prediction,

$$\text{argmin}_{c \in \{1,2\}} R(c \mid X),$$

where

$$R(c \mid X) = \sum_{d=1}^{C} L(d, c) P(Y = d \mid X) \propto \sum_{d=1}^{C} L(d, c) P(X \mid Y = d) P(Y = d).$$

Since there are only two classes, the Bayes classifier predicts class 2 if and only if

$$R(1 \mid X) \geq R(2 \mid X),$$

that is, if and only if

$$L(2, 1) P(Y = 2 \mid X) \geq L(1, 2) P(Y = 1 \mid X).$$

Putting all terms involving the feature vector X on one side, the Bayes classifier predicts class 2 if and only if

$$\frac{P(Y = 2 \mid X)}{P(Y = 1 \mid X)} \geq \frac{L(1, 2)}{L(2, 1)},$$

---

[1] Here, a *statistic* is any function of an observable feature vector, X.

[2] Throughout this chapter, we will identify "class 1" with H_0 and "class 2" with H_a.

or equivalently, if and only if

$$\frac{P(X \mid Y = 2)}{P(X \mid Y = 1)} \geq \frac{L(1,2)}{L(2,1)} \frac{P(Y = 1)}{P(Y = 2)}.$$

Defining a test statistic $S(X)$ and rejection region R either by

$$S(X) = \frac{P(Y = 2 \mid X)}{P(Y = 1 \mid X)} \quad \text{and} \quad R = \left\{ \rho \in \mathbb{R} : \rho \geq \frac{L(1,2)}{L(2,1)} \right\}$$

or by

$$S(X) = \frac{P(X \mid Y = 2)}{P(X \mid Y = 1)} \quad \text{and} \quad R = \left\{ \rho \in \mathbb{R} : \rho \geq \frac{L(1,2)}{L(2,1)} \frac{P(Y = 1)}{P(Y = 2)} \right\}$$

results in a hypothesis test which performs identically to the Bayes classifier (that is, the test rejects H_0 if and only if the Bayes classifier predicts class 2).[3]

12.2   Terminology for Binary Decisions

Statistics, computer science, and various natural and social sciences have given names to many aspects of the problem of making a binary decision from data, whether the problem is regarded as classification or hypothesis testing. Different fields have emphasized different aspects of the problem and in some cases have given multiple, different names to the same thing. These names are shown in Tables 12.1 and 12.2.

Table 12.1 shows the two possible decisions (predict class 1 or class 2, reject or retain H_0) with the two possible states of truth (the true class is 1 or 2, the datum was generated under H_0 or H_a). Each cell of the table contains a probability, a, b, c or d, with $a + b + c + d = 1$. Table 12.2 shows names given certain marginal or conditional probabilities in Table 12.1.

Two important terms do not appear in these tables because they are defined by inequalities. A hypothesis test is a *level-α test* if the size of the test is no greater than α, that is, if P(reject $H_0 \mid H_0$ is true) $\leq \alpha$. The *p-value of an observed statistic $S(X)$* is the smallest value of α such that the observed value $S(X)$ would cause a level-α test to reject the null hypothesis.

12.3   ROC Curves

Let S be a real-valued statistic and consider for the moment making a classification decision of the form "predict class 2 if the observed value of S is greater than or equal to threshold value τ, and otherwise predict class 1." The equivalent form for a

---

[3] Compare this to the solution of Exercise 2.2. Note that the rejection region of the hypothesis test can be interpreted in terms of the relative losses incurred by the two kinds of errors.

Table 12.1   The four possibilities in the decision-making problem described above. The columns reflect the true state of an observation (a datum really is class 1 or class 2, or really was produced under H_0 or H_a). The rows reflect an action taken (we predicted class 1 or class 2, we retained or rejected H_0). The numbers a, b, c, and d represent probabilities with $a + b + c + d = 1$.

	Datum is class 1 H_0 is true	Datum is class 2 H_a is true
Predict class 1 retain H_0	a *true negative* *true nondiscovery*	b *type II error* *false negative* *false nondiscovery*
Predict class 2 reject H_0	c *type I error* *false positive* *false discovery*	d *true positive* *true discovery*

Table 12.2   Names given to marginal probabilities in Table 12.1. Given a classifier or hypothesis test, a statistician might describe its performance in terms of power and size, a computer scientist might describe it in terms of precision and recall, and a physician might describe it in terms of sensitivity and specificity. Although the notation used here is Bayesian (for example, P(reject H_0 | H_0 is true) notationally treats the truth of H_0 as a random variable), the ideas are applicable in both Bayesian and frequentist approaches to making binary decisions.

Probability	Meaning	Names
$\frac{c}{a+c}$	P(reject H_0 | H_0 is true)	*false positive rate, fall-out, size*
$\frac{a}{a+c}$	P(retain H_0 | H_0 is true)	*specificity, true negative rate*
$\frac{d}{b+d}$	P(reject H_0 | H_a is true)	*sensitivity, recall, power, true positive rate*
$\frac{b}{b+d}$	P(retain H_0 | $H_a$is true)	*false negative rate*
$\frac{a}{a+b}$	P(H_0 is true | retain H_0)	*negative predictive value*
$\frac{b}{a+b}$	P(H_a is true | retain H_0)	*false nondiscovery rate, false omission rate*
$\frac{c}{c+d}$	P(H_0 is true | reject H_0)	*false discovery rate*
$\frac{d}{c+d}$	P(H_a is true | reject H_0)	*positive predictive value, precision*
$a + d$	P(prediction is correct)	*accuracy*
$b + c$	P(prediction is incorrect)	*risk, error rate*
$b + d$	P(H_a is true)	*prevalence*

hypothesis test is "reject the null hypothesis H_0 in favor of alternative hypothesis H_a if the observed value of S is greater than or equal to threshold value τ."

The two classes or hypotheses place (presumably different) distributions on test statistic S: let $P(S \mid Y = 1)$ denote the distribution of S when the true class is 1, and let $P(S \mid Y = 2)$ denote the distribution of S when the true class is 2. The *receiver operating characteristic curve*, or *ROC curve*, is the curve parametrized by

$$\{(P(S \geq \tau \mid Y = 1), P(S \geq \tau \mid Y = 2)) : \tau \in \mathbb{R}\}.$$

An example is shown in Figure 12.1.

ROC curves are useful because they illustrate the trade-off which a given classifier or hypothesis test allows between the two kinds of error. ROC curves can thus enable an applied statistician or machine learning practitioner to elicit a loss function from a client or collaborator. Specifically, a client's stated desire to attain a certain operating point on a ROC curve reveals two things: first, the value of the threshold τ which corresponds to that point; and second, the fact that no other point on the curve is preferable, and so the client's loss function implicitly satisifies $\frac{d}{d\tau} R(\hat{f}) = 0$ at that

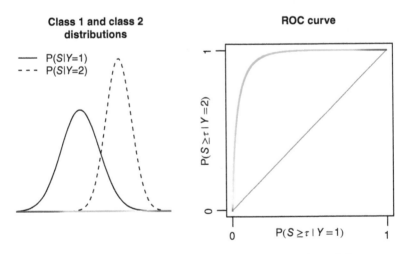

Figure 12.1   Class-1 and class-2 distributions of a statistic $S(X)$ and the corresponding power-vs.-size (ROC) curve. In the left cell, the class-1 and class-2 distributions are both normal, supported on the entire real line. The power-vs.-size curve, drawn in the right-hand cell, is parametrized by $(P(S \geq \tau \mid Y = 1), P(S \geq \tau \mid Y = 2))$ as threshold τ varies over the reals. In this example, the curve touches the vertical axis at $(0, 0)$ when $\tau = \infty$ and touches the horizontal line $y = 1$ at $(1, 1)$ when $\tau = -\infty$: otherwise, it lies above the line $y = x$, which corresponds predicting class 1 or class 2 for each datum based on a fair coin toss. The rainbow coloring of the real line in the left-hand cell corresponds to the values of the threshold τ which yield the points of the ROC curve with the same color.

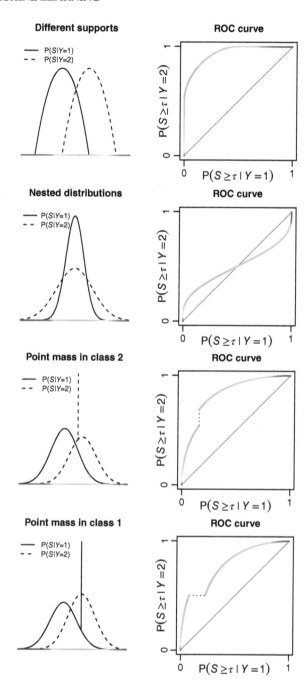

point. Exercise 12.1 shows how a client's ratio of losses $\frac{L(2,1)}{L(1,2)}$ can be recovered from a chosen operating point on the ROC curve, estimates of the density functions of the statistic S for classes $Y = 1$ and $Y = 2$ (typically obtained by histograms or kernel density estimates applied to data used to draw the ROC curve), and the marginal or prior odds of the two classes, $\frac{P(Y=1)}{P(Y=2)}$.

Exercise 12.1 *Suppose classifier $\widehat{f}(X)$ is based on a statistic $S(X)$ (a real-valued function of feature vector X) and a threshold τ, so that*

$$\widehat{f}(X) = \begin{cases} 1 & \text{if } S(X) < \tau \\ 2 & \text{if } S(X) \geq \tau \end{cases}.$$

The ROC curve is

$$\{(P(S(X) \geq \tau \mid Y = 1), P(S(X) \geq \tau \mid Y = 2)) : \tau \in \mathbb{R}\}.$$

(A) Show that the risk of $\widehat{f}$ is connected to a point on the ROC curve by the equation

$$R(\widehat{f}) = L(1,2) P(S(X) \geq \tau \mid Y = 1) P(Y = 1)$$
$$+ L(2,1)(1 - P(S(X) \geq \tau \mid Y = 2)) P(Y = 2).$$

(B) Suppose that the distributions of $S(X) \mid Y = 1$ and $S(X) \mid Y = 2$ have density functions, respectively $P(s \mid Y = 1)$ and $P(s \mid Y = 2)$, so that

$$P(S(X) < \tau \mid Y = 1) = \int_{-\infty}^{\tau} P(s \mid Y = 1) \, ds \quad \text{and}$$

$$P(S(X) < \tau \mid Y = 2) = \int_{-\infty}^{\tau} P(s \mid Y = 2) \, ds.$$

Figure 12.2   The effect of various features of distributions for class 1 or class 2 on power-vs.-size (ROC) curves. The upper-most left cell shows two distributions with overlapping, non-nested, compact support. The ROC curve in the right cell hits the vertical axis at a point other than $(0, 0)$ and hits the horizontal line $y = 1$ at a point other than $(1, 1)$. The second-upper-most left cell shows two distributions with the same mean, but the class-2 distribution has larger variance. The ROC curve in the right cell shows power better than random guessing for small sizes (left of the point where the curve crosses the line $y = x$, one-half in this example) but *worse* than random guessing for large sizes. The second-lower-most left cell shows a distribution for class 2 with a point mass (fattened slightly to make it visible). The ROC curve in the right cell shows a vertical gap, corresponding to a discontinuity in $P(S \geq \tau \mid Y = 2)$ as a function of τ, caused by the point mass. The lower-most left cell shows a distribution for class 1 with a point mass (fattened slightly to make it visible). The ROC curve in the right cell shows a horizontal gap, corresponding to a discontinuity in $P(S \geq \tau \mid Y = 1)$ as a function of τ, caused by the point mass.

Show that $\frac{d}{d\tau}R(\hat{f}) = 0$ if and only if the ratio of losses satisfies

$$\frac{L(2,1)}{L(1,2)} = \frac{P(\tau \mid Y = 1)}{P(\tau \mid Y = 2)} \frac{P(Y = 1)}{P(Y = 2)}.$$

In many applications, we are more concerned about limiting one type of error (for example, misclassifying class 1 as class 2) than about the other type of error (misclassifying class 2 as class 1). In such situations, we seek a classifier which correctly identifies as many data of class 2 data as possible, while holding the misclassification rate for data of class 1 at an acceptable level. This situation is recognized in hypothesis testing, and the names of the hypotheses are assigned so that the goal is to find a test which is most powerful, uniformly with respect to its size, as long as the size is acceptably small.

Figure 12.2 shows pairs of class-1 and class-2 distributions for S and the corresponding power-vs.-size curves. These distributions are chosen to illustrate features which occur in empirical power-vs.-size curves encountered in practice.

12.4   One-Dimensional Measures of Performance

The risk of a given classifier $\hat{f}(X)$ is a one-dimensional value which incorporates both the classifier's propensity for errors and the subjective loss incurred by making different kinds of errors. As discussed in Chapter 2, using a loss function which expresses the real-world consequences of these errors is critical to selecting and training a classifier appropriately.

That said, there are various attempts in the literature to express the performance of a trained classifier as a single number. Two are presented here.

One popular way of reducing the probability of the two types of error to a single, summary number is the *area under a ROC curve*, which is a number between 0 and 1.[4] As shown by the following exercises, the area under a ROC curve can be interpreted as the probability that, when a datum of class 2 and a datum of class 1 are drawn randomly (and independently), the datum of class 2 produces the higher value of test statistic S.

Exercise 12.2 Probability Integral Transform. *Let S be a real-valued random variable with positive density function, so that the cumulative distribution function of S, $F(s) = P(S \le s)$, is continuous and strictly increasing. Let $U = F(S)$. Show that U has the uniform distribution on the interval $(0, 1)$. What changes if $F(s) = P(S \ge s)$?*

---

[4] A ROC curve is considered to exist inside the square $[0, 1] \times [0, 1]$, so the area under a ROC curve is the area under the curve and inside this square.

Exercise 12.3 *Let S_1 be a random variable with the distribution of $S \mid Y = 1$ and let S_2 be a random variable with the distribution of $S \mid Y = 2$, and let S_1 and S_2 be independent. Assume that S_1 and S_2 both have positive density functions. Show that the area under the ROC curve*

$$\{(P(S \geq \tau \mid Y = 1), P(S \geq \tau \mid Y = 2)) : \tau \in \mathbb{R}\}$$

is $P(S_2 \geq S_1)$. **Hint:** *Define function $h : \mathbb{R} \times \mathbb{R} \to (0, 1) \times (0, 1)$ by $h(s_1, s_2) = P(S_1 \geq s_1, S_2 \geq s_2)$, apply h to the joint random variable (S_1, S_2), and note that the ROC curve is the set $\{h(\tau, \tau) : \tau \in \mathbb{R}\}$.*

Measuring the quality of a classifier by the area under a ROC curve implicitly makes the assumption that the practitioner is completely ignorant of the loss function: in binary classification, the ratio $L(1, 2)/L(2, 1)$. This never is (or should never be) the case.

Another way of summarizing performance in a single number, which also takes values between 0 and 1, is the *F-measure* or F_1*-measure*[5] of a classifier or hypothesis test. It is defined as

$$F = 2\frac{\text{precision} \times \text{recall}}{\text{precision} + \text{recall}}.$$

Exercise 12.4 *Show that the F-measure satisfies*

$$F = 2\frac{P(H_a \text{ is true and reject } H_0)}{P(H_a \text{ is true}) + P(\text{reject } H_0)} \in [0, 1].$$

12.5   Confusion Matrices

The performance of a trained classifier on validation (or test) data can be summarized by a $C \times C$ matrix, called the *confusion matrix*, defined by

$$N(d, c) = \text{number of validation data } (\tilde{x}_i, d) \text{ such that } \widehat{f}(\tilde{x}_i) = c.$$

Diagonal elements of this matrix count correctly classified validation data, and off-diagonal element $N(d, c)$ counts the number of times validation data of class d were misclassified as class c by classifier $\widehat{f}$. When a classifier is produced by bagging, each datum can be passed through its out-of-bag classifier, producing an *out-of-bag confusion matrix*.

There is no standard for whether the true class label indexes the rows of the confusion matrix, as defined above, or the columns. When presenting a confusion matrix, care should be taken to make clear what the row index is.

---

[5] The notation F_1 shows the place of this particular measure in one-parameter family of generalizations.

Exercise 12.5 *Show that, in terms of the confusion matrix, the validation estimate of risk defined in Section 7.2 is*

$$\hat{R}_{\text{valid}}(\hat{f}) = \frac{1}{\tilde{n}} \sum_{(d,c) \in C \times C} L(d,c) N(d,c)$$

and the estimate of its variance is

$$\widehat{\text{Var}}[\hat{R}_{\text{valid}}(\hat{f})] = \frac{1}{\tilde{n}} \left(\frac{1}{\tilde{n}} \sum_{(d,c) \in C \times C} L(d,c)^2 N(d,c) - \hat{R}_{\text{valid}}(\hat{f})^2 \right).$$

12.6   Multiple Testing

It is often the case that multiple class predictions are made—that is, a trained classifier is applied to predict the class of more than just one data point—or, equivalently, that multiple hypothesis tests are performed. In some applications, each datum for which the null hypothesis is rejected (data predicted to be of class 2) prompts some kind of action (perhaps further analysis) while each datum for which the null hypothesis is retained (data predicted to be of class 1) prompts no action. Each action incurs a cost, and there is presumably a benefit associated with correctly identifying data of class 2 (rejecting the null hypothesis when it is in fact false).

If T different size-α tests are performed, then the expected number of false positives is αT, which may correspond to an unacceptably high number of cost-incurring actions if T is large. If T is known in advance, it is natural to adjust α so that the expected cost incurred due to false positives is constrained. There are at least two views of how this should be done.

12.6.1   Control the Familywise Error

The *familywise error rate* of T statistical tests is the probability that *any* of the tests incorrectly rejects the null hypothesis. The following exercises develop two methods, known as *Šidák correction* and *Bonferroni correction*, which adjust the size of the individual tests so that the familywise error rate is below a given bound. In applied terms, these methods bound the probability that *any cost at all* is incurred by acting on a false positive, regardless of how much cost is incurred by acting on true positives.

Exercise 12.6 *Assume the null hypothesis is true in $T_0 \leq T$ independent tests of size s. Compute the probability $p(s)$ that at least one test incorrectly rejects the null. Given α, solve $p(s) = \alpha$ for s, and propose a value of s such that the familywise error rate of the T tests is less than or equal to α. This is called the Šidák correction for multiple tests.*

Exercise 12.7 *Assume the null hypothesis is true in $T_0 \leq T$ (not necessarily independent) tests of size s. Use the basic fact*[6] *that* $P(E_1 \cup \cdots \cup E_k) \leq P(E_1) + \cdots + P(E_k)$ *for any set of events* $E_1, \ldots, E_k$ *to find a bound p(s) on the probability that at least one test incorrectly rejects the null. Given* α, *solve p(s) = α for s, and propose a value of s such that the familywise error rate of the T tests is less than or equal to* α. *This is called the* Bonferroni *correction for multiple tests.*

These methods are both conservative in the sense that if $T_0 \ll T$ they will produce a familywise error rate smaller than the target, α. The use of Boole's inequality makes Bonferroni's correction even more conservative, particularly when $s \ll \frac{1}{T}$.

12.6.2   Control the False Discovery Rate

The *false discovery rate*, $P(H_0 \mid \text{reject } H_0)$, is the probability that the null hypothesis is true for a given test, conditional on that test rejecting the null hypothesis. Two slightly different methods have been presented to control the false discovery rate, depending on whether or not the tests are independent:

> (1) let $p_{(1)} \leq \cdots \leq p_{(T)}$ denote the p-values of T tests, sorted into increasing order.
> (2) let k be the largest value of index i such that $p_{(i)} \leq \frac{i}{T}\frac{\alpha}{a_T}$.
> (3) set $s = p_{(k)}$, that is, reject H_0 in exactly those tests with p-value less than or equal to $p_{(k)}$.

where

$$a_T = \begin{cases} 1 & \text{if the tests are independent} \\ \sum_{i=1}^{T} \frac{1}{i} \approx 0.57722 + \log(T) & \text{otherwise} \end{cases}$$

These methods are known as the *Benjamini–Hochberg procedure* for independent tests and the *Benjamini–Hochberg–Yekutieli procedure* for dependent tests. It is proved in Benjamini and Hochberg (1995) and Benjamini and Yekutieli (2001) that these methods result in a false discovery rate less than or equal to $\frac{T_0}{T}\alpha \leq \alpha$ when the null hypothesis is true in T_0 of the T tests.

In applied terms, the Benjamini–Hochberg and Benjamini–Hochberg–Yekutieli methods bound the proportion of the total incurred cost which is incurred by acting on false positives: if the false discovery rate is less than or equal to α, then at least $1 - \alpha$ units of benefit are obtained for each unit of cost incurred by acting on a (true or false) positive. Controlling the false discovery rate is less conservative than

---

[6] This is *Boole's inequality*. It is the simplest of a set of inequalities known as *Bonferroni's inequalities*.

controlling the familywise error rate, in the sense that it is tolerant of false positives as long as sufficient benefit is obtained from true positives.

12.7   Expert Systems

To every consulting statistician or machine learning practitioner, there will come a time like this. You are asked to provide a client with a trained classifier which distinguishes apples from oranges. With a little friendly interrogation, you learn that the client expects only McIntosh apples and navel oranges to be present in the operational environment of the classifier, so the problem is really to distinguish between McIntosh apples and navel oranges. You are promised data appropriate to addressing such a problem.

The data arrive: 20 items labeled *apples* and 300 items labeled *oranges*. Exploratory data analysis reveals that the "apples" consist of 20 bruised Granny Smith apples. The "oranges" consist of two navel oranges, three clementines and 295 polar bears. You call your client and a conversation something like this ensues.

You: "The apples you sent me are rather different from the apples you're looking for."

Client: "Those are the apples we have."

You: "Do you realize you sent me polar bears instead of oranges?"

Client: "Polar bears? What are you talking about? We sent you 300 oranges."

You: "Most of your so-called oranges are white, furry, and eight feet long. They have eaten all of my seal data from another project. I am pretty sure they are polar bears. In any case, I am certain they are not navel oranges."

Client: "You're supposed to be a smart math/stats person: we wouldn't have asked for your help if we didn't think you could solve this problem for us. We will try to get you better data, but we need a solution by next week."

There is a constructive response to this situation: find an expert (ideally, multiple independent experts). An expert in this context is someone who, over the course of her training or working life, has seen many McIntosh apples and many navel oranges. There is a predictive process inside her brain which distinguishes apples from oranges, a process which has been validated and updated by many sequential applications. Parts of this process may be subconscious. In cases like that above, it may be far better to *model the expert* than model the available data. The result of modeling the expert is an *expert system*.

The simplest way to model the expert is to ask the expert how she makes decisions, apple-vs.-orange, based on observations, and to try to mimic her decision process with an algorithm. Naive Bayes and tree classifiers are good frameworks for this. It is also useful, when possible, to observe the expert making decisions about previously unseen apples and oranges, in order to pick up on important but subconscious elements of her decision process. This may take a long time.

Successfully approximating expert behavior can be quite challenging, particularly when assigning weights to different types of evidence. A model elicited from an expert should be validated on marked data, when possible. It may be, however, that the only validation possible is another expert's opinion of "that sounds reasonable."

13

Current Challenges in Machine Learning

Decision makers need forecasts only if there is uncertainty about the future.

—J. Scott Armstrong, *Principles of Forecasting: A Handbook for Researchers and Practitioners*, 2001

This chapter briefly presents a few growth areas in machine learning, generally arising from the changing relative costs of acquiring data, transmitting data, storing data, analyzing data, and computing with data.

13.1 Streaming Data

Streaming data are data which are generated faster or in greater quantity than they can be put in long-term storage. Each datum, on arrival, must be used immediately for whatever purpose is appropriate (training a model, used for prediction, updating a clustering, etc.) and then discarded forever. One area of concern is the ongoing training and assessment of predictive models.

13.2 Distributed Data

Distributed data abstractly comprise a single dataset but physically reside in separate storage devices on a communications network of such high latency that it is infeasible

Machine Learning: a Concise Introduction, First Edition. Steven W. Knox.
© This publication is a US Government work and is in the public domain.
Published 2018 by John Wiley & Sons, Inc.
Companion Website: http://www.wiley.com/go/Knox/MachineLearning

for all of the data, in raw form, to be processed by a single processor. Data may be distributed because it was originally collected in multiple locations, or to reduce access time to a large amount of data by parallelizing the read operation across many hard drives. To be practical, algorithms applied to distributed data may only transmit across the network relatively small summaries of the data on any particular storage device. This is the basis of *cloud computing*.

13.3   Semi-supervised Learning

Semi-supervised learning attempts to improve the performance of a classifier trained on marked data by extracting information from unmarked data. The motivation for semi-supervised learning is situations where marked data are expensive or rare, while unmarked data are cheap or plentiful. An example of a semi-supervised learning problem is training a nearest-cluster classifier, where unmarked data may contribute information on the size, shape, and number of clusters, while marked data also contribute information on the class(es) of data in each cluster.

13.4   Active Learning

Active learning refers to an iterative process in which marked data are acquired sequentially based on uncertainty in predictions made by a classifier. The goal of active learning is to obtain a small (and therefore relatively cheap) marked dataset which is as useful as possible for training classifiers. Active learning begins with an initial set of marked data, $M = \{(x_1, y_1), \ldots, (x_n, y_n)\}$, and a set of feature vectors $U = \{\tilde{x}_1, \ldots, \tilde{x}_k\}$ which are unmarked. Assuming that the true class label of any unmarked datum $\tilde{x}_i$ can be acquired (at some expense), active learning proceeds by iterating the following steps:

---

(1) train a classifier $\widehat{f}$ on the set of marked data, M.

(2) apply $\widehat{f}$ to each feature vector in the unmarked data, U.

(3) determine a subset $S \subset U$ on which $\widehat{f}$ is least certain about its predictions.

(4) acquire the true class labels of the feature vectors in S.

(5) update $M = M \cup S$ and $U = U \setminus S$.

Uncertainty about predictions may be measured by entropy in the estimated probability distribution $(\widehat{P}(Y = 1 \mid X), \ldots, \widehat{P}(Y = C \mid X))$ in likelihood methods, logistic regression, or neural networks; or by large slack variables in support vector machines; or by entropy in the distribution of votes cast by an ensemble; or by a propensity to misclassify marked training data in certain regions of feature space.

13.5   Feature Construction via Deep Neural Networks

Construction of new, informative features by deep neural networks, such as the autoencoders described in Section 11.3.11, is still in its early days. At the time of writing, this is perhaps the fastest-moving part of the field of machine learning.

13.6   Transfer Learning

Transfer learning attempts to learn useful ideas from one classification problem and apply them to another: typically, from a problem in which data are plentiful to a problem in which data are scarce. For example, given a sufficiently large collection of photographs, each labeled "cat" or "dog," one could train a deep autoencoder to construct high-order features which are useful for distinguishing pictures of cats from pictures of dogs. Those features (which is to say, the parameters of the deep autoencoder) may be very useful in a related classification problem (say, distinguishing pictures of groundhogs from pictures of rabbits) for which there is not enough data to train a useful autoencoder.

13.7   Interpretability of Complex Models

The need for accurate and interpretable predictive models will increase as humanity relies more on using machine learning to make potentially life-changing decisions (for example, in self-driving cars or algorithmic medical diagnoses) or decisions with global impact (for example, algorithmic influence on financial markets). Interpretable models will be needed for retrospective analysis, to know who or what is accountable for the consequences of a serious error, and for developing models which are verifiably robust to unforeseen combinations of inputs.

14

R Source Code

> I'm sorry, Dave. I'm afraid I can't do that.
> —HAL 9000 in Arthur C. Clarke and Stanley Kubrick,
> *2001: A Space Odyssey*, 1968

This chapter shows how to implement almost every method of training and applying a classifier described in Chapters 4 and 6, using risk-estimation and model-selection methods described in Chapter 7, and (at least implicitly) optimization methods described in Chapter 10. The purpose of providing the R code in this chapter is to enable the reader, with minimal effort, to learn more about classification in general and the many specific methods described in this book in particular. To that end, the code is written to be both transparent and brief, so that the language of the computer does not form an obstacle between the reader and perception of the mathematical, statistical, and algorithmic ideas being implemented. This led to the following choices.

(1) The code itself relies on R libraries readily available from the Comprehensive R Archive Network (CRAN) at `cran.r-project.org`.

(2) No space is given to checking whether inputs satisfy various requirements (for example, the reader is free to use a negative bandwidth in a classifier which uses kernel density estimates, and accept the consequences). No space is given to protecting against numerical problems such as underflow or overflow.

(3) Much of the discussion around the code is focused on matching the tuning parameters which govern the behavior of the classifiers (and, where relevant, the model parameters estimated by training the classifiers on data) with values

---

Machine Learning: a Concise Introduction, First Edition. Steven W. Knox.
© This publication is a US Government work and is in the public domain.
Published 2018 by John Wiley & Sons, Inc.
Companion Website: http://www.wiley.com/go/Knox/MachineLearning

taken as input or returned as output by the software. That is, matching the ideas behind the classifiers to code parameters, and thence to what the data tell us about these ideas in a particular case.[1]

(4) Several things which could have been made more general, and thus perhaps more useful as software, were intentionally not generalized.

This chapter is not intended to be a general tutorial on the R language, nor to be a substitute for the documentation of the various R functions and libraries which are used.

14.1   Author's Biases

Unlike the other chapters of this book, which are essentially about what *is* (a neural network is one thing, quadratic discriminant analysis is another, and the two are generally not the same), this chapter is about what one *does*. In the author's experience, what people do is affected by many things: habit, bias, and laziness as well as attempts at rational, objective optimization of some subjective goals. In order that the reader may more easily separate the objective requirements of the code in this chapter from the author's biases, several of these biases are listed here.

(1) For computation, my native language is C. I have written well over 100,000 lines of C, and I still prefer the elegant minimalism of C to any other language, despite the convenience many "higher-level" languages offer.

(2) If I am going to invest much time in software development, I prefer to work under a standard. My code written in ANSI-C over 20 years ago still compiles and runs correctly—something which cannot be said of the code written for the first draft of this chapter, to say nothing of my code written for R version 1.

(3) I prefer to put as much code as possible on a screen at one time, using horizontal as well as vertical space to arrange lines. This means I end every line of R with a (usually unnecessary) semicolon.

14.2   Libraries

The code in this chapter uses functions from the R libraries class, e1071, hash, MASS, mclust, nnet, randomForest, rpart, stats, and (optionally)

---

[1] It is one thing to train a support vector machine using the R function svm(), and then to predict the classes of unmarked data using the output of svm() and the R function predict(). It is quite another to extract the meaning of the output from svm() (the support vectors for each class, and the linear boundaries between each pair of classes) to gain some insight about either the training data, or about how a support vector machine performs, or both.

`parallel`.[2] Use of specific libraries will be indicated in each section by loading them with the R `library()` function. These libraries have many functions and datasets which are not used in this chapter, but which the reader may find useful when exploring avenues not followed here.

Although existing R libraries are generally used, in some cases the author does not know of libraries which implement specific methods described in Chapters 4 and 6 or found it preferable and reasonably efficient to implement a method directly in R.

14.3 The Running Example (Section 4.3)

The various classification methods described in Chapters 4 and 6 are illustrated in R code using the data of the example classification problem introduced in Section 4.3. Recall that in this example, data have $m = 2$ real features and belong to one of $C = 3$ classes: orange, blue, and purple. Marginally, the three classes are equally likely:

$$P(Y) = \begin{cases} \frac{1}{3} & \text{if } Y = 1 \text{ (orange)} \\ \frac{1}{3} & \text{if } Y = 2 \text{ (blue)} \\ \frac{1}{3} & \text{if } Y = 3 \text{ (purple)} \end{cases}.$$

Within each class, features are distributed as an equal-weight mixture of three two-dimensional Gaussian distributions with unit covariance matrix and different means. The means of the nine Gaussians are shown in the left-hand cell of Figure 4.1, colored according to class. In polar coordinates, the orange means are $\{(3, \frac{3\pi}{9}), (2, \frac{5\pi}{9}), (1, \frac{7\pi}{9})\}$, the blue means are $\{(3, \frac{9\pi}{9}), (2, \frac{11\pi}{9}), (1, \frac{13\pi}{9})\}$, and the purple means are $\{(3, \frac{15\pi}{9}), (2, \frac{17\pi}{9}), (1, \frac{1\pi}{9})\}$. These means and covariance matrix are defined in the following R code.

```
mus = matrix(NA,9,2); radius = c(3,2,1,3,2,1,3,2,1);
for(i in 1:9) {
    angle = (2*i+1)*pi/9; mus[i,] = radius[i]*c(cos(angle),
    sin(angle));
}
sigma = diag(c(1,1));
```

---

[2] The R code provided in this chapter has been tested using the following versions of R and R libraries: R version 3.4.1 (R Core Team, 2017), `class` version 7.3-14 (Venables and Ripley, 2002), `e1071` version 1.6-8 (Meyer et al., 2017), hash version 2.2.6 (Brown, 2013), MASS version 7.3-47 (Venables and Ripley, 2002), `mclust` version 5.4 (Scrucca et al., 2016), nnet version 7.3-12 (Venables and Ripley, 2002), `parallel` version 3.4.1 (R Core Team, 2017), randomForest version 4.6-12 (Liaw and Wiener, 2002), rpart version 4.1-11 (Therneau et al., 2017), and `stats` version 3.4.1 (R Core Team, 2017).

The means corresponding to class $Y = 1$ are mus[1,], mus[2,], and mus[3,], the means corresponding to class $Y = 2$ are mus[4,], mus[5,], and mus[6,], and the means corresponding to class $Y = 3$ are mus[7,], mus[8,], and mus[9,].

A sample of data from the joint distribution $P(X, Y)$ is drawn in the function draw.sample(), which takes as input a number of samples, ndat, and outputs an ndat × 3 matrix, where each row is a draw (X, Y) from $P(X, Y)$. First, the class label Y of each data point is drawn from the marginal distribution on class labels, which is the uniform distribution on the set $\{1, 2, 3\}$ (or $\{$orange, blue, purple$\}$). This is done in the first line, and stored in the variable cls. Next, the Gaussian mixture component of each data point is drawn from the distribution on mixture components conditional on the class. For each class, this is the uniform distribution on the set $\{1, 2, 3\}$. This is done in the second line, and stored in the variable mix (mix is Z in Section 10.7). Then the feature vector X is drawn from the two-dimensional Gaussian distribution with unit covariance matrix sigma and a mean determined by both the class label and the mixture component within the class, mus[1+3*(cls-1)+(mix-1),]. This is done in the third and fourth lines, using the multivariate normal sampling function mvrnorm() from the R library MASS, and stored in the first two columns of the $n \times (m + 1)$ matrix variable dat. Finally, the class label Y is stored in the third column of dat, and the sample is returned with the rows of dat ordered so that the class labels are non-decreasing (there is no reason to sort the rows of dat, except to make visual inspection of the data easier).

```
library(MASS);
draw.sample = function(ndat) {
  cls = sample(c(1,2,3),ndat,replace=TRUE);
  mix = sample(c(1,2,3),ndat,replace=TRUE);
  dat = matrix(NA,ndat,3);
  dat[,1:2] = t(apply(mus[1+3*(cls-1)+(mix-1),],1,mvrnorm,
    n=1,Sigma=sigma));
  dat[,3] = cls;
  return(dat[order(dat[,3]),]);
}
```

Interpreting the fourth line of draw.sample() from the inside out, the variable 1+3*(cls-1)+(mix-1) is an ndat-long vector with coordinates in the set $\{1, \ldots, 9\}$, and the ith coordinate of this vector indicates which of the nine Gaussian distributions the ith feature vector will be drawn from. The variable mus[1+3*(cls-1)+(mix-1),] is an ndat × 2 matrix: the ith row is the mean of the Gaussian distribution the ith feature will be drawn from. The function mvrnorm() takes as input a mean, covariance matrix, and number of samples, and outputs the given number of samples from a multivariate Gaussian distribution with the given mean and covariance. The function apply(mus[1+3*(cls-1)+(mix-1),],1,mvrnorm,n=1,Sigma=sigma) applies the function mvrnorm() to each row of the matrix mus[1+3*(cls-1)+(mix-1),], drawing one (n=1) sample from a Gaussian distribution with identity covariance matrix (Sigma=sigma, and sigma is the 2×2 identity matrix) and mean equal to a row of mus[1+3*(cls-1)+(mix-1),]. The result of this operation stores the ndat samples as the columns of a $2 \times$ ndat matrix, so the result is transposed by the R function t() to put it in the usual form where feature vectors are rows.

Training and test sets of data, respectively of size $n = 150$ and $\tilde{n} = 50,000$ and called tdat and edat,[3] are drawn using the function draw.sample().

```
nt=150;    tdat = draw.sample(nt);
ne=50000; edat = draw.sample(ne);
```

Some R functions require that feature vectors be rows of an R matrix, while others require that feature vectors be rows of an R data frame. To enhance readability of the code which follows, the feature vectors of the training and evaluation data are stored in data frames tdatDF and edatDF:

```
tdatDF = as.data.frame(tdat[,1:2]);
edatDF = as.data.frame(edat[,1:2]);
```

It will also be useful, when applying the code to other problems, to have the number of classes stored in a variable:

```
nc = 3;
```

The test data (tiny points), training data (medium points), and Gaussian means (large points with thick black boundaries) are shown in Figure 14.1 and can be plotted using the following R code.

```
cols = c("orange","lightblue","purple");
par(mar=c(2,2,2,2)+0.1);  idx=sample(1:ne,ne);
plot(edat[idx,1:2],col=cols[edat[idx,3]],axes=FALSE,xlab="",
    ylab="",pch=".");
points(tdat[,1:2],col=cols[tdat[,3]],pch=20);
points(tdat[,1:2]);
points(mus,col=cols[c(1,1,1,2,2,2,3,3,3)],pch=19,cex=1.5);
points(mus,cex=1.5,lwd=2);
```

In summary, creating training and test samples of data for the example of Section 4.3 defines the following R variables, which will be used throughout this chapter.

R variable	Meaning	Book notation
nt	number of training data	n
tdat[, 1 : 2]	training feature vectors ($n \times 2$ R matrix)	$x_1, \ldots, x_n$
tdatDF	training feature vectors ($n \times 2$ R data frame)	$x_1, \ldots, x_n$

---

[3] The letter t in tdat stands for *training*, and the letter e in edat stands for *evaluation*. If a validation set were used here, it would be called vdat.

R variable	Meaning	Book notation
tdat[, 3]	training class labels	$y_1, \ldots, y_n$
ne	number of test data	$\tilde{n}$
edat[, 1 : 2]	test feature vectors ($\tilde{n} \times 2$ R matrix)	$\tilde{x}_1, \ldots, \tilde{x}_{\tilde{n}}$
edatDF	test feature vectors ($\tilde{n} \times 2$ R data frame)	$\tilde{x}_1, \ldots, \tilde{x}_{\tilde{n}}$
edat[, 3]	test class labels	$\tilde{y}_1, \ldots, \tilde{y}_{\tilde{n}}$
nc	number of classes	C

In the R code which follows, each method will be applied to test data, producing an R vector pred.class of predicted class labels. The following function compares a

Test and training data

Figure 14.1   Test and training data generated by R code in this section. The data are colored by class. Test data are plotted as tiny points, training data are plotted as medium points with black boundaries, and the nine Gaussian means are plotted as large points with black boundaries.

vector of predicted class labels for the test data to the true labels, and reports the test estimate of risk, plus or minus one standard deviation.

```
risk.test = function(pred.class) {
    err = sum(as.numeric(pred.class)!=edat[,3]);
    p = err/ne; sd = round(sqrt(p*(1-p)/ne),4); p = round(p,4);
    print(paste("test estimate of risk:",p,"+/-",sd));
}
```

14.4   The Bayes Classifier (Section 4.1)

Under 0–1 loss, with a uniform prior probability distribution on class labels, the Bayes classifier predicts that a feature vector X has the class which maximizes the conditional likelihood $P(X \mid Y)$, that is, the Bayes classifier predicts

$$\operatorname{argmax}_{c \in \{1,\dots,C\}} P(X \mid Y = c)$$

(this statement is Exercise 4.2). The Bayes classifier is implemented by three R functions. Function bayes.lik.one() inputs a feature vector x and a mean μ, and returns the likelihood function of the Gaussian distribution with mean μ and unit covariance matrix, evaluated at x,

$$\frac{1}{2\pi} e^{-\frac{1}{2}(x-\mu)^{\mathrm{T}}(x-\mu)}.$$

```
bayes.lik.one = function(x,mu) { return(exp(-0.5*(x-mu)%*%
    (x-mu))/(2*pi)); }
```

Function bayes.lik.mix() inputs a feature vector x, a matrix of means

$$\mu = \begin{bmatrix} \mu_1 \\ \vdots \\ \mu_J \end{bmatrix},$$

and vector of non-negative weights $w = (w_1, \dots, w_J)$, and returns the likelihood function of the Gaussian mixture distribution with means given by the rows of μ, unit covariance matrices, and weights w, evaluated at x,

$$\sum_{j=1}^{J} w_j \frac{1}{2\pi} e^{-\frac{1}{2}(x-\mu_j)^{\mathrm{T}}(x-\mu_j)}.$$

```
bayes.lik.mix = function(x,mu,w) {
    liks.one = apply(mu,1,bayes.lik.one,x=x);
    return(sum(w*liks.one));
}
```

The first line of `bayes.lik.mix()` applies the function `bayes.lik.one()` to each row of the input matrix `mu`, producing the J-long vector

$$\left(\frac{1}{2\pi} e^{-\frac{1}{2}(x-\mu_1)^{\mathrm{T}}(x-\mu_1)}, \ldots, \frac{1}{2\pi} e^{-\frac{1}{2}(x-\mu_J)^{\mathrm{T}}(x-\mu_J)} \right).$$

The second line multiplies this vector coordinatewise by the vector of weights $(w_1, \ldots, w_J)$ and returns the sum of the resulting J numbers. The number of mixture components J is not explicitly specified in the R code because it is carried by the dimension of the input matrix `mu` and the length of the input vector `w`.

The Bayes classifier applies function `bayes.lik.mix()` at a given point x, using each set of three means corresponding to each of the three classes, with equal mixture weights in each case. Function `bayes.predict()` outputs the class[4] corresponding to a Gaussian mixture model which produces maximal likelihood at x.

```
bayes.predict.one = function(x) {
  liks.mix = c( bayes.lik.mix(x,mus[1:3,],rep(1/3,3)),
                bayes.lik.mix(x,mus[4:6,],rep(1/3,3)),
                bayes.lik.mix(x,mus[7:9,],rep(1/3,3)) );
  return(max.col(t(liks.mix)));
}
bayes.predict.many = function(x) { return(apply(x,1,
  bayes.predict.one)); }
```

Note that the constant $\frac{1}{2\pi}$ in `bayes.lik.one()` has no effect on the Bayes classifier, and can be omitted to save work, as can the value $\frac{1}{3}$ for the equal weights of the mixture components in each Gaussian mixture in `bayes.lik.mix()`. The Bayes risk can be estimated by applying the Bayes classifier to the test data:

```
pred.class = bayes.predict.many(edat[,1:2]);
risk.test(pred.class);
```

---

[4] The R function `max.col()` applied to a real vector $(v_1, \ldots, v_k)$ returns an element of the set

$$\left\{ i : v_i = \max_{j=1,\ldots,k} v_j \right\},$$

choosing an element uniformly at random if the set contains more than one element. That is,

$$\mathtt{max.col(t}(v)) = \operatorname{argmax}_{i=1,\ldots,k} v_i,$$

with ties broken by selecting an index uniformly at random. This is in contrast to the R function `which.max()`, which breaks ties by choosing the smallest index.

14.5 Quadratic Discriminant Analysis (Section 4.4.1)

A quadratic discriminant analysis (QDA) model is fit using the function qda() in the MASS library:

```
library(MASS);
m = qda(as.factor(tdat[,3])~.,data=tdatDF,method="mle");
```

Fitting the model is equivalent to computing the mean and covariance of the training data for each class separately. The estimated mean for each class is saved as

$$\hat{\mu}_c = \texttt{m\$means[c,]}$$

for $c = 1, \dots, C$. Instead of saving the estimated covariance matrices for each class, $\hat{\Sigma}_1, \dots, \hat{\Sigma}_C$, the qda() function saves the Cholesky factors[5] of the inverse covariance matrices. That is, qda() computes and saves triangular matrices

$$W_c = \texttt{m\$scaling[,,c],}$$

where $W_c W_c^T = \hat{\Sigma}_c^{-1}$, for $c = 1, \dots, C$. This is done for computation of the likelihood function at any point x under the fitted model:

$$\phi(x \mid \hat{\mu}_c, \hat{\Sigma}_c) = (2\pi)^{-\frac{m}{2}} |W_c| e^{-\frac{1}{2}(W_c^T(x-\hat{\mu}_c))^T(W_c^T(x-\hat{\mu}_c))}.$$

Predictions using the fitted model m are made on the test data using the function predict(), and the predictions can be compared to the true class labels of the test data to produce the test estimate of risk.

```
pred.class = predict(m,edatDF)$class;
risk.test(pred.class);
```

14.6 Linear Discriminant Analysis (Section 4.4.2)

A linear discriminant analysis (LDA) model is fit using the function lda() in the MASS library:

```
library(MASS);
m = lda(as.factor(tdat[,3])~.,data=tdatDF,method="mle");
```

As with qda(), the estimated mean for each class is saved in m$means. The function returns a not-necessarily-triangular matrix

$$W = \texttt{m\$scaling,}$$

---

[5] The Cholesky decomposition of a positive-definite real matrix M is a lower-triangular matrix W such that $M = WW^T$. Every positive-definite real matrix has a unique Cholesky decomposition.

with the property that $W W^T = \hat{\Sigma}^{-1}$. Predictions using the fitted model m are made on the test data using the function `predict()`, exactly as for QDA,

```
pred.class = predict(m,edatDF)$class;
risk.test(pred.class);
```

14.7   Gaussian Mixture Models (Section 4.4.3)

A Gaussian mixture model is fit using the function `MclustDA()` in the `mclust` library.

```
library(mclust);
```

The number of mixture components used for each class is represented by a vector $(J_1, \ldots, J_C)$, which is user-specified. In Section 4.4, we considered using either two mixture components for each class or three mixture components for each class,

```
J = c(2,2,2);
```

or

```
J = c(3,3,3);
```

Given J, the model is fit by calling

```
m = MclustDA(tdat[,1:2],tdat[,3],G=as.integer(J),
       modelNames="VVV");
```

Fitting the model is equivalent to, for each class $c = 1, \ldots, C$, finding weights $w_{1c}, \ldots, w_{J_cc}$, means $\mu_{1c}, \ldots, w_{J_cc}$, and covariance matrices $\Sigma_{1c}, \ldots, \Sigma_{J_cc}$ which approximately maximize the likelihood

$$\prod_{i=1}^{n} \left(\sum_{j=1}^{J_{y_i}} w_{jy_i} |2\pi\Sigma_{jy_i}|^{-\frac{1}{2}} e^{-\frac{1}{2}(x-\mu_{jy_i})^T\Sigma_{jy_i}^{-1}(x-\mu_{jy_i})} \right).$$

This is done using the expectation-maximization (EM) algorithm, as described[6] in Section 10.7. The string argument `modelNames="VVV"` indicates that no

---

[6] In fitting the Gaussian mixture models illustrated in Section 4.4.3, the author initialized the EM algorithm by choosing γ_{ij}^1 for $i = 1, \ldots, n$ and $j = 1, \ldots, J$ uniformly at random (provided that $\gamma_{i1}^1 + \gamma_{i2}^1 + \gamma_{i2}^1 = 1$ for each i) and beginning EM with the maximization step, using the lower-level functions `mstep()` and `em()` in the `mclust` library. This was repeated 1000 times, and the Gaussian mixture model parameters which produced the highest expected log-likelihood were retained. In contrast to this approach, the function `MclustDA()` is much more aggressive—it uses a hierarchical clustering algorithm to produce an initial state with high expected log-likelihood and uses EM to climb from that state. In the author's experience, `MclustDA()` is much faster but produces fits with lower expected log-likelihood than the many-random-starts approach. As a result, the "worse" fit produced by `MclustDA()` yields a Gaussian mixture model with higher risk than the many-random-starts approach (risk 0.210 vs. 0.205) when $J = (2, 2, 2)$ because the former is relatively underfit due to worse optimization of the model parameters, but yields a Gaussian mixture model with *lower* risk than the many-random-starts approach (risk 0.209 vs. 0.228) when $J = (3, 3, 3)$ because the former *does not overfit as much as it could,* again due to worse optimization of the model parameters.

constraints are placed on the covariance matrices in the search for optimal parameters.

The estimated weights, means, and covariances for each class $c = 1, \ldots, C$ and each mixture component $j = 1, \ldots, J_c$, are saved as

$$\widehat{w}_{jc} = \texttt{m\$"}c\texttt{"\$parameters\$pro}[j]$$
$$\widehat{\mu}_{jc} = \texttt{m\$"}c\texttt{"\$parameters\$mean}[,j]$$
$$\widehat{\Sigma}_{jc} = \texttt{m\$"}c\texttt{"\$parameters\$variance\$sigma}[,,j].$$

Cholesky factors of the estimated covariance matrices are also saved, with cholsigma in place of sigma in the last line above. Predictions using the fitted model m are made on the test data using the function predict(),

```
pred.class = as.numeric(predict(m,edat[,1:2])$class);
risk.test(pred.class);
```

14.8 Kernel Density Estimation (Section 4.4.4)

Kernel density estimation begins with a kernel function. In Section 4.4, the Gaussian kernel was defined as

```
K = function(x)  { return(exp(-0.5*x%*%x)); }
```

and the Epanechnikov kernel was defined as

```
K = function(x)  { return(max(0,length(x)+4-x%*%x)); }
```

In the code above, the normalization constant $(2\pi)^{-\frac{m}{2}}$ has been omitted from the Gaussian kernel and the normalization constant $\Gamma(\frac{m}{2} + 2)\pi^{-\frac{m}{2}}(m+4)^{-\frac{m}{2}-1}$ has been omitted from the Epanechnikov kernel because these constants do not affect predictions made by the KDE classifier.

Function kde.liks() inputs a point $x \in \mathbb{R}^m$, a set of k points in $\mathbb{R}^m$ stored as the rows of a $k \times m$ matrix

$$\texttt{dat} = \begin{bmatrix} z_1 \\ \vdots \\ z_k \end{bmatrix},$$

and a bandwidth parameter h, and computes the kernel density estimate of a likelihood function at x,

$$\widehat{P}(x) = \frac{1}{k} \sum_{i=1}^{k} \frac{1}{h^m} K\left(\frac{x - z_i}{h}\right).$$

```
kde.liks = function(x,dat,h)  {
    v = t(x-t(dat))/h;
    liks = apply(v,1,K);
    return(mean(h^-dim(dat)[2]*liks));
}
```

The first line of `kde.liks()` computes the vector

$$\left(\frac{x - \text{dat}[1,]}{h}, \ldots, \frac{x - \text{dat}[k,]}{h}\right)$$

and the second line applies the kernel function K to this vector coordinatewise, computing

$$\left(K\left(\frac{x - \text{dat}[1,]}{h}\right), \ldots, K\left(\frac{x - \text{dat}[k,]}{h}\right)\right).$$

The third line scales each coordinate of this vector by h^{-m}, sums the entries of the resulting k-long vector, and divides by k.

Function `kde.predict.one()` inputs a point $x \in \mathbb{R}^m$, a set of n points in $\mathbb{R}^m$ stored as the rows of a $n \times m$ matrix `datx`, an n-long vector of class labels `daty` in the range $1, \ldots, C$, and an C-long vector of bandwidths $h = (h_1, \ldots, h_C)$. In the first line, it estimates the prior (marginal) distribution of class labels based on the counts of vector `daty`,

$$P(Y = c) \propto |\{i : \text{daty}[i] = c\}|,$$

for $c = 1, \ldots, C$. In the second and third lines, it computes kernel density estimates of the likelihood function of data for each class,

$$\widehat{P}(x \mid Y = c) = \frac{1}{n_c} \sum_{\substack{i=1 \\ y_i = c}}^{n} \frac{1}{h_c^m} K\left(\frac{x - x_i}{h_c}\right),$$

for $c = 1, \ldots, C$. In the fourth line it predicts a class with maximal posterior probability,

$$\text{argmax}_{c=1,\ldots,C} \, \widehat{P}(Y = c \mid x) = \text{argmax}_{c=1,\ldots,C} \, \widehat{P}(x \mid Y = c) \, P(Y = c).$$

```
kde.predict.one = function(x,datx,daty,h) {
  t = table(daty); priors = t/sum(t);
  liks = vector("numeric",nc);
  for(cc in 1:nc) {
    liks[cc] = kde.liks(x,datx[daty==cc,],h[cc]); }
  return(max.col(t(priors*liks)));
}
```

Selecting a KDE classifier means selecting a vector of bandwidths $h = (h_1, \ldots, h_C)$ to optimize some estimate of risk. Function `kde.loo.one()` inputs a $n \times m$ matrix of feature vectors `datx`, an n-long vector of class labels `daty`, a C-long vector of bandwidths h, and an index o in the set $\{1, \ldots, n\}$. It predicts the class of the oth datum using the KDE classifier with the bandwidth vector h and all data except the oth. It then compares the prediction to the true class, `daty[o]`. It returns the R Boolean value TRUE (numeric value 1) if the KDE classifier made an incorrect prediction, and returns the R Boolean value FALSE (numeric value 0) if the KDE classifier made the correct prediction.

```
kde.loo.one = function(datx,daty,h,o) {
    pred = kde.predict.one(datx[o,],datx[-o,],daty[-o],h);
    return(pred!=daty[o]);
}
```

Function kde.loo.all() applies the function kde.loo.one() with each datum held out in turn, and returns the average number of times the KDE classifier made an incorrect prediction: that is, kde.loo.all() computes the leave-one-out cross-validation estimate of risk under 0–1 loss for a KDE classifier using a given vector of bandwidths h and given training data datx and daty.

```
kde.loo.all = function(datx,daty,h) {
    errs = sapply(1:dim(datx)[1],kde.loo.one,datx=datx,
        daty=daty,h=h);
    return(mean(errs));
}
```

Introducing the constraint that all bandwidths be equal, $h_1 = \cdots = h_C$, which seems reasonable in the running example of Chapter 4, bandwidth selection is reduced to a one-dimensional optimization. Figure 14.2 shows leave-one-out risk estimates for various bandwidths, for both the Gaussian and Epanechnikov kernel. The plots in Figure 14.2 suggest that any bandwidth roughly in the range [0.3, 1.2] might be equally

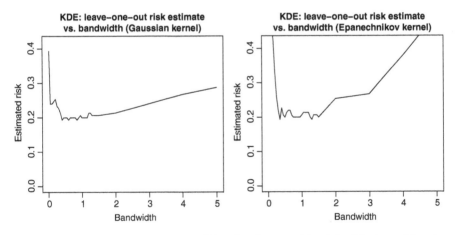

Figure 14.2   Leave-one-out cross-validated estimates of the risk of the kernel density estimate classifier as a function of the bandwidth $h = h_1 = h_2 = h_3$ used for each class.

good, and that from a risk perspective there is not much reason to choose the Gaussian kernel over the Epanechnikov kernel.

```
hcol = c(0.01,0.05,seq(0.1,1.5,0.05),2:5);
hmat = cbind(hcol,hcol,hcol);
errs = apply(hmat,1,kde.loo.all,datx=tdat[,1:2],
   daty=tdat[,3]);
plot(hcol,errs,xlab="Bandwidth",ylab="Estimated Risk",
   type="l",ylim=c(0,0.4*1.05));
```

One need not accept the constraint $h_1 = \cdots = h_C$, and could instead search for a vector of bandwidths $(h_1, \ldots, h_C)$ which minimizes the leave-one-out cross-validated estimate of risk, using an optimization method such as the Nelder–Mead algorithm (described in Section 10.2). This is done by the R function optim(), starting from a user-specified point (starting from $h = (0.8, 0.8, 0.8)$ in the code below).

```
library(stats);
optim(rep(0.8,3),kde.loo.all,method="Nelder-Mead",
   datx=tdat[,1:2],daty=tdat[,3]);
```

In this example, over many starts, Nelder–Mead tends to reach optima roughly in the region $h \in [0.3, 1.2]^3$, and if Nelder–Mead is started at a value in this box then it quickly becomes stuck in a local optimum close to its starting point. This suggests that the objective function (the leave-one-out cross-validation estimate of risk) is sufficiently noisy that there is little or no information to allow us to choose among bandwidth vectors in this region.

Classifiers are often applied to predict the class of more than one point at a time. Function kde.predict.many() is an efficient way to apply kde.predict.one() to many input points at once. The feature vectors to be classified are stored as the rows of the input matrix x.

```
kde.predict.many = function(x,datx,daty,h) {
   return(apply(x,1,kde.predict.one,datx=datx,daty=daty,h=h));
}
```

For example, kde.predict.many() could be used to compute the test estimate of the KDE classifier's risk:

```
pred.class = kde.predict.many(edat[,1:2],tdat[,1:2],tdat[,3],
   rep(0.5,3));
risk.test(pred.class);
```

14.9   Histograms (Section 4.4.5)

Given a feature vector $x = (x_1, \ldots, x_m)$, and a $C \times m$ matrix of bandwidth parameters

$$h = \begin{bmatrix} h_{1,1} & \cdots & h_{1,m} \\ \vdots & & \vdots \\ h_{C,1} & \cdots & h_{C,m} \end{bmatrix},$$

the rectangle $R_c(i_1, \ldots, i_m) \subset \mathbb{R}^m$ which contains x, for each class $c = 1, \ldots, C$, can be found by setting [7]

$$i_j = \left\lfloor \frac{x_j}{h_{c,j}} \right\rfloor$$

for all $j = 1, \ldots, m$ (here, $\lfloor r \rfloor$ represents the integer floor of a real number r). The key to implementing a histogram classifier is constructing an efficient function which inputs a feature vector x and outputs the number of training data in the class-c rectangle $R_c(i_1, \ldots, i_m)$ which contains x, for each class $c = 1, \ldots, C$. One way to do this, which in many cases is efficient, is by constructing a hash table.

For the present purpose, a *hash table* can be thought of as an array where the index, instead of being a non-negative (or positive) integer, is an element of an arbitrary discrete set.[8] The indices of a hash table are called the *keys* of the hash table, and the entries indexed by the keys are the *values* of the hash table.[9] Hash tables are implemented in the R library `hash`.

```
library(hash);
```

Selecting a histogram classifier is done by three functions: `hist.key()`, `hist.insert()`, and `hist.train()`. These functions create and operate on an R data structure (specifically, an R list) which has the following components:

`HT[[1]], ..., HT[[C]]`—a list of C hash tables, one for each class;

`HT$h`—the $C \times m$ matrix of bandwidth parameters, h;

`HT$prior`—the marginal distribution of class labels which occur in the training data.

The data structure `HT` will be a global variable and will not be explicitly passed in and out of the R functions which operate on it.

---

[7] As mentioned in Section 4.4.5, for each class c, the rectangles $R_c(i_1, \ldots, i_m)$ can be translated by any vector in $[0, h_{c,1}) x \ldots x[0, h_{c,m})$. For simplicity, this is omitted in the implementation presented here. It could be added by introducing a $C \times m$ matrix of translation parameters `HT$t` and changing the main line of the function `hist.key()` to read

```
bins = floor(as.numeric((datx-HT$t[cc,])/HT$h[cc,]))
```

The translation parameters `HT$t` and the bandwidth paramters `HT$h` would then all need to be chosen to minimize the leave-one-out cross-validation estimate of risk (or some other risk estimate).

[8] The mathematics and computer science of constructing efficient hash functions and hash tables is extensive. See Cormen et al., Chapter 11, for an introduction.

[9] Part of the practical value of using a histogram classifier is that it enables the use of a hash table as a form of compression of the training data. Indeed, the statement that exactly k specific training data lie in the rectangle $R_c(i_1, \ldots, i_m) \subset \mathbb{R}^m$ may be viewed as a lossy compression of the k data.

Function hist.key() inputs a feature vector x and a class label c, and outputs the index $(i_1, \ldots, i_m)$ of the class-c rectangle $R_c(i_1, \ldots, i_m)$ which contains x. In the output of hist.key(), the index $(i_1, \ldots, i_m)$ is represented as a string (class "character" in R): this string of characters will be used as a key in a hash table which will be constructed in the function hist.train().

```
hist.key = function(datx,cc) {
    bins = floor(as.numeric(datx)/HT$h[cc,]);
    return(deparse(bins));
}
```

Function hist.insert() inputs a feature vector and class label pair (x, y). In the second line, it calls hist.key() to find the index $(i_1, \ldots, i_m)$ of the class-y rectangle $R_y(i_1, \ldots, i_m)$ which contains x. In the third and fourth lines, if no previous feature vector of class y has landed in $R_y(i_1, \ldots, i_m)$, then hist.insert() creates an entry in the class-y hash table recording that one feature vector has landed in $R_y(i_1, \ldots, i_m)$, and otherwise it increments the count of the class-y feature vectors landing in $R_y(i_1, \ldots, i_m)$ by one.

```
hist.insert = function(dat) {
    datx = dat[1:(length(dat)-1)]; daty = dat[length(dat)];
    key = hist.key(datx,daty);
    if(has.key(key,HT[[daty]])==FALSE) { HT[[daty]][key]=1; }
    else { HT[[daty]][key]=values(HT[[daty]][key])+1; }
}
```

Function hist.train() inputs a set of n points in $\mathbb{R}^m$ stored as the rows of a $n \times m$ matrix datx, an n-long vector of class labels daty in the range $1, \ldots, C$, and a $C \times m$ matrix of bandwidths h, and produces a trained histogram classifier by first creating the necessary hash tables, then processing every training point (x, y) in the appropriate hash table using hist.insert(), and finally computing the empirical distribution of class labels and storing it in HT$prior.

```
hist.train = function(datx,daty,h) {
    HT <<- vector("list",nc); HT$h <<- h;
    for(cc in 1:nc) { HT[[cc]] <<-hash(); };
    apply(cbind(datx,daty),1,hist.insert);
    HT$prior <<- as.numeric(table(daty)/length(daty));
}
```

The trained histogram classifier is HT, the structure which contains C hash tables, the bandwidth matrix, and the marginal distribution of classes.

Making predictions with a trained histogram classifier is done with four functions: hist.lookup(), hist.post(), hist.predict.one(), and hist.predict.many(). Function hist.lookup() inputs a feature vector x

and a class label y, and returns the number of training data of class y which fall in the class-y rectangle which contains x. It does this by computing the index $(i_1, \ldots, i_m)$ of the class-y rectangle which contains x in the first line. If this index does not occur as a key in the class-y hash table, hist.lookup() returns the value 0 because the absence of this index as a key in the hash table indicates that no class-y training data fall in $R_y(i_1, \ldots, i_m)$. Otherwise, $(i_1, \ldots, i_m)$ occurs as a key in the class-y hash table, and hist.lookup() returns the value associated with the key, which is the number of class-y training data in the rectangle, $|\{j : y_j = y \text{ and } x_j \in R_y(i_1, \ldots, i_m)\}|$.

```
hist.lookup = function(datx,daty) {
  key = hist.key(datx,daty);
  if(has.key(key,HT[[daty]])==FALSE) { return(0); }
  return(as.numeric(values(HT[[daty]][key])));
}
```

Function hist.post() inputs a feature vector x and returns the number of training data which occur in the class-c rectangle containing x for each class $c = 1, \ldots, C$. This is proportional to the histogram classifier's estimate of the posterior distribution $(\widehat{P}(Y = 1 \mid X = x), \ldots, \widehat{P}(Y = C \mid X = x))$ by Exercise 4.8. If there is a tie among classes with maximal posterior probability (which happens if no training data fall in any rectangle containing x), it is broken by the prior distribution on classes.

```
hist.post = function(datx) {
  posterior = sapply(1:nc,hist.lookup,datx=datx);
  idx = which(posterior==max(posterior));
  if(length(idx)>1) { posterior=rep(0,nc);
    posterior[idx]=HT$prior[idx]; }
  return(posterior);
}
```

Selecting a histogram classifier means selecting a matrix of bandwidths h to optimize some estimate of risk. Function hist.loo.one() inputs a $n \times m$ matrix of feature vectors datx, an n-long vector of class labels daty, a $C \times m$ matrix of bandwidths h, and an index o in the set $\{1, \ldots, n\}$. It predicts the class of the oth datum using the histogram classifier with the bandwidth matrix h and all data except the oth. It then compares the prediction to the true class, daty[o]. It returns the R Boolean value TRUE (numeric value 1) if the histogram classifier made an incorrect prediction, and returns the R Boolean value FALSE (numeric value 0) if the histogram classifier made the correct prediction.

```
hist.loo.one = function(datx,daty,o) {
  posterior = hist.post(datx[o,]);
  posterior[daty[o]] = posterior[daty[o]]-1;
  pred = max.col(t(posterior));
  return(pred!=daty[o]);
}
```

Function `hist.loo.all()` applies the function `hist.loo.one()` with each datum held out in turn, and returns the average number of times the histogram classifier made an incorrect prediction: that is, `hist.loo.all()` computes the leave-one-out cross-validation estimate of risk under 0–1 loss for a histogram classifier using a given vector of bandwidths h and given training data `datx` and `daty`.

```
hist.loo.all = function(datx,daty,h) {
  hist.train(datx,daty,h);
  errs = sapply(1:dim(datx)[1],hist.loo.one,datx=datx,
    daty=daty);
  return(mean(errs));
}
```

Introducing the constraint that all bandwidths be equal, $h_{1,1} = \cdots = h_{C,m}$, which seems reasonable in the running example of Chapter 4, bandwidth selection is reduced to a one-dimensional optimization. Figure 14.3 shows leave-one-out risk estimates for various bandwidths. The plot in Figure 14.3 suggests that any bandwidth roughly in the range $[1.5, 2]$ might be equally good.

Function `hist.predict.one` inputs a feature vector x and predicts a class with maximal posterior probability based on the trained histogram classifier. Function

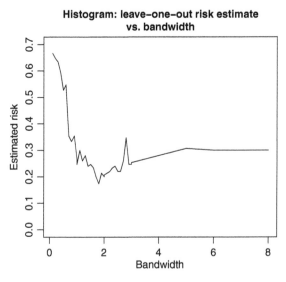

Figure 14.3 Leave-one-out cross-validated estimates of the risk of the histogram classifier, as a function of the common bandwidth used for each feature and each class. Bandwidth is an $m \times C$ matrix h, but we have added the constraint that its entries are all equal to each other.

`hist.predict.many` inputs a $k \times m$ matrix of feature vectors and predicts a class for each.

```
hist.predict.one = function(datx) {
  return(max.col(t(hist.post(datx)))); }
hist.predict.many = function(datx) {
  return(apply(datx,1,hist.predict.one)); }
```

Now a histogram classifier with bandwidths $h_{1,1} = \cdots = h_{C,m} = 2$ can be trained, and a test estimate of its risk can be computed:

```
hist.train(tdat[,1:2],tdat[,3],matrix(2.0,3,2));
pred.class = hist.predict.many(edat[,1:2]);
risk.test(pred.class);
```

14.10   The Naive Bayes Classifier (Section 4.4.6)

Applying the naive Bayes classifier using kernel density estimation for each feature begins with a kernel function. We could use either the Gaussian or Epanechnikov kernel functions as defined in Section 14.8, but since the naive Bayes classifier will apply these kernels with scalar rather than vector input x, it is slightly more efficient to use R's scalar multiplication `x*x` rather than R's vector inner product `x%*%x`. Thus we define one-dimensional versions of the Gaussian and Epanechnikov kernel functions,

```
K = function(x) { return(exp(-0.5*x*x)); }
```

and

```
K = function(x) { return(max(0,length(x)+4-x*x)); }
```

As in Section 14.8, the normalization constant $\sqrt{2\pi}$ has been omitted from the Gaussian kernel and the normalization constant $\dfrac{3}{20\sqrt{5}}$ has been omitted from the Epanechnikov kernel because they do not affect predictions.

Function `kde.liks.one()` is a one-dimensional specialization of the function `kde.liks()` in Section 14.8: it inputs a point $x \in \mathbb{R}$, a set of k points in $z_1, \ldots, z_k \in \mathbb{R}$ stored in a k-long vector `dat`, and a bandwidth h, and computes the one-dimensional kernel density estimate of a likelihood function at x,

$$\widehat{P}(x) = \frac{1}{k} \sum_{i=1}^{k} \frac{1}{h} K\left(\frac{x - z_i}{h}\right).$$

```
kde.liks.one = function(x,dat,h) {
  v = (x-dat)/h;
  liks = K(v);
  return(mean(h^-1*liks)); 
}
```

The first line of `kde.liks.one()` computes the vector

$$\left(\frac{x - \mathrm{dat}[1,]}{h}, \ldots, \frac{x - \mathrm{dat}[k,]}{h} \right)$$

and the second line applies the kernel function K to this vector coordinatewise, computing

$$\left(K\left(\frac{x - \mathrm{dat}[1,]}{h} \right), \ldots, K\left(\frac{x - \mathrm{dat}[k,]}{h} \right) \right).$$

The third line scales each coordinate of this vector by h^{-1}, sums the entries of the resulting k-long vector, and divides by k.

Function `kde.liks.dim()` applies `kde.liks.one()` to one dimension of a multi-dimensional input. Specifically, `kde.liks.dim()` inputs a point $x \in \mathbb{R}^m$, a set of k points in $\mathbb{R}^m$ stored as the rows of a $k \times m$ matrix dat, an m-long vector of bandwidths $h = (h_1, \ldots, h_m)$, and an index $i \in \{1, \ldots, m\}$, and outputs the value of `kde.liks.one()` applied to the ith dimension of the inputs (that is, `kde.liks.dim(x, dat, h, i)` = `kde.liks.one(`x_i`, dat[,i]`, h_i`))`.

```
kde.liks.dim = function(x,dat,h,i) {
    return(kde.liks.one(x[i],dat[,i],h[i])); }
```

Function `nb.kde.liks()` inputs a point $x \in \mathbb{R}^m$, a set of k points in $\mathbb{R}^m$ stored as the rows of a $k \times m$ matrix dat, and an m-long vector of bandwidths $h = (h_1, \ldots, h_m)$, and outputs the naive Bayes estimate of a density function,

$$\widehat{P}(x) = \widehat{P}((x_1, \ldots, x_m)) = \prod_{j=1}^{m} \widehat{P}(x_j),$$

by applying `kde.liks.dim()` to each dimension of the input and multiplying the results.

```
nb.kde.liks = function(x,dat,h) {
    marginal.liks = sapply(1:dim(dat)[2],kde.liks.dim,x=x,
        dat=dat,h=h);
    return(prod(marginal.liks));
}
```

The application of the density estimate to a classifier works exactly as in the KDE classifier of Section 14.8, with one exception: where the KDE classifier used a C-long vector of bandwidth parameters $h = (h_1, \ldots, h_C)$, with bandwidth h_c used to form the density estimate for data of class c, the naive Bayes classifier based on one-dimensional KDE uses a $C \times m$ matrix of bandwidth parameters

$$h = \begin{bmatrix} h_{1,1} & \cdots & h_{1,m} \\ \vdots & & \vdots \\ h_{C,1} & \cdots & h_{C,m} \end{bmatrix},$$

with bandwidth $h_{c,j}$ used to form the density estimate of feature j for data of class c (as for the Histogram classifier of Section 14.9).

Functions for applying the naive Bayes classifier are essentially the same as functions for applying the KDE classifier in Section 14.8. Function nb.kde.predict.one() is identical to function kde.predict.one(), except that the former calls function nb.kde.liks() where the latter calls kde.liks() and a vector of bandwidths $(h_{c,1}, \ldots, h_{c,m})$ is used instead of a scalar bandwidth h_c.

```
nb.kde.predict.one = function(x,datx,daty,h) {
  t = table(daty); priors = t/sum(t);
  liks = vector("numeric",nc);
  for(cc in 1:nc) {
    liks[cc] = nb.kde.liks(x,datx[daty==cc,],h[cc,]); }
  return(max.col(t(priors*liks)));
}
```

Functions kde.loo.one(), kde.loo.all(), and kde.predict.many() from Section 14.8 can be reused simply by replacing the string "kde" with "nb.kde" everywhere it occurs.

```
nb.kde.loo.one = function(datx,daty,h,o) {
  pred = nb.kde.predict.one(datx[o,],datx[-o,],daty[-o],h);
  return(pred!=daty[o]);
}
```

```
nb.kde.loo.all = function(datx,daty,h) {
  errs = sapply(1:dim(datx)[1],nb.kde.loo.one,datx=datx,daty=
    daty,h=h);
  return(mean(errs));
}
```

```
nb.kde.predict.many = function(x,datx,daty,h) {
  return(apply(x,1,nb.kde.predict.one,datx=datx,
    daty=daty,h=h));
}
```

Once a matrix of bandwidths is chosen, nb.kde.predict.many() could be used to compute the test estimate of the naive Bayes classifier's error rate as follows:

```
pred.class = nb.kde.predict.many(edat[,1:2],tdat[,1:2],
  tdat[,3],matrix(0.7,3,2)); risk.test(pred.class);
```

14.11   *k*-Nearest-Neighbor (Section 4.5.1)

A *k*-nearest-neighbor (KNN) classifier is trained using the function knn() in the class library.

```
library(class);
```

Given the training feature vectors `tdat[,1:2]` with associated class labels `tdat[,3]`, and given a value of k, say

```
k = 9;
```

the k-nearest-neighbor classifier predicts class labels for test feature vectors `edat[,1:2]` in via the function call

```
pred.class = knn(tdat[,1:2],edat[,1:2],tdat[,3],k);
risk.test(pred.class);
```

Selecting a KNN classifier means selecting a number of prototypes k to optimize some estimate of risk. Function `knn.loo.one()` inputs a $n \times m$ matrix of feature vectors `datx`, an n-long vector of class labels `daty`, a number of prototypes k, and an index o in the set $\{1, \ldots, n\}$. It predicts the class of the oth datum using the KNN classifier with k prototypes and all data except the oth. It then compares the prediction to the true class, `daty[o]`. It returns the R Boolean value TRUE (numeric value 1) if the KNN classifier made an incorrect prediction, and returns the R Boolean value FALSE (numeric value 0) if the KNN classifier made the correct prediction.

```
knn.loo.one = function(datx,daty,k,o) {
  pred = knn(datx[-o,],datx[o,],daty[-o],k);
  return(pred!=daty[o]);
}
```

Function `knn.loo.all()` applies the function `knn.loo.one()` with each datum held out in turn, and returns the average number of times the KNN classifier made an incorrect prediction: that is, `knn.loo.all()` computes the leave-one-out cross-validation estimate of risk under 0–1 loss for a KNN classifier using a given number of prototypes k and given training data `datx` and `daty`.

```
knn.loo.all = function(datx,daty,k) {
  errs = sapply(1:dim(datx)[1],knn.loo.one,datx=datx,
    daty=daty,k=k);
  return(mean(errs));
}
```

Selecting the number of prototypes is a one-dimensional optimization. The left-hand cell of Figure 14.4 shows leave-one-out cross-validated risk estimates for various numbers of prototypes. This graph suggests that the number of prototypes should be small (about $k = 9$).

```
ks = 1:100; errs = vector("numeric",length(ks));
errs = sapply(ks,knn.loo.all,datx=tdat[,1:2],daty=tdat[,3]);
plot(ks,errs,xlab="Number of Nearest Neighbors",
  ylab="Estimated Risk",type="l",ylim=c(0,0.3*1.05));
```

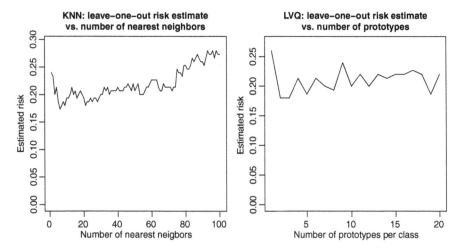

Figure 14.4   Leave-one-out cross-validated estimates of the risk of the k-nearest-neighbor classifier (left) and the learning vector quantization classifier (right), as functions of the number of nearest neighbors or the number of prototypes per class.

14.12   Learning Vector Quantization (Section 4.5.4)

A learning vector quantization (LVQ) classifier is trained using the functions `lvqinit()` and `olvq1()` in the `class` library.

```
library(class);
```

Given the training feature vectors `tdat[,1:2]` with associated class labels `tdat[,3]`, and given a value of the total number of prototypes k, say

```
k = 6;
```

the LVQ classifier is initialized by the function call

```
cd1 = lvqinit(tdat[,1:2],tdat[,3],size=k);
```

This function selects a uniform random sample of training points, without replacement, as the initial set of prototypes of each class. The number of prototypes of the cth class is $k \times \frac{n_c}{n}$, rounded to the nearest integer. Since the training data consists of 49, 48, and 53 points of the three classes respectively, setting $k = 6$ results in two prototypes per class. The LVQ classifier is trained, starting from the initial state `cd1`, by the function call

```
cd2 = olvq1(tdat[,1:2],tdat[,3],cd1,niter=3000*k);
```

It is applied to test data edat using the function lvqtest(),

```
pred.class = lvqtest(cd2,edat[,1:2]);
risk.test(pred.class);
```

The trained LVQ classifier consists of a list of prototypes for each class. For $i = 1, \ldots, k$, the feature vector and class label of the ith prototype are given by the pair

$$(cd2\$x[i,], cd2\$cl[i]).$$

Training an LVQ classifier means selecting a number of prototypes k to optimize some estimate of risk. Function lvq.loo.one() inputs a $n \times m$ matrix of feature vectors datx, an n-long vector of class labels daty, a number of prototypes k, and an index o in the set $\{1, \ldots, n\}$. It predicts the class of the oth datum using the LVQ classifier with k prototypes and all data except the oth. It then compares the prediction to the true class, daty[o]. It returns the R Boolean value TRUE (numeric value 1) if the LVQ classifier made an incorrect prediction, and returns the R Boolean value FALSE (numeric value 0) if the LVQ classifier made the correct prediction.

```
lvq.loo.one = function(datx,daty,k,o) {
  cd1 = lvqinit(datx[-o,],daty[-o],size=k);
  cd2 = olvq1(datx[-o,],daty[-o],cd1,niter=3000*k);
  pred = lvqtest(cd2,datx[o,]);
  return(pred!=daty[o]);
}
```

Function lvq.loo.all() applies the function lvq.loo.one() with each datum held out in turn, and returns the average number of times the LVQ classifier made an incorrect prediction: that is, lvq.loo.all() computes the leave-one-out cross-validation estimate of risk under 0–1 loss for a LVQ classifier using a given number of prototypes k and given training data datx and daty.

```
lvq.loo.all = function(datx,daty,k) {
  errs = sapply(1:dim(datx)[1],lvq.loo.one,datx=datx,
    daty=daty,k=k);
  return(mean(errs));
}
```

Selecting the number of prototypes is a one-dimensional optimization. The right-hand cell of Figure 14.4 shows leave-one-out risk estimates for various numbers of prototypes. This graph suggests that the number of prototypes should be small (about $k = 6$).

```
ks = 3:20; errs = vector("numeric",length(ks));
for(i in 1:length(ks)) {
  errs[i] = lvq.loo.all(tdat[,1:2],tdat[,3],ks[i]);
}
plot(ks,errs,xlab="Number of Prototypes",
  ylab="Estimated Risk",type="l",ylim=c(0,0.3*1.05));
```

14.13   Logistic Regression (Section 4.6)

For polytimous ($C > 2$) classification, a logistic regression classifier is trained using the function `multinom()` in the nnet library.[10]

```
library(nnet);
```

The logistic regression model is trained by the function call

```
m = multinom(as.factor(tdat[,3])~.,maxit=10000,data=tdatDF,
    MaxNWts=3000);
```

It is applied to test data using the function `predict()`,

```
pred.class = predict(m,edatDF,type="class");
risk.test(pred.class);
```

The logistic regression model assumes that the log-odds in favor of each class c relative to a particular reference class (which might as well be class 1) is a linear function of the feature vectors,

$$
\begin{bmatrix}
\log \dfrac{P(Y=1\,|\,X)}{P(Y=1\,|\,X)} \\[2ex]
\log \dfrac{P(Y=2\,|\,X)}{P(Y=1\,|\,X)} \\[2ex]
\log \dfrac{P(Y=3\,|\,X)}{P(Y=1\,|\,X)} \\[1ex]
\vdots \\[1ex]
\log \dfrac{P(Y=C\,|\,X)}{P(Y=1\,|\,X)}
\end{bmatrix}
=
\begin{bmatrix}
0 & 0 & \cdots & 0 \\
\theta_{2,0} & \theta_{2,1} & \cdots & \theta_{2,m} \\
\theta_{3,0} & \theta_{3,1} & \cdots & \theta_{3,m} \\
\vdots & \vdots & & \vdots \\
\theta_{C,0} & \theta_{C,1} & \cdots & \theta_{C,m}
\end{bmatrix}
\begin{bmatrix}
1 \\ X_1 \\ \vdots \\ X_m
\end{bmatrix}.
$$

Fitting a logistic regression model means finding a $C \times (m + 1)$ matrix θ of real parameters ($m + 1$ of which are constrained to be zero) which approximately maximizes the likelihood of the training data. The fitted matrix of parameters, in the format above, can be obtained from the fitted model m as

$$\widehat{\theta} = \texttt{rbind(rep(0,}m+1\texttt{),summary(m)\$coefficients)}.$$

More explicitly, for $i = 2, \ldots, C$ and $j = 0, \ldots, m$,

$$\widehat{\theta}_{i,j} = \texttt{summary(m)\$coefficients[}i-1,j+1\texttt{]}.$$

Selection among multiple competing logistic regression models (say, ones which included different features or combinations of features) could be done by writing

---

[10] For binary classification, a logistic regression classifier can also be trained using the function `glm()` in the `stats` library.

functions for cross-validated risk estimation, but since the parameter estimates are found by maximizing the likelihood of the training data, selection could also be done by choosing a model for which Akaike's information criterion (AIC) is minimal. AIC is computed by the function `AIC()` in the `stats` library,

```
library(stats);
AIC(m);
```

14.14   Neural Networks (Section 4.7)

A single-hidden-layer neural network classifier is trained using the function `nnet()` in the `nnet` library.[11]

```
library(nnet);
```

Given a number k of neurons in the hidden layer, say

```
k = 2;
```

the neural network classifier is trained by the function call

```
m = nnet(as.factor(tdat[,3])~.,size=k,maxit=10000,data=
      tdatDF,MaxNWts=3000);
```

It is applied to test data `edatDF` using the function `predict()`,

```
pred.class = predict(m,edatDF,type="class");
risk.test(pred.class);
```

An equivalent way to do this, using R matrix and vector input instead of the R data frame and formula above, is

```
m = nnet(tdat[,1:2],class.ind(tdat[,3]),size=k,maxit=10000,
      MaxNWts=3000);
pred.class = max.col(predict(m,edat));
risk.test(pred.class);
```

The number of neurons in the hidden layer, k, was selected to minimize the leave-one-out cross-validated estimate of risk. The functions `nnet.onestart()` and `nnet.multistart()` train multiple neural networks on a given set of data, and returns the network which maximizes the likelihood of the data (equivalently, minimizes the training risk with respect to cross-entropy loss). This is done to add some

---

[11] In addition to `nnet`, there are other R libraries for training neural networks of various types: AMORE, `monmlp`, and `neuralnet`, for example. The author is not prepared to describe the differences between these libraries or recommend one over the others for any specific application.

robustness to the gradient descent optimization which trains networks in nnet(), as it can get stuck in local optima.

```r
nnet.onestart = function(i,datx,daty,k) {
  m = nnet(datx,class.ind(daty),size=k,maxit=10000,
       MaxNWts=3000,trace=FALSE);
  return(m);
}


nnet.multistart = function(datx,daty,k,nstart) {
  ms = lapply(1:nstart,nnet.onestart,datx=datx,daty=daty,
       k=k);
  best.idx = which.min(unlist(lapply(ms,getElement,"value")));
  return(ms[[best.idx]]);
}
```

Function nnet.loo.one() inputs a $n \times m$ matrix of feature vectors datx, an n-long vector of class labels daty, number k of neurons in the hidden layer, and an index o in the set $\{1, \ldots , n\}$. It predicts the class of the oth datum using a neural network with k nodes in the hidden layer and all data except the oth. It then compares the prediction to the true class, daty[o]. It returns the R Boolean value TRUE (numeric value 1) if the neural network made an incorrect prediction, and returns the R Boolean value FALSE (numeric value 0) if the neural network made the correct prediction.

```r
nnet.loo.one = function(datx,daty,k,o) {
  m = nnet.multistart(datx[-o,],daty[-o],k,20);
  pred = max.col(t(predict(m,datx[o,])));
  return(pred!=daty[o]);
}
```

Function nnet.loo.all() applies the function nnet.loo.one() with each datum held out in turn, and returns the average number of times the neural network made an incorrect prediction: that is, nnet.loo.all() computes the leave-one-out cross-validation estimate of risk under 0–1 loss for a neural network with k neurons in the hidden layer and given training data datx and daty.

```r
nnet.loo.all = function(datx,daty,k) {
  if(require(parallel)) {
    errs = unlist(mclapply(1:dim(datx)[1],nnet.loo.one,
         datx=datx,daty=daty,k=k,mc.cores=256));
  } else {
    errs = sapply(1:dim(datx)[1],nnet.loo.one,datx=datx,
         daty=daty,k=k);
  }
  return(mean(errs));
}
```

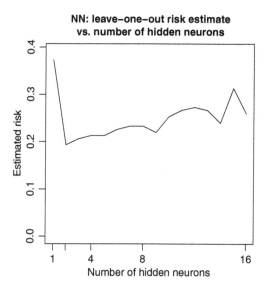

Figure 14.5   Leave-one-out cross-validated estimates of the risk of a single-hidden-layer neural network classifier with various numbers of neurons in the hidden layer.

The plot shown in Figure 14.5 suggests that any number of hidden neurons in the range from two to five might be equally good.

```
ks = 1:16; errs = sapply(ks,nnet.loo.all,datx=tdat[,1:2],
  daty=tdat[,3]);
plot(ks,errs,xlab="Number of Hidden Neurons",
  ylab="Estimated Risk",type="l",ylim=c(0,max(errs)*1.05));
```

Because there are 150 training data in the example problem, and we are using leave-one-out cross-validation, and each neural network is trained from 20 random starting points (values of θ), and 16 different numbers of hidden neurons are considered (k ranging from 1 up to 16), the process described above requires training $150 \times 20 \times 16 = 48,000$ small neural networks. Since none of these networks depends on any of the others, they can all be trained in parallel if that is supported by the available computing environment. Function nnet.loo.all() performs its loop over the training datum left out in parallel using the mclapply() function from the parallel library if it is available, and otherwise performs the loop serially using the sapply() function.

As described in Section 4.7, the parameters of a single-hidden-layer neural network can be written as two matrices, an $N \times (m + 1)$ matrix $\theta^{(1)}$ which governs how the hidden-layer neurons respond to a feature vector, and a $C \times (N + 1)$ matrix $\theta^{(2)}$

which governs how the output functions respond to the vector of hidden-layer neuron outputs. The estimated values of the parameters, $\hat{\theta}^{(1)}$ and $\hat{\theta}^{(2)}$, are recorded in an $(N(m+1)+C(N+1))$-long array, m$wts, as follows. Matrix

$$\hat{\theta}^{(1)} = \begin{bmatrix} \hat{\theta}^{(1)}_{1,0} & \cdots & \hat{\theta}^{(1)}_{1,m} \\ \hat{\theta}^{(1)}_{2,0} & \cdots & \hat{\theta}^{(1)}_{2,m} \\ \vdots & & \vdots \\ \hat{\theta}^{(1)}_{N,0} & \cdots & \hat{\theta}^{(1)}_{N,m} \end{bmatrix} = \begin{bmatrix} \text{m\$wts}\,[1] & \cdots & \text{m\$wts}\,[m+1] \\ \text{m\$wts}\,[m+2] & \cdots & \text{m\$wts}\,[2(m+1)] \\ \vdots & & \vdots \\ \text{m\$wts}\,[(N-1)(m+1)+1] & \cdots & \text{m\$wts}\,[N(m+1)] \end{bmatrix}$$

is obtained as

$$\hat{\theta}^{(1)}_{i,j} = \text{m\$wts}\,[(i-1)(m+1)+j+1] \qquad \text{for} \quad i = 1,\dots,N \quad \text{and} \quad j = 0,\dots,m$$

and, introducing the shorthand $s = N(m+1)$, matrix

$$\hat{\theta}^{(2)} = \begin{bmatrix} \hat{\theta}^{(2)}_{1,0} & \cdots & \hat{\theta}^{(2)}_{1,N} \\ \hat{\theta}^{(2)}_{2,0} & \cdots & \hat{\theta}^{(2)}_{2,N} \\ \vdots & & \vdots \\ \hat{\theta}^{(2)}_{C,0} & \cdots & \hat{\theta}^{(2)}_{C,N} \end{bmatrix}$$

$$= \begin{bmatrix} \text{m\$wts}\,[s+1] & \cdots & \text{m\$wts}\,[s+N+1] \\ \text{m\$wts}\,[s+N+2] & \cdots & \text{m\$wts}\,[s+2(N+1)] \\ \vdots & & \vdots \\ \text{m\$wts}\,[s+(C-1)(N+1)+1] & \cdots & \text{m\$wts}\,[s+C(N+1)] \end{bmatrix}$$

is obtained as

$$\hat{\theta}^{(2)}_{i,j} = \text{m\$wts}\,[s+(i-1)(N+1)+j+1] \quad \text{for} \quad i = 1,\dots,C \quad \text{and} \quad j = 0,\dots,N.$$

14.15   Classification Trees (Section 4.8)

A classification tree is trained using the function rpart() in the rpart library.

```
library(rpart);
```

A tree is trained by the function call

```
m = rpart(as.factor(tdat[,3])~.,method="class",data=tdatDF,
        cp=0.006,minsplit=2,minbucket=1);
```

It is applied to test data using the function predict(),

```
pred.class = predict(m,edatDF,type="class");
risk.test(pred.class);
```

As described in Section 4.8, the function `rpart()` grows and prunes a tree to optimize the cost-complexity criterion

$$\alpha \times (\text{number of leaf nodes}) +$$

$$\sum_{\text{all leaf nodes}\,t} \left(\min_{c\in\{1,\dots,C\}} \sum_{d=1}^{C} L(d,c)\,\widehat{P}(Y = d \mid X \in t) \right) \widehat{P}(X \in t),$$

and this depends on a tuning parameter α which must be selected. In function `rpart()`, one does not specify α directly, but instead specifies a parameter `cp` which is related to α:

$$cp = \frac{\alpha}{\widehat{R}_0},$$

where $\widehat{R}_0$ is the training estimate of risk of a tree consisting of a single leaf node. The value of $\widehat{R}_0$ depends only on the loss function and the prior distribution of classes, $(P(Y = 1), \dots, P(Y = C))$, and it can be extracted from the output of `rpart()` as

$$\widehat{R}_0 = (\text{m\$frame\$dev/m\$frame\$n})\,[1].$$

The estimated risk $\widehat{R}_0$ of the one-leaf can be computed by setting the complexity parameter to infinity and applying the resulting tree to the training data:

```
m = rpart(as.factor(tdat[,3])~.,method="class",data=tdatDF,
        cp=Inf);
pred.class = predict(m,tdatDF,type="class");
rhat0 = mean(pred.class!=tdat[,3]);
```

In Section 4.8, it was shown that in the running example, under 0–1 loss and estimating class priors from the training data, a tree consisting of a single leaf node predicts the purple class and thus has training error $\widehat{R}_0 = \frac{48+49}{150} \approx 0.647$. If left unspecified by the user, `cp` defaults to the value 0.01, which in the running example corresponds to a default value of $\alpha \approx 0.00647$.

The value of α, or equivalently of `cp`, can be selected to minimize a cross-validated estimate of risk. An efficient method to do this, which takes advantage of the fact that a sequence of trees trained on a given dataset with increasing values of α are nested one within the other, is known and implemented in the function `rpart()` (see Breiman et al., 1984, Chapter 10). The function `rpart()` computes a k-fold cross-validated estimate of risk, where k is specified by the optional `rpart()` argument `xval` (the default value of k is 10, and the user can turn off cross-validation by setting $k = 0$). The leave-one-out cross-validation estimate of risk is computed by setting `xval=nt` (recall that `nt` is the number of training data) in the function call

```
m = rpart(as.factor(tdat[,3])~.,method="class",data=tdatDF,
        cp=0,minsplit=2,minbucket=1,xval=nt);
```

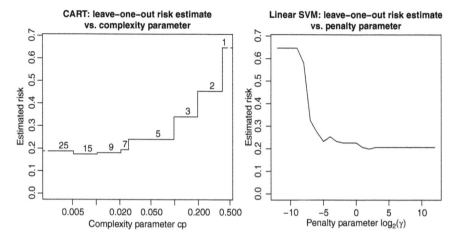

Figure 14.6   Leave-one-out cross-validated estimates of the risk of a classification tree, as a function of the complexity parameter cp (left), and a linear support vector machine, as a function of the penalty parameter γ (right). Both horizontal axes are plotted on a logarithmic scale. The curve plotted in the left-hand cell is drawn as a step function to emphasize that while the complexity parameter cp is real-valued, there are only a finite number of classification tree which can be produced from a given dataset. The number above each line segment of the curve in the left-hand cell is the number of leaf nodes in the tree corresponding to a given range of cp values.

Here, the complexity parameter cp=0 is set to allow the tree to maximally overfit, and the optional arguments minsplit=2 and minbucket=1 are set to prevent the tree-growing process from halting before overfitting has occurred. The cross-validated estimates of risk, and the minimum corresponding values of cp, are stored in the R matrix m$cptable. Specifically, the first column of m$cptable is a set of values of cp, the second column of m$cptable is one less than the number of leaf nodes in the trees corresponding to the values in the first column, and the fourth column of m$cptable is the cross-validated risk estimate of the trees corresponding to the values in the first column. These are displayed graphically by the following code, and shown in the left-hand cell of Figure 14.6.

```
cps = m$cptable[,1]; cps=c(cps[1]*1.1,cps);
        cps[cps==0]=min(cps[cps>0]/2);
errs = m$cptable[,4]*rhat0; errs=c(errs[1],errs);
leaves=1+m$cptable[,2];
plot(cps,errs,xlab="Complexity Parameter cp",ylab="Estimated
    Risk",type="S",ylim=c(0,max(errs)*1.05),log="x");
err = errs[1]; lines(c(max(cps),max(cps)*2),c(err,err),lty=2);
```

```
err = errs[length(errs)]; lines(c(min(cps),min(cps)/2),
    c(err,err),lty=2);
text(((cps[-length(cps)]+cps[-1])/2,errs[-1]+0.025,leaves);
```

As noted in Section 4.8, in this case, selecting a classification tree which minimizes the leave-one-out risk estimate results in selecting a sub-optimal tree (it selects a 15-leaf-node tree, while a 5-leaf-node tree trained on the same data has significantly lower risk).

Classification trees can be represented by a variety of data structures. This section describes the representation used by the R library rpart: the representation used by the R library randomForest is presented in Section 14.20. The function rpart() returns an R object of the class rpart, which contains the trained tree and information about how it was constructed. The trained tree can be recovered from two components of the object m: m$frame and m$splits. Component m$frame is an R data frame which has one row for each node in the tree. The *j*th node of the tree is a leaf if m$frame$var[*j*]=<leaf> and otherwise it is internal, in which case m$frame$var[*j*] is the name of the feature used for the split. Component m$splits is an R matrix which has a variable number of rows: the rows of interest here are those corresponding to internal nodes, which are indexed by the variable internal defined as follows (Therneau et al., 2017, source code for labels.rpart.R).

```
notleaf = (m$frame$var!="<leaf>");
idx = cumsum(c(1,m$frame$ncompete+m$frame$nsurrogate+notleaf));
internal = idx[c(notleaf,FALSE)];
```

Suppose that the *j*th row of m$frame happens to be the *i*th internal node of the tree, counting 1-up from the top of m$frame. Assuming that R's names for the *m* features (stored in m$frame$var) are simply the integers 1, ..., *m*, let

$$b = \text{row.names}(\text{m\$frame})[j] \qquad \tau = \text{m\$splits}[\text{internal,}][i,4]$$
$$k = \text{m\$frame\$var}[j] \qquad s = \text{m\$splits}[\text{internal,}][i,2].$$

A feature vector X which reaches this internal node is sent to the "left" child of the node—that is, the unique node corresponding to the index value $2b$ in row.names(m$frame)—if X_k, τ, and s satisfy

$$(s = -1 \text{ and } X_k < \tau) \text{ or } (s = 1 \text{ and } X_k \geq \tau)$$

and otherwise feature vector X is sent to the "right" child of the node—that is, the unique node corresponding to the index value $2b + 1$ in row.names(m$frame). If, on the other hand, the *j*th row of m$frame corresponds to a leaf node, then any feature vector X which reaches this node is predicted to belong to the class m\$frame\$yval[j]. Thus, for example, the tree illustrated[12] in Figure 4.22 is represented by

$$
m\$frame = \begin{array}{c} 1 \\ 2 \\ 4 \\ 8 \\ 9 \\ 5 \\ 3 \\ 6 \\ 7 \end{array}
\begin{array}{cccc}
\$var & & & \$yval \\
\left[\begin{array}{c} 1 \\ 2 \\ 1 \\ \texttt{<leaf>} \\ \texttt{<leaf>} \\ \texttt{<leaf>} \\ 2 \\ \texttt{<leaf>} \\ \texttt{<leaf>} \end{array} \right.
& \begin{array}{ccc} \cdot & \cdot & \cdot \\ \cdot & \cdot & \cdot \\ \cdot & \cdot & \cdot \\ \cdot & \cdot & \cdot \\ \cdot & \cdot & \cdot \\ \cdot & \cdot & \cdot \\ \cdot & \cdot & \cdot \\ \cdot & \cdot & \cdot \\ \cdot & \cdot & \cdot \end{array}
& \left. \begin{array}{c} 3 \\ 2 \\ 1 \\ 1 \\ 2 \\ 2 \\ 3 \\ 1 \\ 3 \end{array} \right]
& \begin{array}{c} \cdots \\ \cdots \\ \cdots \\ \cdots \\ \cdots \\ \cdots \\ \cdots \\ \cdots \\ \cdots \end{array}
\end{array}
$$

and

$$
m\$splits[internal,] = \begin{bmatrix} \cdot & -1 & \cdot & -0.3105329 & \cdot \\ \cdot & 1 & \cdot & -0.1973331 & \cdot \\ \cdot & 1 & \cdot & -1.8009377 & \cdot \\ \cdot & 1 & \cdot & 1.7666253 & \cdot \end{bmatrix}.
$$

Here, the row names of m\$frame have been written on the left-hand side of the matrix, and values in columns other than one and five in m\$frame and values in columns other than two and four in m\$splits have been suppressed.

14.16   Support Vector Machines (Section 4.9)

A support vector machine is trained using the function svm() in the e1071 library.

```
library(e1071);
```

A linear support vector machine is trained by the function call

```
m = svm(as.factor(tdat[,3])~.,data=tdatDF,kernel="linear",
        cost=2.112);
```

and it is applied to test data using the function predict(),

```
pred.class = predict(m,edatDF);
risk.test(pred.class);
```

The value of the penalty parameter γ (represented by the argument cost in the function svm()) was selected to minimize the leave-one-out cross-validated estimate

---

[12] The terms "left" and "right" used in this section do not correspond to the way in which the tree in Figure 4.22 is drawn.

of risk. Function svm() provides the capability to perform k-fold cross-validation by calling it with the option cross=k, in which case the cross-validated risk estimate can be obtained from the function's output as

$$\hat{R}_{cv} = 1 - \frac{\texttt{m\$tot.accuracy}}{100}.$$

Thus leave-one-out cross-validation can be performed by

```
svmlin.loo.all = function(datx,daty,gamma) {
  m = svm(as.factor(daty)~.,data=datx,kernel="linear",
        cost=gamma,cross=dim(datx)[1]);
  return(1-m$tot.accuracy/100);
}
```

```
gammas = 2^seq(-12,12);
errs = sapply(gammas,svmlin.loo.all,datx=tdatDF,
        daty=tdat[,3]);
plot(log2(gammas),errs,xlab=expression(paste("Penalty
  Parameter ",log[2],"(", gamma,")")),ylab="Estimated Risk",
  type="l",ylim=c(0,max(errs)*1.05));
```

Given a value of γ, function svmlin.loo.all() returns the leave-one-out cross-validated estimate of the risk of a linear support vector machine with penalty parameter γ. The leave-one-out risk estimate is computed for many values of γ, and a value of γ which approximately minimizes this is found by looking at the numbers or plotting a graph, such as that shown in the right-hand cell of Figure 14.6.

Fitting a support vector machine with one of the commonly used kernels introduces one, two, or three additional parameters to be optimized in addition to the penalty parameter γ:

polynomial	$K(x, w) = (\alpha x^T w + \beta)^\delta$
sigmoid	$K(x, w) = \tanh(\alpha x^T w + \beta)$
Gaussian or radial	$K(x, w) = \exp(-\alpha \|x - w\|^2).$

These parameters are all selected to minimize the leave-one-out cross-validated estimate of risk. For example,

```
svmpoly.loo.all = function(datx,daty,theta) {
  m = svm(as.factor(daty)~.,data=datx,kernel="polynomial",
        cost=theta[1],gamma=theta[2],coef0=theta[3],
        degree=theta[4],cross=dim(datx)[1]);
  return(1-m$tot.accuracy/100);
}
library(stats);
opt = optim(c(1,1/nt,0,3),svmpoly.loo.all,method=
        "Nelder-Mead",datx=tdatDF,daty=tdat[,3]);
```

Given a value of θ (now a four-long vector), function svmpoly.loo.all() returns the leave-one-out cross-validated estimate of the risk of a support vector machine with a polynomial kernel, with penalty parameter $\gamma = \theta_1$ and kernel parameters $\alpha = \theta_2$, $\beta = \theta_3$, and $\delta = \theta_4$. Approximately optimal values of these parameters are found using the general-purpose, multi-variate optimization function optim() from the stats library. Function optim() implements versions of several optimization algorithms: Nelder–Mead (Section 10.2), BFGS (Section 10.1.4), conjugate gradient (a quasi-Newton method similar in spirit to BFGS, not covered in Chapter 10), and simulated annealing (Section 10.3). In this application, the Nelder–Mead algorithm is a convenient choice which quickly finds a (local) minimizer of $\widehat{R}_{CV}$. The author was unable to find a better minimizer than the one found by Nelder–Mead, despite some effort. The approximate minimizer of $\widehat{R}_{CV}$ is recovered from the output of optim() as

$\gamma =$ opt\$par[1], $\alpha =$ opt\$par[2], $\beta =$ opt\$par[3], and $\delta =$ opt\$par[4],

and the approximate minimum value is

$$\widehat{R}_{CV} = \text{opt\$value}.$$

The optimal polynomial svm can then be fit on the training data and applied to test data by

```
theta = opt$par;
m = svm(as.factor(tdat[,3])~.,data=tdatDF,kernel="polynomial",
        cost=theta[1],gamma=theta[2],coef0=theta[3],
        degree=theta[4]);
pred.class = predict(m,edatDF);
risk.test(pred.class);
```

As described in Section 4.9, a support vector machine is a binary classifier with class labels in the set $\{-1, 1\}$, and the class label predicted for a new feature vector X by a trained support vector machine is

$$\text{sign}\left(\widehat{\theta}_0 + \sum_{\substack{i : (x_i, y_i) \text{ is a} \\ \text{support vector}}} \widehat{\psi}_i \, y_i \, K(x_i, X) \right),$$

where $\widehat{\theta}_0$ is the estimated intercept parameter and $\widehat{\psi}_1, \dots, \widehat{\psi}_n$ are parameters of a dual optimization problem, where $\widehat{\psi}_i \neq 0$ only if (x_i, y_i) is a support vector. As described in Section 6.1, when faced with data of $C > 2$ classes, the function svm() trains a binary support vector machine to distinguish class c from class d, for all classes $1 \leq c < d \leq C$, and the resulting $\binom{C}{2}$ classifiers vote in a committee. Thus the classifier output by svm() is determined by $\binom{C}{2}$ intercept parameters, $\theta_0^{(c,d)}$, $\binom{C}{2}$ sets of support vectors, and $\binom{C}{2}$ sets of values

$$\{\psi_i^{(c,d)} : (x_i, y_i) \text{ is a support vector for the } (c,d)\text{th classifier}\},$$

where $1 \leq c < d \leq C$. Note that a given training datum (x_i, y_i) may be a support vector for one, several, or none of the $\binom{C}{2}$ binary support vector machines. Within the function svm(), when the C class labels are the integers $1, 2, \ldots, C$, the binary classifier trained to distinguish class c from class d encodes class c as class "1" and class d as class "−1" if and only if $c < d$.

The output of the function svm() contains all the estimated parameters of $\binom{C}{2}$ models concatenated together. For $1 \leq c < d \leq C$, let the paired indices (c, d) be written in the order

$$(1, 2), (1, 3), \ldots, (1, C), (2, 3), \ldots, (2, C), \ldots, (C - 1, C)$$

and let this ordered set of paired indices be identified with the ordered set $1, 2, \ldots, \binom{C}{2}$: explicitly, the map from a paired index (c, d) to a single index i is

$$i = C(c - 1) - \binom{c + 1}{2} + d.$$

The negative of the intercept parameter of the (c, d)th classifier, $-\theta_0^{(c,d)}$, is stored in a $\binom{C}{2}$-long vector m2$rho:

$$-\hat{\theta}_0^{(c,d)} = \texttt{m2\$rho[i]}.$$

The support vectors used by all $\binom{C}{2}$ classifiers are stored as the rows of a single matrix m$SV with m columns. The support vectors are grouped by class in the rows of m$SV: first the support vectors of class 1, then those of class 2, etc. The number of support vectors of each class is stored in the C-long vector m$nSV. Thus the support vectors, as rows of m$SV, are

$$\texttt{m\$nSV[1]} \text{ support vectors of class 1} \begin{cases} \texttt{m\$SV[1,]} \\ \vdots \\ \texttt{m\$SV[m\$nSV[1],]} \end{cases}$$

$$\texttt{m\$nSV[2]} \text{ support vectors of class 2} \begin{cases} \texttt{m\$SV[m\$nSV[1] + 1,]} \\ \vdots \\ \texttt{m\$SV[m\$nSV[1] + m\$nSV[2],]} \end{cases}$$

$$\vdots$$

$$m\$nSV\,[C]\ \text{support vectors of class } C \begin{cases} \texttt{m\$SV[m\$nSV[1] + m\$nSV[2] + \cdots} \\ \texttt{+ m\$nSV[C - 1] + 1,]} \\ \vdots \\ \texttt{m\$SV[m\$nSV[1] + m\$nSV[2] + \cdots} \\ \texttt{+ m\$nSV[C],].} \end{cases}$$

For future reference, we introduce a convenient way of indexing the support vectors of each class. Let

```
idx = c(0,cumsum(m$nSV))
```

so that the support vectors of class c are the rows

```
m$SV[m$nSV[idx[c]+1],]
  ⋮
m$SV[m$nSV[idx[c + 1]],]
```

The binary support vector machine trained to distinguish class c from class d (with $c < d$) makes decisions for new feature vectors X according to

$$\text{sign}\left(\widehat{\theta}_0^{(c,d)} + \sum_{\substack{i\,:\,(x_i, y_i)\text{ is a support vector} \\ \text{for the ``}c\text{ vs. }d\text{'' classifier}}} \widehat{\psi}_i^{(c,d)} y_i^{(c,d)} K(x_i, X) \right),$$

where the superscripts (c, d) indicate that the trained dual parameters $\widehat{\psi}_i^{(c,d)}$ and the assignment of class labels to the set $\{-1, 1\}$ depends on the classes c and d:

$$y_i^{(c,d)} = \begin{cases} 1 & \text{if } y_i = c \\ -1 & \text{if } y_i = d \end{cases}.$$

In the above expression, the sum can be taken over a larger set of vectors (because $\psi_i^{(c,d)} = 0$ unless x_i is a support vector for the "c vs. d" classifier), so the binary support vector machine trained to distinguish class c from class d makes decisions according to

$$\text{sign}\left(\widehat{\theta}_0^{(c,d)} + \sum_{\substack{i\,:\,x_i\text{ is labeled class } c \\ \text{and is a support vector for} \\ \text{at least one classifier}}} \widehat{\psi}_i^{(c,d)} y_i^{(c,d)} K(x_i, X) \right.$$

$$\left. + \sum_{\substack{i\,:\,x_i\text{ is labeled class } d \\ \text{and is a support vector for} \\ \text{at least one classifier}}} \widehat{\psi}_i^{(c,d)} y_i^{(c,d)} K(x_i, X) \right).$$

Now x_i is labeled class c and is a support vector for at least one classifier if and only if $x_i = \texttt{m\$SV[}j\texttt{,]}$ for some $j \in \{\texttt{m\$nSV[idx[c]+1]}, \ldots, \texttt{m\$nSV[idx[c + 1]]}\}$. The corresponding value $\widehat{\psi}_i^{(c,d)} y_i^{(c,d)}$ is stored in the matrix m\$coefs $[j, c]$. Similarly, x_i is labeled class d and is a support vector for at least one classifier if and only if $x_i = $ m\$SV $[j,]$ for some $j \in \{$ m\$nSV[idx[d]+1]$, \ldots, $ m\$nSV[idx[d+1]]$\}$. The corresponding value $\widehat{\psi}_i^{(c,d)} y_i^{(c,d)}$ is stored in the matrix m\$coefs $[j, d-1]$.[13] Thus the binary support vector machine trained to distinguish class c from class d (with $c < d$) makes decisions according to

$$
\text{sign}\left(\widehat{\theta}_0^{(c,d)} + \sum_{j=\text{m\$nSV[idx}[c]+1]}^{\text{m\$nSV[idx}[c+1]]} \text{m\$coefs}[j, c]\, K(\text{m\$SV}[j,], X) \right.
$$

$$
\left. + \sum_{j=\text{m\$nSV[idx}[d]+1]}^{\text{m\$nSV[idx}[d+1]]} \text{m\$coefs}[j, d-1]\, K(\text{m\$SV}[j,], X) \right).
$$

In the case of a linear support vector machine, where $K(x_i, X) = x_i^{\mathrm{T}} X$, the trained classifier distinguishing between class c and class d is

$$
\text{sign}\left(\widehat{\theta}_0^{(c,d)} + \widehat{\theta}^{(c,d)\mathrm{T}} X \right)
$$

where $\widehat{\theta}^{(c,d)}$ is the m-long vector

$$
\widehat{\theta}^{(c,d)} = \sum_{j=\text{m\$nSV[idx}[c]+1]}^{\text{m\$nSV[idx}[c+1]]} \text{m\$coefs}[j, c]\, \text{m\$SV}[j,]
$$

$$
+ \sum_{j=\text{m\$nSV[idx}[d]+1]}^{\text{m\$nSV[idx}[d+1]]} \text{m\$coefs}[j, d-1]\, \text{m\$SV}[j,].
$$

14.17   Bootstrap Aggregation (Section 6.3)

The following two functions enable implementation of any committee classification method by predicting the class which wins a weighted plurality vote. Function weighted.count() inputs class label c, a vector v of class labels, and a vector w of weights (which may be positive or negative, and may or may not all be equal to each

---

[13] Note that for the binary classifier trained to distinguish class c from class d (with $c < d$), the terms $\widehat{\psi}_i^{(c,d)} y_i^{(c,d)}$ are stored in the cth column of m\$coefs (rows idx[c] + 1 through idx[c + 1]) but are stored in the $(d-1)$th column of m\$coefs (rows idx[d] + 1 through idx[d + 1]). The "−1" reflects savings in memory enabled by the fact that there is no need to store parameters for a classifier trained to distinguish class c from itself (Meyer, 2015).

other), and outputs the sum of the weights in w corresponding to the occurrences of class c in v:

$$\sum_{i:v_i=c} w_i.$$

```
weighted.count = function(c,v,w) {
   return(sum(w[which(v==c)])); }
```

Function vote() combines weighted.count() and max.col() to input a vector v of class labels and a vector w of weights and output a class label which receives a maximal sum of weighted votes, with ties decided uniformly at random among all classes which received the same sum of weighted votes.

```
vote = function(v,w) {
   votes = sapply(1:nc,weighted.count,v=v,w=w);
   return(max.col(t(votes)));
}
```

Thus L trained classifiers can be combined into a committee by collecting their votes into a vector $(v_1, \dots, v_L)$, and the weights of their votes into a vector $(w_1, \dots, w_L)$, and applying the function vote().

The committee methods of bagging, boosting, and arcing will all be illustrated using trees as the base learners, specifically stumps. A *stump* is a tree which is constrained to have at most two leaves. The following function applies the tree-training function rpart() from the rpart library to construct a stump.[14]

```
library(rpart);
train.stump = function(y,x,wt=NULL) {
   if(length(wt)==0) { wt=rep(1,length(y)); }
   m = rpart(as.factor(y)~.,data=x,method="class",maxdepth=1,
          cp=0,minsplit=2,weights=wt);
   return(m);
}
```

A committee of L (or in code, nbase) bagged stumps is trained by the following code. Although it would be more efficient to use the R function lapply() (or mclapply(), since bagged classifiers can be trained in parallel), we have used a for loop to simplify comparison of the code for bagging with later code for boosting and arcing. This block of code outputs an L-long R list of trained stumps, called committee, and an $L \times n$ matrix oob. If the training datum (x_i, y_i) is out-of-bag for the lth

---

[14] As written, the function train.stump() can produce a tree with only one leaf (and hence with only one node) if presented with data which is all of one class. Such a tree is called a *root*, and these can arise when bagging with extremely small bag sizes or when one class is represented much more than others in the training data. We allowed roots into the trained ensembles illustrated in Section 6 when they occurred.

classifier, then oob [l, i] is the class predicted by the lth classifier for feature vector x_i. Otherwise, oob [l, i] is the special R value NA to show that (x_i, y_i) is in-bag for the lth classifier (the function votes() ignores values of NA, so using NA as the in-bag indicator simplifies implementation of out-of-bag risk estimation).

```
nbase = 1000; bagsize = nt;
committee = vector("list",nbase); oob = matrix(NA,nbase,nt);
for(i in 1:nbase) {
  idx = sample(1:nt,bagsize,replace=TRUE);
  m = train.stump(tdat[idx,3],tdatDF[idx,]);
  committee[[i]] = m;
  oob[i,setdiff(1:nt,idx)] = predict(m,newdata=tdatDF[-idx,],
    type="class");
}
```

The parameters of a bagged classifier are the number L of classifiers used and the size of the bootstrap sample on which each classifier is trained (and, of course, the choice of classifier and any parameters it may use). As noted in Section 6, the size of the bootstrap sample can be quite important, and can be selected by minimizing the out-of-bag estimate of risk, which is computed by the following code.

```
pred.oob = apply(oob,2,vote,w=rep(1,nbase));
errs = pred.oob!=tdat[,3]; risk.oob = mean(errs);
```

Once L = nbase and bagsize are chosen, the trained bagged classifier can be applied to new data,

```
pred.stumps = do.call(rbind,lapply(committee,predict,
  newdata=edatDF,type="class"));
pred.class = apply(pred.stumps,2,vote,w=rep(1,nbase));
risk.test(pred.class);
```

14.18   Boosting (Section 6.6)

The following code implements a classifier consisting of L = nbase boosted stumps. It uses the same R structures as the code for bagging, and otherwise is a translation of the Adaboost pseudocode shown in Figure 6.7, using the multi-class generalization of Zhu et al. (2009) described in Section 6.6.

```
nbase = 1000; committee = vector("list",nbase);
committee.risk = rep(NA,nbase); data.weights = rep(1/nt,nt);
for(i in 1:nbase) {
  m = train.stump(tdat[,3],tdatDF,data.weights);
  committee[[i]] = m;
```

```
    pred.class = predict(m,tdatDF,type="class");
    idx = which(pred.class!=tdat[,3]);
    committee.risk[i] = risk = sum(data.weights[idx]);
    data.weights[idx] = data.weights[idx] * (1-risk)/risk *
        (nc-1);
    data.weights = data.weights/sum(data.weights);
}
```

Applying a trained, boosted classifier is similar to applying the bagged classifier, except that the individual stumps vote with different weights,

```
pred.stumps = do.call(rbind,lapply(committee,predict,
    newdata=edatDF,type="class"));
committee.weights = log((1-committee.risk)/committee.risk*
    (nc-1));
pred.class = apply(pred.stumps,2,vote,w=committee.weights);
risk.test(pred.class);
```

14.19   Arcing (Section 6.7)

There is only a small difference between boosting and arcing, in terms of the code needed to implement them. An implementation of arcing is exactly the same boosting above, except that the first line of the boosting loop, which is deterministic,

```
m = train.stump(tdat[,3],tdatDF,data.weights);
```

is replaced by a randomized process,

```
idx = sample(1:nt,nt,replace=TRUE,prob=data.weights);
m = train.stump(tdat[idx,3],tdatDF[idx,]);
```

14.20   Random Forests (Section 6.5)

A random forest is trained using the function randomForest() in the randomForest library:

```
library(randomForest);
m = randomForest(as.factor(tdat[,3])~.,data=tdat[,1:2],
        ntree=1000);
```

Selecting a random forest is equivalent to training some number (ntree) of generally over-fit trees. The ith tree in the forest can be viewed by using the function getTree,

```
getTree(m,i)
```

for $i = 1, \ldots,$ ntree. When all features are real-valued, a random forest tree reported by getTree() is represented as a $k \times 6$ matrix

$$\begin{bmatrix} t_{1,1} & t_{1,2} & \cdots & t_{1,6} \\ \vdots & \vdots & & \vdots \\ t_{k,1} & t_{k,2} & \cdots & t_{k,6} \end{bmatrix},$$

where k is the total number of nodes (both internal and leaf) of the tree. Each node of the tree corresponds to one row of the matrix, with

row.names(getTree(m,i)) $= j$ for the jth node of the ith tree and

$t_{j,1}$ = index in $\{1, \ldots, k\}$ of the node's left descendant, or 0 if the node is a leaf

$t_{j,2}$ = index in $\{1, \ldots, k\}$ of the node's right descendant, or 0 if the node is a leaf

$t_{j,3}$ = the index $i \in \{1, \ldots, m\}$ of the variable the node splits on, or 0 if the node is a leaf

$t_{j,4}$ = the threshold τ used for the split, or 0 if the node is a leaf

$t_{j,5}$ = 1 if the node is internal, or -1 if the node is a leaf

$t_{j,6}$ = the class $c \in \{1, \ldots, C\}$ predicted by the node, or 0 if the node is internal.

The terms "left" and "right" are defined to mean that, if the jth node is an internal node, then a feature vector X which enters this node is passed to the left descendant if $X_{t_{j,4}} \le t_{j,5}$ and is passed to the right descendant if $X_{t_{j,4}} > t_{j,5}$. Thus, for example, the tree illustrated in Figure 4.22 is represented in this form by the matrix

$$\begin{bmatrix} 2 & 3 & 1 & -0.311 & 1 & 0 \\ 4 & 5 & 2 & -0.197 & 1 & 0 \\ 6 & 7 & 2 & 1.767 & 1 & 0 \\ 0 & 0 & 0 & 0.000 & -1 & 2 \text{ (blue)} \\ 8 & 9 & 1 & -1.801 & 1 & 0 \\ 0 & 0 & 0 & 0.000 & -1 & 3 \text{ (purple)} \\ 0 & 0 & 0 & 0.000 & -1 & 1 \text{ (orange)} \\ 0 & 0 & 0 & 0.000 & -1 & 2 \text{ (blue)} \\ 0 & 0 & 0 & 0.000 & -1 & 1 \text{ (orange)} \end{bmatrix}.$$

Since random forests are based on bagging, the out-of-bag estimate of risk can be used. The out-of-bag confusion matrix is stored in m$confusion, and the confusion matrix and the out-of-bag risk estimate with respect to 0–1 loss[15] can be obtained from

print(m);

Predictions using the trained random forest m are made on the test data using the function predict(),

pred.class = predict(m,edat);
risk.test(pred.class);

---

[15] The 0–1 loss function is hard-coded in Fortran 77 code underlying the randomForest library. As indicated by Exercise 6.5, a random forest doesn't pay much attention to the loss function.

A

List of Symbols

The following notation is used more-or-less consistently.

$\mathcal{X}$	feature space
X	a feature vector $X \in \mathcal{X}$, thought of as a random variable
x	an observed feature vector $x \in \mathcal{X}$, a realization of X
f	an unknown function on $\mathcal{X}$
Y	a response $Y \in f(\mathcal{X})$, thought of as a random variable
y	an observed response $y \in f(\mathcal{X})$, a realization of Y
E	error, as a random variable
e	observed error, a realization of E
m	the dimension of the feature space $\mathcal{X}$
θ	a vector or matrix of parameters governing a parametric model
k	the dimension of the response space, $f(\mathcal{X})$, in regression; more generally, the length of parameter vector, θ
$|\cdot|$	cardinality, when applied to a set
C	the number of classes in a classification (or clustering) problem, $C = |f(\mathcal{X})|$
$\mathcal{C}$	the set of class labels, $\mathcal{C} = \{1, 2, \dots, C\}$.
c	a particular class, an element of $\mathcal{C}$
n	the number of training data available
n_c	the number of training data belonging to the cth class: $n_1 + \cdots + n_C = n$
$\widehat{f}$	an approximation of f
$\widehat{f}_S$	an approximation of f trained on dataset $S \in (\mathcal{X} \times f(\mathcal{X}))^n$
$(P(Y = 1), \dots, P(Y = C))$	marginal distribution on the set of classes $\mathcal{C} = \{1, \dots, C\}$

Machine Learning: a Concise Introduction, First Edition. Steven W. Knox.
© This publication is a US Government work and is in the public domain.
Published 2018 by John Wiley & Sons, Inc.
Companion Website: http://www.wiley.com/go/Knox/MachineLearning

$P(X \mid Y = c)$	conditional density or likelihood function for feature vectors, given membership in the cth class
$P(Y \mid X)$	conditional density or likelihood function for responses (in regression) or class labels (in classification), given the feature vector X
$L(d, c)$	loss incurred by classifying data of class d as class c
$R(\widehat{f} \mid X = x)$	risk (expected loss) incurred by classifying a datum drawn randomly from the data distribution conditional on the feature vector x, using trained classifier $\widehat{f}$ ($\widehat{f}$ and x fixed, Y random)
$R(\widehat{f})$	risk (expected loss) incurred by classifying a new datum drawn randomly from the data distribution, using trained classifier $\widehat{f}$ ($\widehat{f}$ fixed, X and Y random)
R_n	risk (expected loss) incurred by classifying a new datum drawn randomly from the data distribution, using a given classification method trained on a random set of n independent, identically distributed training data drawn from the data distribution ($\widehat{f}$, X and Y random)
$N(d, c)$	the number of validation data of class d predicted to be class c by a trained classifier, an entry in a confusion matrix
$[\cdot]$	the indicator function of a set S, taking the value 1 at all points in S and the value 0 at all points not in S. Also, the indicator function of the truth of a logical statement.
$I(t)$	impurity of a terminal (leaf) node in a tree
$N(\mu, \sigma^2)$	a normal (Gaussian) distribution with mean μ and variance σ^2
$\phi(x \mid \mu, \Sigma)$	a normal (Gaussian) density function, $\lvert 2\pi\Sigma \rvert^{-\frac{1}{2}} e^{-\frac{1}{2}(x-\mu)^{\mathrm{T}}\Sigma^{-1}(x-\mu)}$
argmax	a maximizer of a function, $\max_{s \in S} g(s) = g\,(\mathrm{argmax}_{s \in S} g(s))$
argmin	a minimizer of a function, $\min_{s \in S} g(s) = g\,(\mathrm{argmin}_{s \in S} g(s))$
.T	the transpose of a matrix (or vector)
$O(\cdot)$	"big-oh" notation, $g(s) = O(h(s))$ means that there exists a positive constant M such that $\lvert g(s) \rvert \le Mh(s)$ for all s

B

Solutions to Selected Exercises

Exercise 2.2

(A) *By Bayes' theorem,*

$$P(Y = 1 \mid X = x) \propto P(X = x \mid Y = 1)P(Y = 1) \propto e^{-\frac{1}{2}(x-\mu_1)^2} p$$
$$P(Y = 2 \mid X = x) \propto P(X = x \mid Y = 2)P(Y = 2) \propto e^{-\frac{1}{2}(x-\mu_2)^2} (1 - p),$$

so, using the fact that $P(Y = 1 \mid X = x) + P(Y = 2 \mid X = x) = 1$,

$$P(Y = 1 \mid X = x) = e^{-\frac{1}{2}(x-\mu_1)^2} p\, S^{-1}$$
$$P(Y = 2 \mid X = x) = e^{-\frac{1}{2}(x-\mu_2)^2} (1 - p)\, S^{-1},$$

where

$$S = e^{-\frac{1}{2}(x-\mu_1)^2} p + e^{-\frac{1}{2}(x-\mu_2)^2} (1 - p).$$

(B) *Using the result of part A,*

$$R(\widehat{f}_\tau \mid X = x) = E_{Y \mid X=x}[L(Y, \widehat{f}_\tau(x))]$$
$$= L(1, \widehat{f}_\tau(x))\, P(Y = 1 \mid X = x) + L(2, \widehat{f}_\tau(x))\, P(Y = 2 \mid X = x)$$
$$= \begin{cases} L(2, 1)\, e^{-\frac{1}{2}(x-\mu_2)^2} (1 - p)\, S^{-1} & \text{if } x \le \tau \\ L(1, 2)\, e^{-\frac{1}{2}(x-\mu_1)^2} p\, S^{-1} & \text{if } x > \tau \end{cases}.$$

(C) *Using the result of part B, and the fact that the marginal density of X is*

$$\frac{1}{\sqrt{2\pi}} e^{-\frac{1}{2}(x-\mu_1)^2} p + \frac{1}{\sqrt{2\pi}} e^{-\frac{1}{2}(x-\mu_2)^2} (1 - p) = \frac{1}{\sqrt{2\pi}} S,$$

Machine Learning: a Concise Introduction, First Edition. Steven W. Knox.
© This publication is a US Government work and is in the public domain.
Published 2018 by John Wiley & Sons, Inc.
Companion Website: http://www.wiley.com/go/Knox/MachineLearning

we see that

$$R(\widehat{f}_\tau) = E_X[R(\widehat{f}_\tau \mid X)]$$

$$= \int_{-\infty}^{\tau} L(2,1)\, e^{-\frac{1}{2}(x-\mu_2)^2} (1-p)\, S^{-1}\, \frac{1}{\sqrt{2\pi}}\, S\, dx$$

$$+ \int_{\tau}^{\infty} L(1,2)\, e^{-\frac{1}{2}(x-\mu_1)^2} p\, S^{-1}\, \frac{1}{\sqrt{2\pi}}\, S\, dx$$

$$= L(2,1)\,(1-p)\, P(Z_2 \le \tau) + L(1,2)\, p\, P(Z_1 > \tau)$$

$$= L(2,1)\,(1-p)\, P(Z_2 \le \tau) + L(1,2)\, p\, (1 - P(Z_1 \le \tau)),$$

where $Z_1 \sim N(\mu_1, 1)$ and $Z_2 \sim N(\mu_2, 1)$.

(D) Differentiating the result of part C with respect to τ,

$$\frac{d}{d\tau} R(\widehat{f}_\tau) = L(2,1)\,(1-p)\, \frac{1}{\sqrt{2\pi}}\, e^{-\frac{1}{2}(\tau-\mu_2)^2} - L(1,2)\, p\, \frac{1}{\sqrt{2\pi}}\, e^{-\frac{1}{2}(\tau-\mu_1)^2}.$$

Setting this equal to zero and solving for τ yields a unique critical point,

$$\tau = \frac{\mu_1 + \mu_2}{2} + \frac{1}{\mu_2 - \mu_1}\, \log\left(\frac{L(1,2)}{L(2,1)} \frac{p}{1-p} \right).$$

The derivative $\frac{d}{d\tau} R(\widehat{f}_\tau)$ approaches zero from below as $\tau \to -\infty$ and approaches zero from above as $\tau \to \infty$, so $\frac{d}{d\tau} R(\widehat{f}_\tau)$ is negative to the left and positive to the right of the unique critical point, which is therefore a minimum. Note that as $\mu_1 \to \mu_2$ from the left, the critical point goes to $\pm\infty$ according to the sign of the log term.

(E) If $L(1,2) = L(2,1)$, the critical point is

$$\tau = \frac{\mu_1 + \mu_2}{2} + \frac{1}{\mu_2 - \mu_1}\, \log\left(\frac{p}{1-p} \right)$$

and if, furthermore, $p = \frac{1}{2}$, the critical point is

$$\tau = \frac{\mu_1 + \mu_2}{2},$$

which is the midpoint between μ_1 and μ_2.

Exercise 2.4 *Consider the following algorithm: given a training data set $\{(x_1, y_1), \ldots, (x_n, y_n)\}$ and a feature vector x to classify, if $x = x_i$ for any i, predict y_i, and otherwise draw the prediction uniformly at random from the set of class labels $\{1, \ldots, C\}$. The training risk for this algorithm is zero, and the actual risk is $\frac{C-1}{C}$.*

Exercise 2.6 *The class-averaged inaccuracy is*

$$\frac{1}{C}\sum_{c=1}^{C} P(\widehat{f}(X) \neq c \mid Y = c) = \sum_{c=1}^{C} \frac{P(\widehat{f}(X) \neq c \text{ and } Y = c)}{C\,P(Y = c)}$$

$$= \int_{\mathcal{X}} \sum_{c=1}^{C} \frac{P(\widehat{f}(x) \neq c \text{ and } X = x \text{ and } Y = c)}{C\,P(Y = c)}\, dx$$

$$= \int_{\mathcal{X}} \sum_{c=1}^{C} \frac{1}{C\,P(Y=c)}[\widehat{f}(x) \neq c]\, P(Y = c \mid X = x)\, P(X = x)\, dx.$$

The last line is recognizable as the risk of approximation $\widehat{f}$, $R(\widehat{f})$, *when for each class c the loss incurred by misclassifying c as any other class is* $\frac{1}{C\,P(Y=c)}$ *(and zero loss is incurred by correctly classifying class c). There are certainly classification problems in which some classes are rare (have small marginal probability) and important (incur high loss for misclassification). But the class-averaged inaccuracy criterion seems to say that* a class is important because it is rare, *or at any rate that the importance of a class is proportional to how rare it is.*

Exercise 3.2 *The gradient of* $\widehat{R}_{\text{train}}(\widehat{f}_\theta)$ *with respect to θ is*

$$\nabla \widehat{R}_{\text{train}}(\widehat{f}_\theta) = \frac{1}{n}(\nabla((\mathbf{y} - \mathbf{x}\theta)^\mathsf{T}(\mathbf{y} - \mathbf{x}\theta)))$$

$$= \frac{1}{n}(\nabla \mathbf{y}^\mathsf{T}\mathbf{y} - \nabla \mathbf{y}^\mathsf{T}\mathbf{x}\theta - \nabla \theta^\mathsf{T}\mathbf{x}^\mathsf{T}\mathbf{y} + \nabla \theta^\mathsf{T}\mathbf{x}^\mathsf{T}\mathbf{x}\theta)$$

$$= \frac{1}{n}(0 - (\mathbf{y}^\mathsf{T}\mathbf{x})^\mathsf{T} - \mathbf{x}^\mathsf{T}\mathbf{y} + 2\mathbf{x}^\mathsf{T}\mathbf{x}\theta)$$

$$= \frac{1}{n}(-2\mathbf{x}^\mathsf{T}\mathbf{y} + 2\mathbf{x}^\mathsf{T}\mathbf{x}\theta).$$

Setting the gradient equal to zero and solving for θ yields a unique critical point,

$$\theta = (\mathbf{x}^\mathsf{T}\mathbf{x})^{-1}\mathbf{x}^\mathsf{T}\mathbf{y},$$

provided that $\mathbf{x}^\mathsf{T}\mathbf{x}$ *is invertible. Since* $\widehat{R}_{\text{train}}(\widehat{f}_\theta) \geq 0$ *and is quadratic, this critical point is the unique global minimum.*

Exercise 3.5 *Let* **1** *denote the n-long vector* $(1, 1, \ldots, 1)$, *and let* v_T, v_R, *and* v_M *be n-long vectors defined by*

$$v_T = \mathbf{y} - \bar{y}\mathbf{1}$$
$$v_M = \widehat{\mathbf{y}} - \bar{y}\mathbf{1} = \mathbf{h}\mathbf{y} - \bar{y}\mathbf{1}$$
$$v_R = \mathbf{y} - \widehat{\mathbf{y}} = \mathbf{y} - \mathbf{h}\mathbf{y} = (\mathbf{i} - \mathbf{h})\mathbf{y} = \widehat{\mathbf{e}}.$$

Observe that

$$v_M + v_R = \widehat{\mathbf{y}} - \bar{y}\mathbf{1} + \mathbf{y} - \widehat{\mathbf{y}} = \mathbf{y} - \bar{y}\mathbf{1} = v_T.$$

Also, v_M and v_R are orthogonal because

$$v_R^T v_M = \mathbf{y}^T(\mathbf{i} - \mathbf{h})\mathbf{h}\mathbf{y} - \mathbf{y}^T(\mathbf{i} - \mathbf{h})\bar{y}\mathbf{1} = \mathbf{y}^T(\mathbf{h} - \mathbf{h}\mathbf{h})\mathbf{y} - \bar{y}\mathbf{y}^T(\mathbf{i} - \mathbf{h})\mathbf{1},$$

and Exercise 3.3 established that $\mathbf{hh} = \mathbf{h}$ (so the first term on the right-hand side is zero) and that $\mathbf{h1} = \mathbf{i1}$ since $\mathbf{1}$ is in the column space of $\mathbf{x}$ (so the second term on the right-hand side is zero). Since the squared Euclidean lengths of v_R, v_M, and v_T are respectively RSS, MSS, and TSS, the Pythagorean theorem establishes that

$$\text{TSS} = \text{MSS} + \text{RSS}.$$

Exercise 3.9 *Here, the values 1 and -1 are stand-ins for any positive and negative numbers, respectively. They need not be equal.*

(A) *$\theta_a = -1$ and $\theta_c = 1$.*

(B) *$\theta_c = 1$ and $\theta_{2c} = -1$.*

(C) *$\theta_a = 1$, $\theta_c = 1$, and $\theta_{(a,c)} = -1$.*

(D) *$\theta_a = 1$, $\theta_c = 1$, and $\theta_{(a,c)} = 1$.*

(E) *The intercept parameter θ_0 is a measure of how much the person likes food, on average.*

(F) *Replace the continuous feature x_b with the binary feature $[x_b > 0]$. Make θ_b large and negative.*

Exercise 4.1 *Let $P(Y \mid X)$ be some conditional distribution with the property that*

$$0 < P(Y \mid X) < 1$$

for at least one value of (X, Y). The Bayes classifier with respect to this conditional distribution is

$$\widehat{f}_{\text{Bayes},P}(x) = \text{argmin}_{c \in \{1,\dots,C\}} R_P(c \mid X = x) = \text{argmin}_{c \in \{1,\dots,C\}} \sum_{d=1}^{C} L(d, c) P(Y = d \mid X),$$

where the notation emphasizes the dependence on P. Let $\widetilde{P}(Y \mid X)$ be the probability distribution which puts probability 1 on $\widehat{f}_{\text{Bayes},P}(X)$, that is,

$$\widetilde{P}(Y = y \mid X = x) = \begin{cases} 1 & \text{if } y = \widehat{f}_{\text{Bayes},P}(x) \\ 0 & \text{else} \end{cases}.$$

Then $\widehat{f}_{\text{Bayes},P}(x) = \widehat{f}_{\text{Bayes},\widetilde{P}}(x)$ for all $x \in \mathcal{X}$ but $\widetilde{P} \neq P$ (because $\widetilde{P}(Y \mid X)$ is always 0 or 1, and $P(Y \mid X)$ is not).

Exercise 4.3 *The solution of part (A) of Exercise 2.2 is:*

$$P(Y = 1 \mid X) \propto e^{-\frac{1}{2}(X-\mu_1)^2} p$$

$$P(Y = 2 \mid X) \propto e^{-\frac{1}{2}(X-\mu_2)^2} (1 - p),$$

so the Bayes classifier is

$$\hat{f}_{\text{Bayes}}(X) = \operatorname{argmin}_{c \in \{1,2\}} R(c \mid X)$$

$$= \operatorname{argmin}_{c \in \{1,2\}} \sum_{d=1}^{2} L(d, c) P(Y = d \mid X)$$

$$= \begin{cases} 1 & \text{if } L(2, 1) e^{-\frac{1}{2}(X-\mu_2)^2} (1 - p) \le L(1, 2) e^{-\frac{1}{2}(X-\mu_1)^2} p \\ 2 & \text{else} \end{cases}$$

$$= \begin{cases} 1 & \text{if } e^{-\frac{1}{2}(X-\mu_2)^2 + \frac{1}{2}(X-\mu_1)^2} \le \dfrac{L(1, 2)}{L(2, 1)} \dfrac{p}{1 - p} \\ 2 & \text{else} \end{cases}$$

$$= \begin{cases} 1 & \text{if } -\dfrac{1}{2}(X - \mu_2)^2 + \dfrac{1}{2}(X - \mu_1)^2 \le \log\left(\dfrac{L(1, 2)}{L(2, 1)} \dfrac{p}{1 - p}\right) \\ 2 & \text{else} \end{cases}$$

$$= \begin{cases} 1 & \text{if } X \le \dfrac{\mu_2 + \mu_1}{2} + \dfrac{1}{\mu_2 - \mu_1} \log\left(\dfrac{L(1, 2)}{L(2, 1)} \dfrac{p}{1 - p}\right). \\ 2 & \text{else} \end{cases}$$

Therefore the answer is yes, the Bayes classifier has the form "predict class 1 if the feature falls below a threshold, and otherwise predict class 2." The solution of part D of Exercise 2.2 is the Bayes classifier.

Exercise 4.5 *The likelihood of* $x_1, \ldots, x_n$ *conditional on the class labels* $y_1, \ldots, y_n$ *is*

$$\prod_{i=1}^{n} |2\pi \Sigma_{y_i}|^{-\frac{1}{2}} e^{-\frac{1}{2}(x_i - \mu_{y_i})^{\mathsf{T}} \Sigma_{y_i}^{-1} (x_i - \mu_{y_i})},$$

so the log-likelihood is

$$-\frac{nm}{2} \log 2\pi + \sum_{i=1}^{n} \left(-\frac{1}{2} \log |\Sigma_{y_i}| - \frac{1}{2}(x_i - \mu_{y_i})^{\mathsf{T}} \Sigma_{y_i}^{-1} (x_i - \mu_{y_i}) \right)$$

$$= -\frac{nm}{2} \log 2\pi + \sum_{c=1}^{C} \left(-\frac{n_c}{2} \log |\Sigma_c| - \frac{1}{2} \sum_{\substack{i=1 \\ y_i = c}}^{n} (x_i - \mu_c)^{\mathsf{T}} \Sigma_c^{-1} (x_i - \mu_c) \right).$$

Maximizing the log-likelihood requires finding the parameters μ_c and Σ_c which maximize the cth term in the sum, for $c = 1, \dots, C$. To find μ_c, note that the cth summand can be written as

$$-\frac{n_c}{2} \log|\Sigma_c| - \frac{1}{2} \sum_{\substack{i=1 \\ y_i=c}}^{n} \left(x_i^{\mathrm{T}}\Sigma_c^{-1}x_i - 2\mu_c^{\mathrm{T}}\Sigma_c^{-1}x_i + \mu_c^{\mathrm{T}}\Sigma_c^{-1}\mu_c \right),$$

so the derivative of the cth summand with respect to μ_c is

$$-\frac{1}{2} \sum_{\substack{i=1 \\ y_i=c}}^{n} \left(-2\Sigma_c^{-1}x_i + 2\Sigma_c^{-1}\mu_c \right) = -\Sigma_c^{-1} n_c \mu_c + \Sigma_c^{-1} \sum_{\substack{i=1 \\ y_i=c}}^{n} x_i.$$

Setting this equal to zero and solving for μ_c yields the unique solution

$$\widehat{\mu}_c = \frac{1}{n_c} \sum_{\substack{i=1 \\ y_i=c}}^{n} x_i.$$

The derivative of the cth summand with respect to Σ_c is

$$-\frac{n_c}{2} \Sigma_c^{-1} + \frac{1}{2} \sum_{\substack{i=1 \\ y_i=c}}^{n} \Sigma_c^{-1}(x_i - \mu_c)(x_i - \mu_c)^{\mathrm{T}}\Sigma_c^{-1}.$$

Setting this equal to zero and solving for Σ_c yields the unique solution

$$\widehat{\Sigma}_c = \frac{1}{n_c} \sum_{\substack{i=1 \\ y_i=c}}^{n} (x_i - \mu_c)(x_i - \mu_c)^{\mathrm{T}},$$

and using the value $\mu_c = \widehat{\mu}_c$ in the above solution causes the derivatives of the log-likelihood with respect to both μ_c and Σ_c to be zero simultaneously.

Exercise 4.7 *The LDA classifier predicts class 1 if and only if predicting class 1 appears to have lower risk than predicting class 2, substituting, for $c = 1, 2$, the estimates*

$$\widehat{P}(x \mid Y = c) = \phi(x \mid \widehat{\mu}_c, \widehat{\Sigma}) = |2\pi\widehat{\Sigma}|^{-\frac{1}{2}} \exp\left(-\frac{1}{2}(x - \widehat{\mu}_c)^{\mathrm{T}}\widehat{\Sigma}^{-1}(x - \widehat{\mu}_c)^{\mathrm{T}} \right)$$

in place of the true but unknown conditional likelihoods $P(x \mid Y = c)$ in the Bayes classifier. Thus the LDA classifier predicts class 1 if and only if

$$L(2,1)P(Y = 2)\,|2\pi\widehat{\Sigma}|^{-\frac{1}{2}} \exp\left(-\frac{1}{2}(x - \widehat{\mu}_2)^{\mathrm{T}}\widehat{\Sigma}^{-1}(x - \widehat{\mu}_2)^{\mathrm{T}} \right)$$

$$\leq L(1,2)P(Y = 1)\,|2\pi\widehat{\Sigma}|^{-\frac{1}{2}} \exp\left(-\frac{1}{2}(x - \widehat{\mu}_1)^{\mathrm{T}}\widehat{\Sigma}^{-1}(x - \widehat{\mu}_1)^{\mathrm{T}} \right),$$

and this inequality holds if and only if

$$-\frac{1}{2}(x - \hat{\mu}_2)^\mathrm{T}\hat{\Sigma}^{-1}(x - \hat{\mu}_2)^\mathrm{T} + \frac{1}{2}(x - \hat{\mu}_1)^\mathrm{T}\hat{\Sigma}^{-1}(x - \hat{\mu}_1)^\mathrm{T} \le \log\left(\frac{L(1,2)}{L(2,1)}\frac{P(Y=1)}{P(Y=2)}\right)$$

which holds if and only if

$$x^\mathrm{T}\hat{\Sigma}^{-1}(\hat{\mu}_2 - \hat{\mu}_1) \le \frac{1}{2}\left(\hat{\mu}_2^\mathrm{T}\hat{\Sigma}^{-1}\hat{\mu}_2 - \hat{\mu}_1^\mathrm{T}\hat{\Sigma}^{-1}\hat{\mu}_1\right) + \log\left(\frac{L(1,2)}{L(2,1)}\frac{P(Y=1)}{P(Y=2)}\right).$$

The LDA classifier therefore predicts class 1 if and only if $x \cdot v \le \alpha$, where

$$v = \hat{\Sigma}^{-1}(\hat{\mu}_2 - \hat{\mu}_1)$$

and

$$\alpha = \frac{1}{2}\left(\hat{\mu}_2^\mathrm{T}\hat{\Sigma}^{-1}\hat{\mu}_2 - \hat{\mu}_1^\mathrm{T}\hat{\Sigma}^{-1}\hat{\mu}_1\right) + \log\left(\frac{L(1,2)}{L(2,1)}\frac{P(Y=1)}{P(Y=2)}\right).$$

That is, the LDA classifier predicts class 1 if and only if x is on one side of the hyperplane

$$\{z \in \mathbb{R}^m : z \cdot v = \alpha\}.$$

When $P(Y = 1) = \frac{1}{2}$ and $L(1,2) = L(2,1)$, the logarithmic term is zero and

$$\alpha = \frac{1}{2}\left(\hat{\mu}_2^\mathrm{T}\hat{\Sigma}^{-1}\hat{\mu}_2 - \hat{\mu}_1^\mathrm{T}\hat{\Sigma}^{-1}\hat{\mu}_1\right).$$

In the setting of Exercise 2.2, $\Sigma = 1$ and $m = 1$ (which means vector inner product is scalar multiplication), so the LDA classifier predicts class 1 if and only if

$$x(\hat{\mu}_2 - \hat{\mu}_1) \le \frac{1}{2}(\hat{\mu}_2^2 - \hat{\mu}_1^2) + \log\left(\frac{L(1,2)}{L(2,1)}\frac{P(Y=1)}{P(Y=2)}\right).$$

If $\hat{\mu}_2 - \hat{\mu}_1 > 0$, the above condition is equivalent to

$$x \le \frac{1}{2}(\hat{\mu}_2 + \hat{\mu}_1) + \frac{1}{\hat{\mu}_2 - \hat{\mu}_1}\log\left(\frac{L(1,2)}{L(2,1)}\frac{P(Y=1)}{P(Y=2)}\right),$$

which is the solution of part D of Exercise 2.2 with $\hat{\mu}_1$ and $\hat{\mu}_2$ substituted for μ_1 and μ_2.

Exercise 4.17 *Let the orange data in Figure 4.31 be class 1 and let the purple data be class 2. In the case of binary classification with 0–1 loss and uniform class prior probabilities $P(Y = 1) = P(Y = 2) = \frac{1}{2}$, quadratic discriminant analysis predicts class 1 if and only if*

$$|2\pi\Sigma_1|^{-\frac{1}{2}}e^{-\frac{1}{2}(x-\mu_1)^\mathrm{T}\Sigma_1^{-1}(x-\mu_1)} \ge |2\pi\Sigma_2|^{-\frac{1}{2}}e^{-\frac{1}{2}(x-\mu_2)^\mathrm{T}\Sigma_2^{-1}(x-\mu_2)},$$

or equivalently (taking logs of both sides and moving terms), if and only if

$$(x - \mu_2)^\mathrm{T}\Sigma_2^{-1}(x - \mu_2) - (x - \mu_1)^\mathrm{T}\Sigma_1^{-1}(x - \mu_1) \ge \log|\Sigma_1| - \log|\Sigma_2|.$$

If we add the restrictions that $\mu_1 = \mu_2$ and $\Sigma_1 = \alpha\Sigma_2$ for some $\alpha > 1$, which appear to be approximately valid in the data illustrated in Figure 4.31, then quadratic discriminant analysis predicts class 1 if and only if

$$(\alpha - 1)(x - \mu_1)^T\Sigma_1^{-1}(x - \mu_1) \geq m \log \alpha.$$

Thus QDA predicts class 1 if and only if the feature vector x lies outside *the ellipsoid*

$$E = \left\{ z \in \mathbb{R}^m : (z - \mu_1)^T\Sigma_1^{-1}(z - \mu_1) = \frac{m \log \alpha}{\alpha - 1} \right\}.$$

Exercise 4.19 *For any real numbers α and β, for any integer $\delta \geq 1$,*

$$K(x, w) = (\alpha x^T w + \beta)^\delta$$

$$= \left(\sum_{j=1}^m \alpha x_j w_j + \beta \right)^\delta$$

$$= \sum_{\substack{(k_1, \ldots, k_m, k_{m+1}) \geq 0 \\ k_1 + \cdots + k_m + k_{m+1} = \delta}} \binom{\delta}{k_1, \ldots, k_m, k_{m+1}} (\alpha x_1 w_1)^{k_1} \cdots (\alpha x_m w_m)^{k_m} \beta^{k_{m+1}}$$

$$= \sum_{\substack{(k_1, \ldots, k_m, k_{m+1}) \geq 0 \\ k_1 + \cdots + k_m + k_{m+1} = \delta}} \binom{\delta}{k_1, \ldots, k_m, k_{m+1}} (x_1 w_1)^{k_1} \cdots (x_m w_m)^{k_m} \alpha^{k_1 + \cdots + k_m} \beta^{k_{m+1}}$$

by the multinomial theorem. Let $\phi(x)$ be defined as a vector indexed by all $(k_1, \ldots, k_m) \geq 0$ such that $k_1 + \cdots + k_m \leq \delta$,

$$\phi(x) = \left(\left(\binom{\delta}{k_1, \ldots, k_m, \delta - k_1 - \cdots - k_m} \alpha^{k_1 + \cdots + k_m} \beta^{\delta - k_1 - \cdots - k_m} \right)^{\frac{1}{2}} x_1^{k_1} \cdots x_m^{k_m} \right)_{\substack{(k_1, \ldots, k_m) \geq 0 \\ k_1 + \cdots + k_m \leq \delta}}.$$

Then

$$K(x, w) = \phi(x)^T \phi(w).$$

If $\beta = 0$ then all terms with $k_{m+1} > 0$ are zero, so the index set runs over all $(k_1, \ldots, k_m) \geq 0$ such that $k_1 + \cdots + k_m = \delta$.

Exercise 5.1 *Following the hint, the risk can be decomposed into six terms:*

$$R = E_{S,X,Y}[(Y - \widehat{f}_S(X))^2]$$

$$= E_{S,X,Y}[(Y - f(X) + f(X) - E_S[\widehat{f}_S(X)] + E_S[\widehat{f}_S(X)] - \widehat{f}_S(X))^2]$$

$$= E_{S,X,Y}[(Y - f(X))^2] + E_{S,X,Y}[(f(X) - E_S[\widehat{f}_S(X)])^2] + E_{S,X,Y}[(E_S[\widehat{f}_S(X)] - \widehat{f}_S(X))^2]$$

$$+ 2E_{S,X,Y}[(Y - f(X))(f(X) - E_S[\widehat{f}_S(X)])] + 2E_{S,X,Y}[(Y - f(X))(E_S[\widehat{f}_S(X)] - \widehat{f}_S(X))]$$

$$+ 2E_{S,X,Y}[(f(X) - E_S[\widehat{f}_S(X)])(E_S[\widehat{f}_S(X)] - \widehat{f}_S(X))].$$

In the first term, the random variable $(Y - f(X))^2$ does not depend on S, so the expectation over S can be dropped. Similarly, in the second term, where the random variable $(f(X) - E_S[\widehat{f}_S(X)])^2$ does not depend on S or Y. In the third term, the random variable $(E_S[\widehat{f}_S(X)] - \widehat{f}_S(X))^2$ does not depend on Y, so the third term may be written as

$$E_{S,X}[(E_S[\widehat{f}_S(X)] - \widehat{f}_S(X))^2] = E_X[E_S[(E_S[\widehat{f}_S(X)] - \widehat{f}_S(X))^2]] = E_X[\text{Var}_S[\widehat{f}_S(X)]]$$

(the first equality used the fact that X is independent of S). The fourth and fifth terms both involve random variables of the form $(Y - f(X))g(X)$ for some function g. These two terms are both equal to zero: since $E[Y \mid X] = f(X)$,

$$E_{X,Y}[(Y - f(X))g(X)] = E_X[g(X) E_{Y \mid X}[(Y - f(X))]] = 0.$$

The sixth term is shown to be zero in a similar way. It is the expected value of a random variable which does not depend on Y, and since X is independent of S,

$$E_{S,X}[(f(X) - E_S[\widehat{f}_S(X)]) (E_S[\widehat{f}_S(X)] - \widehat{f}_S(X))]$$
$$= E_X[(f(X) - E_S[\widehat{f}_S(X)]) E_S[E_S[\widehat{f}_S(X)] - \widehat{f}_S(X)]] = 0.$$

Exercise 6.1 *Under squared-error loss, the risk is the squared bias of Z for θ plus the variance of Z. Since $c_1 + \cdots + c_L = 1$,*

$$\text{Bias}[Z] = \sum_{l=1}^{L} c_l \,\text{Bias}[Z_l] = \beta,$$

and since $Z_1, \ldots, Z_L$ are uncorrelated,

$$\text{Var}[Z] = \sum_{l=1}^{L} c_l^2 \,\text{Var}[Z_l] = \sum_{l=1}^{L} c_l^2 \,\sigma_l^2.$$

Thus minimizing the risk means minimizing

$$R = \beta^2 + \sum_{l=1}^{L} c_l^2 \,\sigma_l^2$$

subject to the constraint $c_1 + \cdots + c_L = 1$. The Lagrangian for this constrained optimization problem is

$$\beta^2 + \sum_{l=1}^{L} c_l^2 \,\sigma_l^2 + \lambda \left(1 - \sum_{l=1}^{L} c_l \right).$$

Differentiating with respect to c_l and setting the derivative equal to zero yields

$$2 c_l \sigma_l^2 - \lambda = 0.$$

That is, at the critical point

$$c_l = \frac{\lambda}{2} \frac{1}{\sigma_l^2} \propto \sigma_l^{-2}.$$

Using the fact that $c_1 + \cdots + c_L = 1$,

$$c_l = \frac{\sigma_l^{-2}}{\sum_{k=1}^{L} \sigma_k^{-2}}.$$

The minimum risk is

$$\beta^2 + \sum_{l=1}^{L} \left(\frac{\sigma_l^{-2}}{\sum_{k=1}^{L} \sigma_k^{-2}} \right)^2 \sigma_l^2 = \beta^2 + \left(\frac{1}{\sum_{k=1}^{L} \sigma_k^{-2}} \right)^2 \sum_{l=1}^{L} \sigma_l^{-2} = \beta^2 + \frac{1}{\sum_{k=1}^{L} \sigma_k^{-2}}.$$

Exercise 6.5 *Recall the notation of classification trees from Section 4.8: n_c is the number of training data of class c and n_c^t is the number of training data of class c which enter node t. At leaf node t, a classification tree applies Bayes' theorem*

$$\widehat{P}(Y = c \mid X \in t) \propto \widehat{P}(X \in t \mid Y = c)\, P(Y = c)$$

and uses the estimate

$$\widehat{P}(X \in t \mid Y = c) = \frac{n_c^t}{n_c}.$$

Node t classifies all data which enter it as the class c which minimizes the estimated posterior risk,

$$\widehat{R}(c \mid X \in t) = \sum_{d=1}^{C} L(d, c)\widehat{P}(Y = d \mid X \in t) \propto \sum_{d=1}^{C} L(d, c)\frac{n_d^t}{n_d} P(Y = d).$$

Now suppose a tree is grown until all leaf nodes have zero impurity, and let t be a leaf node of this tree. All training data in t is of a single class, call it c': that is, $n_{c'}^t > 0$ and $n_c^t = 0$ for all $c \neq c'$. The risk of predicting class c' at leaf node t is

$$\widehat{R}(c' \mid X \in t) \propto \underbrace{L(c', c') \frac{n_{c'}^t}{n_{c'}} P(Y = c')}_{=0} + \sum_{\substack{d=1 \\ d \neq c'}}^{C} L(d, c') \underbrace{\frac{n_d^t}{n_d}}_{=0} P(Y = d) = 0,$$

while the risk of predicting any other class c at leaf node t is

$$\widehat{R}(c \mid X \in t) \propto \underbrace{L(c', c)}_{>0} \underbrace{\frac{n_{c'}^t}{n_{c'}} P(Y = c')}_{>0} + \sum_{\substack{d=1 \\ d \neq c'}}^{C} L(d, c) \underbrace{\frac{n_d^t}{n_d}}_{=0} P(Y = d) > 0.$$

Thus leaf node t predicts class c' regardless of the values taken by the loss function and regardless of the prior distribution on classes.

Exercise 7.1 *For any d, $0 \leq d < n - 1$, approximation $\hat{f}_d$ is found by solving the optimization problem*

$$\underset{(\theta_0, \theta_1, \ldots, \theta_d) \in \mathbb{R}^{d+1}}{\text{minimize}} \sum_{i=1}^{n} \left(y_i - \sum_{j=1}^{d} \theta_j x_i^j \right)^2,$$

and approximation $\hat{f}_{d+1}$ is found by solving the optimization problem

$$\underset{(\theta_0, \theta_1, \ldots, \theta_d, \theta_{d+1}) \in \mathbb{R}^{d+2}}{\text{minimize}} \sum_{i=1}^{n} \left(y_i - \sum_{j=1}^{d+1} \theta_j x_i^j \right)^2.$$

Since any vector $(\theta_0, \theta_1, \ldots, \theta_d)$ considered in the upper problem corresponds to a vector $(\theta_0, \theta_1, \ldots, \theta_d, 0)$ considered in the lower problem, the solution to the lower problem is at least as good as the solution to the upper problem, that is, $\hat{R}_{\text{train}}(\hat{f}_{d+1}) \geq \hat{R}_{\text{train}}(\hat{f}_d)$. If $\hat{R}_{\text{train}}(\hat{f}_{d+1}) = \hat{R}_{\text{train}}(\hat{f}_d)$, then $\hat{\theta}_{d+1} = 0$ in the solution of the lower problem since the solutions to these optimization problems are unique (by Exercise 3.2). The event $\hat{\theta}_{d+1} = 0$ has probability zero since $\hat{\theta}_{d+1}$ is Gaussian-distributed (as we saw in Section 3.6). When $d \geq n - 1$, there are enough parameters $(\theta_0, \theta_1, \ldots, \theta_d)$ to interpolate the points $(x_1, y_1), \ldots, (x_n, y_n)$, at which point $\hat{R}_{\text{train}}(\hat{f}_d) = 0$. Specifically, when $d \geq n - 1$, any parameter vector $(\theta_0, \theta_1, \ldots, \theta_d)$ which solves the system of equations

$$\begin{bmatrix} 1 & x_1 & x_1^2 & \cdots & x_1^d \\ 1 & x_2 & x_2^2 & \cdots & x_2^d \\ \vdots & \vdots & \vdots & & \vdots \\ 1 & x_n & x_n^2 & \cdots & x_n^d \end{bmatrix} \begin{bmatrix} \theta_0 \\ \theta_1 \\ \theta_2 \\ \vdots \\ \theta_d \end{bmatrix} = \begin{bmatrix} y_1 \\ y_2 \\ \vdots \\ y_n \end{bmatrix}$$

produces an approximation $\hat{f}_d$ with zero training risk (since the x_i's are distinct, the rows of the matrix are independent, and the system is solvable when $d \geq n - 1$). In terms of bias and variance, as d increases, the bias of $\hat{f}_d$ goes down and the variance of $\hat{f}_d$ goes up. Selecting a model based on the criterion of minimizing training risk will tend to result in selecting an overfit model.

Exercise 7.5 *By Exercise 7.3,*

$$\text{Var}[\hat{R}_{\text{valid}}(\hat{f})] = \frac{1}{\tilde{n}} R(\hat{f}) (1 - R(\hat{f})).$$

As a function of $R(\hat{f})$, this increases from zero up to a unique maximum at $R(\hat{f}) = \frac{1}{2}$, and then decreases.

(A) We choose $\tilde{n}$ as small as possible so that

$$\frac{1}{\tilde{n}} \rho (1 - \rho) \leq \sigma^2,$$

so $\tilde{n} = \lceil \frac{\rho(1-\rho)}{\sigma^2} \rceil$.

(B) *This is (A) with the ρ chosen to maximize the upper bound on the variance, that is, $\rho = \frac{1}{2}$. This gives $\tilde{n} = \lceil \frac{1}{4\sigma^2} \rceil$.*

(C) *$\tilde{n} = 1875$.*

(D) *The desired value for σ is unattainable unless $R(\widehat{f})$ turns out to be considerably smaller than upper bound provided ($\rho = 0.25$)—a situation we would be unlikely to recognize without using much of the available data for validation. In case (D), either much more than 1800 data are needed, or the target upper bound for the standard deviation ($\sigma = 0.01$) must be relaxed.*

Exercise 10.2 *For any $c = 1, \ldots, C$ and any $j = 0, \ldots, m$,*

$$\frac{\partial}{\partial \theta_{c,j}} \widehat{R}_{\text{train}} = -\sum_{i=1}^{n} \frac{\partial}{\partial \theta_{c,j}} T(x_i, \theta_{y_i}) + \sum_{i=1}^{n} \frac{\sum_{d=1}^{C} \exp(T(x_i, \theta_d)) \frac{\partial}{\partial \theta_{c,j}} T(x_i, \theta_d)}{\sum_{d=1}^{C} \exp(T(x_i, \theta_d))}.$$

For any $c = 1, \ldots, C$, any $d = 1, \ldots, C$, and any $j = 0, \ldots, m$,

$$\frac{\partial}{\partial \theta_{c,j}} T(X, \theta_d) = \begin{cases} 0 & \text{if } c \neq d \\ 1 & \text{if } c = d \text{ and } j = 0 \\ X_j & \text{if } c = d \text{ and } j > 0 \end{cases}.$$

Thus for any $c = 1, \ldots, C$,

$$\frac{\partial}{\partial \theta_{c,0}} \widehat{R}_{\text{train}} = -\sum_{\substack{i=1 \\ y_i = c}}^{n} 1 + \sum_{i=1}^{n} \frac{\exp(T(x_i, \theta_c))}{\sum_{d=1}^{C} \exp(T(x_i, \theta_d))}$$

and for any $j = 1, \ldots, m$,

$$\frac{\partial}{\partial \theta_{c,j}} \widehat{R}_{\text{train}} = -\sum_{\substack{i=1 \\ y_i = c}}^{n} x_{ij} + \sum_{i=1}^{n} x_{ij} \frac{\exp(T(x_i, \theta_c))}{\sum_{d=1}^{C} \exp(T(x_i, \theta_d))}.$$

Exercise 10.4 *The halting criterion is as follows. Having proposed the parameter value θ_{i+1}, apply the level-α one-sided Z-test developed in part (C) of Exercise 7.5 to test the null hypothesis $R(\widehat{f}_{\theta_{i+1}}) \geq R(\widehat{f}_{\theta_i})$ against the alternative hypothesis $R(\widehat{f}_{\theta_{i+1}}) < R(\widehat{f}_{\theta_i})$. If this test retains the null hypothesis, halt and report θ_i as an optimal value. If this test rejects the null hypothesis, continue the optimization. If it is known in advance that at most I iterations will be performed, then applying Bonferroni correction is equivalent to performing level-$\frac{\alpha}{I}$ tests in the halting criterion.*

Exercise 10.5 *Let $\alpha = E[X]$. Since g is concave, there is a line through the point $(\alpha, g(\alpha))$ such that the curve parametrized by $(y, g(y))$ is always on or below the line. Let s be the slope of such a line, so*

$$g(y) \leq g(\alpha) + s(y - \alpha)$$

for all $y \in \mathbb{R}$. Then

$$E[g(X)] \leq E[g(\alpha) + s(X - \alpha)] = g(\alpha) + sE[X] - s\alpha = g(E[X]).$$

If g is strictly concave, then

$$g(y) < g(\alpha) + s(y - \alpha)$$

except at the point $y = \alpha$, so

$$E[g(X)] < g(E[X])$$

unless $P(X = \alpha) = 1$.

Exercise 10.6 *Let X be a random variable with density P_0 and let Z be a random variable with density P_1. We observe that*

$$E\left[\frac{P_1(X)}{P_0(X)}\right] = \int \frac{P_1(x)}{P_0(x)} P_0(x)\,dx = \int_{x:P_0(x)>0} P_1(x)\,dx = P(P_0(Z) > 0) \leq 1,$$

with equality if and only if

$$P(P_0(Z) > 0) = 1.$$

Now

$$-E\left[\log\left(\frac{P_0(X)}{P_1(X)}\right)\right] = E\left[\log\left(\frac{P_1(X)}{P_0(X)}\right)\right],$$

and applying Jensen's inequality to the random variable $\frac{P_1(X)}{P_0(X)}$, since log is strictly concave on the positive reals,

$$E\left[\log\left(\frac{P_1(X)}{P_0(X)}\right)\right] \leq \log\left(E\left[\frac{P_1(X)}{P_0(X)}\right]\right) \leq 0$$

with equality if and only if $P(\frac{P_1(X)}{P_0(X)} = c) = 1$ for some constant c and $P(P_0(Z) > 0) = 1$. The equality conditions imply that for any set S, $P(X \in S) = c\,P(Z \in S)$. The particular case $S = \{x : P_0(x) > 0\}$ has

$$1 = P(X \in S) = c\,P(Z \in S) = c,$$

so $c = 1$. Therefore

$$E\left[\log\left(\frac{P_0(X)}{P_1(X)}\right)\right] \geq 0$$

with equality if and only if $P(\frac{P_1(X)}{P_0(X)} = 1) = 1$.

Exercise 10.8 *The Lagrangian for maximizing the log-likelihood subject to the constraint* $w_1 + \cdots + w_J = 1$ *is*

$$\sum_{j=1}^{J} \left(\sum_{\substack{i=1 \\ z_i=j}}^{n} \log \left(w_j \, |2\pi\Sigma_j|^{-\frac{1}{2}} e^{-\frac{1}{2}(x_i-\mu_j)^{\mathrm{T}}\Sigma_j^{-1}(x_i-\mu_j)} \right) \right) + \lambda \left(1 - \sum_{j=1}^{J} w_j \right).$$

Neglecting constants, this is

$$\sum_{j=1}^{J} \left(|\{i : z_i = j\}| \log w_j - \frac{1}{2} |\{i : z_i = j\}| \, \log |\Sigma_j| - \frac{1}{2} \sum_{\substack{i=1 \\ z_i=j}}^{n} (x_i - \mu_j)^{\mathrm{T}}\Sigma_j^{-1}(x_i - \mu_j) \right)$$
$$+ \lambda \left(1 - \sum_{j=1}^{J} w_j \right).$$

The derivative with respect to w_j *is*

$$\frac{|\{i : z_i = j\}|}{w_j} - \lambda,$$

and setting this equal to zero and solving for w_j *yields the solution*

$$w_j = \frac{|\{i : z_i = j\}|}{\lambda}.$$

Since

$$1 = \sum_{j=1}^{J} w_j = \sum_{j=1}^{J} \frac{|\{i : z_i = j\}|}{\lambda} = \frac{n}{\lambda},$$

it follows that $\lambda = n$ *and so for all j, the unique critical point for* w_j *is*

$$\widehat{w}_j = \frac{|\{i : z_i = j\}|}{n}.$$

Maximization of the Lagrangian with respect to $\mu_1, \ldots, \mu_J, \Sigma_1, \ldots, \Sigma_J$ *when* $z_1, \ldots, z_n$ *are known is identical to maximizing the log-likelihood of the model used in the quadratic discriminant classifier: this was done in Exercise 4.5.*

Exercise 11.2 *Since X is uniformly distributed in the unit ball*

$$B = \left\{ (z_1, z_2, \ldots, z_m) : z_1^2 + z_2^2 + \cdots + z_m^2 \le 1 \right\},$$

the density of X_1 *at the point* x_1 *is equal to the* $(m-1)$-*dimensional volume of the intersection of B with the hyperplane*

$$H = \left\{ (z_1, z_2, \ldots, z_m) : (z_1, z_2, \ldots, z_m) \cdot (1, 0, \ldots, 0) = x_1 \right\}.$$

The intersection $B \cap H$ is empty (so the volume is zero) unless $x_1 \in [-1, 1]$, in which case the intersection $B \cap H$ is an $(m-1)$-dimensional ball centered at $(x_1, 0, \ldots, 0)$ with radius $\sqrt{1 - x_1^2}$. Thus the density of X_1 at x_1 is

$$V\left(m - 1, \sqrt{1 - x_1^2}\right) = \frac{\pi^{\frac{m-1}{2}} \left(1 - x_1^2\right)^{\frac{m-1}{2}}}{\Gamma\left(\frac{m-1}{2} + 1\right)} \propto \left(1 - x_1^2\right)^{\frac{m-1}{2}}.$$

for $x_1 \in [-1, 1]$. The density of X_1 is symmetric about zero, so X_1 has the distribution of $N \times |X_1|$, where the sign N is uniformly distributed on the set $\{-1, 1\}$ and $|X_1|$ is a random variable supported on the interval $[0, 1]$, independent of N. This implies that

$$\mathrm{E}[X_1] = 0 \quad \text{and} \quad \mathrm{Var}[X_1] = \mathrm{E}\left[X_1^2\right] - \mathrm{E}[X_1]^2 = \mathrm{E}\left[X_1^2\right].$$

The distribution of X_1^2 is obtained by

$$P\left(X_1^2 \le x\right) = P\left(|X_1| \le \sqrt{x}\right) \propto \int_0^{\sqrt{x}} \left(1 - x_1^2\right)^{\frac{m-1}{2}} dx_1 = \int_0^x (1 - u)^{\frac{m-1}{2}} \frac{1}{2} u^{-\frac{1}{2}} du,$$

using the substitution $x_1 = u^{\frac{1}{2}}$ in the last integral. From this we recognize that $X_1^2 \sim$ Beta$(\frac{1}{2}, \frac{m+1}{2})$, and therefore

$$\mathrm{Var}[X_1] = \mathrm{E}\left[X_1^2\right] = \frac{\frac{1}{2}}{\frac{1}{2} + \frac{m+1}{2}} = \frac{1}{m+2}.$$

Exercise 11.4 *Let D be the distance between the origin and a point uniformly distributed the unit ball centered at the origin. For $r \in [0, 1]$, the density of D is proportional to the surface area of an m-dimensional sphere of radius r,*

$$S(m, r) = \frac{\pi^{\frac{m}{2}} m\, r^{m-1}}{\Gamma\left(\frac{m}{2} + 1\right)} \propto r^{m-1}.$$

From this we recognize that D is distributed Beta$(m, 1)$. For the squared distance,

$$P(D^2 \le x) = P(D \le \sqrt{x}) \propto \int_0^{\sqrt{x}} r^{m-1}\, dr = \int_0^x u^{\frac{m-1}{2}} \frac{1}{2} u^{-\frac{1}{2}} du,$$

using the substitution $r = u^{\frac{1}{2}}$ in the last integral. From this, we recognize that $D^2 \sim$ Beta$(\frac{m}{2}, 1)$.

Exercise 11.7 *The inner sphere is tangent to the radius-$\frac{1}{2}$ sphere centered at $(\frac{1}{2}, \frac{1}{2}, \ldots, \frac{1}{2})$ at the point $(x, x, \ldots, x)$, where x is the smaller of the two solutions to the equation*

$$m \left(x - \frac{1}{2} \right)^2 = \left(\frac{1}{2} \right)^2$$

that is, $x = \frac{1}{2} - \frac{1}{2\sqrt{m}}$. The radius of S is the distance from $(x, x, \ldots, x)$ to the origin, which is

$$\sqrt{m \left(\frac{1}{2} - \frac{1}{2\sqrt{m}} \right)^2} = \frac{\sqrt{m} - 1}{2}.$$

This radius exceeds 1 (and so S contains a point outside C) for all $m \geq 10$.

Exercise 11.10 *Let $\mathbf{1}$ denote the n-long column vector of all 1's. Multiplication of $\mathbf{X}$ on the left by the $n \times n$ matrix of all 1's, $\mathbf{11}^T$, results in a matrix with constant columns, and each entry in the ith column of $\mathbf{11}^T\mathbf{X}$ is the sum of all elements in the ith column of $\mathbf{X}$. Thus each entry in the ith column of $\frac{1}{n}\mathbf{11}^T\mathbf{X}$ is the mean of all elements in the ith column of $\mathbf{X}$, so*

$$\frac{1}{n}\mathbf{11}^T\mathbf{X} = \begin{bmatrix} \bar{x} \\ \bar{x} \\ \vdots \\ \bar{x} \end{bmatrix}.$$

Therefore,

$$\mathbf{HX} = \left(\mathbf{I} - \frac{1}{n}\mathbf{11}^T \right) \mathbf{X} = \mathbf{X} - \frac{1}{n}\mathbf{11}^T\mathbf{X} = \mathbf{X} - \begin{bmatrix} \bar{x} \\ \bar{x} \\ \vdots \\ \bar{x} \end{bmatrix}$$

is the matrix formed by subtracting $\bar{x}$ from each row of $\mathbf{X}$. The idempotency of $\mathbf{H}$ could be said simply to follow from the above property, but formally it is shown by

$$\mathbf{H}^2 = \left(\mathbf{I} - \frac{1}{n}\mathbf{11}^T \right)^2 = \mathbf{I} - \frac{2}{n}\mathbf{11}^T + \frac{1}{n^2}\mathbf{1}\underbrace{\mathbf{1}^T\mathbf{1}}_{=n}\mathbf{1}^T = \mathbf{I} - \frac{1}{n}\mathbf{11}^T = \mathbf{H}.$$

The rows of $\mathbf{HX}$ are $(x_1 - \bar{x}, x_2 - \bar{x}, \ldots, x_n - \bar{x})$, so

$$\frac{1}{n}(\mathbf{HX})^T(\mathbf{HX}) = \frac{1}{n} \sum_{i=1}^{n} (x_i - \bar{x})(x_i - \bar{x})^T = \mathbf{S}.$$

Exercise 11.12 *Since* **Q** *is an orthogonal matrix, its columns are all mutually orthogonal unit vectors, so (1) is satisfied. For (2), let z be an arbitrary m-dimensional unit vector. The sample variance of* **HX**z *is, by Exercise 11.10,*

$$\frac{1}{n}(\mathbf{X}z)^{\mathsf{T}}\mathbf{H}(\mathbf{X}z) = z^{\mathsf{T}}\left(\frac{1}{n}\mathbf{X}^{\mathsf{T}}\mathbf{H}\mathbf{X}\right)z = z^{\mathsf{T}}\mathbf{S}z = z^{\mathsf{T}}\mathbf{Q}\mathbf{\Lambda}\mathbf{Q}^{\mathsf{T}}z = (\mathbf{Q}^{\mathsf{T}}z)^{\mathsf{T}}\mathbf{\Lambda}(\mathbf{Q}^{\mathsf{T}}z).$$

Note that since z is a unit vector and **Q** *is orthogonal,* $\mathbf{Q}^{\mathsf{T}}z$ *is also a unit vector (because* $\|\mathbf{Q}^{\mathsf{T}}z\|^2 = z^{\mathsf{T}}\mathbf{Q}\mathbf{Q}^{\mathsf{T}}z = z^{\mathsf{T}}z = \|z\|^2 = 1$*). Since* $\mathbf{\Lambda} = \mathrm{diag}(\lambda_1, \lambda_2, \dots, \lambda_m)$*, the last expression for the sample covariance of* **HX**z *can be written as*

$$\sum_{i=1}^{m}\lambda_i(\mathbf{Q}^{\mathsf{T}}z)_i^2.$$

Since $\lambda_1 \geq \lambda_2 \geq \cdots \geq \lambda_m \geq 0$*, the above expression for the sample covariance of* **HX**z *is maximized when z is chosen so that*

$$\mathbf{Q}^{\mathsf{T}}z = \begin{bmatrix} 1 \\ 0 \\ \vdots \\ 0 \end{bmatrix}$$

or equivalently, multiplying on the left by **Q***, when*

$$z = \mathbf{Q}\begin{bmatrix} 1 \\ 0 \\ \vdots \\ 0 \end{bmatrix} = Q_1,$$

unless $\lambda_1 = 0$*. But if* $\lambda_1 = 0$ *then for all z,*

$$\sum_{i=1}^{m}\lambda_i(\mathbf{Q}^{\mathsf{T}}z)_i^2 = \sum_{i=1}^{m}0(\mathbf{Q}^{\mathsf{T}}z)_i^2 = 0$$

and we are free to choose $z = Q_1$ *as the (non-unique) maximizer. For (3), suppose we have shown that (3) holds for all $j = 1, \dots, h$. We will show that (3) holds for $j = h + 1$. Let z be an arbitrary m-dimensional unit vector, and observe that the sample covariance between* **HX**Q_j *and* **HX**z *is*

$$\frac{1}{n}(\mathbf{HX}Q_j)^{\mathsf{T}}\mathbf{HX}z = \dots \text{(as above)} \dots = Q_j^{\mathsf{T}}\mathbf{Q}\mathbf{\Lambda}\mathbf{Q}^{\mathsf{T}}z.$$

Since **Q** *is orthogonal,*

$$Q_j^{\mathsf{T}}\mathbf{Q}\mathbf{\Lambda}\mathbf{Q}^{\mathsf{T}}z = \underbrace{[0, \dots, 0, 1, 0, \dots, 0]}_{\text{1 in position } j}\mathbf{\Lambda}\mathbf{Q}^{\mathsf{T}}z = \lambda_j(\mathbf{Q}^{\mathsf{T}}z)_j.$$

Thus if the sample covariance between **HX**Q_j *and* **HX**z *is zero for $j = 1, \dots, h$ then*

$$\lambda_j(\mathbf{Q}^{\mathsf{T}}z)_j = 0 \qquad \text{for } j = 1, \dots, h.$$

As in (2), finding z which maximizes the sample variance of $\mathbf{H}\mathbf{X}z$ is equivalent to finding z which maximizes

$$\sum_{i=1}^{m} \lambda_i (\mathbf{Q}^{\mathrm{T}}z)_i^2,$$

and if the sample covariance between $\mathbf{H}\mathbf{X}Q_j$ and $\mathbf{H}\mathbf{X}z$ is zero for $j = 1, \ldots, h$ then the expression to be maximized becomes

$$\sum_{i=h+1}^{m} \lambda_i (\mathbf{Q}^{\mathrm{T}}z)_i^2.$$

The argument that $z = Q_{h+1}$ maximizes this expression (whether $\lambda_{h+1} > 0$ or $\lambda_{h+1} = 0$) is the same as the argument for $z = Q_1$ in (2).

Exercise 11.15 For part (A), let $c_\lambda = h(\widehat{\theta})$ and let $\tilde{\theta}$ be a solution to the constrained optimization problem

$$\text{minimize over } \theta: \quad g(\theta)$$
$$\text{subject to:} \quad h(\theta) \le c_\lambda.$$

If $g(\tilde{\theta}) < g(\widehat{\theta})$ then, since $h(\tilde{\theta}) \le h(\widehat{\theta})$,

$$g(\tilde{\theta}) + \lambda h(\tilde{\theta}) < g(\widehat{\theta}) + \lambda h(\widehat{\theta}),$$

contradicting the fact that $\widehat{\theta}$ minimizes $g(\widehat{\theta}) + \lambda h(\widehat{\theta})$. So $g(\tilde{\theta}) \ge g(\widehat{\theta})$, that is, $\widehat{\theta}$ is a solution to the constrained problem. For part (B), let $\widehat{\theta}$ be a solution to the constrained optimization problem

$$\text{minimize over } \theta: \quad g(\theta)$$
$$\text{subject to:} \quad h(\theta) \le c$$

(if this constrained optimization problem has more than one solution, take $\widehat{\theta}$ so that $h(\widehat{\theta})$ is as small as possible). If $h(\widehat{\theta}) < c$, then $\widehat{\theta}$ is a local minimum of g. Since g is convex, $\widehat{\theta}$ is a global minimum of g, and therefore $\widehat{\theta}$ is a solution to the unconstrained optimization problem

$$\text{minimize over } \theta: \quad g(\theta) + \lambda_c h(\theta)$$

for the value $\lambda_c = 0$. If $h(\widehat{\theta}) = c$, then $\widehat{\theta}$ is a solution to the constrained optimization problem

$$\text{minimize over } \theta: \quad g(\theta)$$
$$\text{subject to:} \quad h(\theta) = c.$$

Let $\partial H = \{\theta : h(\theta) = c\}$ be the boundary of the set $H = \{\theta : h(\theta) \le c\}$. At every point $\theta \in \partial H$, the gradient $\nabla h(\theta)$ is orthogonal to ∂H and points outside of H (since $h(\theta)$ increases as θ moves from inside $H = \{\theta : h(\theta) \le c\}$ across the boundary $\partial H = \{\theta :$

$h(\theta) = c\}$ to the complement of H, which is $\{\theta : h(\theta) > c\}$. In particular, $\nabla h(\widehat{\theta})$ is orthogonal to H at $\widehat{\theta}$. Also, $\nabla g(\widehat{\theta})$ is orthogonal to H at $\widehat{\theta}$, because if it were not, then a small move within H would reduce the value of g, and $\widehat{\theta}$ would not be a solution to the constrained optimization problem. That is, there is a scalar λ such that

$$\nabla g(\widehat{\theta}) = \lambda \nabla h(\widehat{\theta}).$$

Let $\partial G = \{\theta : g(\theta) = g(\widehat{\theta})\}$ be the boundary of the set $G = \{\theta : g(\theta) \le g(\widehat{\theta})\}$ (G is also a convex set). At every point $\theta \in \partial G$, the gradient $\nabla g(\theta)$ is orthogonal to ∂G and points outside of G. The interior of H and G have empty intersection, because if they did not, there would exist a point θ such that $g(\theta) < g(\widehat{\theta})$ and $h(\theta) < c$, and then $\widehat{\theta}$ would not be a solution to the constrained optimization problem. Thus at $\widehat{\theta}$, which is in both ∂H and ∂G, the gradients $\nabla g(\widehat{\theta})$ and $\nabla h(\widehat{\theta})$ point in opposite directions, that is, $\lambda < 0$. Let $\lambda_c = -\lambda$. Then $\lambda_c \ge 0$ and

$$\nabla g(\widehat{\theta}) + \lambda_c \nabla h(\widehat{\theta}) = 0.$$

Since $\lambda_c \ge 0$, $g(\theta) + \lambda_c h(\theta)$ is a convex function. Since $\nabla(g(\theta) + \lambda_c h(\theta))|_{\theta=\widehat{\theta}} = 0$, $\widehat{\theta}$ is a local, and hence global, minimum of $g(\theta) + \lambda_c h(\theta)$. That is, $\widehat{\theta}$ is a solution of the unconstrained optimization problem.

Exercise 12.1 *For part (A),*

$$
\begin{aligned}
R(\widehat{f}) &= E_{(X,Y)}[L(Y,\widehat{f}(X))] \\
&= L(1,2)\,P(Y=1,\widehat{f}(X)=2) + L(2,1)\,P(Y=2,\widehat{f}(X)=1) \\
&= L(1,2)\,P(\widehat{f}(X)=2 \mid Y=1)\,P(Y=1) + L(2,1)\,P(\widehat{f}(X)=1 \mid Y=2)\,P(Y=2) \\
&= L(1,2)\,P(\widehat{f}(X)=2 \mid Y=1)\,P(Y=1) + L(2,1)\,(1 - P(\widehat{f}(X)=2 \mid Y=2))\,P(Y=2) \\
&= L(1,2)\,P(S(X) \ge \tau \mid Y=1)\,P(Y=1) + L(2,1)\,(1 - P(S(X) \ge \tau \mid Y=2))\,P(Y=2).
\end{aligned}
$$

For part (B), we apply part (A) to solve

$$
\begin{aligned}
0 &= \frac{d}{d\tau} R(\widehat{f}) \\
&= L(1,2)\,\frac{d}{d\tau} P(S(X) \ge \tau \mid Y=1)\,P(Y=1) \\
&\quad + L(2,1)\,\frac{d}{d\tau}(1 - P(S(X) \ge \tau \mid Y=2))\,P(Y=2) \\
&= L(1,2)\,\frac{d}{d\tau}(1 - P(S(X) < \tau \mid Y=1))\,P(Y=1) \\
&\quad + L(2,1)\,\frac{d}{d\tau} P(S(X) < \tau \mid Y=2)\,P(Y=2) \\
&= L(1,2)\,(-P(\tau \mid Y=1))\,P(Y=1) + L(2,1)\,P(\tau \mid Y=2)\,P(Y=2).
\end{aligned}
$$

Putting the losses on one side yields

$$\frac{L(2, 1)}{L(1, 2)} = \frac{P(\tau \mid Y = 1)}{P(\tau \mid Y = 2)} \frac{P(Y = 1)}{P(Y = 2)}.$$

Exercise 12.2 *Since F is a cumulative distribution function,* $\lim_{s \to -\infty} F(s) = 0$ *and* $\lim_{s \to \infty} F(s) = 1$, *and since F is continuous and strictly increasing, it is a one-to-one (hence invertible) and onto map of* $(-\infty, \infty)$ *to* $(0, 1)$. *For any* $u \in (0, 1)$,

$$P(U \leq u) = P(F(S) \leq u) = P(S \leq F^{-1}(u)) = F(F^{-1}(u)) = u.$$

Thus U is uniformly distributed on $(0, 1)$. *Nothing changes if* $F(s) = P(S \geq s)$ *(that is,* $U = F(S)$ *is still uniformly distributed on* $(0, 1)$*).*

Exercise 12.3 *By application of Exercise 12.2, the distribution of* $(U_1, U_2) = h(S_1, S_2)$ *is uniform on* $(0, 1) \times (0, 1)$ *since each coordinate is uniformly distributed on* $(0, 1)$ *and the two coordinates are independent. By definition of the uniform distribution, the area under the ROC curve is the probability that the point* (U_1, U_2) *is under the ROC curve, and since h is one-to-one, this is the probability that h maps* (S_1, S_2) *to a point under the ROC curve. Now h maps a point* (s_1, s_2) *under the ROC curve if and only if the point* $(P(S_1 \geq s_1), P(S_2 \geq s_2))$ *is below the point* $(P(S_1 \geq s_1), P(S_2 \geq s_1))$, *that is, if and only if* $P(S_2 \geq s_2) \leq P(S_2 \geq s_1)$. *Since* $P(S_2 \geq s)$ *is a strictly decreasing function of s, h maps a point* (s_1, s_2) *under the ROC curve if and only if* $s_2 \geq s_1$. *Thus*

$$P((U_1, U_2) \text{ is under the ROC curve}) = P(S_2 \geq S_1).$$

Exercise 12.7 *Let* E_i *be the event that the ith test, out of the* $T - T_0$ *tests in which the null hypothesis is false, incorrectly rejects the null. By Boole's inequality, the probability that at least one test incorrectly rejects the null is*

$$p(s) = P(E_1 \cup \cdots \cup E_{T-T_0}) \leq P(E_1) + \cdots + P(E_{T-T_0}) = (T - T_0) s.$$

The solution to the equation $p(s) = \alpha$, *for* $0 < \alpha < 1$, *is*

$$s = \frac{\alpha}{T - T_0}.$$

The value of T_0 *is unknown, but since* $p(s)$ *is a decreasing function of* T_0, *the value of s obtained by replacing* T_0 *with zero,*

$$s_0 = \frac{\alpha}{T},$$

provides a computable value such that $p(s_0) \leq \alpha$.

C

Converting Between Normal Parameters and Level-Curve Ellipsoids

Let Z be a m-dimensional normal random variable with mean μ and covariance matrix Σ. The density function for Z is

$$\phi(z) = (2\pi)^{-\frac{m}{2}} |\Sigma|^{-\frac{1}{2}} e^{-\frac{1}{2}(z-\mu)^{\mathrm{T}}\Sigma^{-1}(z-\mu)},$$

so the level curves of the density can be written as

$$\{z : \phi(z) = c\} = \left\{ z : (z-\mu)^{\mathrm{T}}\Sigma^{-1}(z-\mu) = -2\log\left(c(2\pi)^{\frac{m}{2}}|\Sigma|^{\frac{1}{2}}\right) \right\},$$

so level curves of $\phi(z)$ are level curves of $(z-\mu)^{\mathrm{T}}\Sigma^{-1}(z-\mu)$.

By a well-known theorem,[1] the random variable $(Z-\mu)^{\mathrm{T}}\Sigma^{-1}(Z-\mu)$ is distributed χ_m^2. Thus the ellipsoid centered at μ, bounded by a level curve of the density, and containing total probability mass ρ is that given by the equation

$$(z-\mu)^{\mathrm{T}}\Sigma^{-1}(z-\mu) = k^2, \tag{C.1}$$

where k^2 is the ρ-quantile of a χ_m^2 random variable.

---

[1] See, for example, Mardia et al. (1979, Theorem 2.5.2).

Machine Learning: a Concise Introduction, First Edition. Steven W. Knox.
© This publication is a US Government work and is in the public domain.
Published 2018 by John Wiley & Sons, Inc.
Companion Website: http://www.wiley.com/go/Knox/MachineLearning

C.1 Parameters to Axes

To compute the axes of the ellipsoid, given ρ (and hence k) and covariance matrix Σ, let $\Lambda = \text{diag}(\lambda_1, \dots, \lambda_m)$ be the diagonal matrix of eigenvalues of Σ and let Γ be the corresponding matrix of eigenvectors (in columns) so that

$$\Gamma \Lambda \Gamma^{\text{T}} = \Sigma.$$

Note that Γ is orthonormal, and that all the eigenvalues are positive since Σ is positive definite, so $\Sigma^{-1} = \Gamma \Lambda^{-1} \Gamma^{\text{T}}$.

Let $w = \Gamma^{\text{T}}(z - \mu)$, so (C.1) is equivalent to

$$k^2 = (z - \mu)^{\text{T}} \Gamma \Lambda^{-1} \Gamma^{\text{T}}(z - \mu) = w^{\text{T}} \Lambda^{-1} w.$$

The ellipsoid

$$\{w : w^{\text{T}} \Lambda^{-1} w = k^2\}$$

has axes

$$\{e_i k \sqrt{\lambda_i} : i = 1, \dots, m\},$$

where $e_1, \dots, e_m$ are the standard basis vectors of $\mathbb{R}^m$. The axes are the columns of matrix $k \Lambda^{\frac{1}{2}}$. The volume of the ellipsoid is

$$\frac{\pi^{\frac{m}{2}}}{\Gamma\left(\frac{m}{2} + 1\right)} \prod_{i=1}^{m} k \sqrt{\lambda_i} = \frac{\pi^{\frac{m}{2}}}{\Gamma\left(\frac{m}{2} + 1\right)} k^m |\Lambda|^{\frac{1}{2}} = \frac{\pi^{\frac{m}{2}}}{\Gamma\left(\frac{m}{2} + 1\right)} k^m |\Sigma|^{\frac{1}{2}}.$$

The axes of ellipsoid (C.1) are obtained by transforming back by $z = \Gamma w + \mu$. They are the columns of $\Gamma k \Lambda^{\frac{1}{2}}$ (and the ellipsoid is centered at μ).

C.2 Axes to Parameters

To compute the covariance matrix, given k and a set of axes $\{a_1, \dots, a_m\}$, let Γ be the $m \times m$ matrix whose ith column is $\frac{a_i}{\|a_i\|}$ and let Λ be the $m \times m$ diagonal matrix whose ith diagonal element is $\frac{\|a_i\|^2}{k^2}$. Then $\Sigma = \Gamma \Lambda \Gamma^{\text{T}}$. For computational convenience, we note that

$$\Sigma_{ij} = k^{-2} \sum_{l=1}^{m} a_{li} a_{lj} \qquad (\Sigma^{-1})_{ij} = k^2 \sum_{l=1}^{m} a_{li} a_{lj} \|a_l\|^{-4} \qquad \text{and} \qquad |\Sigma| = \prod_{l=1}^{m} \left(\frac{\|a_l\|}{k}\right)^2.$$

The volume of the ellipsoid is

$$\frac{\pi^{\frac{m}{2}}}{\Gamma\left(\frac{m}{2} + 1\right)} \prod_{i=1}^{m} \|a_i\|.$$

D

Training Data and Fitted Parameters

D.1   Training Data

The training data used in the examples of Chapters 4 and 6 are:

Orange		Blue		Purple	
1.01835311	3.858188069	−2.44778619	0.411762949	0.88920445	−1.554771660
−0.39035021	2.296152712	−1.81633020	0.956820553	0.59253129	−2.200991648
1.45409603	2.767220184	−3.71879213	0.656435644	0.81555510	−3.534221374
1.25139303	2.240148404	−4.33296530	1.865524891	0.74919674	−2.554551343
1.47861376	4.169890444	−2.95165877	−1.981955555	1.01707661	−3.740811041
1.97106252	3.309064594	−3.23600711	0.318457605	0.83830882	−2.892823356
1.29525413	3.664758067	−3.71472179	1.963290297	0.04673084	−5.136697938
2.36633865	3.886386797	−0.67750270	0.573221485	1.81426495	−4.178348176
0.61478730	2.941948574	−3.20171872	1.851323283	1.09740306	−3.540756942
1.13013934	1.769883249	−4.72701125	1.157517690	2.57366436	−3.829619656
3.08806139	2.460464018	−4.17015401	2.875329033	1.74152363	−4.129447431
1.65043358	2.074489002	−3.04809093	−0.775681901	0.80962318	−2.734405293
1.13657335	2.817216261	−2.38590381	−1.403671955	1.04180389	−2.818153236
1.21845986	2.893188673	−3.93859341	1.315428603	1.57861364	−1.891101028
0.51819402	2.294952866	−2.73051526	0.817989003	1.42890558	−1.583289100
2.24860514	4.081035106	−2.76453011	−0.291580652	2.29935588	−2.998218571
2.02139794	1.975443811	0.10086777	−1.546832786	2.01047969	−3.146778337
0.65409179	1.920205104	−1.81167675	−0.534785884	3.26547873	−0.587171020
2.67129310	1.404452541	−0.80292510	−1.965567682	1.92613576	−1.995552239
0.66700023	1.107842837	−0.07977799	−0.206200508	2.07894932	−1.814050173

(continued)

Machine Learning: a Concise Introduction, First Edition. Steven W. Knox.
© This publication is a US Government work and is in the public domain.
Published 2018 by John Wiley & Sons, Inc.
Companion Website: http://www.wiley.com/go/Knox/MachineLearning

Orange		Blue		Purple	
−0.72131160	2.432526464	−1.32543573	−1.136373467	2.55846461	−2.670704773
−1.78554518	0.958900921	−2.11904040	0.142818093	2.28421459	−0.562091196
−0.38147151	1.696933085	−1.29248964	−1.680869124	2.81930129	−0.897591518
−1.63970921	1.195835127	−2.70512615	−1.698475625	0.81160670	−0.017597401
0.16660581	1.627306919	−1.42575626	0.491183425	1.00021220	1.369779746
−0.53473335	0.256732142	−0.34499844	−1.478875991	1.85579676	−0.780971996
0.77922983	2.658307727	−0.41313214	−2.606355508	2.94224740	−0.917127449
−0.43405071	1.155635446	−1.73804314	−0.377478946	3.39946795	−1.290240370
−0.00392283	2.786281150	−3.34726854	−0.489081734	1.61400622	−0.098490359
−1.48783130	2.842362043	−3.33693741	0.652810034	3.07596402	−2.355845314
−1.62056323	2.471772577	−0.99798094	−0.197343843	2.70316623	−0.784568415
−1.13040474	3.993191633	−0.81619694	−0.904100285	0.16866374	0.087303778
−0.94676657	2.107545261	−0.83144496	−2.106851992	2.36020820	0.386671144
−0.87149783	0.443262467	−0.05076807	−0.942751092	1.54411490	1.270567501
0.72172938	1.330088990	0.40901775	−0.150548721	0.84342988	1.192702586
−1.48759633	2.142702781	−0.86619007	−0.422721220	−0.09665570	1.763367271
−1.30630746	0.337073803	0.33547868	−0.368116275	1.08326952	−0.506463053
−0.46927054	1.544676753	−0.42808889	−2.245273519	1.08068246	−0.110448148
−0.70760372	0.947117303	−1.02428998	−0.978266671	1.88326233	1.701906397
1.43817519	1.770816447	0.50581813	−0.924577068	1.68723111	0.455089492
−2.37831742	−0.464470754	−1.05376056	−0.235850726	1.82308565	0.805090510
0.74073626	0.883323110	0.38703888	0.472247048	1.90900463	−0.681547255
−1.02523935	1.694383192	−1.13726330	−1.158928528	1.04463161	0.587939704
−2.62367442	−0.095448930	−0.14537709	0.706053317	1.73276164	0.323584212
−1.72811292	0.300693402	−0.59091457	−0.202037204	−0.20000141	−0.107531745
−1.55782155	−0.197322454	1.56382176	1.917287127	−0.09333630	−0.127257567
−1.66553512	1.551425239	−1.23286663	−0.517321830	−0.27606741	3.713758001
−0.93240616	0.997272107	0.52671043	−2.443710226	0.71040903	1.743478628
		−0.56358878	−1.396337990	0.19262828	−0.008076803
				1.74211005	1.064850079
				0.33966526	0.692246616
				−0.15690328	0.054194159
				0.85525127	1.068336589

D.2   Fitted Model Parameters

This section contains fitted parameters for some of the models fit in Chapter 4.

D.2.1   Quadratic and Linear Discriminant Analysis

$\hat{\mu}_1 = (0.09313711, 1.9437887)$ $\hat{\mu}_2 = (-1.56152789, -0.2902658)$

$\hat{\mu}_3 = (1.39352262, -0.9527820)$

$\hat{\Sigma}_1 = \begin{pmatrix} 2.0367611 & 0.9371364 \\ 0.9371364 & 1.3460017 \end{pmatrix}$ $\hat{\Sigma}_2 = \begin{pmatrix} 2.2583093 & -0.8557902 \\ -0.8557902 & 1.5960710 \end{pmatrix}$

$\hat{\Sigma}_3 = \begin{pmatrix} 0.8889359 & -0.3959931 \\ -0.3959931 & 3.5267115 \end{pmatrix}$

$\hat{\Sigma} = \begin{pmatrix} 1.703569 & -0.119592 \\ -0.119592 & 2.198208 \end{pmatrix}$

D.2.2   Logistic Regression

The approximate maximum-likelihood estimate of the parameter θ is

$$\hat{\theta} = \begin{pmatrix} 0 & 0 & 0 \\ 0.4198989 & -0.8577562 & -1.560357 \\ 0.3935905 & 1.2712873 & -1.542454 \end{pmatrix}.$$

Thus the linear functions which define the log-odds in favor of class 2 or class 3 over class 1 are, respectively,

$$T_2 = T((x_1, x_2), \hat{\theta}_2) = 0.4198989 - 0.8577562\,x_1 - 1.560357\,x_2$$

and

$$T_3 = T((x_1, x_2), \hat{\theta}_3) = 0.3935905 + 1.2712873\,x_1 - 1.542454\,x_2.$$

D.2.3   Neural Network

The fitted parameters of a single-hidden layer neural network with two hidden neurons are as follows. For the hidden layer,

$$\hat{\theta}_{1,0}^{(1)} = -5.27 \qquad\qquad \hat{\theta}_{1,\star}^{(1)} = (0.70, -1.46)$$

$$\hat{\theta}_{2,0}^{(1)} = 2.72 \qquad\qquad \hat{\theta}_{2,\star}^{(1)} = (1.99, 1.23)$$

$$\hat{\theta}_{1,0}^{(2)} = 7.93 \qquad\qquad \hat{\theta}_{1,\star}^{(2)} = (-655.57, -5.94)$$

$$\hat{\theta}_{2,0}^{(2)} = 9.72 \qquad\qquad \hat{\theta}_{2,\star}^{(2)} = (311.05, -11.44)$$

$$\hat{\theta}_{3,0}^{(2)} = -16.89 \qquad\qquad \hat{\theta}_{3,\star}^{(2)} = (344.26, 16.93).$$

As functions of the features,

$$T_1 = 7.93 - 655.57\,\sigma(-5.27 + 0.70x_1 - 1.46x_2) - 5.94\,\sigma(2.72 + 1.99x_1 + 1.23x_2)$$

$$T_2 = 9.72 + 311.05\,\sigma(-5.27 + 0.70x_1 - 1.46x_2) - 11.44\,\sigma(2.72 + 1.99x_1 + 1.23x_2)$$

$$T_3 = -16.89 + 344.26\,\sigma(-5.27 + 0.70x_1 - 1.46x_2) + 16.93\,\sigma(2.72 + 1.99x_1 + 1.23x_2).$$

D.2.4   Classification Tree

See Figure 4.22.

References

Where do we go from here? Would books help us?
—Guy Montag in Ray Bradbury, *Fahrenheit 451*, 1953

Agresti, A. (1984). *Analysis of Ordinal Categorical Data*. John Wiley & Sons, Inc.

Akaike, H. (1974). Information theory and an extension of the maximum likelihood principle. In: 2nd International Symposium on Information Theory, reprinted in Breakthroughs in Statistics, vol. 1, pp. 599–624, edited by S. Kotz and N. L. Johnson, 1992.

Anguita, D., Ghelardoni, L., Ghio, A., Oneto, L., and Ridella, S. (2012). The "K" in K-fold cross validation. In: Proceedings of the European Symposium on Artificial Neural Networks, Computational Intelligence and Machine Learning, Bruges, Belgium, pp. 441–446.

Aristotle. (350 BCE). *Politics*, translated by B. Jowett in 1885. The Internet Classics Archive. Available at classics.mit.edu/Aristotle/politics.mb.txt

Arlot, S. and Celisse, A. (2010). A survey of cross-validation procedures for model selection. *Statistics Surveys*, 4, 40–79.

Armstrong, J. (2001). *Principles of Forecasting: A Handbook for Researchers and Practitioners*. Springer.

Ash, R. (1965). Information theory. In: *Interscience Tracts in Pure and Applied Mathematics*, vol. 19. Interscience Publishers.

Austen, J. (2004). *Pride and Prejudice*. Dalmation Press.

Battiti, R. (1989). Accelerated backpropagation learning: Two optimization methods. *Complex Systems*, 3, 331–342.

Bartholomew, D. (2013). *Unobserved Variables: Models and Misunderstandings*. Springer.

Bellman, R. (1957). *Dynamic Programming*. Princeton University Press.

Bengio, Y. and Grandvalet, Y. (2004). No unbiased estimator of the variance of K-fold cross-validation. *Journal of Machine Learning Research*, 5, 1089–1105.

Benjamini, Y. and Hochberg, Y. (1995). Controlling the false discovery rate: A practical and powerful approach to multiple testing. *Journal of the Royal Statistical Society, Series B (Methodological)*, 57(1), 289–300.

Benjamini, Y. and Yekutieli, D. (2001). The control of the false discovery rate in multiple testing under dependency. *Annals of Statistics*, 29(4), 1165–1188.

Bentley, J. L. (1975). Multidimensional binary search trees used for associative searching. *Communications of the ACM*, 18(9), 509–517.

Biau, G. and Devroye, L. (2010). On the layered nearest neighbor method, the bagged nearest neighbor estimate, and the random forest method in regression and classification. *Journal of Multivariate Analysis*, 101(10), 2499–2518.

Biau, G., Devroye, L., and Lugosi, G. (2008). Consistency of random forests and other averaging classifiers. *Machine Learning*, 9, 2015–2033.

Billingsley, P. (1986). *Probability and Measure*, 2nd ed. John Wiley & Sons, Inc.

Borg, I. and Groenen, P. (1997). *Modern Multidimensional Scaling: Theory and Applications*. Springer.

Box, G. E. P. and Draper, N. R. (1987). *Empirical Model Building and Response Surfaces*. Wiley.

Bradbury, R. (1953). *Fahrenheit 451*. Ballantine Books.

Breiman, L. (1995). Better subset selection using the nonnegative garrote. *Technometrics*, 37(4), 373–384.

Breiman, L. (1996a). Bagging predictors. *Machine Learning*, 26, 123–140.

Breiman, L. (1996b). Bias, variance and arcing classifiers. Technical Report 460, Statistics Department, University of California at Berkeley, pp. 801–849.

Breiman, L. (1998). Arcing classifiers. *Annals of Statistics*, 23(3), 801–849.

Breiman, L. (2001a). Random forests. *Machine Learning*, 45, 5–32.

Breiman, L. (2001b). Statistical modeling: The two cultures. *Statistical Science*, 16(3), 199–231.

Breiman, L. (2004). Consistency for a simple model of random forests. Technical Report 670, Statistics Department, University of California at Berkeley.

Breiman, L., Friedman, J. H., Olshen, R. A., and Stone, C. J. (1984). *Classification and Regression Trees*. Wadsworth International Group.

Brown, C. (2013). hash: Full feature implementation of hash/associated arrays/dictionaries. R package version 2.2.6. Available at https://CRAN.R-project.org/package=hash

Buck, R. C. (1943, November). Partition of space. *The American Mathematical Monthly*, 50(9), 541–544.

Burges, C. J. C. (1998). A tutorial on support vector machines for pattern recognition. *Data Mining and Knowledge Discovery*, 2, 121–167.

Bylander, T. (2002). Estimating generalization error on two-class datasets using out-of-bag estimates. *Machine Learning*, 48(1–3), 287–297.

Carlisle, A. and Dozier, G. (2000). Adapting particle swarm optimization to dynamic environments. In: International Conference on Artificial Intelligence, Las Vegas, NV, vol. 1, pp. 429–434.

Casella, G. and Berger, R. L. (2002). *Statistical Inference*, 2nd ed. Duxbury.

Chawla, N. V., Hall, L. O., Bowyer, K. W., and Kegelmeyer, W. P. (2004). Learning ensembles from bites: A scalable and accurate approach. *Journal of Machine Learning Research*, 5, 421–451.

Clark, A. and Kubrick, S. (1968). *2001: A Space Odyssey*. MGM.

Conover, W. J. (1999). *Practical Nonparametric Statistics*, 3rd ed. John Wiley & Sons, Inc.

Cormen, T. H., Leiserson, C. E., Rivest, R. L., and Stein, C. (2009). *Introduction to Algorithms*, 3rd ed. MIT Press.

Cover, T. and Hart, P. (1967). Nearest neighbor pattern classification. *IEEE Transactions on Information Theory*, 13(1), 21–27.

Cover, T. M. and Thomas, J. A. (2006). *Elements of Information Theory*. John Wiley & Sons, Inc.

Cox, D. R. and Lewis, P. A. W. (1966). *The Statistical Analysis of Series of Events*. Chapman & Hall.

D'Agostino, R. B. and Stephens, M. A. (1986). *Goodness-of-Fit Techniques*. Dekker.

Dasgupta, S. and Anupam, G. (2003). An Elementary Proof of a Theorem of Johnson and Lindenstrauss. *Random Structures and Algorithms*, 22(1), 60–65.

DeGroot, M. (1970). *Optimal Statistical Decisions*. McGraw-Hill.

Dempster, A. P., Laird, N. M., and Rubin, D. B. (1977). Maximum likelihood from incomplete data via the EM algorithm. *Journal of the Royal Statistical Society, Series B (Methodological)*, 39(1), 1–38.

Devroye, L., Györfi, L., and Lugosi, G. (1996). *A Probabilistic Theory of Pattern Recognition*. Springer.

Dietterich, T. G. (2000). An experimental comparison of three methods for constructing ensembles of decision trees: Bagging, boosting, and randomization. *Machine Learning*, 40, 139–157.

Domingos, P. (1999). The role of Occam's razor in knowledge discovery. *Data Mining and Knowledge Discovery*, 3(4), 409–425.

Domingos, P. (2000). A unified bias-variance decomposition for zero-one and squared loss. In: Proceedings of the 17th International Conference on Machine Learning, Stanford, CA, pp. 231–238.

Duda, R. O., Hart, P. E., and Stork, D. G. (2001). *Pattern Classification*, 2nd ed. John Wiley & Sons, Inc.

Eckert, C. and Young, G. (1936). The Approximation of One Matrix by Another of Lower Rank. *Psychometrika*, 1(3), 211–219.

Efron, B. (1979). Bootstrap methods: Another look at the jackknife. *Annals of Statistics*, 7, 1–26.

Efron, B. (1982). *The Jackknife, the Bootstrap, and Other Resampling Plans*, vol. 38. Philadelphia Society for Industrial and Applied Mathematics.

Efron, B. (1983, June). Estimating the error rate of a prediction rule: Improvement on cross-validation. *Journal of the American Statistical Association*, 78, 316–331.

Efron, B. (1986, June). How biased is the apparent error of a prediction rule? *Journal of the American Statistical Association*, 81(394), 461–470.

Efron, B. (2004, September). The estimation of prediction error: Covariance penalties and cross-validation. *Journal of the American Statistical Association*, 99, 619–632.

Efron, B. and Tibshirani, R. (1997, June). Improvements on cross-validation: The .632+ bootstrap method. *Journal of the American Statistical Association*, 92(438), 548–560.

Epanechnikov, V. A. (1967). Non-parametric estimation of a multivariate probability density. *Theory of Probability and Its Applications*, 14(1), 153–158 (translated by B. Seckler).

Feller, W. (1967). *An Introduction to Probability Theory and Its Applications*, vols. 1 (3rd ed.) and 2 (2nd ed.). John Wiley & Sons, Inc.

Ferguson, T. (1996). *A Course in Large Sample Theory*. Chapman & Hall.

Feynman, R. (2001). *What Do You Care What Other People Think?* W. W. Norton & Co.

Fisher, R. A. (1937). *The Design of Experiments*, Second Edition. Oliver and Boyd.

Fisher, R. A. (1938). Presidential Address. *Sankhyā: The Indian Journal of Statistics*, 4(1), 14–17.

Fisher, R. A. (1950). *Statistical Methods for Research Workers*, 11th ed. Hafner Publishing Co.

Fix, E. and Hodges, J. L. (1951). Discriminatory analysis, nonparametric discrimination: Consistency properties. Technical Report 4, USAF School of Aviation Medicine.

Freund, Y. and Schapire, R. E. (1997). A decision-theoretic generalization of on-line learning and an application to boosting. *Journal of Computer and System Sciences*, 55(1), 119–139.

Friedman, J. H. (1997a). Data mining and statistics: What's the connection? In: Proceedings of the 29th Symposium on the Interface between Computer Science and Statistics, Houston, TX.

Friedman, J. H. (1997b). On bias, variance, 0/1-loss, and the curse-of-dimensionality. *Data Mining and Knowledge Discovery*, 1(1), 55–77.

Friedman, J. H. and Tukey, J. W. (1974). A projection pursuit algorithm for exploratory data analysis. *IEEE Transactions in Computing*, C-23(9), 881–889.

Friedman, J., Hastie, T., and Tibshirani, R. (2000). Additive logistic regression: A statistical view of boosting. *Annals of Statistics*, 28(2), 337–407.

Fung, G. and Mangasarian, O. L. (2001). Proximal support vector machines. In: *KDD 2001: Proceedings of the Seventh ACM SIGKDD International Conference on Knowledge Discovery and Data Mining*, San Francisco, CA, pp. 77–86.

Furnival, G. M. and Wilson Jr., R. W. (1974, November). Regression by leaps and bounds. *Technometrics*, 16(4), 499–511.

Galton, F. (1886). Regression towards mediocrity in hereditary stature. *Anthropological Miscellanea*, 15, 246–263.

Galton, F. (1907). Vox populi. *Nature*, 75, 450–451.

Gan, G., Ma, C., and Wu, J. (2007). *Data Clustering: Theory, Algorithms, and Applications*. SIAM.

Geman, S., Bienenstock, E., and Doursat, R. (1992). Neural networks and the bias/variance dilemma. *Neural Computation*, 4(1), 1–58.

Gentle, J. E. (1998). *Numerical Linear Algebra for Applications in Statistics*. Springer.

Geurts, P., Ernst, D., and Wehenkel, L. (2006). Extremely randomized trees. *Machine Learning*, 63(1), 3–42.

Golub, G. H. and Van Loan, C. F. (1996). *Matrix Computations*, 3rd ed. Johns Hopkins.

Gonick, L. (1993). *The Cartoon Guide to Statistics*. Harper Perennial.

Green, P. J. (1995, December). Reversible jump Markov chain Monte Carlo computation and Bayesian model determination. *Biometrika*, 82(4), 711–732.

Grenander, U. (1993). *General Pattern Theory: A Mathematical Study of Regular Structures.* Clarendon Press.

Grenander, U. (1996). *Elements of Pattern Theory.* Johns Hopkins University Press.

Hamming, R. (1995). n-Dimensional Space. Online video. Youtube.securitylectures, August 8, 2012.

Hand, D. J. and Yu, K. (2007). Idiot's Bayes—Not so stupid after all? *International Statistical Review*, 69(3), 385–398.

Hart, P. (1968). The condensed nearest neighbor rule. *IEEE Transactions on Information Theory*, 18(1), 515–516.

Hartigan, J. A. (1975). *Clustering Algorithms.* John Wiley & Sons, Inc.

Hastie, T., Tibshirani, R., and Friedman, J. (2001). *The Elements of Statistical Learning: Data Mining, Inference, and Prediction.* Springer.

Hinton, G. E. and Salakhutdinov, R. R. (2006). Reducing the dimensionality of data with neural networks. *Science*, 313(5786), 504–507.

Ho, T. K. (1995). Random decision forests. In: Proceedings of the 3rd International Conference on Document Analysis and Recognition, Montreal, Quebec, Canada, pp. 278–282.

Howard, J. (2012, December). *Down with Experts.* New Scientist.

Huber, P. J. (1985). Projection Pursuit. *The Annals of Statistics*, 13(2), 435–475.

Huff, D. (1954). *How to Lie with Statistics.* Norton.

Jacobs, R. A., Jordan, M. I., Nowlan, S. J., and Hinton, G. E. (1991). Adaptive mixtures of local experts. *Neural Computation*, 3, 79–87.

James, G. M. (2003). Variance and bias for general loss functions. *Machine Learning*, 51, 115–135.

James, G. M. and Hastie, T. (1997). Generalizations of bias/variance decompositions for prediction error. Technical Report, Department of Statistics, Stanford University.

Jeffreys, H. (1931). *Scientific Inference.* Cambridge University Press.

Jeffreys, H. (1948). *Theory of Probability.* Clarendon Press.

Johnson, N. L., Kotz, S., and Balakrishnan, N. (1993). *Discrete Univariate Distributions*, 2nd ed. John Wiley & Sons, Inc.

Johnson, N. L., Kotz, S., and Balakrishnan, N. (1994). *Continuous Univariate Distributions*, vol. 1, 2nd ed. John Wiley & Sons, Inc.

Johnson, N. L., Kotz, S., and Balakrishnan, N. (1997). *Discrete Multivariate Distributions.* John Wiley & Sons, Inc.

Johnson, W. B. and Lindenstrauss, J. (1984). Extensions of Lipschitz Mappings into a Hilbert Space. *Contemporary Mathematics*, 26, 189–206.

Kaufman, L. and Rousseeuw, P. J. (1990). *Finding Groups in Data: An Introduction to Cluster Analysis.* John Wiley & Sons, Inc.

Kennedy, J. and Eberhart, R. (1995). Particle swarm optimization. In: Proceedings of the IEEE International Conference on Neural Networks, Perth, Western Australia, pp. 1942–1948.

Kernighan, B. W. and Ritchie, D. M. (1988). *The C Programming Language.* Prentice Hall.

Kleinberg, J. (2002). An impossibility theorem for clustering. In: Advances in Neural Information Processing Systems 15.

Kohavi, R. (1995). A study of cross-validation and bootstrap for accuracy estimation and model selection. In: Proceedings of the International Joint Conference on Artificial Intelligence, Montreal, Quebec, Canada, pp. 1137–1143.

Kohavi, R. and Wolpert, D. H. (1996). Bias plus variance decomposition for zero-one loss functions. In: Proceedings of the Thirteenth International Conference on Machine Learning, Bari, Italy, pp. 275–283.

Kohonen, T. (1986). Learning vector quantization for pattern recognition. Technical Report TKK-F-A601, Helsinki University of Technology.

Kolmogorov, A. N. (1956). *Foundations of the Theory of Probability*. Chelsea.

Kolmogorov, A. N. (1968). Three approaches to the quantitative definition of information. *International Journal of Computer Mathematics*, 2, 157–168.

Kong, E. B. and Dietterich, T. G. (1995). Error-correcting output coding corrects bias and variance. In: International Conference on Machine Learning, pp. 313–321.

Kotz, S., Balakrishnan, N., and Johnson, N. L. (2000). *Continuous Multivariate Distributions*, vol. 1, 2nd ed. John Wiley & Sons, Inc.

Kullback, S. and Leibler, R. A. (1951, March). On information and sufficiency. *Annals of Mathematical Statistics*, 22(1), 79–86.

Le Borgne, Y.-A. (2005). Bias–variance trade-off characterization in a classification problem: What differences with regression? Technical Report 534, Machine Learning Group, Université Libre de Bruxelles.

Liaw, A. and Wiener, M. (2002). Classification and regression by randomForest. *R News*, 2(3), 18–22.

Liu, F. T., Ting, K. M., Yu, Y., and Zhou, Z.-H. (2008). Spectrum of variable-random trees. *Journal of Artificial Intelligence Research*, 32, 355–384.

Mardia, K. V., Kent, J. T., and Bibby, J. M. (1979). *Multivariate Analysis*. Academic Press.

Meyer, D. (2015). svm() internals. In: E. Dimitriadou, K. Hornik, F. Leisch, D. Meyer, and A. Weingessel, e1071: Misc Functions of the Department of Statistics (e1071), TU Wien

Meyer, D., Dimitriadou, E., Hornik, K., Weingessel, A., and Leisch, F. (2017). e1071: Misc functions of the Department of Statistics, Probability Theory Group (Formerly: E1071), TU Wien. R package version 1.6-8. Available at https://CRAN.R-project.org/package=e1071

Miller, D. S. and Day, C. H. (1986). *Berry Finder: A Guide to Native Plants with Fleshy Fruits*, 2nd ed. Nature Study Guild Publishers.

Mosteller, F. and Wallace, D. L. (1963, June). Inference in an authorship problem. *Journal of the American Statistical Association*, 58(302), 275–309.

Pagano, M. and Anoke, S. (2013). Mommy's baby, daddy's maybe: A closer look at regression to the mean. *Chance*, 26(3), 4–9.

Paulos, J. A. (2001). *Innumeracy: Mathematical Illiteracy and Its Consequences*. Hill & Wang.

Pearson, K. (1901). On Lines and Planes of Closest Fit to Systems of Points in Space. *Philosophical Magazine*, 2, 559–572.

Press, W., Teukolsky, S., Vetterling, W., and Flannery, B. (1992). *Numerical Recipes in C: The Art of Scientific Computing*, 2nd ed. Cambridge University Press.

Radicati, S. and Levenstein, J. (2013). Email Statistics Report, 2013–2017. The Radicati Group.

Rawlings, J. O., Pantula, S. G., and Dickey, D. A. (2001). *Applied Regression Analysis: A Research Tool*, 2nd ed. Springer.

R Core Team. (2017). R: A language and environment for statistical computing. R Foundation for Statistical Computing, Vienna, Austria. Available at https://www.R-project.org/

Rebonato, R. (2007). *Plight of the Fortune Tellers: Why We Need to Manage Financial Risk Differently*. Princeton University Press.

Rissanen, J. (1978). Modeling by shortest data description. *Automatica*, 15(5), 465–471.

Rodriguez, J. D., Perez, A., and Lozano, J. A. (2010). Sensitivity analysis of k-fold cross validation in prediction error estimation. *IEEE Transactions on Pattern Analysis and Machine Intelligence*, 32(3), 569–575.

Ross, S. M. (1996). *Stochastic Processes*. John Wiley & Sons, Inc.

Sakamoto, Y., Ishiguro, M., and Kitagawa, G. (1986). *Akaike Information Criterion Statistics*. D. Reidel Publishing Co.

Salamon, P., Sibani, P., and Frost, R. (2002). *Facts, Conjectures, and Improvements for Simulated Annealing*. SIAM.

Schapire, R. E. (2013). Explaining AdaBoost. In: *Empirical Inference: Festschrift in Honor of Vladimir N. Vapnik*, pp. 37–52, edited by B. Schölkopf, Z. Luo, and V. Vovk. Springer.

Schapire, R. E. and Freund, Y. (2012). *Boosting: Foundations and Algorithms*. MIT Press.

Schclar, A. and Rokach, L. (2009). Random projection ensemble classifiers. *Lecture Notes in Business Information Processing*, 24, 309–316.

Schervish, M. (1995). *Theory of Statistics*. Springer.

Schwartz, G. (1978). Estimating the dimension of a model. *The Annals of Statistics*, 6(2), 461–464.

Scott, D. W. (1992). *Multivariate Density Estimation: Theory, Practice and Visualization*. John Wiley & Sons, Inc.

Scrucca, L., Fop, M., Murphy, T. B., and Raftery, A. E. (2016). mclust 5: Clustering, classification and density estimation using Gaussian finite mixture models. *The R Journal*, 8(1), 289–317.

Searle, S. R. (1971). *Linear Models*. John Wiley & Sons, Inc.

Shannon, C. E. (1948). A mathematical theory of communication. *Bell System Technical Journal*, 27, 379–423. Additional content from October 1948 issue, pp. 623–656.

Silver, N. (2012). *The Signal and the Noise*. Penguin.

Smith, E. E. (1943). *Second Stage Lensmen*, Fantasy Press. Reprinted in Smith, E. E. (1999). *Chronicles of the Lensmen*, Vol. 2, SFBC.

Solomonoff, R. J. (1964a). A formal theory of inductive inference: Part I. *Information and Control*, 7(1), 1–22.

Solomonoff, R. J. (1964b). A formal theory of inductive inference: Part II. *Information and Control*, 7(2), 224–254.

Stone, M. (1974). Cross-validatory choice and assessment of statistical predictions. *Journal of the Royal Statistical Society, Series B (Methodological)*, 36(2), 111–147.

Stone, M. (1977). An asymptotic equivalence of choice of model by cross-validation and Akaike's criterion. *Journal of the Royal Statistical Society, Series B (Methodological)*, 39(1), 44–47.

Strang, G. (1988). *Linear Algebra and Its Applications*, 3rd ed. Harcourt Brace Jovanovich.

Sugar, C. A. and James, G. M. (2003). Finding the number of clusters in a dataset: An information-theoretic approach. *Journal of the American Statistical Association*, 98(463), 750–763.

Suits, D. B. (1957, December). Use of dummy variables in regression equations. *Journal of the American Statistical Association*, 52(280), 548–551.

Taylor, H. M. and Karlin, S. (1994). *An Introduction to Stochastic Modeling*, revised ed. Academic Press.

Tenenbaum, J. B., De Silva, V., and Langford, J. C. (2000). A global geometric framework for nonlinear dimensionality reduction. *Science*, 290(5500), 2319–2323.

Therneau, T., Atkinson, B., and Ripley, B. (2017). rpart: Recursive partitioning and regression trees. R package version 4.1-11. Available at https://CRAN.R-project.org/package=rpart

Thode Jr., H. C. (2002). *Testing for Normality*. Marcel Dekker.

Tibshirani, R. (1996a). Bias, variance, and prediction error for classification rules. Technical Report, Department of Statistics, University of Toronto.

Tibshirani, R. (1996b). Regression shrinkage and selection via the lasso. *Journal of the Royal Statistical Society, Series B*, 58(1), 267–288.

Tibshirani, R. and Knight, K. (1999). Model search by bootstrap "bumping." *Journal of Computational and Graphical Statistics*, 8(4), 671–686.

Torgerson, W. S. (1952). Multidimensional scaling: I. Theory and method. *Psychometrika*, 17(4), 401–419.

Tufte, E. R. (2001). *The Visual Display of Quantitative Information*, 2nd ed. Graphics Press.

Tufte, E. R. (2003a). *The Cognitive Style of PowerPoint*. Graphics Press.

Tufte, E. R. (2003b). *Visual and Statistical Thinking*. Graphics Press.

Tukey, J. (1962). The Future of Data Analysis. *Annals of Mathematical Statistics*, 33(1), 1–67.

Tukey, J. (1986). Sunset Salvo. *The American Statistician*, 40(1), 72–76.

Turing, A. (1950, October). Computing Machinery and Intelligence. *Mind*, LIX(236), 443–460.

van der Vaart, A. W. (2000). *Asymptotic Statistics*. Cambridge University Press.

Venables, W. N. and Ripley, B. D. (2001). *Modern Applied Statistics with S-PLUS*, Third Edition, Springer.

Verhulst, P. F. (1838). Notice sur la loi que la population suit dans son accroissement. In: *Mathématique et Phsyique de L'Observatoire de Bruxelles, Tome Quatrième*, pp. 113–121. Hauman & Co.

Verhulst, P. F. (1844). Recherches in mathématiques sur la loi d'accroissement de la population. *Nouveaux Mémoires de l'Académie Royale des Sciences et Belles-Letters de Bruxelles*, Tome XVIII, pp. 1–42.

Voss, W. and Evers, L. (2005, August). Course Notes for M.Sc. in Bioinformatics Module 13: Statistical Data Mining, Oxford Bioinformatics Programme, University of Oxford.

Wasserman, L. (2004). *All of Statistics: A Concise Course in Statistical Inference*. Springer.

Wasserman, L. (2006). *All of Nonparametric Statistics*. Springer.

Watterson, B. (1998, June 2). Calvin and Hobbes.

Webb, G. I. (1996). Further experimental evidence against the utility of Occam's razor. *Journal of Artificial Intelligence Research*, 4, 397–417.

Wilks, S. S. (1938). The large-sample distribution of the likelihood ratio for testing composite hypotheses. *Annals of Mathematical Statistics*, 9(1), 60–62.

Wolpert, D. H. (1992). Stacked generalization. *Neural Networks*, 5(2), 241–259.

Young, G. and Householder, A. S. (1938). Discussion of a Set of Points in Terms of their Mutual Distances. *Psychometrika*, 3(1), 19–22.

Zamyatin, Y. (1924). *We*. Translated by Ginsburg, M. (1972). Bantam Books.

Zhu, J., Rosset, S., Zou, H., and Hastie, T. (2009). Multi-class AdaBoost. *Statistics and Its Interface*, 9, 349–360.

Index

Machine Learning: a Concise Introduction, First Edition. Steven W. Knox.
© This publication is a US Government work and is in the public domain.
Published 2018 by John Wiley & Sons, Inc.
Companion Website: http://www.wiley.com/go/Knox/MachineLearning